A Teacher's Miscellany

A Teacher's Miscellany

An Anthology of Short Writings from Diverse Countries and Many Centuries

Bernard E. Farber
Editor

McFarland & Company, Inc., Publishers
Jefferson, North Carolina, and London

Britis

Libra

A Teacher's miscellany : an anthology of short writings from diverse countries and many centuries / [compiled] by Bernard E. Farber.
p. cm.
Includes indexes.
ISBN 0-89950-517-1 (lib. bdg. : 50# alk. paper) ∞
1. Quotations, English. 2. Education—Quotations, maxims, etc.
I. Farber, Bernard E., 1914– .
PN6081.T35 1990
082—dc20 89-43697
CIP

Manufactured in the United States of America

McFarland & Company, Inc., Publishers
Box 611, Jefferson, North Carolina 28640

To Ellen, Marsha and Scott
With a father's love

Table of Contents

Preface

The encompassing process of teaching and learning commonly called education has been with us since the dawn of history. Adam and Eve had no teacher; left to their own devices, they were compelled to discover how to survive in a new universe through trial and error. Unquestionably they also learned from one another. Their sons were more fortunate; they had parents to teach them and models to emulate.

Although the process of education has since become institutionalized, in essence its aims have changed little over the centuries: the transmission of heritage and knowledge, and the development of skills and attitudes that lead to personal well-being and social usefulness.

During the last millennium, a common thread has run through most of the schools of the world. Though separated by many miles and centuries, they have been boring, autocratic and oppressive, and generally disliked by students. There have been a few notable exceptions to this dreary situation, and their stories are heartwarming. Exceptional also are writers like Quintilian and Montaigne who were advocates of a more liberal and humane education, notions that fell outside the mainstream of educational thought and practice of their time.

In the United States, and in some other parts of the world, contemporary education has been greatly influenced by the writings of Froebel, Montessori, Dewey and others, with the happy consequence that schools have become more child-centered and less authoritarian and repressive. However, although the physical cruelties of earlier times have to a large extent disappeared, vestiges of some undesirable practices still linger.

This book had its genesis some years ago when I was the principal of a large urban elementary school. To keep the staff informed of approaching report card and vacation dates, class schedule changes and other pertinent information, I would issue a weekly faculty bulletin. It was my habit always to append an inspirational or challenging quotation, or a synopsis of some relevant educational research or interesting article. The quotations especially proved to be popular, and they slowly accumulated until the notion of arranging them into book form began to take shape. The pursuit of that notion resulted initially in the publication of *A Teacher's*

Treasury of Quotations. The publication of *A Teacher's Miscellany* furthers that idea.

As its title implies, this anthology is directed primarily toward educators, *i.e.*, everyone engaged in the process of education, whether formal or informal: teachers, professors, administrators, librarians, psychologists, social workers, clergy, and others. It should be of interest as well to the non-professional (especially parents)—indeed, to anyone who enjoys reading for the sheer joy of reading and who takes pleasure in the adventure of browsing along backroads that often lead to unexpected and delightful surprises. It should be noted that most of the writers represented in this book were *not* professional educators.

These selections have been drawn from the literature of diverse countries and many centuries. Their sources include biographies and autobiographies, journals, letters, speeches, history, novels, poetry, drama, magazine and newspaper articles—in short, any lode that might yield a quotable gem was mined. The quotes abound with informative commentary and descriptions of schools, teaching, family relationships, and child-rearing practices. They detail more than bare experiences; they reveal also the participants' thoughts, their anxieties, their fears and their exultations. Thus the course of educational thought and practice becomes illuminated for us; we comprehend the past, and we understand more clearly today's education and our own world.

Although this collection endeavors to be "scholarly," it attempts to avoid both dullness and pedantry. Each selection chosen was subjected to the same criteria that were employed in *A Teacher's Treasury of Quotations:* Is it interesting and informative? Might it be of historical interest? Does it evoke memories of things past? Is it profound, provocative or witty? Is it written or said in an engaging style? Admittedly, these are subjective guidelines. While their application may be inadvertently influenced by the compiler's biases and preferences, it is also well to remember Oscar Wilde's statement that "it is only an auctioneer who can equally and impartially admire all schools of Art." In the end, as Cervantes wrote, "Every production must resemble its author."

The compiler should function as an editor, not as a censor, critic or advocate. To quote a writer is not necessarily to agree with him. Therefore, many points of view, sometimes in direct contradiction, are presented. This, I believe, is a desirable situation, for, faced with the abrasion and conflict of ideas, the reader is encouraged to evaluate these views carefully and then make reasonable choices.

Those who desire to use this reference reader as an aid for talks, papers and the like will find that pertinent information such as source and date of publication is given. The Table of Contents, Author Index and Subject Index are designed to facilitate the rapid location of desired material. On occasion a note has been appended to clarify a word's meaning, to present an interesting sidelight, or to draw the reader's attention to a similar or contrasting selection.

Richard Pace, in his preface to *The Benefit of a Liberal Education* (1517), wrote, "If anyone happens to object to my mixing so many jokes with such serious matter, I don't see that it would hurt him to laugh a little." He was expounding a basic educational principle – that education need not be, and should not be, a somber affair. More than fifty years ago Dr. Frederick Gorton, my undergraduate astronomy professor, expressed this thought so succinctly that it has remained etched in my memory ever since. When his class of spring-fevered tittering seniors reacted to one student's pranks while the professor's back was turned, Dr. Gorton faced the group and, with a kindly smile and an inquisitive look, waited patiently to be made privy to the cause of our laughter. When no explanation was forthcoming, he chuckled, shrugged his shoulders and said gently, "Oh well, if it's funny, it's good." I have tried to follow this dictum by interspersing the leavening and spice of some relevant humorous or offbeat material throughout the book.

Bernard E. Farber
Longboat Key, Florida
June 1990

A Teacher's Miscellany

Administrator

See Principal

Adolescence

(*See also* Youth and Age)

1. To be left alone on the tightrope of youth unknowing is to experience the excruciating beauty of full freedom and the threat of eternal indecision. Few, if any, survive their teens. Most surrender to the vague but murderous pressure of adult conformity. It becomes a constant battle with the superior forces of maturity.

—Maya Angelou, *I Know Why the Caged Bird Sings* (1970), 264.

2. A child's suffering can be very real and very deep and all the worse since a child has neither the wisdom nor the resources of mature men and women. His misery fills the whole of his world, leaving no space for other things. He has only emotions with no reason, with no cynicism or resignation to dull the edges of his jealousy or suffering. Those people who think of adolescence as a happy, carefree time either possess deficient emotions or inadequate memories.

—Louis Bromfield, *The Wild Country* (1948), 59.

3. Early youth is a baffling time. The present moment is nice but it does not last. Living in it is like waiting in a junction town for the morning limited; the junction may be interesting but some day you will have to leave it and you do not know where the limited will take you. Sooner or later you must move down an unknown road that leads beyond the range of imagination, and the only certainty is that the trip has to be made. In this respect early youth is like old age; it is a time of waiting before a big trip

to an unknown destination. The chief difference is that youth waits for the morning limited and age waits for the night train.

—Bruce Catton, *Waiting for the Morning Train,* (1972), 39.

4. Naturally good until now, I had never lied, for nothing tempted me to lie except fear of wounding and I had nothing to fear. But now with the advent of young men—benign serpents—came the apple . . . and many little lies to save her [Mother's] disappointment in me. I felt that it was for happiness, and the only difficulties of the untruths were the crimson blushes and fears of detection. Childhood was over.

—Diana Cooper, *The Rainbow Comes and Goes* (1958), v.

5. I was thirteen years old, and it had not been a good day.

To begin with, I had botched up my first-period math test. Then, at noon, I had discovered that my lunch ticket had run out, and I had forgotten to take money to buy another. My combination lock had stuck, so I hadn't been able to get my gym clothes out of my locker and had received another demerit in P.E.

After school I'd gone to the orthodontist to have my braces tightened and had been told that I'd have to wear them for at least another year because my teeth weren't lining up properly. Tonight was Carol Johnson's slumber party, and I had not been invited; why, I didn't know—I had thought Carol liked me.

All in all, I was in a rotten mood as I slammed into the house and dropped my books in a heap on the coffee table.

—Lois Duncan, *Chapters: My Growth as a Writer* (1949), 3.

6. The future accumulates like a weight upon the past. The weight upon the earliest years is easier to remove to let that time spring up like grass that has been crushed. The years following childhood become welded to their future, massed like stone, and often the time beneath cannot spring back into growth like new grass; it lies bled of its green in a new shape with those frail bloodless sprouts of another, unfamiliar time, entangled one with the other beneath the stone.

—Janet Frame, *An Angel at My Table* (1984), II.13.

7. Sensuality is burgeoning. . . . I feel at once grave, ill at ease and happy as I watch our children—our *children*—growing to meet the greatest of instincts. May it have mercy on them!

—Käthe Kollwitz, *Diary and Letters,*
May 5, 1910, ed. Hans Kollwitz (1955).

8. Adolescence always has its tragic aspects. It is only a question of degree.

—Agnes E. Meyer, *Out of These Roots* (1953), 27.

9. A few days after Kate had turned fourteen, she told me that a boy in her school, a basketball star named Nuri Adour, had said to her, "You certainly are a pretty thing. Maybe we'll go out sometime."

"He's very nice, Dad," said Kate. "He's a senior and he's six feet *three.*"

"Isn't he a little . . . well, *high* for you?" I said, seeing him dribbling her into bed.

"Dad, he's really a together guy and you should feel flattered because he likes me better than any of the Lebanese girls."

I had no objection to Kate going out with an Arab, just as long as it wasn't a boy. . . .

That evening, Judy told me that Kate had confessed to her, woman-to-woman, a bit more sweet talk that Nuri had spoken: she was the only girl in the school with a behind as cute as her face.

"For this I'm sweating to send her to college," I said. "So she can develop her rectal allure."

"She feels good about his attention," Judy said. "He's a celebrity and he's more mature than the other boys."

"That's what I'm afraid of. Aren't there any eunuchs on that team?"

But beneath my flippancy was despair, for Kate's childhood seemed to be ending, a termination I couldn't accept. Perhaps I was being unreasonable, but I wanted my daughters to forever be chaste companions of mine, kissing me only and an occasional uncle or two. For years American children had been trying to lower the age of puberty; there was mascara on the lollipops, and tourniquets called training bras; so I was determined to keep my girls children for at least another twenty years, and the effort I gave to this cause was both pathetic and intense.

—Ralph Schoenstein, *Yes, My Darling Daughters,* (1976), 8.

Autobiography

See Biography

Biography

(*See also* Writing)

10. Anyone who sits down to write his autobiography should, I think, ask himself why he is doing it. Those three or four hundred pages devoted to his probably quite undistinguished life and doings call for some explanation. It is not enough to say with Sartre that in subjectivity one discovers other people as well as oneself. The fact remains that the autobiographer is asking a large number of men and women whom he does not know to take an interest in his personal affairs.

—Gerald Brenan, *A Life of One's Own: Childhood and Youth* (1962), preface.

11. I, Daniel Harmon Brush, having by favor of a good Providence attained to three-fourths of a century in age—still, however, strong and lusty in health—commence in this book the jotting down of items that have transpired in a somewhat busy and extended life, as recollected by me or derived from other reliable sources, of small importance or interest to the passing crowd, but which, in the relation, may tend to beguile a tedious hour and afford some recreation in the remaining shadowy days allotted me.

—Daniel Harmon Brush, *Growing Up with Southern Illinois: 1820 to 1861* (1944), opening sentence.

12. I hope my readers will not think me vain for writing my life since there have been many that have done the like, as Caesar, Ovid, and many more, both men and women, and I know no reason I may not do it as well as they: but I verily believe some censuring Readers will scornfully say, why hath this Lady writ her own life? since none cares to know whose daughter she was or whose wife she is, or how she was bred, or what fortunes she had, or how she lived, or what humour or disposition she was of? I answer that it is true, that 'tis to no purpose to the Readers, but it is to the Authoress, because I write it for my own sake, not theirs.

—Margaret Cavendish, Duchess of Newcastle, 1655, in Mary Ellen Chase, *A Goodly Heritage* (1932), prologue.

13. All men of whatsoever quality they be, who have done anything of excellence, or which may properly resemble excellence, ought, if they are persons of truth and honesty, to describe their life with their own hand; but they ought not to attempt so fine an enterprise till they have passed the age of forty. . . . It is true that men who have laboured with some show of excellence, have already given knowledge of themselves to the world; and this alone ought to suffice them: I mean the fact that they have proved their manhood and achieved renown. Yet one must needs live like others; and so in a work like this there will always be found occasion for natural bragging.

—Benvenuto Cellini, *The Life of Benvenuto Cellini, Written by Himself* (written 1558–62; published 1728), I.i.ii, tr. John Addington Symonds.

14. When Nasrettin Hoca, celebrated jester or stupid-shrewd man, was asked why he sat on his donkey backward, he said he wanted to see where he had been. Most donkey riders prefer to see where they are going, though it would seem that a little flexibility of the neck might permit anyone to look in both directions more or less at the same time. Certainly in that universal travel we call life all of us manage to keep an eye pretty constantly on both where we have been and where we are going, the chief difference between the two views being that the backward is considerably clearer than the forward. Yet most of this day-to-day looking back is fragmentary and evanescent. When our donkey is resting after the day's journey, perhaps on a little hill, we can take a more leisurely and lasting survey.

—Robert Francis, *The Trouble with Francis: An Autobiography* (1971), opening paragraph.

15. Anyone turning biographer commits himself to lies, to concealment, to hypocrisy, to flattery, to events hiding his own lack of understanding, for biographical truth is not to be had, and even if it were it couldn't be used.

—Sigmund Freud, letter to Arnold Zweig dissuading him from writing a proposed biography of Freud, May 31, 1936, in Ronald W. Clark, *Freud: The Man and the Cause* (1980), 64. *See* Shaw, **#18.**

16. The great difficulty when one writes one's journal . . . is to forget that one does not write it for others, or rather not to forget that one writes it for oneself, or rather to forget that one does not write it for a time when one will have become someone else, or rather not to forget that one is someone else in writing it, or rather not to forget that its only interest must be for oneself immediately, which is to say for someone who does not exist since one is someone else as soon as one begins to write.

—Robert Pinget, "Monsieur Songe," in May Sarton, *At Seventy: A Journal* (1984), 34.

17. What I don't know would fill a book. And, dear reader, it's going to.

—Billy Rose, opening sentence of his autobiography, *Wine, Women, and Words* (1946).

18. All autobiographies are lies. I do not mean unconscious, unintentional lies: I mean deliberate lies. No man is bad enough to tell the truth about himself during his lifetime, involving, as it must, the truth about his family and his friends and colleagues. And no man is good enough to tell the truth to posterity in a document which he suppresses until there is nobody left alive to contradict him.

—George Bernard Shaw, *Sixteen Self Sketches* (1949), 71. *See* Freud, #15.

19. Only when one has lost all curiosity about the future has one reached the age to write an autobiography.

—Evelyn Waugh, *A Little Learning: An Autobiography* (1964), opening sentence

20. This Autobiography, in spite of all the pains I have taken and research I have put into it, is necessarily fiction. The fact that names, dates, and places seem to correspond with such things that may have occurred in real life does not guarantee the truth of these stories. So, in all candor, I wish to warn the reader not to confuse this story with reality. For God only knows the truth. I am hereby trying, in my finite way, to set down some facts which seem real and true to me. At best, this is only a tale that is told!

—William Allen White, *Autobiography* (1946), preface.

Book

(*See also* Book Preface; Library; Literature; Reader; Reading; Textbook)

21. There are three kinds of book owners. The first has all the standard sets and best sellers—unread, untouched. (This deluded individual owns wood-pulp and ink, not books.) The second has a great many books—a few of them read through, most of them dipped into, but all of them as clean and shiny as the day they were bought. (This person would probably like to make books his own, but is restrained by a false respect for their physical appearance.) The third has a few books or many—every one of them dog-eared and dilapidated, shaken and loosened by continual use, marked and scribbled from front to back. (This man owns books.)

—Mortimer J. Adler, "How to Mark a Book," *The Saturday Review*, July 6, 1940. *See* Brown, #23.

Book 7

22. [In monasteries] Special curses were uttered against those who mutilated books or absconded with them. "This book belongs to [the monastery of] St. Mary of Robert's Bridge," warns a twelfth-century manuscript of Saint Augustine and Ambrose, "whoever shall steal it, or sell it, or in any way alienate it from this house, or mutilate it, let him be forever cursed. Amen." Below this, in the manuscript, now in the Bodlein Library at Oxford, we can read in a fourteenth-century hand: "I, John, Bishop of Exeter, know not where the aforesaid house is, nor did I steal this book, but acquired it in a lawful way."

—Daniel Boorstin, *The Discoverers* (1983), 492.

23. As a writer, I hold uncut pages to be comment on an owner and an insult to an author. A book for me is something to be read, not kept under glass or in a safe. I want to dog-ear it, to underline it, to annotate it, and mark my favorite passages, and make my own index on the blank pages at the back.

—John Mason Brown, "Seeing Things," *The Saturday Review*, Sept. 22, 1951. *See* Adler, #21.

24. The appearance of a new book is an indication that another man has found a mission, has entered upon the performance of a hefty duty, activated by the noblest impulses that can spur the soul of man to action. It is the proudest boast of the profession of literature, that no man ever published a book for selfish purposes or with ignoble aim. Books have been published for the consolation of the distressed; for the guidance of the wandering; for the relief of the destitute; for the hope of the penitent; for uplifting the burdened soul above its sorrows and fears; for the general amelioration of the condition of all mankind; for the right against wrong; for the good against bad; for the truth. This book is published for two dollars per volume.

—Robert J. Burnette, *The Rise and Fall of the Moustache* (1877).

25. These [books] are the masters who instruct us without rods and ferules, without hard words and anger, without clothes or money. If you approach them, they are not asleep; if, investigating, you interrogate them, they conceal nothing; if you mistake them, they never grumble; if you are ignorant, they cannot laugh at you.

—Richard de Bury (1287–1345), *Philobiblon* (1473), autobiographical sketch designed as a handbook on collecting and preserving books.

26. This morning I put leather polish on the bindings of a number of nice old books which I am lucky enough to own. This is a regular yearly rite with me. There are people who would not dream of starving a child who will starve a fine old binding, and think nothing of it. But a child, be it ever so stuffed with vitamins, may grow up to be a sorrow, and a disgrace to you, whereas a good book will always be a credit and a friend. Let the admirers of the younger generation chew on that one!

—Robertson Davies, *The Table Talk of Samuel Marchbanks* (1949), 16.

27. A precious—mouldering pleasure—'t is—
To meet an Antique Book—
In just the Dress his Century wore—
A privilege—I think—

His venerable Hand to take—
And warming in our own—
A passage back—or two—to make—
To Times when he—was young—

His quaint opinions—to inspect—
His thought to ascertain
On Themes concern our mutual mind—
The Literature of Man—

What interested Scholars—most—
What Competitions ran—
When Plato—was a Certainty—
And Sophocles—a Man—

When Sappho—was a living Girl—
And Beatrice wore
The Gowns that Dante—deified—
Facts Centuries before

He traverses—familiar—
As One should come to Town—
And tell you all your Dreams—were true—
He lived—where Dreams were born—

His presence is Enchantment—
You beg him not to go—

Book 9

Old Volumes shake their Vellum Heads
And tantalize—just so—

—Emily Dickinson, c. 1862,
Complete Poems, ed. Thomas H. Johnson (1960), 371.

28. The great thing about a book is having it in one's home like a medicine or an analgesic, a stimulus or a soporific when the drugstores are all closed. Late at night one's private library is like a medicine chest. One cannot tell what one will be in the mood for or what one's spirit will most urgently crave. Or if the analogy seems too medicinal, perhaps the refrigerator or cookie jar will do.

—Irwin Edman, "Unrequired Reading,"
The Saturday Review, Nov. 4, 1950.

29. So deeply did the Jews respect their books that they were not destroyed when they became frayed and torn. When books of importance (and for two thousand years there were no other books for the Jews) were too worn for use, they were given honorable burial in a vault beneath the synagogue. In the Jewish hierarchy of values, a *Beth haMidrash* (a house of study: thus, a house of books) takes precedence over a *Beth haKnesset* (a house of assembly: a synagogue). Therefore, ruled the Rabbis, it is proper to change a synagogue into a house of study, which would be moving it upward in importance, but improper to change a house of study into a synagogue, which would be moving it downward.

—Harry Gersh, *The Sacred Books of the Jews* (1968), foreword.

30. Here lies poor Ned Purdom, from misery freed,
Who long was a bookseller's hack;
He led such a damnable life in this world,
I don't think he'd wish to come back.

—Oliver Goldsmith (1730?–74), "On a Bookseller,"
in William Cole, ed., *Pith and Vinegar: An Anthology of Short Humorous Poetry* (1969).

31. I visit Sosius' publishing house, close by in the Forum, at the corner of the Tuscan quarter. The open patio holds some eighty desks, at each of which a scribe sits, bent over a long parchment scroll. A clear-voiced reader delivers the text which these slaves are copying: Claudius' own learned *History of the Etruscans*. He spells it out, letter by letter, warning them beforehand where each line ends; so that all copies will be uniform and mistakes easily checked. The book is about to consist of twenty scrolls, at five denarii a scroll [about $30 for 150,000 words].

—Robert Graves, *Collected Short Stories:* "The Tenement: A Vision of Imperial Rome" (1968), 143.

32. It happened July 3, 1886, in the back shop of the New York Tribune where [Ottmar] Merganthaler, who was 32, had set up the first production model of his [Linotype] machine. Whitelaw Reid, the Tribune's publisher, picked up the first slug the machine cast, a sliver of lead the width of a news column with its face shaped into eight words of type.

"Ottmar," he said, "you've done it. A line of type."

For 400 years until that day, printing had been done essentially the way Gutenberg set his Bible, one character at a time. The process was so tedious that the largest daily newspapers were limited to eight pages.

The "eighth wonder" changed that. Within a generation U.S. newspaper circulation leaped from 3.6 million to 33 million. Inexpensive magazines appeared—weekly. Schoolbooks, once handed down as family treasures, became available to all. Public libraries became commonplace. The nation's literacy rate soared.

—Jules Loh, "Linotype Machine Imprints on History," *Sarasota Herald-Tribune*, June 28, 1986.

33. The love of learning, the sequestered nooks,
And all the sweet serenity of books.

—Henry Wadsworth Longfellow, "Morituri Salutamus" (1875), st.xxi, *Poems of Henry Wadsworth Longfellow*, ed. Louis Untermeyer (1943), 432.

34. The habit of reading is one of the greatest resources of mankind; and we enjoy books that belong to us much more than if they are borrowed. A borrowed book is like a guest in the house; it must be treated with punctiliousness, with a certain considerate formality. You must see that it sustains no damage; it must not suffer while under your roof. You cannot leave it carelessly, you cannot mark it, you cannot turn down the pages, you cannot use it familiarly. And then, some day, although this is seldom done, you really ought to return it.

—William Lyon Phelps, radio address, Apr. 6, 1933.

35. The enormous multiplication of books in every branch of knowledge is one of the greatest evils of this age; since it presents one of the most serious obstacles to the acquisition of correct information, by throwing in the reader's way piles of lumber in which he must painfully grope for the scraps of useful matter, peradventure interspersed.

—Edgar Allan Poe, *Marginalia* (1844–49).
See Eliot, **#1153**, and Mendelssohn, **#1163**, under "Writing."

36. But one thing is certain. Though books, as Milton says, may be the embalming of mighty spirits, they are also the resurrection of rebellious, reactionary, fantastical, and wicked spirits! In books dwell all the demons and all the angels of the human mind. It is for this reason that a bookshop—especially a second-hand bookshop—is an arsenal of explosives, an armoury of revolutions, an opium den of reactions. And just because books are repository of all the redemptions and damnations, all the sanities and insanities, of the divine anarchy or the soul, they are still, as they have always been, an object of suspicion to every kind of ruling authority. In a second-hand bookshop are the horns of the altar where all the outlawed thoughts of humanity can take refuge! Here, like desperate bandits, hide all the reckless progeny of our wild, dark, self-lacerating hearts. A bookshop is a powder-magazine, a dynamite-shed, a drugstore of poisons, a bar of intoxicants, a den of opiates, an island of sirens. Of all the "houses of ill fame" which a tyrant, a bureaucrat, a propagandist, a moralist, a champion of law and order, an advocate of keeping people ignorant for their own good, hurries past with averted eyes or threatens with his minions, a bookshop is the most flagrant. Plato, that poetical enemy of poets, would certainly recommend his philosopher-kings to abolish second-hand bookshops. A second-hand bookshop can blow sky-high the machinations of centuries of first-hand politicians. It sets the prophet against the priest, the prisoner against society, the has-nothing against the has-all, the individual against the universe! It is as heavily charged with the sweet mischiefs of sex as the privy-walls of a railway station, or the imagination of St. Anthony. Here are the poisons to kill, the drugs to soothe, the fire-water to madden, the ichor to inflame, the nectar to imparadise! The infinite pathos of all the generations lies here, their beatings against the wall, their desperate escapes, their triumphant reconciliations.

—John Cowper Powys,
Enjoyment of Literature (1938), xii.

37. In the futile attempts we make to tidy up our lives and our surroundings, nothing is more difficult than throwing out a book. I can't even bring myself to throw out a terrible book. I have all I can do to throw out a magazine. It has to be done, though, and I'm trying to develop some plan. At about age forty, each of us should resolve to throw away or give away one book for each new book we acquire. There are books we will never part with and shouldn't. If you've read and liked a book and taken a little of it into your life, you should keep it forever. It doesn't take up much room, it's attractive on the bookshelf, it doesn't take much dusting and it provides evidence to visitors in your house that you're literate. Even though you may never actually take it down and read it again, the presence of its title staring out at you every day is a reminder of its contents. The books we should throw out are the junk books we acquire and the books that were good in their time but have no lasting value. This includes most popular novels. No one reads a novel twice and most of them are read as entertainment and diversion. Nothing that is merely entertaining and diverting is worth saving.

—Andrew A. Rooney, *Pieces of My Mind:* "Casting Out Books" (1982), 6.

38. People had different habits of concentration years ago. When I browse in used-book stores, I'm struck by how small the print is in old books. You wonder how people read them! If you take the successive editions of a Henry James novel, the first thing you notice is that the print gets bigger and bigger with later editions.

—Susan Sontag, in *U.S. News and World Report,* July 9, 1979.

39. Books and friends, few and good.

—Spanish proverb.

40. I am from that library which Maximillian, Duke of Bavaria, took as a prize of war from captured Heidelberg and sent as a trophy to Gregory XV.

—Inscription in every book that General Johan Tilly, Flemish field marshal, stole from Heidelberg after capturing the city in 1623 and sent to the Vatican.

41. O for a Booke and a shadie nooke, eyther in-a-doore or out;
With the grene leaves whisp'ring overhede, or the Streete cries all about.
Where I maie Reade all at my ease, both of the Newe and Olde;
For a jollie goode Booke whereon to looke, is better than Golde.

—John Wilson (?–1889), motto in his second-hand book catalogue. Found in Sir John Lubbock, *Pleasures of Life* (1887–89), and in John Ireland (1879–1962), *Enchiridion,* where it is given as an old song.

42. Few or no Books are to be found in this vast Country, beside the Assembly, Catechism, Watts Hymns, Bunyans Pilgrims Progress—Russells—Whitefields and Erkine Sermons. Nor do they delight in Historical Books or in having them read to them, as do our Vulgar in England, for these People despise Knowledge, and instead of honouring a Learned Person, or any one of Wit or Knowledge, be it in the Arts, Sciences, or Languages, they despise and Ill treat them—And this Spirit prevails even among the Principals of this Province.

—Charles Woodmason, an Anglican minister, describing Carolina of the 1760s and 1770s, in Richard Hofstadter, *Anti-intellectualism in American Life* (1963), 75.

43. It is simple enough to say that since books have classes—fiction, biography, poetry—we should separate them and take from each what it is right that each should give us. Yet few people ask from books what books can give us. Most commonly we come to books with blurred and divided minds, asking of fiction that it shall be true, of poetry that it shall be false, of biography that it shall be flattering, of history that it shall enforce our own prejudices. If we could banish all such preconceptions when we read, that would be an admirable beginning. Do not dictate to your author; try to become him. Be his fellow-worker and accomplice. If you hang back, and reserve and criticise at first, you are preventing yourself from getting the fullest possible value from what you read. But if you open your mind as widely as possible, then signs and hints of almost imperceptible fineness, from the twist and turn of the first sentences, will bring you into the presence of a human being unlike any other. Steep yourself in this, acquaint yourself with this, and soon you will find that your author is giving you, or attempting to give you, something far more definite.

—Virginia Woolf, *The Second Common Reader:* "How Should One Read a Book?" (1932), 235.

Book Preface

(*See also* Biography; Textbook)

44. You may depend upon my bare word, reader, without any further security, that I could wish this offspring of my brain were as ingenious, sprightly, and accomplished, as yourself could desire; but the mischief on't is, nature will have its course. Every production must resemble its author, and my barren and unpolished understanding can produce nothing but what is very dull, very impertinent, and extravagant beyond imagination.

—Miguel de Cervantes,
Don Quixote (1615), preface.

45. No part of a book is so intimate as the Preface. Here, after the long labor of the work is over, the author descends from his platform, and speaks with his reader as man to man, disclosing his hopes and fears, seeking sympathy for his difficulties, offering defence or defiance, according to his temper, against the criticisms which he anticipates. It thus happens that a personality which has been veiled by a formal method throughout many chapters, is seen suddenly face to face in the Preface; and this alone, if there were no other reason, would justify a volume of Prefaces.

—Charles W. Eliot, ed. *The Harvard Classics: Prefaces and Prologues to Famous Books,* "Introductory Note" (1909).

46. foreword, preface. *F.* is a word invented in the 19th c. as a Saxonism by anti-latinists, and caught up as a vogue word by people who love a new name for an old thing. *P.* has a 500-year history behind it in English, and, far from being antiquated, is still *the* name for the thing. The vogue now seems to be passing, and it looks as though a decent retirement might be found for *f.* by confining it to the particular kind of preface that is supplied by some distinguished person for a book written by someone else who feels the need of a sponsor.

—H.W. Fowler, *A Dictionary of Modern English Usage,* 2nd ed., (1965), 207.

47. A *preface* . . . is most often a personal comment by the author apologizing for writing the work, or for being alive; in fact, a couple of centuries ago, the *preface* was often called the *apology.*

—William Safire, "Forwards March,"
The New York Times Magazine, Nov. 3, 1985.

48. Persons attempting to find a motive in this narrative will be prosecuted; persons attempting to find a moral in it will be banished; persons attempting to find a plot in it will be shot.

By Order of the Author,
Per G.G., Chief of Ordnance.

—Mark Twain, *The Adventures of Huckleberry Finn:* "Notice" (1884).

Censorship

(*See also* Freedom, Academic; Sex)

49. There exists I believe throughout the whole Christian world a law which makes it blasphemy to deny or doubt the divine inspiration of all the books of the old and new Testaments from Genesis to Revelations. . . . Now what free enquiry when a writer must surely encounter the risk of fine or imprisonment for adducing any argument for investigation into the divine authority of these books? . . . I think such laws a great embarrassment, great obstructions to the improvement of the human mind. Books that cannot bear examination certainly ought not to be established as divine inspiration by penal laws. It is true few persons appear desirous to put such laws in execution and it is also true that some few persons are hardy enough to venture to depart from them; but as long as they continue in force as laws the human mind must make an awkward and clumsy progress in its investigations. I wish they were repealed.

—John Adams, letter to Thomas Jefferson,
Jan. 23, 1825, in Lester J. Cappon, ed.,
The Adams-Jefferson Letters (1959), 607.

50. 'Never mind, one day we'll have lots of books again.'

'No, never,' she said. 'That will never be. I have no faith anymore. In this world there's neither goodness nor good sense. The world is governed by evil minded idiots. And books are always being burnt. The library at Alexandria went up in flames, the Inquisitors had their bonfires, Radishchev* was burnt, books were burnt under Stalin, there have been bonfires in the squares under Hitler, and there will be more and more of them burnt. There are always more people to burn books than to write them. You have your life ahead of you, Tolya, so just remember that this is the first sign of trouble—if books are banned, that means things are going wrong. It means that you are surrounded by force, fear and ignorance, that power is in the hands of barbarians. My God, just to think . . . It's bad enough when bands of vandals start throwing books onto a fire in the main square, but that's not the worst that can happen. It's always possible there is only a limited number of them—the vandals, that is. But when every single person in every home starts shaking with fright and burning his own books . . . to reduce a whole nation to that level! That takes some doing! I ask myself why on earth did I ever have you? To have to live in such a world. . .'

—A. Anatoli [Kuznetsov], *Babi Yar*,
tr. David Floyd (1970), 158. *Alexander Radishchev

(1749–1802), writer and thinker, regarded as the founder of the revolutionary tradition in Russia.

51. Your honor, this book is a bucket of swill;
It portrays a young couple alone on a hill,
And a woman who lived in a shoe as a house
With her brood—but not once does it mention her spouse,
I submit that this book is obscene, vile and loose
And demand its suppression. Its name? "Mother Goose."

—Anonymous, in Henry Ehlers and Gordon C. Lee, *Crucial Issues in Education*, 3rd ed. (1964), 46.

52. I met Monsignor Podgorc who had been our professor of religion in Teacher's College [Austria]. He stopped me and asked: "Where are you going in such a hurry?"

I answered in haste: "I am already late for the lecture in theosophy, given at the Sandwirt Hotel."

"A lecture in theosophy?" Monsignor Podgorc mumbled, rubbing his chin persistently. "Do you know that you are not allowed to hear this lecture?"

"Who should forbid me to attend it?" I asked briskly. One could easily imagine how provoked I felt.

But Msgr. Podgorc answered sternly: "If you were Doctor Andrea Huber, you probably could obtain permission from our bishop to go to the meeting. But you are not Dr. Huber. If you go there you will commit a severe sin and you would, continuing such activities, become automatically excommunicated."

"Excommunicated?" I gasped. "How can I ever find the truth if I am not permitted to search for it? I will go and nobody can hold me back," I snapped and hastily I turned around and stormed towards the stairway.

—Andrea U. Baum, *Between Two Continents* (1969), 42.

53. A list of two hundred books which it is proposed to purchase for the library of the Lincoln School has been referred to a committee of the Board of Education, with power to reject any objectionable volumes. As it is not probable that the members of the committee are familiar with a half-dozen volumes comprised in this list or any other, it may reasonably be affirmed that a conscientious performance of their duty will require the first intellectual labor they have ever done in all their lives. It is to be hoped the works are printed in large, clear type, with the syllables properly estranged.

—Ambrose Bierce, "Purifying the School Libraries" (1871), in Ernest Jerome Hopkins, ed., *The Ambrose Bierce Satanic Reader* (1968), 103.

54. I never heard of anyone who really loved books who wanted to suppress any of them. Censors only read a book with great difficulty, moving their lips as they puzzle out each syllable, when somebody tells them that the book is unfit to read.

—Robertson Davies, *The Table Talk of Samuel Marchbanks* (1949), 208.

55. Theologians are all alike, of whatever religion or country they may be; their aim is always to wield despotic authority over man's consciences; they therefore persecute all of us who have the temerity to unveil the truth.

—Frederick the Great, King of Prussia, letter to Voltaire, Nov. 4, 1736.

56. He was forbidden to read certain books, but he read them all the same. This is what has occurred to thousands upon thousands of children all the world over since books were first printed.

—W. Somerset Maugham, introduction (1949) to Stendhal's *The Red and the Black* (1831).

57. The peculiar evil of silencing the expression of an opinion is, that it is robbing the human race; posterity as well as the existing generation; those who dissent from the opinion, still more than those who hold it. If the opinion is right, they are deprived of the opportunity of exchanging error for truth: if wrong, they lose, what is almost as great a benefit, the clearer perception and livelier impression of truth, produced by its collision with error. . . . The opinion which it attempted to suppress by authority may possibly be true. Those who desire to suppress it, of course deny its truth; but they are not infallible. They have no authority to decide the question for all mankind, and exclude every other person from the means of judging. To refuse to hear an opinion, because they are sure it is false, is to assume that *their* certainty is the same thing as *absolute* certainty. All silencing of discussion is an assumption of infallibility.

—John Stuart Mill, *On Liberty* (1859), ii.

58. Knowledge cannot defile, nor consequently the books, if the will and conscience be not defil'd. . . . Wholesome meats to a vitiated stomack differ little or nothing from unwholesome; and best books to a naughty mind are not unappliable to occasion of evill. . . .

If it be true, that a wise man like a good refiner, can gather gold out of the drossiest volume, and that a fool will be a fool with the best book, yea or without book, there is no reason that we should deprive a wise man of any advantage to his wisdome, while we seek to restrain from a fool, that which being restrain'd, will be no hindrance to his folly.

—John Milton, *Areopagitica* (1644), sec.11,14.

59. All censorships exist to prevent any one from challenging current conceptions and existing institutions. All progress is initiated by challenging current conceptions, and executed by supplanting existing institutions. Consequently the first condition of progress is the removal of censorships. There is the whole case against censorship in a nutshell.

—George Bernard Shaw, preface
(1902) to *Mrs. Warren's Profession* (1894).

60. It was a fine spring morning on Lady Day, in the year 1811, when I went to [Percy Bysshe] Shelley's rooms: he was absent; but before I had collected our books he rushed in. He was terribly agitated. I anxiously inquired what had happened.

"I am expelled," he said, as soon as he had recovered himself a little, "I am expelled! I was sent for suddenly a few minutes ago; I went to the common room, where I found our master and two or three of the fellows. The master produced a copy of the little syllabus, and asked me if I were the author of it. He spoke in a rude, abrupt, and insolent tone. I begged to be informed for what purpose he put the question. No answer was given; but the master loudly and angrily repeated, 'Are you the author of this book?' If I can judge from your manner, I said, you are resolved to punish me, if I should acknowledge that it is my work. If you can prove that it is, produce your evidence; it is neither just nor lawful to interrogate me in such a case and for such a purpose. Such proceedings would become a court of inquisitors, but not free men in a free country. 'Do you choose to deny that this is your composition?' the master reiterated in the same rude and angry voice." Shelley complained much of his violent and ungentlemanlike deportment, saying, "I have experienced tyranny and injustice before, and I well know what violence is; but I never met with such unworthy treatment. I told him calmly, but firmly, that I was determined not to answer any questions respecting the publication on the table. He immediately repeated his demand; I persisted in my refusal; and he said furiously, 'Then you are expelled; and I desire you will quit the college early to-morrow morning at the latest.' One of the fellows took up two papers, and handed one of them to me; here it is." He produced a regular sentence of expulsion, drawn up in due form, under the seal of the college.

—Percy Bysshe Shelley, in Thomas Jefferson Hogg,
The Life of Percy Bysshe Shelley (1858). During his

second year at Oxford, Shelley and his friend Hogg
were expelled for circulating a pamphlet on *The Necessity of Atheism* which was published anonymously by a local bookseller.

61. Even in matters where there is no risk to faith and devotion, no one shall introduce new questions in matters of great moment, or any other opinion which does not have suitable authority, without first consulting his superiors; he shall not teach anything opposed to the axioms of learned men or the general belief of scholars.

—Society of Jesus (Jesuit Order), *Ratio Stuiorum* (1599).

62. Be it enacted—that it shall be unlawful for any teacher in any ... schools ... which are supported ... by the public school funds of the State, to teach any theory that denied the story of the Divine Creation of man as taught in the Bible, and to teach instead that man has descended from a lower order of animals.

—Statute of the State of Tennessee.
John T. Scopes taught the theory of evolution in defiance of this law, thus precipitating the famous Dayton, or Scopes trial, July 1925. The law was repealed in 1967.

63. If you were to bother to read my books, to behave as educated persons would, you would learn that they are not sexy, and do not argue in favor of wildness of any kind. They beg that people be kinder and more responsible than they often are. It is true that some of the characters speak coarsely. That is because people speak coarsely in real life. Especially soldiers and hardworking men speak coarsely, and even our most sheltered children know that. And we all know, too, that those words really don't damage children much. It was evil deeds and lying that hurt us.

After I have said all this, I am sure you are still ready to respond, in effect, "Yes, yes—but it still remains our right and our responsibility to decide what books our children are going to be made to read in our community." This is surely so. But it is also true that if you exercise that right and fulfill that responsibility in an ignorant, harsh, un-American manner, then people are entitled to call you bad citizens and fools. Even your own children are entitled to call you that....

If you and your board are now determined to show that you in fact have wisdom and maturity when you exercise your powers over the education of our young, then you should acknowledge that it was a rotten lesson you taught young people in a free society when you denounced and then burned books—books you haven't even read. You should also resolve to expose your children to all sorts of opinions and information, in order that they will be better equipped to make decisions and to survive.

—Kurt Vonnegut, letter to Charles McCarthy, chairman of the Drake, North Dakota, school board, Nov. 16, 1973, *Palm Sunday* (1981), 6, 7.

Child Rearing

(*See also* Discipline; Parent; Punishment; Punishment, Corporal; Punishment, Corporal [Con]; Punishment, Corporal [Pro]).

64. When I did well, I heard it never;
When I did ill, I heard it ever.

—Anonymous

65. [They] rank their children, in their earliest years,
Among their cats and dogs, their bulls and bears,
Mere animals whose gambols now and then
May raise a laugh, and turn the rising spleen
Ere reason dawn'd, or Cunning Learnt disguise.

—Anonymous, poem printed in England, 1775, in Dorothy Uris, *Say It Again* (1979), 34.

66. Johnny was an adopted child. . . .

The miller and his wife had offered to raise him, after his own folks died, and that was a good deed on their part. But, as soon as he lost his baby teeth and started acting the way most boys act, they began to come down on him like thunder, which wasn't so good. They were good people, according to their lights, but their lights were terribly strict ones, and they believed that the harder you were on a youngster, the better and brighter he got. Well, that may work with some children, but it didn't with Johnny Pye.

He was sharp enough and willing enough—as sharp and willing as most boys in Martinsville. But, somehow or other, he never seemed to be able to do the right things or say the right words—at least when he was home. Treat a boy like a fool and he'll act like a fool, I say, but there's some folks need convincing. The miller and his wife thought the way to smarten Johnny was to treat him like a fool, and finally they got so he pretty much believed it himself.

—Stephen Vincent Benét, *Selected Works of Stephen Vincent Benét:* "Johnny Pye and the Fool-Killer" (1942), II.90.

67. How do the dear girls go on? I would have them taught geometry, which is of all sciences in the world the most entertaining; it expands the mind more to the knowledge of all things in nature, and better teaching to distinguish between truths and such things as have the appearance of being truths, yet are not, than any other.

Their education, and the proper cultivation of the sense which God has given them, are the objects on which my happiness most depends. To inspire them with a love of everything that is honourable and virtuous, though in rags, and with contempt for vanity in embroidery, is the way to make them the darlings of my heart. They should not only read, but it requires a careful selection of books; nor should they ever have access to two at the same time; but when a subject is begun, it should be finished before anything else is undertaken. How would it enlarge their minds, if they should acquire a sufficient knowledge of mathematics and astronomy to give them an idea of the beauty and wonders of creation! I am persuaded that the generality of people, and particularly fine ladies, only adore God because they are told it is proper and the fashion to go to church; but I would have my girls obtain such knowledge of the works of creation, that they may have a fixed idea of the nature of that Being who could be the Author of such a world. Whenever they have that, nothing on this side of the moon will give them much uneasiness of mind. I do not mean that they should be Stoics, or want the common feelings for the sufferings that the flesh is heir to; but they would then have a source of consolation for the worst that could happen.

—Lord Collingwood, while at sea, letter to
Lady Collingwood about the education of their daughters,
June 16, 1806, in E.V. Lucas, ed., *The Gentlest Art* (1908), 334.

68. It is well to remember that the majority of men have never invented the device of beating children into submission. Some of the American Plains Indian tribes were . . . deeply shocked when they first saw white people beat their children. In their bewilderment they could only explain such behavior as part of an over-all missionary scheme—an explanation also supported by the white people's method of letting their babies cry themselves blue in the face. It all must mean, so they thought, a well-calculated wish to impress white children with the idea that this world is not a good place to linger in, and that it is better to look to the other world where perfect happiness is to be had at the price of having sacrificed this world.

—Erik H. Erikson, *Young Man Luther* (1958), 69.
See Mead, **#611**, under "Punishment, Corporal."

69. [In China, 1250–1276] Earliest childhood was one of the happiest times of life. Children were allowed to roam about the streets in groups. They were never beaten, and to silence the really naughty ones nothing more stern was done than to threaten them with some sort of a bogeyman. One of these was Liu-the-Barbarian, with a dark skin like an Indian or a Malay. In the Huai valley and in Hupei, children were frightened into being good by warning them that Big-eyes Yang with the terrible voice would come. In southern Kiangsu, on the other hand, appeal was made to a kind of demon who had the power of curing malaria. To judge by the number of sweetsellers and toysellers who went about the street of the town, children must have been more often spoilt than punished. It was not until a fairly advanced age, about seven years, that they were sent to school, or in wealthy families, given a tutor.

—Jacques Gernet, *Daily Life in China on the Eve of the Mongol Invasion 1250–1276*, tr. H.M. Wright (1962), 153.

70. For success in training children the first condition is to become as a child oneself, but this means no assumed childishness, no condescending baby-talk that the child immediately sees through and deeply abhors. What it does mean is to be as entirely and simply taken up with the child as the child himself is absorbed by his life.

—Ellen Key, *The Century of the Child* (1909), iii.

71. I didn't know mothers were supposed to use psychology on children. I knew they used whatever was immediately available, like shaving strops, wooden ladles, or the ever-ready palm of the hand which wise Mother Nature had shaped to fit perfectly over the rear of a kid. Wise Mother Levenson simply applied wise Mother Nature's wisdom on us.

I didn't know that fathers were not supposed to hit kids if they were bad. Most fathers hit kids—anybody's. The kid whose father didn't hit him felt that his father either wasn't interested in him or wasn't his real father. Besides, as any honest kid will tell you under oath, there are days when kids can be quite impossible—like Monday through Sunday, for instance. Come to think of it, the only perfect kid I ever heard of was my father when he was a kid.

—Sam Levenson, *Everything But Money* (1949), 15.

72. Let therefore your *rules* to your son be as few as possible, and rather fewer than more that seem absolutely necessary. For if you burden him with many rules, one of these two things must necessarily follow; that either he must be very often punish'd, which will be of ill consequence, by making punishment too frequent and familiar; or else you must let the transgressions of some of your rules go unpunish'd, whereby they will of course grow contemptible, and your authority become cheap to him.

—John Locke, *Some Thoughts concerning Education* (1693), 65.

73. Parents neglect this duty [to educate their children] from various causes. In the first place, there are some who are so lacking in piety and uprightness that they would not do it if they could, but, like an ostrich, harden themselves against their offspring, and do nothing for them. In the second place, the great majority of parents are unqualified for it, and do not understand how children should be brought up and taught. In the third place, even if parents were qualified and willing to do it themselves, yet on account of the other employments and household duties, they have no time for it, so that necessity requires us to have teachers for public schools, unless each parent employ a private instructor.

—Martin Luther, *Letter to the Mayors and Aldermen* (1524), tr. F.V. Painter (1928).

74. Let no parent who prefers one child to the other think that the children are unaware of the situation. It cannot be concealed. It betrays itself in the glance of an eye, in the tones of the voice, and in all the other irrepressible symptoms of natural affinity. It is very hard on the other children. It can be even harder on the child who knows himself to be the center of parental interest. An increased understanding of human psychology, which we owe chiefly to Freud, has made modern parents painfully and in many cases so absurdly aware of the dangers of the Oedipus complex that they warn all their relatives and friends not to reflect their own secret preference for little Susie or Jimmie. This of course destroys all spontaneity and is probably worse for the children than the rankest favoritism. When parents really achieve perfect justice in relationship to their children, I am sure life will be saner but it will also be very dull.

—Agnes E. Meyer, *Out of These Roots* (1953), 13.

75. Nature in her wisdom has attached the parent to the child and bound them spiritually together with a Herculean knot. This tie is the source of my consideration for your immature minds, a consideration which causes me to take you often into my arms. This tie is the reason why I regularly fed you cake and gave you ripe apples and fancy pears. This tie is the reason why I used to dress you in silken garments and why I never could endure to hear you cry. You know, for example, how often I kissed you, how seldom I whipped you. My whip was invariably a peacock's tail. Even this I wielded hesitantly and gently so that sorry welts might not disfigure your tender seats. Brutal and unworthy to be called father is he who does not himself weep at the tears of his child. How other fathers act I do not know, but you know well how gentle and devoted is my manner toward you, for I have always profoundly loved my own children and I have always been an indulgent parent – as every father ought to be.

– Thomas More, letter to his daughters, probably in 1517, in Richard Marius, *Thomas More* (1984), 225.

76. I think she must have been strictly brought up, she's so desperately anxious to do the wrong thing correctly.

– Saki (H.H. Munro), *Reginald:* "Reginald on Worries" (1904).

77. Long as I have lived, I have never heard any persons converse as my father and mother did, and, as my mother never suffered her children to interrupt conversation, we were compelled to listen, whether willing or not. My father not only conversed in a superior way himself, but he gave the tone to all his visitors and to all his pupils. I can hardly say how young I was when I got ideas of other countries and times, and other modes of life, such as by the modern style of education could never possibly be obtained, and this through the simple means of listening to my father's conversation.

And while this system of improvement was going forward, whenever the family was assembled, there was a private discipline of such undeviating strictness, carried on with me by my excellent mother, that it might have appeared that no other person in the world could have been so well fitted to bring a mere child of many imaginations under regulations as was my ever honored parent. Lady Jane Grey speaks of the severities to which she was subjected by her noble parent, the nips, and bobs, and pinches; but I experienced what I thought much worse. It was the fashion then for children to wear iron collars around the neck, with backboards strapped over the shoulders. To one of these I was subjected from my sixth to my thirteenth year. I generally did all my lessons standing in stocks, with this same collar around my neck; it was put on in the morning, and seldom taken off till late in the evening; and it was Latin which I had to study! At the same time I had the plainest possible food; dry bread and cold milk were my principal food, and I never sat on a chair in my mother's presence. And yet I was a very happy child, and when relieved from my collar, I not unseldom manifested my delight by starting from our hall door and taking a run for half a mile through the woods which adjoined our pleasure grounds.

– Mary Martha Sherwood, *Memoirs* (1854).
For Lady Jane Grey's description of her upbringing,
See Ascham, #952, under "Teacher, Praise for."

78. If by some strange chance not a vestige of us descended to the remote future save a pile of school-books or some college examination papers, we may imagine how puzzled an antiquary of the period would be on finding in them no sign that the learners were ever likely to be parents. "This must have been the *curriculum* for their celibates," we may fancy him concluding. "I perceive here an elaborate preparation for many things; . . . but I find no reference whatever to the bringing up of children. They could not have been so absurd as to omit all training for this gravest of responsibilities. Evidently then, this was the school-course of one of their monastic orders."

—Herbert Spencer, *What Knowledge Is of Most Worth?* (1859).

79. Every citizen's son, the child of a chaste mother, was from the beginning reared, not in the chamber of a purchased nurse, but in that mother's bosom and embrace, and it was her special glory to study her home and devote herself to her children. . . . But in our day we entrust the enfant to a little Greek servant-girl who is attended by one or two, commonly the worst of all slaves, creatures utterly unfit for any important work.

—Tacitus, *A Dialogue on Oratory* (c. A.D. 81), xxviii, xxix.

80. Before I got married I had six theories about bringing up children; now I have six children and no theories.

—John Wilmot, 2nd Earl of Rochester (1647–80).
He was the most notorious of the Restoration rakes.

Childhood

(*See also* Adolescence; Children; Youth and Age)

81. Childhood in seventeenth-century America was not easy. Families were large, infant mortality high, and medicine medieval. One recommended cure for infantile diseases was a tonic consisting largely of snails, earthworms, and "The Strongest Ale." Discipline was severe. In many households children were not to sit while eating, as did their elders, but stood at the table during meals—in silence. School days were long. Lessons were shrouded in somber theology and warnings of impending doom. *The New England Primer*, first published in 1683, was liberally illustrated with symbols of the grave and carried such rhymed couplets as "Xerxes did die, And so must I" and "While Youth do cheer, Death may be near."

—*The American Heritage History of Colonial Antiques*
(1967), 30. See *The Youth's Instructor*, #1047, under "Textbook."

82. In medieval society the idea of childhood did not exist; this is not to suggest that children were neglected, forsaken, or despised. The idea of childhood is not to be confused with affection for children: It corresponds to an awareness of the particular nature of childhood, that particular nature of childhood which distinguishes the child from the adult, even the young adult. In medieval society this awareness was lacking. This is why, as soon as the child could live without the constant solicitude of his mother, his nanny, or his cradle-rocker, he belonged to adult society.

—Philippe Ariès, *Centuries of Childhood* (1962), 128. *See* Illich, **#84.**

83. It is difficult, impossible, I am told, for anyone to recall his boyhood exactly as it was. It could not have been what it seems to the adult mind, since we cannot escape from what we are . . . and in going back we must take our present selves with us: The mind has taken a different color, and this is thrown back upon our past.

—W.H. Hudson, *Far Away and Long Ago* (1918). *See* Rinehart, **#89.**

84. Childhood as distinct from infancy, adolescence, or youth was unknown to most historical periods. Some Christian centuries did not even have an eye for its bodily proportions. Artists depicted the infant as a miniature adult seated on his mother's arm. Children appeared in Europe along with the pocket watch and the Christian moneylenders of the Renaissance. Before our century neither the poor nor the rich knew of children's dress, children's games or the child's immunity from the law. Children belonged to bourgeoisie. The worker's child, the peasant's child, and the nobleman's child all dressed the way their fathers dressed, played the way their fathers played, and were hanged by the neck as were their fathers. After the discovery of "childhood" by the bourgeoisie all this changed. . . .

Until the last century, "children" of middle-class parents were taught at home with the help of preceptors and private schools. Only with the advent of industrial society did the mass production of "childhood" become feasible and come within the reach of the masses. The school system is a modern phenomenon, as is the childhood it produces.

—Ivan D. Illich, *Deschooling Society* (1970), 26. *See* Ariès, **#82.**

85. Long before our formal education began, our generation went to school in our backyards in Rockwell's Woods. Tagging at our parents' heels we learned to tell black oak from white, and both from red. We learned to recognize beech, ash, poplar, and pepperidge tree. Science was in its infancy and there came to us the early classifications of botany, the erudite story of the heavenly bodies, the dramatic history of the earth written in hill, valley, and drumlin in quartz, amethyst, and garnet. There were birds to discover and commit to heart, and fish to call by name as they swam undisturbed by our peering eyes. Turtles and peep frogs, woodchucks and chipmunks, snakes and toads were our familiars—all the wondrous commonplaces of the freshly discovered outdoors.

—Gerard E. Jensen, *A Boyhood in the Nineties: Reminiscences of Norwich, Connecticut,* in Oliver Jensen, ed., *The Nineties* (1967), 91.

86. It's odd how large a part food plays in memories of childhood. There are grown men and women who still shudder at the sight of spinach, or turn away with loathing from stewed prunes and tapioca.... Luckily, however, it's the good taste one remembers best.

—Caroline Lejeune, *Thank You for Having Me* (1964), i.

87. How recapture for modern youngsters the flavor of American village life before the dubious influence of automobiles, telephones, moving pictures, radios and television? Our favorite haunt after school was the blacksmith shop where it was a high privilege to be allowed to blow the bellows and watch the coals glow in the open grate. Nobody had yet thought up the dull process called vocational training. It was still something we absorbed as tools and agricultural implements were mended and horses shod. While this was going on we lent half an ear to the leisurely discussion by the grownups of village and national politics, of human tragedies and comedies, of the many decent, homely interests of decent, homely people who then as now were sure the country would go to the dogs unless the Republicans were re-elected.

—Agnes E. Meyer, *Out of These Roots* (1953), 18.

88. All through my boyhood I had a profound conviction that I was no good, that I was wasting my time, wrecking my talents, behaving with monstrous folly and wickedness and ingratitude—and all this, it seemed, was inescapable, because I lived among laws which were absolute, like the law of gravity, but which it was not possible for me to keep.

—George Orwell, *A Collection of Essays* (1970).

89. Men deceive themselves; they look back on the children who were once themselves, and attempt to reconstruct them. But they can no longer think like a child, and against the unpleasant and the horrid the mind has set up the defensive machinery of forgetfulness.

—Mary Roberts Rinehart, *My Story* (1931), 3. *See* Hudson, **#83.**

90. We have thought that because children are young they are silly. We have forgotten the blind stirrings, the reaching outward of our own youth.

—Mabel Louise Robinson, "Writing for the Younger Generation," in Helen Hull, ed., *The Writer's Book* (1950).

91. There is the myth that you can explain neurotic behavior by attributing it to an unhappy childhood. But *all* childhood is unhappy; all childhood is charged with uncertainty and fear, with conflict and frustration, with unbearable rage and unattainable desire. It makes little sense to talk about unhappy childhoods unless we ask why some people emerge from childhood with their productive capacities enriched, while others remain paralyzed by unresolved and infantile dilemmas.

—Leo Rosten, *The Many Worlds of Leo Rosten:* "The Free Mind" (1964), 207.

92. An indescribably sweet breeze blows over the friendships of childhood. They are tender, delicate, pale blue petals that tremble with each stir of the childish soul and whose roots even then already penetrate down to the deep layers in which inherited instincts and tempting desires fertilise the soil of the passions. Its first friendship is a revelation for the child. . . .

Say what you will, only a child can be a child's friend! . . .

The child is surrounded by so much authority, so much school, so much dignity, so much law, that it would have to break down under the weight of all these restraints if it were not saved from such a fate by meeting with a friend.

—William Stekel, *The Depths of the Soul* (1921), 73, 76. *See* Disraeli, **#801,** under "Student."

93. Certainly Adam had not more sweet and curious apprehensions of the world, then I when I was a child.

—Thomas Traherne (1637?–1674), *Centuries of Meditation* (published 1908). Discovered at the end of the 19th century, this was once mistaken for the work of Henry Vaughan.

94. The difference between a childhood and a boyhood must be this: our childhood is what we alone have had; our boyhood is what any boy in our environment would have had.

—John Updike, *Assorted Prose:* "Environment" (1965).

95. Oh for boyhood's painless play,
Sleep that wakes in laughing day,
Health that mocks the doctor's rules,
Knowledge never learned of schools,
Of the wild bee's morning chase,
Of the wild-flower's time and place,
Flight of fowl and habitude
Of the tenants of the wood.

—John Greenleaf Whittier, "The Barefoot Boy" (1855), st.ii,
The Complete Poetical Works of John Greenleaf Whittier (1892).

96. I find it difficult to say whether my childhood was happy. I suspect that most childhoods are more alike than we suppose. Children have very little capacity for sustained happiness. Dr. Johnson suggested that happiness and misery are always pretty much alike for every human being, and the happiness of a great general who has saved his country is exactly the same as the happiness of a girl attending her first dance. This is certainly true of children. They can be made miserable and cheerful, but really miserable or really happy childhoods must be rare exceptions. Most of them alternate between the two, with the same pleasures, the same embarrassments and guilts, the same pride, the same enthusiasm.

—Colin Wilson, *Voyage to a Beginning:
An Intellectual Autobiography* (1969), 16.

97. "What are *you* going to be when you grow up, Joey?" Walter asked.

"Why, a farmer, of course," Joey answered. "What else would I be? I'm one already. Like my pa, and my grandpa, and his pa. Rogers are always farmers." . . .

"What are you going to be, Walter?" Joey finally inquired.

Walter answered slowly, "I don't know. I haven't made up my mind. Maybe a minister, like Pa. Or maybe a schoolmaster. I want to do something," he hesitated a moment seriously, "whatever it is, that will *help* people."

"You better not be a schoolmaster, then," Joey advised drily, recalling his own regrettable educational experiences in which a hickory stick had figured largely.

—L.N. Wood, *Walter Reed: Doctor in Uniform* (1943), 10–11.

Children

(*See also* Adolescence; Childhood)

98. Children are so much the goods, the possessions of their parents, that they cannot, without a kind of theft, give away themselves without the allowance of those that have a right to them.

—Richard Allestree, *The Whole Duty of Man* (1663). *Contrast* Gilman **#108.**

99. *Mrs. Darling:* Peter . . . let me adopt you.
Peter: Would you send me to school?
Mrs. Darling: Yes.
Peter: And then to an office?
Mrs. Darling: I suppose so.
Peter: Soon I should be a man?
Mrs. Darling: Very soon.
Peter: I don't want to go to school and learn solemn things. No one is going to catch me, lady, and make me a man. I want always to be a little boy and have fun.

—James M. Barrie, *Peter Pan* (1904), V.

100. Since children are spotted with evil manners, and think on things that be, and regard not of things that shall be, they love playing, and games, and vanity, and forsake learning and profit; and things most worthy they repute least worthy, and least worthy most worthy. They desire things that be to them contrary and grievous, and set more store by the image of a child than the image of a man, and make more sorrow and woe, and weep more for the loss of an apple, than for the loss of their heritage; and the goodness that is done for them they let pass out of mind. They desire all things that they see, and pray and ask with voice and with hand. They love talking and counsel of such children as they be, and avoid company of old men. They keep no counsel, but they tell all they hear and see. Suddenly they laugh and suddenly they weep. Always they cry, jangle, scorn, or disdain, that hardly they be still while they sleep. When they are washed of filth, straightaway they defile themselves again. When the mother washeth and combeth them, they kick and sprawl, and put with feet and hands, and withstandeth with all their might. For they think only on belly joy.

—Friar Bartholomew the Englishman (fl.1230–50), in Derek Brewer, *Chaucer in His Time* (1963), 120.

101. Children are sacred and pure. Even among cutthroats and crocodiles they maintain their angelic rank. We may crawl into any pit you like, but we are in duty bound to envelop them in an atmosphere befitting their rank. You can't be foul-mouthed in their presence with impunity, or insult the servant, or tell Natalya Aleksandrovna with rancor, "Get out! To the devil with you! I'm not holding you!"

You can't make children the plaything of your mood, now kissing them tenderly, then stamping your feet at them in a frenzy. It is better not to love than to love with a despotic love.

—Anton Chekhov, letter to Aleksandr, his eldest brother, Jan. 2, 1889, in Avrahm Yarmolinsky, ed., *Letters of Anton Chekhov* (1973), 105. Natalya Aleksandrovna was Aleksandr's second wife. *Contrast* Edwards, **#105**, and Spring, **#116.**

102. Until one looks back on one's own past one fails to realize what an extraordinary view of the world a child has. The angle of vision is entirely different from that of an adult; everything is out of proportion.

Children can make a shrewd appraisal of what is going on around them, and have a quite good judgment of character and people. But the *how* and *why* of things seem never to occur to them.

—Agatha Christie, *An Autobiography* (1977), 57.

103. Much may be learned about any society by studying the behaviour and accepted ideas of its children, for children—and sometimes adults—are shadows of their parents, and what they believe and what they do are often what their parents believe in their hearts and would do if society would put up with it.

—Robertson Davies, *What's Bred in the Bone* (1985), 154.

104. Children are profoundly observant and perceptive. In fact, their perception is the means by which they catch up to the world because they find everyone in advance of where they are. The perception becomes sort of an act of betrayal. The kid is dependent on everyone around him, on the parents, but begins to hone his capacity to perceive and make judgments, which is independence. So he gets trapped in the tension between dependence and independence and feels very guilty about what he knows.

—E.L. Doctorow, in *Sarasota Herald-Tribune,* Dec. 15, 1985.

105. All children are by nature children of wrath, and are in danger of eternal damnation in Hell.

—Jonathan Edwards, *Sermon to Children* (1740). *See* Chekhov, **#101**, and Spring, **#116.**

106. I suppose to some extent all children have a touch of magic about them—like some mysterious lens, they seem to have the capacity to focus the light into the darkest and gloomiest of places. . . . Perhaps it's the newness of the young, or perhaps it's just because the shine hasn't worn off, but they can and do (if you give them half a chance) make a dent in the toughest armor of life. If you're very lucky they can dissolve away all those protective barricades so carefully erected over years of living.

—Fynn *[pseud.], Mister God, this is Anna* (1974), 60.

107. A kid is a guy I never write down to. He's interested in what I say if I make it interesting. He is also the last container of a sense of humor, which disappears as he gets older, and he laughs only according to the way the boss, society, politics, or race, want him to. Then he becomes an adult. And an adult is an obsolete child.

—Theodor Geisel (Dr. Seuss), *New York Mirror,* May 18, 1958.

108. There is no more brilliant hope on earth today than this new thought about the child . . . the recognition of the child, children as a class, children as citizens with rights to be guaranteed only by the state; instead of our previous attitude toward them of absolute personal ownership—the unchecked tyranny, or as unchecked indulgence, of the private home.

—Charlotte Perkins Gilman,
The Home (1903). *Contrast* Allestree, **#98.**

109. If I were asked what is to be accounted the great discovery of this century, I would pass by all the splendid achievements that men have wrought in wood and stone and iron and brass . . . the printing press, the loom, the steam-engine, the steamship, the ocean cable, the telegraph, the wireless telegraphy, the telephone, the phonograph . . . the planets that have been added to our solar sytem . . . the Roentgen ray that promises to revolutionize the study of the human brain . . . the labor-saving machines and devices . . . above and beyond all these the index finger of the world's progress, in the march of time, would point unerringly to the little child as the one great discovery of the century now speeding to its close.

—G.R. Glenn, "What Manner of Child Shall This Be?,"
National Education Association, *Proceedings,* 1900.

110. Not for me, thank you. I wouldn't want to be a child again, even for one night. I wasn't miserable exactly but I don't look back on laughing, carefree days, either. I was no merry grig. I was no gloomy grig. Never at ease with other children, wary of grown-ups, I wasn't popular and didn't really yearn to be. I enjoyed being alone, except for my grandmother.... The truth is that I was an oddball child.

—Helen Lawrenson, *Stranger at the Party* (1972), 11.

111. Never imagine that children who don't say, or ask, don't know. In their blank eyes and heedless ears is hidden their attempt to make away with what they cannot swallow. Unable to become shock-proof except by cutting off response, they must go deaf and blind. Some remain so, learning self-protection all too well.

—Rosamond Lehmann, *The Swan in the Evening* (1967), 52.

112. Ah! what would the world be to us
If the children were no more?
We should dread the desert behind us
Worse than the dark below.

—Henry Wadsworth Longfellow, "Children" (1849), st.iv,
The Poetical Works of Henry Wadsworth Longfellow (1870).

113. The hearts of small children are delicate organs. A cruel beginning in this world can twist them into curious shapes. The heart of a child can shrink so that forever afterward it is hard and pitted as the seed of a peach. Or again, the heart of such a child may fester and swell until it is a misery to carry within the body, easily chafed and hurt by the most ordinary things.

—Carson McCullers, *The Member of the Wedding* (1946).

114. Of all the dear sights in the world, nothing is so beautiful as a child when it is giving something. Any small thing it gives. A child gives the world to you . . . it opens the world for you as if it were a book you'd never been able to read. But when a gift must be found, it is always some absurd little thing, pasted on crooked . . . an angel looking like a clown. . . . A child has so little that it can give, because it never knows it has given you everything.

—Margaret Lee Runbeck, *Our Miss Boo:*
"The Sum," (1942), 224. *See* Orwell, **#1002,** under "Teaching."

115. A baby is God's opinion that life should go on. . . . Never will a time come when the most marvelous invention is as marvelous as a newborn baby. The finest of our precision watches, the most supercolossal of our supercargo planes, don't compare with a newborn baby in the number and ingenuity of coils and springs, in the flow and change of chemical solutions, in timing devices and interrelated parts that are irreplaceable.

—Carl Sandburg, *Remembrance Rock*, "Prologue" (1948), 7.

116. All children have wicked hearts when they are born: and that makes them so wicked when they grow up in life. Even little infants, that appear so innocent and pretty, are God's little enemies at heart.

—Samuel Spring, *Three Sermons to Little Children* (1819). *See* Chekhov, **#101**, and Edwards, **#105.**

117. The greatest terror a child can have is that he is not loved, and rejection is the hell of fears. . . . And with rejection comes anger, and with anger some kind of crime in revenge. . . . One child, refused the love he craves, kicks the cat and hides his secret guilt: and another steals so that money will make him loved; and a third conquers the world—and always the guilt and revenge and more guilt.

—John Steinbeck, *East of Eden* (1952).

118. Always obey your parents, when they are present. This is the best policy in the long run, because if you don't they will make you. Most parents think they know better than you do, and you can generally make more by humoring this superstition than you can by acting on your own better judgment.

Be respectful to your superiors, if you have any, also to strangers and sometimes to others. . . .

Go to bed early, get up early—that is wise—although I once knew a man who got up at sunrise and a horse bit him. . . . Some authorities say get up with the sun; others say get up with one thing, some another. But a lark is really the best thing to get up with. It gives you a splendid reputation with everybody to know that you get up with the lark, and if you can get the right kind of lark, and work him right, you can easily train him to get up at half past nine, every time.

—Mark Twain, speech to young people, in Albert Bigelow Paine, ed., *Mark Twain's Speeches* (1910), 104.

119. There was a child went forth every day,
And the first object he looked upon or received with wonder or pity or love or dread, that object he became,
And that object became part of him for the day or a certain part of the day . . . or for many years or stretching cycles of years.

—Walt Whitman, *Leaves of Grass* (1855), xxiv.

College

(*See also* Degree, Academic; Freedom, Academic; Professor; School Rules; Student, College; Student Pranks; Student Songs)

120. [Oxford University:] Home of lost causes, and forsaken beliefs, and unpopular names, and impossible loyalties.

—Matthew Arnold, preface to *Essays in Criticism,* (1865), I.

121. A university, in its perfect extent, is one of the noblest results of human intelligence. It aims at nothing else than to furnish a concentration of all useful knowledge; to collect, to digest, to diffuse all the learning which can in any manner be made the fit subject of public instruction and promote the honor and advantage of the nation. An individual is plainly incompetent to fulfill any but a small part of such a purpose. It requires joint action; it requires that which, more than anything else, constitutes the happiness of liberal minds—the extensive cooperation of good men in furthering good designs. To such an institution belongs a library, collections in natural history, hospitals; men learned in the professions and in the arts; the inquisitive and ambitious of the young.

A university is not devoted exclusively to any one department of knowledge. It opens its gates wide to the reception of all valuable truth; and sustaining no particular branch of science by the sanction of prescription, by the continuance of favoritism, or by the dead letter of intellectual mortmains, it allows to each division of human knowledge that degree of prominence which its intrinsic merits can obtain. In the true social spirit, it receives and takes an interest in everything that belongs to the human understanding.

Neither is it a mere system of lectures adapted to the curious and the idle. It is designed not to afford pastime but to excite and encourage severe industry; not to furnish amusement but to diffuse and also to advance science.

Nor does it attach itself to any sect in religion. God forbid that the day should ever arrive when there should be a separation of pure morality and deep religious conviction from our public places of education; but the character of a university requires that it should be subordinate to no religious party, subservient to no religious sect. It must be established independently, on its own merits.

—George Bancroft, *Journal of the Proceedings of a Convention of Literary and Scientific Gentlemen,* 1831, in *The Annals of America* (1968), V.380.

122. Speaking of bathrooms, the first bathtubs to appear in Harvard dormitories were installed in the basement of Matthews Hall in the 1870s. Up until the sixties there was no water supply of any kind in the Yard. Neither was there any sewer. For bathing purposes the students carried water to their rooms in pails from one of the two pumps in the yard. Perhaps they heated some water on their own fire—otherwise they had nice, cold water. Consequently "the amount of bathing done in the college was very limited."

—Richard Bissell, *You Can Always Tell a Harvard Man* (1962), 198.

123. This College is for all conditions and classes of men without regard to color, nationality, race, or religion. A man white, black, or yellow; Christian, Jew, Mohammedan, or heathen, may enter and enjoy all the advantages of this insitution for three, four, or eight years, and go out believing in one God, in many gods, or in no God. But it will be impossible for anyone to continue with us long without knowing what we believe to be the truth and our reasons for that belief.

—Daniel Bliss, credo for the American University of Beirut, 1871.

124. [At Harvard College in 1815] It was true that the standard of learning was not too lofty. In this, as in certain other respects, the well-known "Harvard indifference" resembled that of Oxford and Madrid. Intellectual things took second place. The object of study was to form the mind, but this was to form the character; and Massachusetts knew what its character was and took a certain satisfaction in it. Everyone was aware of the best Boston and Cambridge type, the type that Josiah Quincy represented, or the late Chief Justice Dana, formed on the classic models. A clear, distinct mentality, a strong distaste for nonsense, steady composure, a calm and gentle demeanour, stability, good principles, intelligence, a habit of understatement, a slow and cautious way of reasoning, contempt for extravagance, vanity and affection, kindness of heart, purity, decorum, profound affections, filial and paternal. A noble type, severely limited, which Boston celebrated in its marble busts.

—Van Wyck Brooks, *The Flowering of New England, 1815–1865* (1936), 34.

125. The king to Oxford sent a troop of horse,
For Tories know no argument but force;

With equal skill to Cambridge books he sent,
For Whigs admit no force but argument.

—Sir William Browne (1692–1774), in *The Faber Book of Comic Verse,* ed. Michael Roberts (1967), 67. A response to Trapp's poem #**153.**

126. More than once I went a considerable distance out of my way to pass the corner of Lexington Avenue and Twenty-Third Street, where that edifice [City College of New York] stood. I would . . . gaze at its red, ivy-clad walls, mysterious high windows, humble spires; I would stand watching the students on the campus . . . and go my way, with a heart full of reverence, envy, and hope. . . .

It was not merely a place in which I was to fit myself for the battle of life, nor merely one in which I was going to acquire knowledge. It was a symbol of spiritual promotion as well. University-bred people were the real nobility of the world. . . . The red, church-like structure . . . was the synagogue of my new life [in America].

—Abraham Cahan, *The Rise of David Levinsky* (1917), 168.

127. A university studies politics, but it will not advocate fascism or communism. A university studies military tactics, but it will not promote war. A university studies peace, but it will not organize crusades of pacifism. It will study every question that affects human welfare, but it will not carry a banner in a crusade for anything except freedom of learning.

—Lotus Delta Coffman, *Journal of the American Association of University Women,* January 1936.

128. *Jeremy.* Sir, I have the Seeds of Rhetorick and Oratory in my Head—I have been at *Cambridge.*

Tattle. Ay: 'tis well enough for a Servant to be bred at an University: But the Education is a little too pedantick for a Gentleman.

—William Congreve, *Love for Love* (1695), V.iii.22.

129. We went [to Harvard College], expecting to see something unusual as it is the only college, or would-be academy of the Protestants in America, but we found eight or ten young fellows sitting around, smoking tobacco . . . the whole house smelt so strong of it that I said "It certainly must be also a tavern." We inquired how many professors there were and they replied not one. . . . They knew hardly a word of Latin. . . . They took us to the library, where there was nothing particular.

—Jasper Danckaerts, *Journal,* 1968, in Richard Bissell, *You Can Always Tell a Harvard Man* (1962), 147.

130. The house in which classes are taught at present is situated in a pleasant part of the Town, and is sixty feet long and twenty-three broad. Three large rooms are finished for the purpose of teaching; there is also a library room and an apartment for the philosophical apparatus.

The library already consists of two thousand, seven hundred and six volumes, in Hebrew, Greek, Latin, English, French, German, Low Dutch and Italian languages, the donations of gentlemen in England, Scotland and Philadelphia.

The philosophical apparatus contains a complete electrical machine, a camera obscura of a new construction, a prism, a telescope, a solar microscope, a barometer and thermometer, upon one scale, and a large and elegant set of globes. . . . The tuition money is only five pounds per annum to be paid half-yearly, and twenty-five shillings entrance; boarding can be had at twenty-six pounds per annum, in general houses, including washing, mending, fire and candles; twelve boarding houses are now open, equal to any at other seminaries, and the greatest attention will be paid to the morals of the students by Dr. Nesbit and Dr. Davidson, who officiate in the Presbyterian Church on Sundays.

By order of the board
JOHN ARMSTRONG, PRESI. PRO TEM

—Advertisement published by the Trustees of Dickinson College (Pennsylvania), in Walker Lewis, *Without Fear of Favor* (1965), 16. In contrast, Dr. Charles Nesbit, its first president, wrote to Dr. Benjamin Rush that "the town is situated in a deep clay swamp" and students "are obliged to lodge in small, narrow and inconvenient apartments."—*Ibid.*, 15.

131. Enter to grow in wisdom.

—Inscription on the outside of the Gate to Harvard Yard, 1890.

Depart to serve better thy country and mankind.

—Inscription on the inside of the Gate.
—Charles William Eliot

132. It is said that once, on his way to breakfast, the master of Adams House [Harvard] saw a boy and a girl leaving the boy's room, and without skipping a beat, said, "Good morning, gentlemen." At this point, I think, co-residential housing was inevitable.

—Anne Fadiman, *Life* Magazine, September 1966.

133. We keep the students within view of their parents; we save them the toils and long foreign journeys; we protect them from robbers. They used to be pillaged while traveling abroad; now, they may study at small cost and short wayfaring, thanks to our liberality.

—Frederick II, Holy Roman Emperor,
charter of foundation of the University of Naples, July 1224.

134. Erfurt was the most modern German university of its day [1501].... Erfurt University even took the unprecedented step of giving the faculty of philosophy pride of place over the faculty of theology, which reigned undisputed everywhere else.... Unlike other universities Erfurt had not followed the example of Paris and divided its students by grouping compatriots together; on his arrival every student had to enrol in a *Burse*, or students' hostel, where he lived as a boarder under strict supervision. Jealously as the students paraded their status before the townspeople, they had to toe the line like schoolboys in their hostels, where life was almost monastic, their meals, their prayers, their coming and going being prescribed and supervised. The syllabus of work was controlled; any student wishing to attend a lecture that was not compulsory had to get permission from the rector. The students wore uniforms, to make them easily identifiable in the town; university bulldogs, as well as proctors, kept a lookout. The choice of books was not left to students, and we may safely assume that Luther hardly ever held a book in his hand which deviated, however slightly, from what his professors regarded as the true path.... [He] rose with the bell at four o'clock each morning and went to bed, in obedience to the rules, at eight o'clock at night.

—Richard Friedenthal, *Luther: His Life and Times* (1970), 18.

135. [At Harvard] It was still necessary, in the second half of that [eighteenth] century for the student to carry his own knife and fork to the dining room, and when he had dined he wiped them on the tablecloth....

The food was scant, poorly cooked, and the service primitive.... Necessity, the mother of invention, drove these often underfed boys to "pin to the surfaces of the table by a two-pronged fork some slices of meat from the previous day's dinner." This practice of forking meat to the underside of the pine tables seems to have been almost general college custom, for we find it reported in accounts of life at Princeton, where the historian, Varnum Lansing Collins, tells us that ownership of these dividends from yesterday's dinner was "strictly respected, stray dogs alone excepted."

At Yale "the breakfast consisted of ollapodrida hashed up from the remains of yesterday's dinner and fried into a consistency that baffled digestion. This compound was known as slum. To these accommodations a senior or a tutor would prefix and suffix a grace, during the telling of which two forks were sometimes observed sticking into each potato on the table."...

—Christian Gauss, "The Good Old Times," in A.C. Spectorsky, ed., *The College Years* (1958), 85, 87. [ollapodrida=*a highly seasoned stew made of one or more meats and several vegetables*].

136. At Bowdoin, and probably in America generally, blackboards were used for the first time in 1824. Before that date, at Bowdoin and probably at most other American colleges, college men did much of their work on slates.

—Christian Gauss, *ibid.*

137. Surely it was of this place, now Cambridge [University] but formerly known by the name of Babylon, that the prophet spoke when he said, "The wild beasts of the desert shall dwell there, and their houses shall be full of doleful creatures, and owls shall build there; and satyrs shall dance there; their forts and towers shall be a den for ever, a joy of wild asses."

—Thomas Gray, letter to Richard West, December 1736.

138. When any scholar is able to read Tully [Cicero] or such like classical Latin author *extempore*, and make and speak true Latin in verse and prose *suo (ut aiunt) Marte* [without any assistance whatever], and decline perfectly the paradigms of nouns and verbs in the Greek tongue, then may he be admitted into the College, nor shall any claim admission before such qualifications.

—Harvard College requirements for admission, 1642, in Josiah Quincy, *The History of Harvard University* (1840), I.515.

139. The word university originally meant a corporation or gild in general, and the Middle Ages had many such forms of corporate life. Only gradually did the term become narrowed so as to denote exclusively a learned corporation or society of masters and scholars, *universitas societas magistrorum discipulorumque*, as it is expressed in the earliest and still the best definition of a university. In this general sense there might be several universities in the same town, just as there were several craft gilds, and these separate universities of law or of medicine were each jealous of their corporate life and were slow to coalesce into a single university with its special faculties. Speaking broadly, the nucleus of the new development was in Northern Europe a gild of masters and in the South a gild of students, but in both cases the point of chief importance centres about admission to the gild of masters or professors. Without such admission there could be no license to teach; until then one could be only a student, thereafter one was a master, in rank if not by occupation, and had passed out of the journeyman stage. In order to guard against favoritism and monopoly, such admission was determined by an examination, and ability to pass this examination was the natural test of academic attainment in the several subjects of study. This license to teach *(licentia docendi)* was thus the earliest form of academic degree. Historically, all degrees are in their origin teachers' certificates, as the names doctor and master still show us; a Master of Arts was a qualified teacher of arts, a Doctor of Laws or Medicine was a certified teacher of these subjects. Moreover the candidate regularly gave a specimen lecture, or, as it was said, incepted, and this inception is the origin of the modern commencement, which means commencing to teach. An examination presupposes a body of material upon which the candidate is examined, usually a set of standard textbooks, and this in turn implies systematic teaching and a minimum period of study. Curriculum, examinations, commencement, degrees are all part of the same system; they are all inherited from the Middle Ages, and in some form they go back to the twelfth century.

—Charles Homer Haskins,
The Renaissance of the Twelfth Century (1927), 369
See first Anonymous, **#188,** under "Degree, Academic."

140. When the High Lama asked him whether Shangri-La was not unique in his experience, and if the Western world could offer anything in the least like it, he answered with a smile: "Well, yes—to be quite frank it reminds me very slightly of Oxford, where I used to lecture. The scenery is not so good, but the subjects of study are often just as impractical, and though even the oldest of the dons is not quite so old, they appear to age in a somewhat similar way."

—James Hilton, *Lost Horizon* (1933), 159.

141.

HERE WAS BURIED
THOMAS JEFFERSON
AUTHOR
OF THE DECLARATION OF
AMERICAN INDEPENDENCE
OF
THE STATUTE OF VIRGINIA
FOR RELIGIOUS FREEDOM AND
FATHER OF THE UNIVERSITY

OF VIRGINIA
BORN APRIL 2D
1743 O.S.
DIED [JULY 4]
[1826]

—Thomas Jefferson, inscription for his tombstone, written by himself. April 2d, "O.S.," or Old Style, is April 15, New Style. Note that he did not include that he was also President of the United States of America.

142. It is not brick and mortar, books and laboratories that make a university. These are its vegetative organs. Its spirit is given by its teachers. It is not what is their fame, what their degrees, what they have published, but *what can they do?*... The best teacher, other things being equal, is the one most human. The ultimate aim of education is the regulation of human conduct. Its justification is the building up of an enlightened common sense. It is to help make right action possible and prevalent that the university exists.

—David Starr Jordan (1851–1931), in Mary A. Hill, *Charlotte Perkins Gilman: The Making of a Radical Feminist, 1860–1896* (1980), 246.

143. [No rule should be made that would] exclude any person of any Religious Denomination whatever from Equal Liberty and advantage of Education, or from any the Degrees, Liberties, Privileges, Benefits, or Immunities, on account of his particular Tenets in matters of Religion.

—Charter of King's College (later Columbia University), 1754.

144. Does a College education pay? Does it pay to feed in pork trimmings at five cents a pound in the hopper and draw out nice, cunning, little "country" sausages at the other end? Does it pay to take a steer that's been running loose on the range and living on cactus and petrified wood till he's just a bunch of barb-wire and sole-leather, and feed him corn till he's just a solid hunk of porterhouse steak and oleo oil?

—George Horace Lorimer, *Letters from a Self-Made Merchant to His Son* (1902)

145. There was no heat in any of the buildings [of Harvard University], except that supplied by the open fireplaces in each study. Students bought their own coal, kept it in a locked closet in the cellar, except in Gray's hall where the closets were outside of each room, and during the winter fires were kept going day and night in the little coal grates. This kind of heat had its advantages over present methods, for not only was it pleasant, healthy heat, as the chimmey kept taking the bad air out of the room, removing all need of modern air-conditioning gadgets, but the fire was a delightful place for the midnight saucepan of hot chocolate, made with condensed milk; nor is there any modern way of making toast as delicious as the eleven o'clock Sunday morning toast, made after the fire had been raked, fresh coal put on, the window closed, and two roommates had crawled under the covers until the room warmed up and the fire was right. For toast made this way the bread had to be fresh, slices cut thick, a hole poked in the slice so it can be hung on the poker (it will not be right if toasted on the gridiron); the butter should be sweet butter, kept on the window ledge inside the double window, so that it cannot be "fished" up by the thieves living in the room overhead, though it will taste better if it has been secured by that method from the room below; the fire should be very hot and the toast crisp on both sides, soft in the middle, buttered hot, and eaten instantly. If funds are in, a few lamb chops cooked the same way, but impaled on a stolen fork lashed to the poker, will taste as no other chops ever tasted; they too must be eaten as hot as fingers can hold them or should be torn limb from limb without benefit of knife or fork. Now Harvard heats these buildings, fireplaces are dark, and toast cannot be made on a radiator.

—William G. Morse, Harvard '99,
Pardon My Harvard Accent (1941).

146. The view taken of a University in these Discourses is the following: — That it is a place of *teaching* universal *knowledge*. This implies that its object is, on the one hand, intellectual, not moral; and on the other, that it is the diffusion and extension of knowledge rather than the advancement. If its object were scientific and philosophical discovery, I do not see why a University should have students; if religious training, I do not see how it can be the seat of literature and science.

—John Henry Newman, *The Idea of a University* (1873), preface.

147. [*Circa* 1660] A college would often have its own particular resort, and [William] Prideaux tells an agreeable story of an inn over against Balliol College, 'a dingy, horrid, scandalous alehouse, fit for none but draymen and tinkers. . . . Here the Balliol men continually lie and by perpetual bubbling add art to their natural stupidity to make themselves perfect sots. The head, being informed of this, called them together, and in a grave speech informed them of the mischiefs of that hellish liquor called ale.' One of them, however, replied that 'the Vice-Chancellor's men drank ale at the Split Cow, and why not they?' The Master then went to the Vice-Chancellor, but he 'being an old lover of ale himself was unsympathetic; and the Master, returning to his college, called the fellows again and told them that he had been with the Vice-Chancellor and that he told him there was no hurt in ale; truly, he thought there was, but now, being informed of the contrary, since the Vice-Chancellor gave his men leave to drink ale, he would give them leave to [sic]; so that now they may be sots by authority.'

—William Prideaux, in Graham Greene,
Lord Rochester's Monkey (1974), 29.

148. My sovereign Lord, think not that I have placed him in that lousy college, which they call Montague. I had rather have put him amongst gravediggers of Sanct Innocent, so enormous is the cruelty and villainy I have known there; for the galley-slaves are far better amongst the Moors and Tartars, the murderers in criminal dungeons, yea, the very dogs in your house, than are the poor wretched students in aforesaid college. And if I were King of Paris, the devil take me if I would not set it on fire and burn both the Principal and the Regents for suffering this inhumanity to be exercised before their eyes.

—François Rabelais (c. 1490–1553), in Paul Eldridge,
François Rabelais: The Great Storyteller (1971), 25.

149. *Normal school* is a literal translation of French *école normale.* Both the French and English forms of *normal* are derived from the Latin *norma,* signifying carpenter's rule, pattern or model. The French called colleges for the training of teachers normal schools because they were intended to be the model schools whose methods of instruction were for imitation in other institutions. The first *école normale* was founded in 1685 at Rheims, France, by Abbe de la Salle, founder of "The Brothers of the Christian Schools," who desired to train teachers for the schools of the order, which were designed to offer free religious primary education to the children of the working classes.

—George Stimpson, *A Book
About a Thousand Things* (1946), 262.

150. UNIVERSITY *n.* Institution where people incapacitated by an intellectual disposition can be put out of society's way.

—Graham Storr, "A (Fairly) Concise Science
Dictionary," *New Scientist* (London), Dec. 23, 1982.

151. Waggish non-Yale men never seem to weary of calling "For God, for Country and for Yale," the outstanding single anti-climax in the English language.

—*Time* Magazine, June 11, 1951.

152. Balliol College is a Victorian Gothic pile of no great distinction.... Yet it sits at the head of Oxford's intellectual table—a proud hatchery of Prime Ministers, archbishops, cardinals and viceroys.

—*Time* Magazine, July 12, 1963, on the 700th anniversary of one of Oxford's best known colleges.

153. King George, observing with judicious eyes
The state of both his Universities,
To Oxford sent a troop of horse; and why?
That learned body wanted loyalty.
To Cambridge books he sent, as well discerning
How much that loyal body wanted learning.

—Joseph Trapp (1679–1747), *The Faber Book of Comic Verse,* ed. Michael Roberts (1974), 67. In 1715, George I presented 30,000 books to Cambridge, about the same time a troop of horse was sent to Oxford to arrest some Jacobites. *See* Browne's reply, **#125.**

154. Theologians may disagree, but I am persuaded that God concocted college class reunions to make us feel old.

—Carll Tucker, "Aging Blues," *The Saturday Review,* July 22, 1978.

Critic, of the Arts

(*See also* Criticism, of the Arts)

155. As Christopher Hampton once said: 'Asking a working actor what he thinks about critics is like asking a lamp-post how he feels about dogs.' It does happen and some playwrights have a ready answer. This was Brendan Behan's: 'Critics are like eunuchs in a harem. They're there every night, they see it done every night, they see how it should be done every night, but they can't do it themselves.'

—Gyles Brandreth, *Great Theatrical Disasters* (1982), 119.

156. I am rather wretched and ill. In my 'literary life' I have taken the last step of infamy, and become—a reviewer! I have undertaken to 'do' great slabs of minor poetry for *The Cambridge Review.* I have read volumes of them, all the same, and all exactly the stuff I write. I frequently wonder whether I have not written several of them myself under a pseudonym, and forgotten about it.

—Rupert Brooke, letter to St. John Welles Lucas-Lucas,
in Christopher Hassall, *Rupert Brooke: A Biography* (1964), 116.

157. Critics—appall'd I venture on the name,
Those cut-throat bandits in the path of fame.

—Robert Burns, "[Third Epistle]
To Robert Graham of Fintry, Esq." (1789), viii,
The Poetical Works of Burns, ed. Raymond Bentman (1974).

158. Critics are like horse-flies which prevent the horse from ploughing.

—Anton Chekhov (1860–1904),
in W. Somerset Maugham's introduction to
The Complete Short Stories of W. Somerset Maugham (1953).

159. He praised the Thing he understood;
'Twere well if every Critic would.

—Austin Dobson, "The 'Squire
at Vauxhall," *At the Sign of the Lyre* (1889).

160. They, who write ill, and they, who ne'er durst write,
Turn critics, out of mere revenge and spite:
A playhouse gives them fame; and up there starts,
From a mean fifth-rate wit, a man of parts.

—John Dryden, *The Conquest
of Granada,* prologue to the second part (1760)

161. If thou dislk'st the Piece thou light'st on first,
Thinke that of All that I have writ, the worst;
But if thou read'st my book unto the end,
And still do'st this, and that verse, reprehend:
O Perverse man! If all disgustfull be,
The Extreme Scabbe take thee, and thine, for me.

—Robert Herrick,
"To the soure Reader," *Hesperides* (1648).

162. I ask't thee oft, what Poets thou hast read,
And lik'st the best? Still thou reply'st, The dead.

I shall, ere long, with green turfs cover'd be;
Then sure thou't like, or thou wilt envie me.

—Robert Herrick, "Upon the same," *ibid.*

163. A critic is the haunter of unquiet graves. He tries to evoke the presence of a living art, but usually succeeds only in disturbing the peace of the dead.

—Matthew J.C. Hodgart, *The Ballads* (1966), i.

164. What is the modern Poet's fate?
To write his thought upon a slate;
The critic spits on what is done,
Gives it a wipe—and all is gone.

—Thomas Hood (1799–1845), "The Poet's Fate."

165. With much ado you fail to tell
The requisites for writing well;
But, what bad writing is, you quite
Have proved by every line you write.

—Walter Savage Landor (1775–1864), "A Critic," in Richard Coniff, ed., *The Devil's Book of Verse* (1983), 84.

166. He could gauge the old books by the old set of rules,
And his very old nothings pleased very old fools;
But give him a book, fresh out of heart,
And you put him at sea without compass or chart.

—James Russell Lowell, *A Fable for Critics* (1848).

167. You damn every poem I write,
Yet publish not one of your own.
Now kindly let yours see the light,
Or else leave my damned ones alone.

—Martial, *Epigrams* (A.D. 93), I.91.

168. I am sitting in the smallest room in my house. I have your review in front of me. Soon it will be behind me.

—Max Reger (1873–1916), reply to a music critic, in Robert Hendrickson, *The Literary Life and Other Curiosities* (1981), 206.

169. It is only an auctioneer who can equally and impartially admire all schools of art.

—Oscar Wilde, *Intentions:* "The Critic as Artist" (1891).

170. The Poor in Wit or Judgement, like all Poor,
Revile, for having least, those who have more;
So, 'tis the Critick's Scarcity of Wit
Makes him traduce them who have most of it.

—William Wycherley (1640?–1716), "The Envious Critick," in William Cole, ed., *Pith and Vinegar* (1969).

171. You who scribble, yet hate all that write,
And keep each other company in spite,
As rivals in your common mistress, fame,
And with faint praises one another damn.

—William Wycherley, *The Plain Dealer:* "Prologue" (written 1665–66; produced 1674?).

Criticism, of the Arts

(*See also* Critic, of the Arts)

172. Your comedy I've read, my friend,
And like the half you pilfer'd best;
But sure the piece you yet may mend:
Take courage, man! and steal the rest.

—Anonymous, "To a Living Author," in Russell Baker, ed., *The Norton Book of Light Verse* (1986), 86.

173. In your otherwise beautiful poem there is a verse which reads, "Every moment dies a man, Every moment one is born." It must be manifest that, were this true, the population of the world would be at a standstill. In truth the rate of birth is slightly in excess of that of death. I would suggest that in your next edition of the poem you have it read, "Every moment dies a man, Every moment one and one-sixteenth is born."

Strictly speaking this is not correct. The actual figure is a decimal so long I cannot get it in the line, but I believe one and one-sixteenth will be sufficiently accurate for poetry.

—Charles Babbage (1792–1871), English mathematician, letter to Tennyson after reading "The Vision of Sin."

174. The beastliness of the author is set forth in his own description of himself, and we can conceive of no better reward than the lash for such a violation of decency. The author should be kicked from all decent society as below the level of the brute. He must be some escaped lunatic raving in pitiable delirium.

—*Boston Intelligencer,* 1855, reaction to the first edition of Whitman's *Leaves of Grass,* in Donald Hall, ed., *The Oxford Book of American Literary Anecdotes* (1981), 93.

175. Your Poem must *eternal* be,
Eternal! it can't fail,
For 'tis *incomprehensible,*
And without head or tail.

—Samuel Taylor Coleridge, "To Mr. Pye" (1800), *The Complete Works of Samuel Taylor Coleridge,* ed. Ernest Hartley Coleridge (1912), II.956.

176. Swans sing before they die:—'twere no bad thing
Should certain persons die before they sing.

—"On a Volunteer Singer" (1800), *ibid.,* II.960.

177. It seems to me much better to read a man's own writing than to read what others say about him, especially when the man is first-rate and the "others" are third-rate.

—George Eliot, letter to Sara Hennell, Oct. 28, 1865.

178. Criticism should not be querulous and wasting, all knife and root-puller, but guiding, instructive, inspiring, a south wind, not an east wind.

—Ralph Waldo Emerson, *Journals,* June, undated, 1847.

179. Eartham, March 4, 1793
Honored king of bards,

Since you deign to demand the observations of an humble and unexperienced servant of yours, on a work of one who is so much superior (as he is ever ready to serve you with all his might) behold what you demand! but let me desire you not to censure me for my unskilful and perhaps (as they will undoubtedly appear to you) ridiculous observations; but be so kind as to receive them as a mark of respectful affection from your obedient servant.

—Thomas Hayley, age twelve, letter to William Cowper pointing out defects in Cowper's translation

of Homer, in E.V. Lucas, *The Gentlest Art* (1908), 10-13.
In a letter to Hayley written ten days later, Cowper responded
to each criticism and thanked "my dear little censor."

180. Dr. [John] Donne's verses are like the peace of God; they pass all understanding.

—James I of Great Britain and VI of Scotland (1566–1625),
saying recorded by Archdeacon Thomas Plume (1630–1704).

181. Mr. James Macpherson,—

I received your foolish and impudent letter. Any violence offered me I shall do my best to repel; and what I cannot do for myself, the law shall do for me. I hope I shall not be deterred from detecting what I think a cheat by the menaces of a ruffian.

What would you have me retract? I thought your book an imposture; I think it an imposture still. For this opinion I have given my reasons to your public, which I here dare you to refute. Your rage I defy. Your abilities, since your Homer, are not so formidable: and what I hear of your morals inclines me to pay regard, not to what you shall say, but to what you shall prove. You may print this if you will.

—Samuel Johnson, in James Boswell,
The Life of Samuel Johnson, 1775 (1791),
xxv. Johnson doubted the authenticity of
Macpherson's alleged translations of *Fingal*
and *Temora* from the Gaelic of the 3rd-century poet Ossian.

182. Literary criticism can be no more than a reasoned account of the feeling produced upon the critic by the book he is criticizing. Criticism can never be a science: it is, in the first place, much too personal, and in the second, it is concerned with values that science ignores. The touchstone is emotion, not reason. We judge a work of art by its effect on our sincere and vital emotion, and nothing else. All the critical twiddle-twaddle about style and form, all this pseudo-scientific classifying and analysing of books in an imitation-botanical fashion, is mere impertinence and mostly dull jargon.

—D.H. Lawrence,
Selected Literary Criticism: "John Galsworthy" (1956), 118.

183. You read us your verse with your throat wrapped in wool.
The reason we're anxious to know.
To us it appears

That some wool in our ears
  Would really be more apropos.

—Martial, *Epigrams* (A.D. 93), IV.41.

184. Dear Mrs. Tynan:

I don't make a practice of writing to married women, especially if the husband is a dramatic critic, but I had to tell someone (and it might as well be you since you're the author) how much I enjoyed The Dud Avocado. It made me laugh, scream and guffaw (which, incidentally, is a great name for a law firm).

If this was actually your life, I don't see how the hell you ever got through it.

Sincerely yours,
Groucho Marx

—Letter to Elaine Tynan, Sept. 30, 1959, in *The Groucho Letters* (1967), 141. After Tynan thanked him "for the delightful things you said," Groucho wrote back, "I was delighted that you were delighted that I was delighted about your book." (Nov. 20, 1959).

185. "I told Raymond," said Bowbong, "about the man rebuked for sleeping through a play he was to give his opinion about. The man said, 'Sleep is an opinion.'"

—Carl Sandburg, *Remembrance Rock:* "Prologue" (1948), 7.

186. You dont expect me to know what to say about a play when I dont know who the author is, do you?

—George Bernard Shaw, *Fanny's First Play*, "Epilogue" (1911).

187. Robert Creeley's poems have two main characteristics: (1) they are short; (2) they are not short enough.

—John Ivan Simon, *Acid Test* (1963).

Curriculum

See College; English Language; Geography; Grammar; Handwriting; History; The Humanities; Language; Literature; Mathematics; Negroes, Education of; Orthography; Philosophy; Poetry; Reading; School, Advertisements for; School, American; School, British; Science; Speech; Studies; Teaching; Women, Education of

Degree, Academic

188. Inasmuch as you have been presented to me for examination in both (Civil and Canon) Laws and for the customary approval, by the Most Illustrious and the Most Excellent D.D. [naming the Promotors], Golden Knights, Counts Palatine, Most Celebrated Doctors, and inasmuch as you have since undergone an arduous and rigorous examination, in which you bore yourself with so much learning and distinction that that body of Most Illustrious and Excellent Promotors without one dissenting voice—I repeat, without one dissenting voice—have judged you worthy of the laurel, therefore by the authority which I have as Archdeacon and senior Chancellor, I create, publish and name you, N.N., Doctor in the aforesaid Faculties, giving to you every privilege of lecturing, of ascending the Master's chair, of writing glosses, of interpreting, of acting as Advocate, and of exercising also the functions of a Doctor here and everywhere throughout the world; furthermore, of enjoying all those privileges which those happy individuals, who have been so deserving in these fostering colleges, are accustomed to use and enjoy.

And I trust that all these things will forever result in the increase of your fame and the honour of our colleges, to the praise and glory of Almighty God and of the ever blessed Virgin Mary.

—Anonymous, sample of the formula used for granting degrees in law at a medieval university, in Hastings Rashdall, *Universities of Europe in the Middle Ages* (1936), II. The "master's degree" of the medieval university became the Ph.D. of modern times. The present master's degree is a more recent introduction. [gloss=*an explanation, by means of a marginal or interlinear note or translation, of a technical or unusual expression in a manuscript text*]. *See* Haskins, **#139**, under "College."

189. A maiden at college, Miss Breeze,
Had B.A.'s and M.A.'s and Lit. D.'s.
Said her doctor, "It's plain
You'll collapse from the strain,
For you're killing yourself by degrees."

—Anonymous, In Louis Untermeyer, *A Treasury of Laughter* (1946), 430.

190. On completion of the required course of studies, the student is given a B.A. or, if he has avoided all impractical courses, the B.S. He is now entitled to put his degree after his name, like an M.D., but will be subjected to considerable ridicule if he does, unless he lives in England.

The degree is proof of the fact that the student is Educated, despite doubts raised by his inability to write clearly, keep his bank account balanced, or be logical in an argument. When people ask him, "Where did you go?" he is able to tell where he went.

The degree is formally conferred at Commencement, the final test of the student's stamina and fortitude. Commencement takes place in June, the weather determining whether it is held indoors or outdoors. If it is held indoors, in the college gym, which is without air conditioning and smells of sweat socks, it will be the hottest day of the year, while if it is held outdoors there will be a steady downpour, beginning almost the instant the College Chaplain opens the ceremony with the invocation. Possibly what sounds like "Let us spray" is heard by some ancient rain god.

Students wear academic robes, which are black because students are supposed to be in mourning at having to leave college after four happy years of examinations, term papers, and required physical education. On their heads are mortarboards, a type of headgear which has never caught on for everyday use. While the glee club is singing, a wind inevitably rises and students must hold onto their mortarboards or graduate bareheaded.

—Richard Armour, *Going Around in Academic Circles:* "The Degree" (1965), 95.

191. The problem of [academic] degree names [for women] proved . . . critical: many people considered it inappropriate to call women graduates *bachelors* or *masters*. . . .

According to D.C. Gilman [in 1885], president of Johns Hopkins University, hundreds of weak and inefficient colleges were actually manufacturing—"with an inventive skill that is truly American"—new degrees for their clientele. In the same year, the *Pall Mall Gazette* [March 5, 1885] satirizes the new feminine degrees:

> Silly fellows are constantly poking fun, for instance, at the insult it would be to an ungraduated husband to be married to a "master," and at the incongruity of giving clever but otherwise marriageable girls the title of "bachelor." The Americans have cut the knot in their usual practical fashion, and talk of Miss Bluestocking not as "Bachelor of Arts" or "Bachelor of Science," but as "Maid of Philosophy," "Maid of Science," "Maid of Arts," while a girl who has taken degrees in all the faculties is, we suppose, called a "Maid of All Work," what in this

aristocratic country is a badge of servitude being in the free democracy of the West a prize of intellect.

—Dennis Baron, *Grammar and Gender* (1986), 173. *See* Merriam, #197.

192. There were some gentlemen that invited me to go to Cambridge, where the big college or university is; where they keep ready-made titles or nicknames to give people. I would not go, for I did not know but they might stick an LL.D. on me before they let me go; and I had no idea of changing "Member of the House of Representatives of the United States," for what stands for "lazy lounging dunce," which I am sure my constituents would have translated my new title to be, knowing that I had never taken any degree, and did not own to any, except a small degree of good sense not to pass for what I was not.

—Davy Crockett (1786–1836), *The Autobiography of Davy Crockett*, ed. Hamlin Garland (1923), 90.

193. Every scholar, that on proof is found able to read the original of the Old and New Testament into the Latin tongue, and to resolve them logically, withal being of honest life and conversation, and at any public act hath the approbation of the Overseers and Master of the College, may be invested with his first degree.

Every scholar, that giveth up in writing a synopsis or summary of Logic, Natural and Moral Philosophy, Arithmetic, Geometry, and Astronomy, and is ready to defend his thesis or positions, withal skilled and studious, at any public act after trial he shall be capable of the second degree, of Master of Arts.

—Degree requirements of Harvard College, in Josiah Quincy, *The History of Harvard University* (1840), I.515.

194. [In China] The doctorate of letters . . . was certainly the most sought after. It was the one that conferred most prestige and which opened the way to most brilliant careers. But there were also doctorates . . . of philology, of history and ritual, and of law, . . . [and] examinations for military and medical officials.

—Jacques Gernet, *Daily Life in China . . . 1250–1276* (1962), 157.

195. Because His Majesty wants to remedy as much as possible the abuses which are being committed in his kingdom, having recognized that confusion has spread among letters as well as other arts, professors granting indifferently the degree of *licenciés*, *bacheliers*, and *docteurs* to all those who appear providing they have money, His Majesty orders that there will be eight professors at the college, each of whom shall be paid by said college five hundred écus yearly, four of whom will be in medicine and four in jurisprudence, and who, having judged the students and others who present themselves before them as worthy of the above-mentioned degrees, shall pass them without taking anything from them; and so that there be no fraud committed, these professors may not admit anyone to said degrees without his having taken a public examination which four of the [Jesuit] fathers shall attend and who will sign with the professors the degree which the student shall receive.

—Henry IV of France, conditions for the establishment of La Flèche, 1603, in Jack R. Vrooman, *René Descartes* (1970), 28.

196. [Stephen] Leacock treasured his Ph.D. . . . It represented the fruit of much hard work and financial strain on his part and he didn't propose to let people forget it. As a pose, he spoofed the accomplishment, and in all likelihood there was a particle of truth in the amusing tale he told of how he decided to take his Ph.D. to Europe with him. The only way to do this, of course, was to sign himself on the ship's passenger list as Doctor Leacock.

> I was just settling down in my cabin when the steward rapped, opened the door, and announced: "Dr. Leacock? The Captain's compliments, doctor, will you please come and have a look at the second stewardess' knee?" I was off like a shot. But it was no use. Another fellow got there ahead of me. He was a Doctor of Divinity.

—David M. Legate, *Stephen Leacock* (1970), 35.

197. Widespread jokes of the time [c. 1837] suggested that female graduates be awarded degrees of MPM—Mistress of Pudding Making—and RW—Respectable Wife.

—Eve Merriam, *Growing Up Female in America* (1971), 13. *See* Baron, **#191.**

198. Once you have the cap and gown all you need do is open your mouth. Whatever nonsense you talk becomes wisdom and all the rubbish, good sense.

—Molière, *The Imaginary Invalid* (1673), III.

199. In Latin, *gradus* meant a step, and *degradus* a step in an ascent or descent, a rung on a ladder. From the first we get our word "graduation"; from the second, "degree" . . . .

The graduation ceremony, originally consisting of two parts, has been greatly reduced since medieval times. The first part conferred the preliminary license to teach, or bachelor's degree. This was followed six months later by the candidate's inception and first formal lecture, or disputation, before the assembled faculty. After that, he received the teacher's cap (biretta) and a token book in recognition of his scholarship in reading and thinking, lecturing and disputing. That is why a book is still the perfect graduation gift, and why Harvard, even in its early years, gave each graduate a book (which had to be returned right after commencement).

—Michael Olmert, "Points of Origin," *Smithsonian* Magazine, June 1986. *See* Haskins, #139, under "College."

200. A gentle rain after long drought,
Meeting an old friend in a foreign clime,
The joys of the wedding day,
One's name on the list of successful candidates.

—Quoted in Margaret R. Thiele, *None but the Nightingale: An Introduction to Chinese Literature* (1967), 43. These were considered the "four happinesses of life." The highest scholastic degree, Academician, and membership in the "Forest of Pencils" (Imperial Academy) were attained by the one half of one per cent of the candidates who passed the fourth examination.

201. A few months ago I was told that Johns Hopkins University had given me a degree. I naturally supposed this constituted me a Member of the Faculty, and so I started to help what I could there. I told them I believed they were perfectly competent to run a college as far as the higher branches of education are concerned, but what they needed was a little help here and there from a practical commercial man. I said the public is sensitive to little things and they wouldn't have full confidence in a college that didn't know how to spell John.

—Mark Twain, *Notebook,* Jan. 7, 1889 (1935).

Discipline

(*See also* Child Rearing; Punishment, Corporal; Punishment, Corporal [Con]; Punishment, Corporal [Pro]; Punishment, Corporal [by Students]; Teaching Method)

202. A pretty school-mistress named Beauchamp
Said, "These awful boys, how shall I teachamp?

For they will not behave,
Although I look grave
And with tears in my eyes I beseauchamp."

—Anonymous.

203. Our sole delight was play; and for this we were punished by those who yet themselves were doing the like. But elder folks' idleness is called "business"; that of boys, being really the same, is punished by those elders.

—St. Augustine, *Confessions* (c. A.D. 400), I.

204. Milton [Academy, c. 1909] had long since abandoned "caning" as an un-American activity and in its place had substituted, as had many schools, a system of punishment known as "marks." Not "black marks" or "demerits." Simply "marks." A boy was allowed in a half week to collect five of these. If he got six or more, he had to "serve" them, ten minutes for each "mark" up to nine, by sitting in the schoolroom Wednesday afternoon or Saturday morning. He did not have to study. He had only to sit still enough not to acquire more "marks" from the master who used the time to get papers corrected. More than nine "marks" meant that a boy had to work them off on Saturday morning walking around the track, a lap to a "mark," under the supervision of a bored teacher. Few boys had to do this, and to do it at all was held to be a sign of a fairly low character. . . . At Milton there was another kind of punishment known as "hot-ovens". . . . This was a form of running the gauntlet in which a boy would have to get on his hands and knees and crawl through two lines of other boys while they beat him. It was not fun, either. It . . . hurt, though not abiding.

—John Mason Brown, *The Worlds of Robert E. Sherwood: Mirror to His Times, 1896–1939* (1962), 61, 63.

205. She had a deep sense of justice and sometimes this made her feel as uncomfortable in her spirit if she deserved a whipping and did not get it as she felt in her body if she did get it, and of the two she preferred to suffer in body.

—Elizabeth Goudge, *The Child from the Sea* (1970), I.i.

206. [In Philadelphia, c. 1765, an English schoolmaster named Dove, rarely applied the birch in the usual way, but it] was generally stuck into the back part of the collar of the unfortunate culprit, who, with this badge of disgrace towering from his nape, was compelled to take his stand upon the top of the form [bench] for such a period of time as his offence was thought to deserve. He had another contrivance for boys who were late in their morning attendance. This was to dispatch a committee of five or six scholars for them, with a bell and lighted lantern; and in this odd equipage, in broad daylight, the bell all the while tingling, were they escorted through the streets to school. As Dove affected a strict regard to justice in his dispensations of punishment, and always professed a willingness to have an equal measure of it meted out to himself in case of his transgressing, the boys took him at his word; and one morning, when he had overstaid his time, he found himself waited on in the usual form. He immediately admitted the justice of the procedure, and, putting himself behind the lantern and the bell, marched with great solemnity to school, to the no small gratification of the boys and the entertainment of the spectators.

—Alexander Graydon, in Clifton Johnson,
Old-time Schools and School-books (1904), 41.

207. One of the chief factors in education is discipline, the purport of which is to break down the child's self-will and thereby eradicate his purely natured and sensuous self. We must not expect to achieve this by mere goodness, since it is just the immediate will which acts on immediate fancies and caprices, not on reasons and representative thinking. If we advance reasons to children, we leave it open to them to decide whether the reasons are weighty or not, and thus, we make everything depend on their whim. So far as children are concerned, universality and the substance of things reside in their parents, and this implies that children must be obedient. If the feelings of subordination, producing the longing to grow up, is not fostered in children, they become forward and impertinent.

—Georg Wilhelm Friedrich Hegel,
Philosophy of Right (1821), *Additions*, par. 174.

208. No more fiendish punishment could be devised, were such a thing physically possible, than that one should be turned loose in society and remain absolutely unnoticed by all the members thereof.

—William James, *The Principles of Psychology* (1890), 293.

209. Like all children he looked upon restraints as the exercise of outrageous tyranny, and when he was obliged to learn his lessons, and when he was not allowed to do exactly as he liked, regarded himself as treated with monstrous cruelty.

—W. Somerset Maugham, introduction
(1949) to Stendahl's *The Red and the Black* (1831).

210. I have always disliked the discipline of our schools. They might have erred less harmfully by leaning towards indulgence. They are a regular jail of imprisoned youth. They make them slack, by punishing them for slackness before they show it. Go in at lesson time: you hear nothing but cries, both from tortured boys and from masters drunk with rage. What a way to arouse zest for their lesson in these tender and timid souls, to guide them to it with a horrible scowl and hands armed with rods! Wicked and pernicious system! Besides, as Quintilian very rightly remarked, this imperious authority leads to dangerous consequences, and especially in our manner of punishment. How much more fittingly would their classes be strewn with flowers and leaves than with bloody stumps of birch rods!

—Michel de Montaigne, *Essays:* "Of the Education of Children" (1580), I.xxvi, tr. Donald M. Frame.

211. The broad effects which can be obtained by punishment in man and beast, are the increase of fear, the sharpening of the sense of cunning, the mastery of the desires; so it is that punishment tames man, but does not make him "better."

—Friedrich Nietzsche, *The Geneology of Morals* (1887), Essay I.ix.

212. [At the turn of this century] From the standpoint of discipline the physical cruelties of the earlier day had to a large degree disappeared, but the control exercised over the pupils was at least negative. The business of the school being what it was, any movement, any conversation, any communication, were out of order. The spirit of control was military and repressive, not constructive and cooperative. Long rows of seats, military evolutions of classes, stated appearances for recitations, with the rest of the school time devoted to narrowly prescribed exercises, had for their moral equivalent being quiet, industrious at assigned tasks, and submissive to the rule of the drill-sergeant in skirts who unflinchingly governed her little kingdom of learn-by-heart-and-recite-by-rote.

—Edward H. Reisner, *The Evolution of the Common School* (1930).

213. What makes obedience seem necessary in schools is the large classes and overworked teachers demanded by a false economy. Those who have no experience of teaching are incapable of imagining the expense of spirit entailed by any really living instruction. They think that teachers can reasonably be expected to work as many hours as bank clerks. Intense fatigue and irritable nerves are the result, and an absolute necessity of performing the day's task mechanically. But the task cannot be performed mechanically except by exacting obedience.

—Bertrand Russell, *Principles of Social Reconstruction:* "Education" (1916).

Educated Person

(*See also* Education, Effect [Result] of; Intellectual; Scholar)

214. An educated person is a person with whom you could be seated for a two-hour train ride without being bored.

—Anonymous, in Donald W. Robinson, "What Is Liberal Education?" *Phi Delta Kappan* Magazine, May 1979.

215. The problem of devising successful substitutes for common sense has not yet been solved. . . . [Yet] there are certain lessons that we can take to heart. . . . It seems to me that, as a minimum, we henceforth cannot regard a man as well educated who does not intuitively recognize that common sense is not to be taken for granted, or who does not handle his thinking as a tool in the awareness that every tool has limitations built into it. Such a man, looking to the past, can only be amazed that the human brain has, by cut-and-try methods, evolved procedures as effective as it has for dealing with the world around us; looking to the present, sees perhaps the most important reason for the present internal social difficulties of the human race in its uncritical use of the traditional habits of thought; and looking to the future, can feel only optimism for the time when we shall have learned how to substitute consciously directed control of our thinking for the blind procedures of common sense.

—Percy Williams Bridgman (1882–1961), "Science and Common Sense," in Leo Hamalian and Edmond L. Volpe, eds., *Great Essays by Nobel Prize Winners* (1960), 324.

216. It is important to remember that, in strictness, there is no such thing as an uneducated man. Take an extreme case. Suppose that an adult man, in the full vigour of his faculties, could be suddenly placed in the world, as Adam is said to have been, and then left to do as he best might. How long would he be left uneducated? Not five minutes. Nature would begin to teach him, through the eye, the ear, the touch, the properties of objects. Pain and pleasure would be at his elbow telling him to do this and avoid that; and by slow degrees the man would receive an education which, if narrow, would be thorough, real, and adequate to the circumstances though there would be no extras and very few accomplishments.

—Thomas Henry Huxley, lecture, "A Liberal Education and Where to Find It" (1868), *Collected Essays* (1894).

217. Whom, then, do I call educated. . . ? First, those who manage well the circumstances which they encounter day by day, and who possess a judgement which is accurate in meeting occasions as they arise and rarely miss the expedient course of action; next, those who are decent and honourable in their intercourse with all with whom they associate, tolerating easily and good-naturedly what is unpleasant or offensive in others and being themselves as agreeable and reasonable to their associates as it is humanly possible to be; furthermore, those who hold their pleasures always under control and are not unduly overcome by their misfortunes, bearing up under them bravely and in a manner worthy of our common nature; fourthly, and most important of all, those who are not spoiled by their successes and do not desert their true selves and become arrogant, but hold their ground steadfastly as intelligent men, not rejoicing in the good things which have come to them through chance rather than in those which through their own nature and intelligence are theirs from their birth. Those who have a character which is in accord, not with one of these things, but with all of them—these, I contend are wise and complete men, possessed of all the virtues.

—Isocrates, *Panathenaicus* (339 B.C.), tr. George Norlin (1929).

218. A University training is the . . . the education which gives a man a clear conscious view of his own opinions and judgments, a truth in developing them, an eloquence in expressing them, and a force in urging them. It teaches him to see things as they are, to go right to the point, to disentangle a skein of thought, to detect what is sophistical, and to discard what is irrelevant. It prepares him to fill any post with credit, and to master any subject with facility. It shows him how to accommodate himself to others, how to throw himself into their state of mind, how to bring before them his own, how to influence them, how to come to an understanding with them, how to bear with them. He is at home in any society, he has common ground with every class; he knows when to speak and when to be silent; he is able to converse, he is able to listen; he can ask a question pertinently, and gain a lesson seasonably, when he has nothing to impart himself; he is ever ready, yet never in the way; he is a pleasant companion, and a comrade you can depend upon; he knows when to be serious and when to trifle, and he has a sure tact which enables him to trifle with gracefulness and to be serious with effect. He has the repose of mind which lives in itself, while it lives in the world, and which has resources for its happiness at home when it cannot go abroad. He has a gift which serves him in public, and supports him in retirement, without which good fortune is but vulgar, and with which failure and disappointment have a charm.

—John Henry Newman,
The Idea of a University, Discourse VII (1873).

219. The Educated Guy . . . finds when he gets his post graduate course that all the other Professors have got one too, and lots of them a half dozen. He begins to wonder if he hasent (sic) spent all his time wondering if he knows anything or not. He wishes he had took up some other line. He talks with an old broad minded man of the world of experience, and he feels lost. So I guess he gets to wondering what education really is, after all. For there is nothing as stupid as an educated man if you get off the thing that he was educated in.

—Will Rogers, *The Autobiography of Will Rogers* (1926), 248.

220. Most [learned men] are like courtiers themselves. They are sometimes as greedy, as treacherous, as cruel; and the only difference between the pests of the court and the pests of the school is that the latter are more ridiculous.

—Voltaire, letter to Frederick the Great,
Aug. 26, 1736, in Richard Aldington, tr.,
Letters of Voltaire and Frederick the Great (1927), 25.

Education

(*See also* Learning; Study)

221. Education! Oh Education! The greatest Grief of my heart, and the greatest Affliction of my Life! To my mortification I must confess, that I have never closely thought, or very deliberately reflected on the Subject, which never occurs to me now, without producing a deep Sigh, an heavy groan and sometimes Tears.

—John Adams, letter to Thomas Jefferson, July 16, 1814,
in Lester J. Cappon, ed., *The Adams-Jefferson Letters* (1959), 438.

222. Education is painful. Few people enjoy much of it, still fewer the whole process. Most of us think of it as a period of captivity, of frustration, of boredom; relieved, if we are fortunate, by moments of happiness. Others loathe it with a passionate hatred. "No power on earth," said the Lord Salisbury, who was Prime Minister in Queen Victoria's reign, when asked to visit Eton, "would induce me to go back even for a single afternoon to that existence among devils that I remember as a boy." But he sent his own son to Eton; where else could a person of such ancestry be sent? Besides, one was not supposed to be happy at school.

—Gillian Avery, *School Remembered* (1967), introduction. *See* Guitry, **#514,** and Huxley, **#516,** under "Parent."

223. 'Tis granted, and no plainer truth appears,
Our most important are our earliest years;
The mind impressible and soft, with ease
Imbibes and copies what she hears and sees,
And through life's labyrinth holds fast the clue
That Education gives her, false or true.
Plants raised with tenderness are seldom strong;
Man's coltish disposition asks the thong;
And, without discipline, the favourite child,
Like a neglected forester, runs wild.
But we, as if good qualities would grow
Spontaneous, take but little pains to sow;
We give some Latin, and a smatch of Greek;
Teach him to fence and figure twice a week;
And having done, we think, the best we can,
Praise his proficiency, and dub him man.

—William Cowper (1731–1800), "The Progress of Error," *The Poetical Works of William Cowper*, ed. H.F. Cary (no date), I.55.

224. Getting education is like getting measles; you have to go where measles is.

—Abraham Flexner, to Albert Jay Nock, in Clifton Fadiman, *The American Treasury* (1955), 287.

225. Educate.... Those who like to remind their audiences on school speech days [commencement] that education is a drawing out and not a putting in are not quite right in their etymology. It is true that the Latin word *educere,* the primary meaning of which is to draw out, was also used in the sense to rear, but that word would have given us *eduction.*

Education is derived from a different word, *educare,* the primary meaning of which is to bring up, to educate.

—H.W. Fowler, *A Dictionary of Modern English Usage,* 2nd ed. (1983), 145.

226. [In the early 1300s] The children [in England,] boys or girls, of freemen, villeins, and the less important members of the middle classes such as rural craftsmen and urban shopkeepers and minor merchants received no formal education at all, unless there was a particularly conscientious priest in the community—a rare situation after the Black Death killed off up to two-thirds of those in religious orders.

Prior to 1348 the chances of getting some kind of religious and semi-religious education, even to learn to read and write, were fairly good in the larger villages, for at that time one in fifty-two of all persons over fourteen years of age were servants of the Church, and had a real sense of being servants of their people whose lives and souls were in their care. By the time boys of the same age as Alice could have hoped for some education of this kind there was only one priest, monk or friar for every one hundred and fifty adults. Not only the practical benefits of education were lost; the moral precepts suffered too.

Families with some social position in the community did expect to have their children educated in a rudimentary sort of way. In theory, lessons were for boys only, but instances are known where a sister attended the lessons as well. More usually the girl was instructed in the social graces, routine of housewifery and so on, by her mother or an older female relative.

—F. George Kay, *Lady of the Sun: The Life and Times of Alice Perrers* (1966), 39.
She was mistress of Edward III of England. Died 1400.
[villein=*(in the feudal system) a member of a class of persons who were serfs with respect to the lord but had the rights and privileges of freemen with respect to others*].

227. How did all this [education] come about? Our system of education arose out of the mediaeval Latin schools and the church. It still carries, like a fossil snake in stone, the mark of its original structure. Not that this was the earliest kind of education. But the others were different. Greek education included music and dancing and what we call the arts. It was supposed to fit people to live. Mediaeval education was supposed to fit people to die. Any school-boy of to-day can still feel the effect of it.

Greek education was free from the problems that have beset our own. It didn't include the teaching of languages, the Greeks despising all foreigners as barbarians. It avoided everything "practical" like the plague, and would have regarded a professor of Engineering as a child of the devil, misusing truth. Mathematics, crippled by the want of symbols, became a sort of dream—intense, difficult and proudly without purpose. Greek education carried with it no "exams" and "tests" for entry to the professions. A Greek dentist didn't have to pass in Latin. He used a hammer.

—Stephen Leacock, *Too Much College* (1939).

228. The greatest and most important difficulty of human science is the education of children. For, as in agriculture, the husbandry that is to precede the planting, as also planting itself, is certain, plain, and well known; but after that which is planted comes to life, there is a great deal more to be done, more art to be used, more care to be taken, and much more difficulty to cultivate and bring it to perfection; so it is with men; it is no hard matter to get children; but after they are born, then begins the trouble, solicitude, and care rightly to train, principle, and bring them up.

—Michel de Montaigne, *Essays:*
"Of the Education of Children" (1580), I.xxvi, tr. Charles Cotton.

229. I remember seeing a picture of education.... It represented a glorious woman with a wise and fearless face stooping over her children and pointing them to far horizons.... She was telling them, one felt, of the great prospect of life that opened before them, of the spectacle of the world, the splendours of the sea and mountain they might travel and see, the joys they might acquire, of effort and pride of effort and the devotions and nobilities it was theirs to achieve. Perhaps even she whispered of the warm triumphant mystery of love that comes at last to those who have patience and unblemished hearts.

—H.G. Wells, *The History of Mr. Polly* (1909), 9.

Education, Aims of

(*See also* Women, Education of)

230. There is a sameness, both dreadful and reassuring, in the statements one is pelted with these days on the aims of American education.... The young college president, freshly in office, must pale at the thought of the miles and miles of clichés that stand between him and that final baccalaureate address, twenty years hence, when he will say: essentially the same thing.

—William F. Buckley Jr.,
Quotations From Chairman Bill (1970), 65.

231. Education as such has no aims. Only persons, parents and teachers, etc., have aims, not an abstract idea like education. And consequently their purposes are indefinitely varied, differing with different children, changing as children grow and with the growth of experience on the part of the one who teaches. Even the most valid aims which can be put in words will, as words, do more harm than good unless one recognizes that they are not aims but rather suggestions to educators as to how to observe, how to look ahead, and how to choose in liberating and directing the energies of the concrete situations in which they find themselves.

—John Dewey, *Democracy and Education* (1916), 125.

232. If we indoctrinate the young person in an elaborate set of fixed beliefs, we are insuring his early obsolescence. The alternative is to develop skills, attitudes, habits of mind, and the kinds of knowledge and understanding, that will be the instruments of continuous change. . . . All too often we are giving young people cut flowers when we should be teaching them to grow their own plants. We are stuffing their heads with the products of earlier innovation rather than teaching them how to innovate.

—John W. Gardner, in Carnegie
Corporation of New York, *Annual Report* (1962), 11.

233. Naturally, one has to go to school, and one does get something out of it. Of my own three aims, as declared at the time of starting, two seem to have been accomplished—I did study, at school, and I did learn French rather thoroughly during a total of twelve years of it. But I never learned to sweep, alas, and I can't yet.

—Nancy Hale, *A New England Girlhood* (1936), 45.

234. Men are men before they are lawyers, or physicians, or merchants, or manufacturers; and if you make them capable and sensible men, they will make themselves capable and sensible lawyers or physicians. What professional men should carry away with them from an University, is not professional knowledge, but that which should direct the use of their professional knowledge, and bring the light of general culture to illuminate the technicalities of a special pursuit.

—John Stuart Mill, inaugural address
as Rector of University of St. Andrews, Feb. 1, 1867.

235. How are they to be reared and educated? Is not this an inquiry which may be expected to throw light on the greater inquiry which is our final end: How do justice and injustice grow up in States?

—Plato, *Republic* (c. 375 B.B.), II.

236. Education, then, briefly is the leading human souls to do what is best, and making what is best out of them; and these two objects are always attainable together, and by the same means; the training which makes men happiest in themselves, also makes them most serviceable to others. True education, then, has respect, first to the ends which are proposable to the man, or attainable by him; and secondly, to the material of which the man is made. So far as it is able, it chooses the end according to the material: but it cannot always choose the end, for the position of many persons in life is fixed by necessity; still less can it choose the material; and therefore, all it can do, is to fit the one to the other as wisely as may be.

But the first point to be understood, is that the material is as various as the ends; that not only one man is unlike another, but *every* man is essentially different from *every* other, so that no training, no forming, no informing, will ever make two persons alike in thought or in power. Among all men, whether of the upper or lower orders, the differences are eternal and irreconcilable, between one individual and another, born under absolutely the same circumstances. One man is made of agate, another of oak; one of slate, another of clay. The education of the first is polishing; of the second, seasoning; of the third, rending; of the fourth, moulding. It is of no use to season the agate; it is vain to try to polish the slate; but both are fitted, by the qualities they possess, for services in which they may be honored.

—John Ruskin, *The Stones of Venice*
(1851–53), III, App. 7, 220.

237. Miss Ophelia's ideas of education, like all her other ideas, were very set and definite, and of the kind that prevailed in New England a century ago, and which are still preserved in some very retired and unsophisticated parts, where there are no railroads. As nearly as could be expressed, they could be comprised in a few words: to teach them to mind when they were spoken to; to teach them the catechism, sewing, and reading; and to whip them if they told lies. And though, of course, in the flood of light that is now poured on education, these are left far away in the rear, yet it is an undisputed fact that our grandmothers raised some tolerably fair men and women under this régime.

—Harriet Beecher Stowe, *Uncle Tom's Cabin* (1852), 245.

Education, Criticism of

238. Accurs'd the man, whom fate ordains, in spite,
And cruel parents teach, to Read and Write!
What need of letters? Wherefore should we spell?
Write our names? A mark will do as well.

Much are the precious hours of youth misspent,
In climbing Learning's rugged steep ascent;
When to the top the bold advent'rer's got,
He reigns, vain monarch, o'er a barren spot,
While in the *vale of Ignorance* below,
FOLLY and VICE to rank luxuriance grow;
Honours and wealth pour in on ev'ry side,
And proud Preferment rolls her golden tide.

O'r crabbed authors life's gay prime to waste,
To cramp wild genius in the chains of taste,
To bear the slavish drudgery of schools,
And tamely stoop to ev'ry pedant's rules,
For seven long years debarr'd of lib'ral ease,
To plod in college trammels to *degrees*,
Beneath the weight of solemn toys to groan,
Sleep over books, and leave mankind unknown,
To praise each senior blockhead's thread-bare tale,
And laugh till reason blush, and spirits fail,
Manhood with vile submission to disgrace,
And *cap* the fool, whose merit is his Place;
VICE CHANCELLORS, whose knowledge is but small,
And CHANCELLORS, who nothing know at all.

—Charles Churchill, "The Author" (1763), st.i–iii, *The Poetical Works of Charles Churchill*, ed. Douglas Grant (1956).

239. To the University of Oxford I acknowledge no obligation; and she will as cheerfully renounce me for a son, as I am willing to disclaim her for a mother. I spent fourteen months at Magdalen College; they proved the fourteen months the most idle and unprofitable of my whole life.

—Edward Gibbon, *Memoirs of His Life and Writings* (1796).

240. Education in America and in other countries of the West is an inspiring achievement: all those light, healthy schools, those myriad colleges, so many youngsters having a fine time and not working too hard. Yet it has a couple of weaknesses. One is that education has become almost too easy to get. It is accepted like a supply of pure water: no one expects to get much stimulus or nourishment from it, but it is used to keep the tissues well filled and the outer surface clean. The other is that it does not often carry over into mature life. The average American would rather be driving a car along a crowded highway than reading a book and thinking. The average Frenchman would rather be drinking an extra bottle of wine than watching a play by Racine. The average Britisher would rather fill up a football-pool form than listen to Elgar's *Enigma.* Why this should be so, I cannot tell. It must be something wrong with education. Probably it is the cult of the average; the idea that schools exist in order to make everyone pretty much the same, and that happiness consists in sharing a group life, sweet, humming, undifferentiated, and crowded like bees in a hive.

—Gilbert Highet, *Man's Unconquerable Mind* (1954), 42.

241. Literary or scientific, liberal or specialist, all our education is predominantly verbal and therefore fails to accomplish what it is supposed to do. Instead of transforming children into fully developed adults, it turns out students of the natural sciences who are completely unaware of Nature as the primary fact of experience, it inflicts upon the world students of the humanities who know nothing of humanity, their own or anyone else's.

—Aldous Huxley, *The Doors of Perception* (1954), 74.

242. I myself have been consulted of late by so many who profess themselves to be at a loss how to breed their children, and the early corruption of youth is now become so general a complaint that he cannot be thought wholly impertinent who brings the consideration of this matter on the stage, and offers something, if it be but to excite others, or afford matter of correction: for errors in education should be less indulged than any.

—John Locke, *Some Thoughts concerning Education* (1693), introduction.

243. The materials for education are much like those by means of which a plant grows: The arts and sciences may be compared to earth, air and water. But whereas it is now commonly held that the materials themselves are the education, so that a person who has stored up certain facts and ideas is thereby educated, the truth is that they are no more the education than the air and earth and water are the growth of the plant. The analogy between plant nourishment and what we call education would hold if plants could store up large chemical supplies while remaining shriveled, wizened, small, undeveloped: a thing unknown in botany. We must realize that education is a process of growth, lasting throughout life and coeval with life. If we are wise we shall not try to force it or hasten it. We will give up the whole medal-awarding, diploma-bestowing, scholarship-granting, pupil-punishing rigmarole: and we will direct our efforts toward seeing that the environment is so ordered that the natural processes may be carried on in the most favorable way.

—Lewis Mumford, *My Works and Days* (1979), 28.

244. Soon I must shuffle off this mortal coil, but I hope that coming generations will look back at the education of our time and marvel at its barbarity, its destruction of human potentialities, its insane concern about formal learning. I hope against everything that makes me pessimistic: the wars, the religious suppression, the crimes. Cannot those who yell for the hanging of criminals see that they are treating a ruptured appendix with aspirin? Will not society recognize that it is our repressive system, plus the poverty of our mean streets, plus our soulless, acquisitive society, that is making criminals and neurotics?

—A.S. Neill, *"Neill! Neill! Orange Peel!"* (1972), 20.

245. The papers today say that illiteracy has decreased. The more that learn how to read the less learn how to make a living. That's the one thing about a little education. It spoils you for actual work. The more you know the more you think somebody owes you a living.

—Will Rogers, *The Autobiography of Will Rogers* (1926), 252.

246. I did not learn anything at school. . . . I did not learn my school lessons, having much more important ones in hand, with the result that I have not wasted my life trifling with literary fools in taverns as Johnson did when he should have been shaking England with the thunder of his spirit. My schooling did me a great deal of harm and no good whatever: it was simply dragging a child's soul through the dirt.

—George Bernard Shaw, preface to *Misalliance* (1914).

247. One of the accepted convictions I had heard most frequently was that education was the way to cure our evils. I did not believe that. Educated people were the slowest to move toward any change. It seemed to me that education was a hindrance to reform, but maybe our education was bad. Mine was, and thinking back over my school and college courses, I could see that one trouble with our education was that it did not teach us what was not known, not enough of the unsolved problems of the sciences, of the arts, and of life. It did not aim, apparently, to make us keen with educated, intelligent curiosity about the unknown, not eager to do the undone; it taught most of us only what was known. It gave us positive knowledge when there was no certain knowledge, and worst of all, when we did not particularly want it. We were not curious as students, and we are not curious enough now as men and women. It seemed to me, as I thought and talked it over with others, that curiosity was the beginning and end of education and that if one could arouse that in the minds of college students, they might reverse their relations with their teachers. The students would be asking the questions, not the professors; the students would be learning instead of the teacher teaching.

—Lincoln Steffens,
The Autobiography of Lincoln Steffens (1931), 44.

248. Much is said about the universal diffusion of education in America, and a vast deal of genuine admiration is felt and expressed at the progress of mind throughout the Union. They believe themselves in all sincerity to have surpassed, to be surpassing, and to be about to surpass, the whole earth in the intellectual race. I am aware that not a single word can be said, hinting a different opinion, which will not bring down a transatlantic anathema on my head; yet the subject is too interesting to be omitted....

From every enquiry I could make, and I took much pains to obtain accurate information, it appeared that much is attempted, but very little beyond reading, writing, and book-keeping, is thoroughly acquired. Were we to read a prospectus of the system pursued in any of our [English] public schools, and that of a first-rate seminary in America, we should be struck by the confined scholastic routine of the former, when compared to the varied and expensive scope of the latter; but let the examination go a little further, and I believe it will be found that the old fashioned school discipline of England has produced something higher, and deeper too, than that which roars so loud, and thunders in the index.

—Frances Trollope, *Domestic Manners of the Americans* (1832), ed. Donald Smalley (1949), 327. She was the mother of Anthony Trollope.

249. How little those formalities, to which
With overweening trust alone we give
The name of Education, have to do
With real feeling and just sense.

—William Wordsworth, *The Prelude*
(completed 1805; published posthumously 1850).

Education, Effect (Result) of

(*See also* Educated Person)

250. Not that I had any special reason for hating school! Strange as it may seem to my readers, I was not unpopular there. I was a modest, good-humoured boy. It is Oxford that has made me insufferable.

—Max Beerbohm, *More:* "Going Back to School" (1899). *See* Saki, #265.

251. Give a man a fish and you feed him for a day. Teach a man to fish and you feed him for a lifetime.

—Chinese proverb. *See* Kuan Chung, #256.

252. We might say that a well-directed system of education rectifies natural inequality in ability instead of strengthening it, just as good laws remedy natural inequality in the means of subsistence, and just as in societies where laws have brought about this same equality, liberty, though subject to a regular constitution, will be more widespread, more complete, than in the total independence of savage life.

—Marquis de Condorcet, *Sketch for a Historical Picture of the Progress of the Human Mind* (1795).

253. Nothing has a more direct tendency to advance the happiness and glory of a community than the founding of public schools and seminaries of learning for the education of youth, and adorning their minds with useful knowledge and virtue. Hereby, the rude and ignorant are civilized and rendered humane; persons who would otherwise be useless members of society are qualified to sustain with honor the offices they may be invested with for the public service; reverence for the Deity, filial piety, and obedience to laws are inculcated and promoted.

—Samuel Davies and Gilbert Tennent, *A General Account of the Rise and State of the College, Lately Established in the Province of New-Jersey* [The College of New Jersey, now Princeton University] (1754).

254. The little value Indians set on what we prize so highly, under the name of learning, appears from a pleasant passage that happened some years since, at a treaty between some colonies and the Six Nations. When everything had been settled to the satisfaction of both sides, and nothing remained but a mutual exchange of civilities, the English commissioners told the Indians that they had in their country a college for the instruction of youth, who were there taught various languages, arts, and sciences; that there was a particular foundation in favor of the Indians to defray the expense of the education of any of their sons who should desire to take the benefit of it; and said, if the Indians would accept the offer, the English would take half a dozen of their brightest lads and bring them up in the best manner.

The Indians, after consulting on the proposals, replied that it was remembered that some of their youths had formerly been educated at that college, but that it had been observed that for a long time after they returned to their friends, *they were absolutely good for nothing*—being neither acquainted with the true methods of killing deer, catching beavers, or surprising an enemy. The proposition they looked on, however, as a mark of kindness and goodwill of the English to the Indian nations, which merited a grateful return; and, therefore, if the English gentlemen would send a dozen or two of their children to Onondago, the Great Council would take care of their education, bring them up in what was really the best manner, and make men of them.

—Benjamin Franklin, letter to
Peter Collinson, May 9, 1753, in Jared Sparks, ed.,
The Works of Benjamin Franklin (1836–40), VII.68–73.

255. The best and briefest reason for a good education is that the more effort you expend in sharpening the ax, the less effort you have to expend in chopping the wood.

—Sydney J. Harris, *The Best of Sydney Harris* (1976), 307.

256. If you plan for a year, plant a seed. If for ten years, plant a tree. If for a hundred years, teach the people. When you sow a seed once, you will reap a single harvest. When you teach the people, you will reap a hundred harvests.

—Kuan Chung (died 643 B.C.),
Kuan-tzu (Book of Master Kuan), in Ling Juheng, ed.,
Kuan-tzu chi p'ing (1970), I.12. *See* Chinese proverb, **#251.**

257. I don't know, Ma'am, why they make all this fuss about education; none of the Pagets can read or write, and they get on well enough.

—Attributed to William Lamb,
Viscount Melbourne (1779–1848), to Queen Victoria.

258. Knowledge is power by whomsoever possessed. . . .

Give the people knowledge, therefore, and you give them power.

Education must ever be the grand safeguard of our liberties – the palladium of our political institutions – of all our rights and privileges. In every country on the globe where the mass of the people are best instructed will be found the most liberty, the most virtue, and the most happiness.

– Philip Lindsley, inaugural address at Cumberland College (now University of Nashville), Jan. 12, 1825, in *The Annals of America* (1968), V.157.

259. Education, then, beyond all other devices of human origin, is the great equalizer of the conditions of men, – the balance wheel of the social machinery.... It does better than to disarm the poor of their hostility toward the rich: it prevents being poor. Agrarianism is the revenge of poverty against wealth.... Education prevents both the revenge and the madness.... The spread of education, by enlarging the cultivated class or caste, will open a wider area over which the social feelings will expand; and, if this education should be universal and complete, it would do more than all things else to obliterate factitious distinctions in society.

– Horace Mann, *Twelfth Annual Report of the Massachusetts Board of Education,* 1848.

260. Our ... alternative is education. It works slowly, in an evolutionary manner. It creates no sudden Utopias. It offers no magic remedies. It gives no categorical promises. It demands effort and discipline. It awakens man to his own creative possibilities – to what William James called the "wider self." Education, rightly considered, is man's most formidable tool for survival.

– Frederick Mayer, *A History of Educational Thought* (1960), 8.

261. Since a student wants to turn out to be a learned man, he must give himself over entirely to work at first. But the work finally ends up in honorable pleasure. So also a boy first learning the rudiments in school undergoes some difficulty, which is increased considerably (if I may mention this in passing) if it's his luck to have an inexperienced teacher like the ones I know we used to have a lot of – and probably still do. For if one of them sees a boy who's slow in learning, he thinks the only thing he can do about it is beat him. An ignorant man thinks beatings can do more than nature itself. He doesn't know that it's often the case that slower minds retain things better and produce better fruit than those that are premature.... Of course, a boy in school has to put up with some trouble. Yet, when he grows up to be a man and is a little more mature, he'll consider it more deeply and see that the trouble he had is compensated for by an increase in virtue and that it's completely transformed into inward happiness. The only thing he'll be sorry for is that he didn't suffer more. And no doubt he's weighed it carefully, because the hard, rough, rugged foot of the mountain finally brought him to the level, delightful, flowery summit. He finds so many things there, such various beauty, that he can't go down even if he wants to, the virtue of learning is so engrained in him. Socrates, who was a unique pattern of wisdom in his age, advised young men, to good advantage, to look at themselves often in the mirror, and if they seemed somewhat ugly, to make themselves handsome with learning, and if they seemed handsome, to increase it with learning. For this is the power of learning: it raises humble things to the heights, and it makes things that are already high equal to the divine. And it also has this virtue: if Fortune smiles on you, learning makes you even more splendid. But if you meet adversity, it's a great consolation—as I've often learned in my own case. Moreover, since most people set a value on utility in human affairs, the young should consider and examine how many people there used to be and how many there are now who were born into obscurity and who have become famous and noble through learning. For true nobility is surely created by virtue, and not by a long and famous line of ancestors.

—Richard Pace, *The Benefit of a Liberal Education* (1517), tr. and ed. Frank Manley and Richard S. Sylvester (1967), 123. Pace, a good friend of Thomas More and Erasmus, was an ardent advocate of the new humanistic learning in England.

262. But what do we find...? The schoolrooms packed with children wasting their time and playing at learning; our recent graduates disgracing themselves in public life and, what is worst of all, the very things that they mislearned when young, they are reluctant to confess in old age.

—Petronius, *Satyricon* (c. A.D. 60), i.5.

263. My education finished 9th. July. Whatever moral good and general knowledge I may have got from it, I have retained no literal rules. I don't believe I can repeat a single line of any language.... I regret German very much, history I can read alone, French is still going on, the rules of geography and grammar are tiresome, there is no general word to express the feelings I have always entertained towards arithmetic.

—Beatrix Potter, entry of July 10, 1885, *The Journal of Beatrix Potter from 1881 to 1897,* transcribed by Leslie Linder (1966).

264. Do you know, Carter, that I can actually write my name in the dust on the table?

Faith, Mum, that's more than I can do. Sure there's nothing like education, after all.

—*Punch* Magazine, 1902.

265. But, good gracious, you've got to educate him first. You can't expect a boy to be vicious till he's been to a good school.

—Saki (H.H. Munro), *Reginald in Russia:* "A Baker's Dozen" (1910). *See* Beerbohm, **#250.**

Education, Financial Support of

See Education, Government Support of

Education, Government Support of

(*See also* School, Establishment of)

266. Great is the mistake which is current on this subject that colleges are designed exclusively for the rich; that none but the rich can be benefited by them and, therefore, that the state ought not to patronize or endow them; that funds for their support ought not to be drawn from the public treasury or the other people's purse, because this would be to tax the many for the advantage of the few. Nothing can be more groundless and fallacious than such a representation; no course more injurious to the people were it adopted.

—Philip Lindsley, inaugural address at Cumberland College (now University of Nashville), Jan. 12, 1825, in *The Annals of America* (1968), V.158.

267. Religion, morality, and knowledge, being necessary to good government and the happiness of mankind, schools and the means of education shall forever be encouraged.

—Northwest Ordinance, passed by U.S. Congress, July 13, 1787.

268. Education for the masses [in England] was considered unnecessary and in 1837 £20,000 was all the Government voted towards the education of children throughout the entire country. A cynic observed that an item of £50,000 was voted for the rebuilding of the royal stables.

—Alvin Redman, *The House of Hanover* (1960), 316.

269. Call upon the rulers of our country to lay the foundations of their empire in *knowledge* as well as virtue. Let our common people be compelled by law to give their children (what is commonly called) a good English education. Let schoolmasters of every description be supported in part by the public, and let their principles and morals be subjected to examination before we employ them. Let us have colleges in each of the states, and one federal university under the patronage of Congress, where the youth of all the states may be melted (as it were) together into one mass of citizens after they have acquired the first principles of knowledge in the colleges of their respective states. Let the law of nature and nations, the common law of our country, the different systems of government, history, and everything else connected with the advancement of republican knowledge and principles, be taught by able professors in this university. This plan of general education alone will render the American Revolution a blessing to mankind. As you have staked your reputation upon this great event, with the world and with posterity, you must not desert us till you see the curtain drop and the last act of the drama closed.

—Benjamin Rush, letter to Richard Price, May 25, 1786, *Letters of Benjamin Rush,* ed. L.H. Butterfield (1951), I.388.

270. Though the common people cannot, in any civilised society, be so well instructed as people of some rank and fortune, the most essential parts of education, however, to read, write, and account can be acquired at so early a period of life that the greater part even of those who are to be bred to the lowest occupations have time to acquire them before they can be employed in those occupations. For a very small expense the public can facilitate, can encourage, and can even impose upon almost the whole body of the people the necessity of acquiring the most essential parts of education.

—Adam Smith, *The Wealth of Nations* (1776), II.V.ii.266.

271. I maintain that Government ought to provide for the education of all children who would otherwise be brought up, or rather grow up, in ignorance.

In the first place the welfare of the individual, and in the second that of the community demand it. It is as much the duty of the parent to educate, as it is to feed and clothe, the child. For on what, I would ask, depends this last duty? Why is the child to be fed and clothed, if not to enable him to receive and make proper use of—an education? an education which he is no better able to obtain for himself, than he is to supply his physical wants. Indeed the culture of the physical is important only so far as it is subservient to that of the intellectual man. No one disputes this. Should then poverty or neglect threaten to rob the child of this right—a right more dear and more worthy to be cherished and defended than any he can enjoy—in such a case, it appears to me to be the duty of that neighbor whose circumstances will allow of it, to take the part of the child, and act the part of the parent. The duty in this instance amounts to a moral obligation, and is as much a duty as it is a duty to preserve the life of the infant whose unnatural parents would suffer it to starve by the road-side. What can it profit a man that he hath enough to eat and to drink, and the wherewithal he may be clothed, provided he lose his own soul?

But as these wealthy neighbors can accomplish more good by acting in concert, can more effectively relieve the unfortunate by a community of good offices, it is their duty, or, in other words, the duty of the community, so to do. Thus much for the welfare of the child.

That such a course, in the second place, is consistent with, nay, is necessary to, the greatest good of the community, scarcely admits of a doubt.

I shall not undertake to prove that the community ought to do what is for its own good; this is entirely unnecessary; since the welfare of posterity is certainly to be consulted.

—Henry David Thoreau, Oct. 1836,
in Joseph Moldenhauer and Edwin Moser,
with Alexander C. Kern, ed., *Henry D. Thoreau: Early Essays and Miscellanies* (1975), 60.

272. Whereas sundry laws and statutes by act of Parliament established have with great wisdom ordained, for the better educating of youth in honest and profitable trades and manufactures, as also to avoid sloth and idlness wherewith such young children are easily corrupted, as also for relief of such parents whose poverty extends not to give them breeding, that the justices of the peace should, at their discretion, bind out children to tradesmen or husbandmen to be brought vp in some good and lawfull calling. And whereas God Almighty, among many of his other blessings, has vouchsafed increase of children to this colony, who are now multiplied to a considerable number, who if instructed in good and lawfull trades may much improve the honor and reputation of this country, and no less their own good and their parents' comfort; but forasmuch as for the most part the parents, either through fond indulgence or perverse obstinacy, are most averse and unwilling to part with their children. Be it therefore enacted by authority of this Grand Assembly, according to the aforesaid laudable custom in the Kingdom of England, that the commissioners of the several counties respectively do, at their discretion, make choice of two children in each country of the age of eight or seven years, at the least, either male or female, which are to be sent up to James City, between this and June next, to be employed in the public flax houses under such master and mistress as shall there be appointed, in carding, knitting and spinning, etc. And that such children be furnished from the said county with six barrels of corn, two coverlets, or one rug and one blanket, one bed, one wooden bowl or tray, two pewter spoons, a sow shoat of six months old, two laying hens, [and] with convenient apparent both linen and woolen, with hose and shoes. And for the better provision of housing for the said children, it is enacted, that there be two houses built by the first of April next forty foot long apiece with good and substantial timber; the houses to be twenty foot broad apiece, eight foot high in the pitch, and a stack of brick chimnies standing in the middle of each house, and that they be lofted with sawn boards and made with convenient partitions. And it is further thought fit that the commissioners have caution not to take up any children but from such parents who by reason of their poverty are disabled to maintain and educate them. Be it likewise agreed, that the governor has agreed with the Assembly for the sum of 10,000 pounds of tobacco, to be paid him next crop, to build and furnish the said houses in the manner and form expressed.

—Edgar Wallace and Clifton Hall,
Readings in American Educational History (1951), 9.

273. If I had an archangel's trumpet—the blast of which could startle the living of all the world—I would snatch it at this moment and sound it in the ears of all the people of the ... States which have a solitary poor "unwashed and uncombed" child untaught at a free school.

Tax yourselves.... To educate your children—every one of them—at common primary free schools at State charge.

—Henry A. Wise, address in West Virginia
1844, *Report of the Commissioner of Education for the Year 1899–1900* (Washington, D.C., 1901).

Education, Universal and Compulsory

274. There may be such a thing under a despotism as compulsory education, but not in a Republic.... The proposition just introduced into the [Michigan] Senate is simply an absurdity. In States where there are no free schools and people are too poor to pay even their rate bills, the proposition to fine them for not sending their children to school is really a stupid absurdity. The idea is based on the assumption that all parents have the means of sending their children to school, and the neglect to do so is a criminal fault on their part. Nothing can be further from the truth.

—*Detroit Free Press,* Feb. 18, 1871.
The 1871 state law required all Michigan children between the ages of 8 and 14 to attend school 12 weeks a year.

275. The new state law [in Illinois] that extended the education of every child through the eighth grade angered the Amish farmers, who looked upon education as a necessary evil and regarded the extension as a waste of time and energy on the child's part. . . . Father shared the objections of the majority of the Amish community. Amishmen were destined to be farmers; therefore, why all the hue and cry about an eighth-grade education! From generation to generation the Amish had developed their sons to be expert farmers. And all this without a lot of fancy book "larning."

I heard Father say, "Who in the world thinks that an Amish farmer has enough *time* to sit and read?" I suppose that remark reflected well enough the general feeling of his community: till the soil; be frugal; plan each year for the family; pay your debts; work hard; work harder.

Such was the attitude under which I started my first day of school [in 1916].

—Jesse W. Hofer, *An Amish Boy Remembers* (1973), 32. He was later to earn Ph.D. and M.D. degrees.

276. Now surely nothing but universal education can counterwork this tendency to the domination of capital and the servility of labor. If one class possesses all the wealth, and the education, while the residue of society is ignorant and poor, it matters not by what name the relation between them may be called: the latter, in fact and in truth, will be the servile dependents and subjects of the former. But, if education be equally diffused, it will draw property after it by the strongest of all attractions; for such a thing never did happen, and never can happen, as that an intelligent and practical body of men should be permanently poor.

—Horace Mann, *Twelfth Annual Report of the Massachusetts Board of Education,* 1848.

277. Learning is of the greatest importance to the support of a free government; and to prevent this the few are always crying up the advantges of costly colleges, national academies, and grammar schools in order to make places for men to live without work, and to strengthen their party; but are always opposed to cheap schools and women's schools, the only or principal means by which learning is spread among the many.

—William Manning, *The Key of Libberty* (1798).

278. Less than half a century ago, citizens could be found in abundance who would "sacrifice the last dollar, sir," before they would submit to "the injustice of being taxed for the benefit of other people's children." Much more recently, individuals would proclaim their willingness to "rot in jail before sending my boy to school, if I don't want to."

—Henry C. Morrison, *School Revenue* (1930), 84.

279. *Resolved,* that education is one of the strongest safeguards of the Republican Party, the bulwark of American citizens, and a defense against the invasion of the rights of man; its liberal distribution to all, without regard to race, creed, or sex, is necessary for the well-being and advancement of society, and all should enjoy its blessing alike in each of the states and territories of the United States; that . . . there shall be a liberal free-school system enacted by the legislatures of the several states for the benefit of all the inhabitants thereof.

—Platform of the Negro National Labor Union, Jan. 1, 1980, in J.J. Adler, C. Van Doren and G. Ducas, eds., *The Negro in American History* (1969), II.253.

280. There can be no real liberty without a wide diffusion of real intelligence; that the members of a republic, should all be alike instructed in the nature and character of their equal rights and duties, as human beings, and as citizens; and that education, instead of being limited as in our public poor schools, to a simple acquaintance with words and cyphers, should tend, as far as possible, to the production of a just disposition, virtuous habits, and a rational self governing character.

—Report of a committee of Philadelphia workingmen, *Working Man's Advocate,* Mar. 6, 1830.

281. In laying the foundations of a new state, it is all important to provide not only for the education of every individual of the present, but of each one of all succeeding generations. Unless ample provision is made for each individual of all classes, we can have no security that the great mass will ever be educated; for the great whole is made up of individuals. The neglect of one individual may lead to the neglect of many individuals: and thus the great interests of the whole community be endangered. It is confidently believed to be a radical error to contemplate human beings merely in the mass; and consequently all legislation founded upon such a view of man, must be fundamentally wrong.

—John D. Pierce, first annual report of the first Superintendent of Public Instruction of the State of Michigan, 1837.

282. The common village school is New England's fairest boast—the brightest jewel that adorns her brow. The principle that society is bound to provide for its members' education as well as protection, so that none need be ignorant except from choice, is the most important that belongs to modern philosophy. It is essential to a republican government. Universal education is not only the best and surest, but the only sure foundation for free institutions. True liberty is the child of knowledge; she pines away and dies in the arms of ignorance.

—Sergeant Smith Prentiss, address to the New England Society of New Orleans, Dec. 22, 1845.

283. Every friend to the prosperity of Pennsylvania must view with pleasure the establishment and success of those seminaries of learning which are intended to diffuse knowledge through the states; but useful as these colleges and academies are, they are not sufficiently extensive in their objects to spread literature through the humble and indigent classes of people: they are calculated chiefly for the benefit of the affluent and independent part of the citizens of the state.

The blessings of knowledge can be extended to the poor and laboring part of the community only by the means of FREE SCHOOLS....

To a people enlightened in the principles of liberty and Christianity, arguments, it is to be hoped, will be unnecessary to persuade them to adopt these necessary and useful institutions. The children of the poor form a great proportion of all communities. Their ignorance and vices when neglected are not confined to themselves; they associate with and contaminate the children of persons in the higher ranks of society. Thus they assist after they arrive at manhood in choosing the rulers who govern the whole community. They give a complexion to the morals and manners of the people. In short, where the common people are ignorant and vicious, a nation, and above all a republican nation, can never be long free and happy. It becomes us, therefore, as we love our offspring and value the freedom and prosperity of our country, immediately to provide for the education of the poor children who are so numerous in the thick-settled parts of the state.

—Benjamin Rush, "To the Citizens of Philadelphia: A Plan for Free Schools," March 28, 1787, in L.H. Butterfield, ed., *Letters of Benjamin Rush* (1951), I.412.

284. Education, once the peculiar privilege of the few, must in our best earthly estate become the valued possession of the many. It is a natural and inalienable right of human souls. The gift of imagination, of memory, of reason, of invention, of constructive and executive power, carries with it both prerogative and obligation. No man dare with impunity surrender, as to himself, this endowment, nor deny to his neighbor the right and obligation which it involves. Given, intellectual potentiality; required, intellectual discipline and power. The law holds among leaders of thought, teachers and lawmakers; among nobles and favorites of fortune. It holds no less among the lowly—the plebians and the peasants of society.

—John H. Vincent, *The Chautauqua Movement* (1886).

Education: What It Is

285. This long, slow process of building one's mind and spirit was what was meant by education. . . . Education was the constant, often unconscious, rescue within oneself of the life from death, beginning long before one was aware of it in the associations made possible through the places in which one found oneself, through the persons one knew, and, as Dr. Johnson had well said, through the books one read and loved.

—Mary Ellen Chase, *Windswept* (1941), III.

286. *Paideia* in Greek means education (it is the same word we see in encyclopaedia); but it also means civilization—culture, in the highest sense. This is because the Greeks believed that all civilization and all progress were based on education, lifelong education, enjoyment and improvement of all the highest powers of the mind. Other nations have held that their own civilization meant power—or service to God—or service to the divine monarch—or wealth and comfort. Several nations in our own day sometimes seem to believe that if everyone had plenty to eat and drink and owned a motorcar and a few other machines, life would be perfect. The Greeks too enjoyed life with all its delights, wine, women, and song, sports and dancing: many of them gave up their whole existence to light pleasures; but, centrally, they knew what was better, and their greatest men pursued and maintained it. This was simply the improvement of the mind. It was in order to help men think that their great poets composed, their philosophers and historians wrote, their orators spoke. They were teachers. Homer, Aeschylus, Aristophanes; Thucydides, Plato, Aristotle; Pindar, Simonides, Menander: these and many more were, first and foremost, doctors of the soul.

—Gilbert Highet, *Man's Unconquerable Mind* (1954), 18.

287. Education is a matter of holding a balance between discipline and laxity, between over-solicitude and neglect, between spartanism and indulgence, between attachment and independence: that is true in one's self-development and true in the relations of parent and teacher, too. There is no single prescribed path for creating this equilibrium; and the right measure for one moment will be the wrong measure for the next.

—Lewis Mumford, *Green Memories: The Story of Geddes Mumford* (1947), 166.

288. Education is not *one* of man's activities: it comprises all of them; it is man singing, painting, wondering, feeling, dreaming, working, loving in that terrible comedy we call life. It is man experimenting with fire, in the stone age, or at the kitchen stove; it is man carving the first hieroglyphics, or writing his first ABC's, man wondering at the stars, or plotting them or forecasting their returns; man cackling in treetops, or spreading the good word through the printed page.

—Lewis Mumford, *My Works and Days* (1979), 32.

289. Let us not leave the meaning of education ambiguous or ill-defined. At present . . . we call one man educated and another uneducated, although the uneducated man may be sometimes very well educated for the calling of a retail trader, or of a captain of a ship, and the like. For we are not speaking of education in this narrower sense, but of that other education in virtue from youth upwards, which makes a man eagerly pursue the ideal perfection of citizenship, and teaches him how rightly to rule and to obey.

—Plato, *Laws* (c. 367–347 B.C.), I.643.

290. It makes me gladsome to be getting some education, it being like a big window opening.

—Mary Webb, *Precious Bane* (1924), I.v.

Educator

See Principal; Professor; Teacher

English Language

See Grammar; Language; Orthography

Examination

291. It would be fun to send you some of my examination papers. My rule in making them up is to ask questions which I can't myself answer. It astounds me to see how some of my students answer questions which would play the deuce with me.

—Henry Brooks Adams (1838–1918),
letter to Charles Milnes Gaskell, in Louis Kronenberger,
Animal, Vegetable, Mineral (1972), 161.

292. With anxiety and in great excitement I awaited with the other [Austrian] students the big day of our oral examinations, when we had to prove in verbal battles the value of our knowledge and the extent of our wisdom. But when the deciding hour came, I was confident and calm. I succeeded again in receiving top honors. Showered with hearty congratulations and praise, I could hardly wait for the end. Then I dashed out of the room, beaming with glory and happiness, gliding down the hall in enthralled enthusiasm, dancing and whirling into a new life of rapture and ecstasy. Now—I was a teacher.

—Andrea U. Baum, *Between Two Continents* (1969), 7.

293. Candidates are required to enter their apartments on the day preceding the examination and are not allowed to leave until the day after it is closed.... Candidates are not allowed to get drunk and behave disorderly during the examination.... On entering the examination-hall the candidate shall be subjected to a search, and if he is found to have with him any precomposed essay, or miniature copy of the classics, he shall be punished by wearing the wooden collar, and shall lose his first degrees and be incapacitated from standing as a literary candidate for ever. Moreover both the parents and the tutor of the delinquent shall be prosecuted and punished.

—Elijah Coleman Bridgman, rules governing literary
examinations in China, *Description of the City of Canton* (1839).

294. I never got a mark higher than 75 per cent in my life; and I have a strong prejudice against any boy who can get such marks. It means low ambitions. An endeavor to please the elders is at the bottom of high marks and mediocre careers.

—John J. Chapman, letter to S.S. Drury, May 18, 1914,
in Clifton Fadiman, *The American Treasury* (1955), 287.

295. [During] my Entrance Examination to Harrow ... I was found unable to answer a single question in the Latin paper. I wrote my name at the top of the page. I wrote down the number of the question 'I'. After much reflection I put a bracket round it thus '(I)'. But thereafter I could not think of anything connected with it that was either relevant or true. Incidentally there arrived from nowhere in particular a blot and several smudges. I gazed for two whole hours at this sad spectacle: and then merciful ushers collected my piece of foolscap with all the others and carried it up to the Headmaster's table. It was from these slender indications of scholarship that Dr. Weldon drew the conclusion that I was worthy to pass into Harrow. It is very much to his credit. It showed that he was a man capable of looking beneath the surface of things: a man not dependent upon paper manifestations. I have always had the greatest regard for him.

—Winston Churchill, *My Early Life: A Roving Commission* (1938), 15. *See* Halle, **#301**, and Stein, **#304**.

296. The masters appointed, should devote every Saturday to examination into the acquirements of the preceding five days: And the trustees of the school should be required to attend at least all quarterly examinations. This should be a duty exacted under a penalty. At these quarterly examinations, specimens of proficiency, produced on the spot, on momentary requisition, should be demanded from each pupil. The secret of all proficiency, is frequent and rigid examination.

—Thomas Cooper, *Lectures on the Elements of Political Economy* (1826).

297. Attendant upon a West Point Inquisition. In preparing for this last, I believe for two weeks previous, that I scarcely lifted my eyes from my book, except to eat and sleep my six hours, and even then after such close application I shuddered to obey the call of "turn out first section second class." This however was not the trying time, although my heart palpitated strong enough to have shaken the Alleghenies had they been placed upon it.

—George W. Cullum, letter to Alfred Huidekoper about West Point examinations, Jan. 21, 1832, in Sidney Forman, *West Point* (1950).

298. The long agony is at length over, & it may well be called "The agony": for I have never seen more anguish depicted in the countenances of any than the U.S. Corps of Cadets have manifested.

—William Dutton, letter to his cousin Lucy J. Mathews, June 22, 1843, in Forman, *ibid.*

299. If this boy passes the examinations he will be admitted; and if the white students choose to withdraw, all the income of the college will be devoted to his education.

—Edward Everett, answer, as president of Harvard, to students who protested the admission of Beverly Williams, a Negro student, in 1848.

300. If I were an examiner—which heaven forfend!—I should not take much stock of the candidate's knowledge. What can a youth of sixteen be expected to know? Either he gabbles, like a parrot, things that he does not understand, or he talks out of his head. Imagine the case vice versâ, and the examiner having the same questions put him instead of the examinee! No: if I had to pass or reject a candidate, I should not go upon the correctness of his replies, but upon his general appearance. I should take note whether his physiognomy was more or less pleasing, and consider the generosity of his facial angle, the brightness of his eye, the timbre of his voice. I should engage him in a little conversation without any pretensions to strict science. I should not say to myself: "Can this youth tell me without hesitation the phases of the Thirty Years' War or the laws of Solon." I should say to myself: "You have a marriageable daughter. Would you give her to this young man?" That is the true touchstone.

—Anatole France (1844–1924), in Jean Jacques Brousson, *Anatole France Himself*, tr. John Pollock (1925), 285.

301. 1893–: Sent to a crammer in London for six months—where his tutor, Captain James, is said to have concluded, "That lad couldn't have gone through Harrow, he must have gone under it."

—Kay Halle, *Irrepressible Churchill* (1966), 20. Winston Churchill had twice failed the entrance examinations to Sandhurst. *See* Churchill, #295.

302. The day of examination [for a teaching position in a Swiss village] arrived. One candidate, older than myself, exhibited his learning. He was ordered to read the first chapter of the New Testament and write some lines, a task which took him half an hour to perform. I was called in. The examiner placed before me a genealogical table from Adam to Abraham, as a reading exercise. He then handed me an unmended quill pen, desiring me to write something. "But what shall I write?" said I. "Write the Lord's prayer, or whatever you like," was the reply. As I had no knowledge, either or parts of speech or orthography, or of punctuation the result of my scribbling may be imagined. This was all the examination, and after it we retired. When we were recalled, the chairman informed us that neither had been found overburdened with learning; that one of us was better in reading, the other in writing; but, that since my rival was already forty years old, while I was only eighteen, they thought I would sooner acquire the necessary knowledge. Moreover, since my dwelling (the town had no schoolhouse) was better adapted for a school than that of my competitor, they had appointed me schoolmaster. No doubt I felt happy at this unexpected decision, though I had no reason to be very proud of my salary, which was only one dollar per week, while my vanquished opponent was appointed policeman, with one and a half dollars per week.

—Hermann Krüsi (1775–1844),
Pestalozzi: His Life and Work (1927), 467.

303. "But sir, I don't think I really deserve it, it was mostly bull, really." This disclaimer from a student whose examination we have awarded a straight "A" is wondrously depressing. Alfred North Whitehead invented its only possible rejoiner: "Yes sir, what you wrote is nonsense, utter nonsense. But ah! It's the right *kind* of nonsense!"

—William G. Perry, Jr., "Examsmanship
and the Liberal Arts: A Study in Educational Epistomology,"
in *Examining in Harvard College: A Collection of Essays* (1963).

304. It was a very lovely spring day, Gertrude Stein had been going to the opera every night and going also to the opera in the afternoon and had been otherwise engrossed and it was the period of the final examinations, and there was the examination in William James' course. She sat down with the examination paper before her and she just could not. Dear Professor James, she wrote at the top of her paper. I am sorry but really I do not feel a bit like an examination paper in philosophy to-day, and left.

The next day she had a postal card from William James saying, Dear Miss Stein, I understand perfectly how you feel. I often feel like that myself. And underneath it he gave her work the highest mark in his course.

—Gertrude Stein, *The Autobiography of
Alice B. Toklas* (1933), 79. *See* Churchill, **#295.**

305. Let it be known to you, that I have tested Miss Lucinda Foote, aged twelve, by way of examination, proving that she has made laudable progress in the language of the learned, viz., The Latin and the Greek; to such an extent that I found her translating and expounding with [perfect] ease, both words and sentences in the whole of Vergil's Aeneid, in selected orations of Cicero, and in the Greek testament. I testify that were it not for her sex, she would be considered fit to be admitted as a student . . . of Yale University.

—Ezra Stiles, president of Yale, official proclamation, 1783, in Lynn Sherr and Jurate Kazickas, *American Women's Gazetteer* (1976).

306. No one cause has done so much to render the occupation of teacher distasteful as the old system of annual examinations. Teachers were condemned to be tried, not by a jury of their peers, but too often by men who knew little or nothing of practical teaching, and who unfrequently made the annual examination a guillotine for decapitating any unlucky pedagogue who had fallen under the ban of their petty displeasure. . . . The annual examinations of experienced teachers offered an annual insult to intelligence, by lumping character, aptness to teach, moral and social culture, in tabular statements of "percentage" on arithmetic and spelling, in which infinitesimal details counted everything, character and success nothing at all.

—John Swett, Superintendent of Public Instruction of California, *Thirteenth Annual Report*, 1863.

Freedom, Academic

(*See also* Censorship)

307. *An inviolable refuge from tyranny should be found in the university.* It should be an *intellectual experiment station*, where new ideas may germinate and where their fruit, though still distasteful to the community as a whole, may be allowed to ripen until finally, perchance, it may become a part of the accepted intellectual food of the nation or of the world.

—Declaration of the First Committee on Academic Freedom of the American Association of University Professors, 1915.

308. The [Feinberg] law inevitably turns the school system into a spying project. Regular loyalty reports on the teachers must be made out. The principals become detectives; the students, the parents, the community become informers. Ears are cocked for tell-tale signs of disloyalty. The prejudices of the community come into play in searching out the disloyal. This is not the usual type of supervision which checks a teacher's competency; it is a system which searches for hidden meanings in the teacher's utterances.

What happens under the law is typical of what happens in a police state. Teachers are under constant surveillance; their pasts are combed for disloyalty; their utterances are watched for clues to dangerous thoughts. A pall is cast over the classrooms. There can be no real academic freedom in that environment. . . .

This, I think, is what happens when a censor looks over a teacher's shoulder. This system of spying and surveillance with its accompanying reports and trials cannot go hand and hand with academic freedom. It produces standardized thought, not the pursuit of truth. Yet it was the pursuit of truth which the First Amendment was designed to protect.

—Justice William O. Douglas, dissenting U.S. Supreme Court opinion, *Adler v Board of Education* (1952). The New York Board of Regents compiled a list of "subversive organizations" in which present membership would constitute *prima facie* evidence of disqualification for employment as a public school teacher. Past membership would be presumptive evidence of present membership.

309. If at times it appears that our university colleagues protest overly much about "academic freedom," they do so because it is the one indispensable condition of their existence. Without it, their professional careers, the purposes to which they have dedicated their lives, would become meaningless. Either we have academic freedom or we have academic slavery. There is no middle ground for a true university.

—Grayson Kirk, "Academic Responsibilities," in R.E. Summers, ed., *Freedom and Loyalty in Our Colleges* (1954).

310. It is a matter of primary importance in the cultivation of those sciences, in which truth is discoverable by the human intellect, that the investigator should be free, independent, unshackled in his movements; that he should be allowed and enabled, without impediment, to fix his mind intently, nay, exclusively, on his special object, without the risk of being distracted every other minute in the process and progress of his inquiry, by charges of temerariousness, or by warnings against extravagance or scandal.

—John Henry Newman, *Christianity and Scientific Investigation* (1855).

311. Statistical evidence shows that the greater the intellectual freedom, and the higher the general average intelligence in a community, the greater is also the number of suicides.

—Svend Ranulf, *The Jealousy of the Gods and Criminal Law at Athens,* ii (1934).

312. The fact that society at large permits activities to be carried on freely or ideas to be circulated freely does not obligate colleges to give them hospitality under the guise of academic freedom or of constitutional rights.

Prize fights, burlesque shows, and propagandizing are not proper college activities, no matter how acceptable they may be elsewhere.

—Harold W. Stoke, "The Invitation of Speakers to the College Campus," *School and Society*, Mar. 10, 1962.

Genius

313. It is not enough to be the possessor of genius—the time and the man must conjoin. An Alexander the Great, born into an age of profound peace, might scarce have troubled the world—a Newton, grown up in a thieves' den, might have devised little but a new and ingenious picklock.

—John Cleveland Cotton, *Diversions of Historical Thought*, in *Selected Works of Stephen Vincent Benét:* "The Curfew Tolls" (1942), II.383.

314. He knew that he was different, that he was gifted, and like all gifted people he knew it was not profitable to be different.

—Ralph De Boissière, *Crown Jewel* (1952), 36.

315. Time, Place, and Action may with pains be wrought,
But Genius must be born; and never can be taught.

—John Dryden, "To My Dear Friend, Mr. Congreve" (1694), ln.59, *The Works of John Dryden*, ed. A.B. Chambers and William Frost (1974), IV.

316. Profound knowledge is good, but profound genius is better, because one obtains with greater ease all the thoughts of all wise men, which the other obtains slowly by adding himself conclusion to conclusion. Yet in the end when both have arrived at the same amount of knowledge the latter is much the richest.... Considered with relation to our whole existence, that, habits of thought are better than knowledge—was the original position of my rhetoric.

—Ralph Waldo Emerson, *Journals*, Jan. 25, 1824, in W.H. Gilman, A.R. Ferguson, and M.R. Davis, *The Journals and Miscellaneous Notebooks* (1961), II.

317. Talents differ; all is well and wisely put;
If I cannot carry forests at my back,
Neither can you crack a nut.

—Ralph Waldo Emerson (1803–82), "Fable" ("The Mountain and the Squirrel"), *Poems* (1904), 75.

318. The great despise men of genius who have nothing but genius: men of genius despise the great who have nothing but greatness: the upright pity both, who have either greatness or genius without virtue.

—Jean de La Bruyère, *Les Caractères* (1688), ix.

319. Geniuses should always be given dinners when they are struggling; it gives them encouragement. If you wait till they are recognized it only gives them indigestion.

—Charlotte Mansfield, *Girl and the Gods* (1907).

320. I have always thought geniuses much inferior to the plain sense of a cookmaid, who can make a good pudding and keep the kitchen in order.

—Lady Mary Wortley Montagu, letter to the Countess of Pomfret, March 1739, *The Letters and Works of Lady Mary Wortley Montagu,* ed. Lord Wharncliffe (1898), II.41.

321. He came up from Brazen Nose College,
Just caught, as they call it, this spring;
And his head, love, is stuffed full of knowledge
Of every conceivable thing.
Of science and logic he chatters
As fine and as fast as he can;
Though I am no judge of such matters,
I'm sure he's a talented man.

—Winthrop Mackworth Praed (1802–39), "The Talented Man," in Burton Egbert Stevenson, ed., *The Home Book of Verse* (1953), 1807.

322. Could we teach taste or genius by rules, they would be no longer taste or genius.

—Joshua Reynolds, *Discourses,* III, lecture at the Royal Academy, London, Dec. 14, 1770.

323. A genius is a person who, seeing farther and probing deeper than other people, has a different set of ethical valuations from theirs, and has energy enough to give effect to this extra vision and its valuations in whatever manner best suits his or her specific talents.

—George Bernard Shaw, *Saint Joan,* preface (1924).

Geography

324. Geography had no place in the medieval catalogue of the "seven liberal arts." Somehow it fit neither into the quadrivium of mathematical disciplines (arithmetic, music, geometry, and astronomy) nor into the trivium of logical and linguistic disciplines (grammar, dialectic, and rhetoric). For a thousand years of the Middle Ages no common synonym for "geography" was in ordinary usage, and the word did not enter the English language until the mid-sixteenth century. Lacking the dignity of a proper discipline, geography was an orphan in the world of learning. The subject became a ragbag filled with odds and ends of knowledge and pseudo-knowledge, of Biblical dogma, travelers' tales, philosophers' speculations, and mythical imaginings.

—Daniel J. Boorstin, *The Discoverers* (1983), 100.

Girls, Education of

See Women, Education of

Grammar

(*See also* Language; Orthography)

325. For many years the pronoun *she* was used in educational circles to refer to all schoolteachers (a similar situation pertained in nursing and in secretarial studies). The pronoun choice was clearly motivated by the predominance at the time of women teachers, a situation which led to the word *teacher* to be interpreted as a covert feminine noun. The generic masculine pronoun was invariably retained, however, in reference to pupils, school administrators, and the professoriate.

—Dennis Baron, *Grammar and Gender* (1986), 176.

326. I am about to—or I am going to—die. Either expression is used.

—Dominique Bouhours,
a grammarian, last words, in Robert Hendrickson,
The Literary Life and Other Curiosities (1981), 109.

327. And therein to content ourselves, if we can but obtaine so much of many, as to be able to understand and make use of the [grammar] rules, or to turn them though they can not say them readily; for we see most schollers, when they come to the Universities, to forget that perfectnesse in their Grammars, and most learned men can not say the rules; yet so long as they have full understanding & remembrance to make use in resolving, writing or speaking, this suffieth.

—John Brinsley,
Ludus Literarius, or The Grammar School (1622).

328. Grammar made me more trouble than any other study. Somehow I never could learn grammar, and it always made me angry when I tried. My parents and teachers told me that I could never write or speak unless I learned grammar, and so I tried and tried, but even now I can hardly tell an adverb from an adjective, and I do not know that I care. When a little boy, I used to think that if I really had anything to tell I could make myself understood; and I think so still. The longer I live the surer I am that the chief trouble of writers and speakers is the lack of interesting thoughts, and not of proper words.

—Clarence Darrow, *The Story of My Life* (1932).

329. I had a wrangle today with a man who said that there is no such thing as grammar, and that "the living speech" was good speech. He talked about "Everyman's grammar"—meaning anything anybody cares to say—as the only guide to usage. Humph! I wouldn't particularly like to trust myself to Everyman's medicine or Everyman's ideas of the law. Why should I accept Everyman's grammar?

—Robertson Davies,
The Table Talk of Samuel Marchbanks (1949), 54.

330. Grammer beinge but an introduction to the understanding of autors, if it be made to longe or exquisite to the lerner, hit in a maner mortifieth his corage: And by that time he cometh to the most swete and pleasant redinge of olde autors, the sparkes of feruent desire of lernynge is extincte with the burdone of grammer, lyke as a lyttel fyre is sone quenched with a great heape of small stickes: so that it can neuer come to the principall logges where it should longe bourne in a great pleasaunt fire.

—Sir Thomas Elyot,
The Boke Named the Governour (1531), I.x.

331. The adjective is the banana peel of the parts of speech.

—Clifton Fadiman, in *Reader's Digest,* September 1956.

332. Split infinitive. The English-speaking world may be divided into (1) those who neither know nor care what a split infinitive is; (2) those who do not know, but care very much; (3) those who do know and condemn; (4) those who know and approve; and (5) those who know and distinguish.

—H.W. Fowler, *A Dictionary of Modern English Usage*, 2nd ed. (1983), 579.

333. To forestall any accusations that I am anti-democratic in my predilection for the King's English, let me explain that I am a grammarian by necessity rather than by choice. All through my education I had teachers who were martinets and who beat grammar and spelling into me. Not only was I tongue-lashed for mistakes like "between you and I," but also I was endlessly drilled in such mnemonics as:

1. "I before E except after C and in nEIther lEIsurely forEIgner sEIzed thEIr wEIrd hEIght."
2. "Tie the can to DIFFERENT THAN."
3. "With might and main, use LIE-LAY-LAIN."

These mnemonics made little sense in themselves, but somehow it never occurred to me to wonder why any lEIsurely forEIgner should want to bestir himself to sEIze a wEIrd hEIght, or how silly a Busch Bavarian container would look dangling from a THAN. I heard them repeated over and over, and they stuck in my memory. When I hear somebody misusing the tenses of LIE, I duck sympathetically for him as if expecting a blackboard eraser to be fired in my direction. And as for telling my dog "Lay down" instead of "Lie down," an automatic mechanism in my brain would register TILT the second I started to mouth the wrong word. (My dog, incidentally, is agrammatical: she will neither lay down nor lie down upon command!) . . . So please try if you can to be understanding of my built-in antipathy to the way of speaking of my fellow Americans. If you catch me some time seeming to cringe from an imaginary blow, or with a tic ticking in my cheek, or with an uncontrollable itching in the heifer of my leg, think nothing of it. Somebody has probably just split an infinitive within my earshot, and I am reacting.

—Daniel R. Howe, *Howe About This and That:* "In Defense of the King's English" (1967), 265.

334. I'm glad you like adverbs—I adore them; they are the only qualifications I really respect.

—Henry James, letter to Miss M. Betham Edwards, Jan. 5, 1912, in Percy Lubbock, ed., *The Letters of Henry James* (1920), II.

335. Where strictness of grammar does not weaken expression, it should be attended to in complaisance to the purists of New England. But where by a small grammatical negligence, the energy of an idea is condensed, or a word stand for a sentence, I hold grammatical rigor in contempt.

—Thomas Jefferson, letter to President James Madison, in Karl Lehmann, *Thomas Jefferson: American Humanist* (1947), 82.

336. There are grammatical errors even in his silence.

—Stanislaw J. Lec, *Unkempt Thoughts*, tr. Jacek Galazka (1962).

337. The principal design of a Grammar in any Language is to teach us to express ourselves with propriety in that Language, and enable us to judge of every phrase and form of construction whether it be right or wrong. The plain way of doing this, is to lay down rules, and to illustrate them by examples. But, besides shewing what is right, the matter may be further explained by pointing out what is wrong.

—Robert Lowth, *A Short Introduction to English Grammar* (1762).

338. English grammar is very difficult and few writers have avoided making mistakes in it. So heedful a writer as Henry James, for instance, on occasion wrote so ungrammatically that a schoolmaster, finding such errors in a schoolboy's essay, would be justly indignant. It is necessary to know grammar, and it is better to write grammatically than not, but it is well to remember that grammar is common speech formulated. Usage is the only test. I would prefer a phrase that was easy and unaffected to a phrase that was grammatical.

—W. Somerset Maugham, *The Summing Up* (1938), 40.

339. A grammarian's daughter made love with a man, and the poor creature gave birth to a child who was, in orderly sequence: masculine, feminine, and neuter.

—Palladas, Greek epigrammatist of Alexandria (early 5th cent. A.D.).

340. This sentence demonstrates alot of the to frequent errors that occur in my freshman composition classes its not just there willingness to gleefully split an infinitive or end a sentence with a preposition which are problems kindly boarding school masters used to be concerned with. Its true my students arent the good mannered middle class bunch who I went to school with, there more often cops or shoesalesmens or garbagemens (pardon me, sanitationmens) sons and daughters, and yet there a sharp group, wary, skeptical, bright.

So when I knock myself out day after day. class after class. explaining the genitive case in english, the proper position of commas, the runon sentence, the distinction between the three theres and still these mistakes appear even in the work of the best of them. I wonder.

—Robert Pattison, "Being a Disquisition wherein were told whats happening to english including examples written by a man who no's;", *New York Times*, Dec. 19, 1974.

341. Grammar and logic free language from being at the mercy of the tone of voice. Grammar protects us against misunderstanding the sound of an uttered name; logic protects us against what we say having a double meaning.

—Eugen Rosenstock-Huessy, in W.H. Auden, *A Certain World: A Commonplace Book* (1970), 226.

342. Damn the subjunctive. It brings all our writers to shame.

—Mark Twain, *Notebook*, July 2, 1896 (1935).

Handwriting

343. It was very pleasant to me to get a letter from you the other day. Perhaps I should have found it pleasanter if I had been able to decipher it. I don't think that I mastered anything beyond the date (which I knew) and the signature (which I guessed at). There's a singular and perpetual charm in a letter of yours; it never grows old, it never loses its novelty. . . . Other letters are read and thrown away and forgotten, but yours are kept forever—unread. One of them will last a reasonable man a lifetime.

—Thomas Bailey Aldrich (1836–1907), letter to Professor Edward Sylvester Morse.

344. There must be special care, that every one who is to write, have all necessaries thereunto; as to pen, ink, paper, ruler, plummet, ruling pen, pen-knife, etc.

The like care must be, that their ink be thin, black, clear; which will not run abroad nor blot; their paper good; that is, such as white, smooth, and which will bear ink, and also that it be made in a book. Their writing books should be kept fair, straight ruled, and each to have a blotting paper to keep their books from soiling, or marring under their hands.

Cause every one of them to make his own pen, otherwise the making and mending of pens will be a very great hindrance, both to the masters and to the scholars. Besides that, when they are away from their masters they will write naught, because they know not how to make their pens themselves.

The best manner of making the pen is thus:

a. Choose the quill of the best and strongest of the wing, which is somewhat harder, and will cleave.

b. Make it clean with the back of the pen-knife.

c. Cleave it straight up the back; first with a cleft made with your pen-knife, after with another quill put into it, rive it further a little and little, till you see the cleft to be very clean . . . [then make] the nib and cleft both about one length, somewhat above a barley-corn breadth, and small, so as it may let down the ink, and write clean. Cut the nib first slant downwards to make it thin, and after straight over thwart. Make both sides of equal bigness, unless you be cunning to cut that side, which lieth upon the long finger thinner and shorter; yet so little, as the difference can hardly be discerned. But both of equal length is accounted the surest.

—John Brinsley,
Ludus Literarius, or the Grammar School (1622), 29.

345. The rules of penmanship at that time [c. 1900] provided that you had to lean your head over to the left, wind up like they [sic] was nobody on second base, and when you finally touched pen to paper, your head followed through from left to right so that when you come to the end of the line, your right ear laid flat on the desk. I was a complete flop under this system and in after yrs. I changed my stance, kept my head still, took a slower back swing and seemed to improve a little, though 2 of my gal friends told me when I was 20 that my mash notes looked like the output of a 3 yr. old child with a satisfied craving for brandy. The ultimate results of my long battle with the wiles of penmanship is that during the last 15 yrs. I ain't used pen and ink, except to sign letters of apology to golf clubs.

—Ring Lardner,
"What I Ought to of Learnt in High School,"
The American Magazine, Nov. 1923, in Matthew J. Bruccoli
and Richard Layman, eds., *Some Champions:
Sketches and Fiction by Ring Lardner* (1976), 5.

Headmaster

See Principal

Historian

(*See also* History)

346. Bias, point of view, fury—are they then so dangerous and must be ironed out of history, the hills flattened and the contours leveled? The professors talked about passion and point of view of history as a Calvinist talks about sin in the bedroom. There they sat, trying to get the heat out of history and here I sat, trying to get in. There must surely be a balance between us somewhere, a place for us to meet. . . . Perhaps it all depends on what one looked for in reading it. A point of view and special lighting are not distortions, says Santayana. "They are conditions of vision, and spirit can see nothing not focused in some living eye."

—Catherine Drinker Bowen, *Adventures of a Biographer* (1946), 93. *See* Nash, **#352,** below.

347. One intellectual excitement has . . . been denied me. Men wiser and more learned than I have discovered in history a plot, a rhythm, a predetermined pattern. These harmonies are concealed from me. I can see only one emergency following upon another as wave follows wave, only one great fact with respect to which, since it is unique, there can be no generalizations, only one safe rule for the historian: that he should recognize in the development of human destinies the play of the contingent and the unforeseen. This is not a doctrine of cynicism and despair. The fact of progress is written plain and large on the page of history; but progress is not a law of nature. The ground gained by one generation may be lost on the next. The thoughts of men may flow into the channels which lead to disaster and barbarism.

—Herbert A.L. Fisher, *A History of Europe* (1935), preface.

348. "I came, sir," said I to him, "to ask for the advice that a man of your experience can give. I am taking the utmost trouble in composing a history and I reach no result whatever."

He answered me, shrugging his shoulders:

"What is the good, my dear sir, of giving yourself so much trouble, and why compose a history when all you need to do is to copy the best-known ones in the usual way? If you have a fresh view or an original idea, if you present men and things from an unexpected point of view, you will surprise the reader. And the reader does not like being surprised. He never looks in a history for anything but the stupidities that he knows already. If you try to instruct him you only humiliate him and make him angry. Do not try to enlighten him; he will only cry out that you insult his beliefs.

"Historians copy from one another. Thus they spare themselves trouble and avoid the appearance of presumption. Imitate them and do not be original. An original historian is the object of distrust, contempt, and loathing from everybody. . . .

"One word more. If you want your book to be well received, lose no opportunity for exalting the virtues on which society is based – attachment to wealth, pious sentiments, and especially resignation on the part of the poor, which latter is the very foundation of order. Proclaim, sir, that the origins of property – nobility and police – are treated in your history with all the respect which these institutions deserve. Make it known that you admit the supernatural when it presents itself. On these occasions you will succeed in good society."

– Anatole France, *Penguin Island* (1908), 4, tr. A.W. Evans.

349. A trend in history is like a wave to a swimmer in the ocean: He does not see it until it is about to engulf him; this is why social historians possess only 20-20 hindsight.

– Sydney J. Harris,
syndicated column, *Detroit Free Press*, June 2, 1983.

350. There was a young person whose history,
Was always considered a mystery;
She sat in a ditch, although no one knew which,
And composed a small treatise on history.

– Edward Lear, in Thomas Byron, ed., *Nonsense and Wonder: The Poems and Cartoons of Edward Lear* (1977), 118.

351. The perfect historian is he in whose work the character and spirit of the age is exhibited in miniature. He relates no fact, he attributes no expression to his characters, which is not authenticated by sufficient testimony. But, by judicious selection, rejection, and arrangement, he gives to truth those attractions which have been usurped by fiction. In his narrative a due subordination is observed: some transactions are prominent; others retire. But the scale on which he represents them is increased or diminished, not according to the dignity of the persons concerned in them, but according to the degree in which they elucidate the condition of society and the nature of man. He shows us the court, the camp, and the senate. But he shows us also the nation. He considers no anecdote, no peculiarity of manner, no familiar saying, as too insignificant for his notice which is not too insignificant to illustrate the operation of laws, of religion, and of education, and to make the progress of the human mind. Men will not merely be described, but will be made intimately known to us. The changes of manners will be indicated, not merely by a few general phrases or a few extracts from statistical documents, but by appropriate images presented in every line.

—Thomas Babington Macaulay, "History," *Edinburgh Review*, May 1828.

352. A historian on the American side of the Atlantic received a fitting rebuke to his implied assumption that to be outside a particular tradition made an unbiased view of controversial questions possible. In conducting oral examination of a Mormon student who was submitting a Ph.D. thesis on a particular period of Mormon history, the historian asked the student if, he being a Mormon, considered himself sufficiently unprejudiced to write a thesis of Mormon history. The somewhat daring student appositely remarked, "Yes, if you, not a Mormon, consider yourself unprejudiced enough to examine it."

—Arnold S. Nash, *The University and the Modern World* (1943). *See* Bowen, **#346.**

353. It is right for a good man to love his friends and his country, and to hate the enemies of both. But when a man takes upon him to write history, he must throw aside all such feelings, and be prepared, on many occasions, to extol even an enemy, when his conduct deserves applause; nor should he hesitate to censure his dearest and most esteemed friends, whenever their deeds call for condemnation. For as an animal, if it be deprived of sight, is wholly useless; so if we eliminate truth from history, what remains will be nothing but an idle tale.

—Polybius, *Histories* (c. 125 B.C.), I.

History

(*See also* Historian)

354. History has a long-range perspective. It ultimately passes stern judgment on tyrants and vindicates those who fought, suffered, were imprisoned, and died for human freedom, against political oppression and economic slavery. Pioneers who were reviled, persecuted, ridiculed, and abused when they fought for free public schools, woman's suffrage against chattel slavery, for labor unions, are honored and revered today.

—Elizabeth Gurley Flynn, *Labor's Own: William Z. Foster* (1949).

355. History fades into fable; fact becomes clouded with doubt and controversy; the inscription moulders from the tablet: the statue falls from the pedestal. Columns, arches, pyramids, what are they but heaps of sand; and their epitaphs but characters written in the dust?

—Washington Irving,
The Sketch-Book: "Westminster Abbey" (1820).

356. History: A nearly defunct field of study that is of value only to the extent that it glorifies everything previously debased, and vice versa.

—Bernard Rosenberg, *Dictionary for the Disenchanted* (1972).

357. *Swindon:* What will History say?
Burgoyne. History, sir, will tell lies, as usual.

—George Bernard Shaw, *The Devil's Disciple* (1897), III.

358. I am determined to apply myself to a study that is hateful & disgusting to my very soul, but which is above all studies, necessary for him who would be listened to as a member of antiquated abuses.—I mean that record of crimes & miseries—History.

—Percy Bysshe Shelley, letter to Thomas Hookham,
Dec. 17, 1812, in Frederick L. Jones, ed., *Letters* (1964), I.

359. History, poetry and philosophy I commonly read on horseback, having other employment at other times.

—John Wesley, *Journal,* Mar. 19, 1770.

Homework

360. Every evening except in summer, once the supper dishes had been cleared away and washed, our orderly and harmonious routine began. My father settled himself in his big chair in the library, an oracle who might be consulted in times of calamity or doubt. My mother procured her enormous mending-basket, heaped with underwear and stockings. As we grew older and entered the academy, the freight of this great basket was always weighed with books—her own Caesar, Cicero, and Vergil. We always studied in the dining-room, each having his proper place around the lamp in the centre of the table and my mother sitting as at meal-times at the head. Even although the smaller children were required before their earlier bed-time to put but fifteen minutes upon their spelling or sums, my mother insisted that they sit with the group for that space of time. Half-sized ones of grammar-school age wrestled in comparative silence with abstruse problems concerning the cube root of monstrous numbers; or the manual talents of Mr. A., Mr. B., and Mr. C.; or the ways, means, and price of papering a room with many annoying windows of differing sizes. My father in the library adjoining was usually too much engrossed in his book or too tired to throw much light on such practical matters, although he was always glad to explain the Monroe Doctrine or the Alien and Sedition Acts.

—Mary Ellen Chase, *A Goodly Heritage* (1932), 224.

361. Homework, as such, must be a comparatively recent development in the educational field. Personally, I don't remember hearing much about it during my hitch in grade school. Perhaps we were less well trained than the scholars of today—or maybe we were just smarter and didn't need to spend all day and half the night getting our lessons. It might possibly have been the way a country school was run, with all the students sitting there listening to the others recite. Under that system, you picked up learning by a sort of osmosis. Besides, you could always do your homework while the classes in which you had no interest were reciting.

So, lacking homework, and having neither radio nor TV, it was no wonder we turned to reading aloud on those long winter evenings at home.

—Loula Grace Erdman, *Life Was Simpler Then* (1963), 134.

362. I didn't know I needed some quiet place where I could do my homework. My brothers used to sit around the dining-room table in the evening doing homework en masse, noisily, bothering each other, correcting, helping. They didn't know they were doing it all wrong. . . . I didn't know I had to *feel* like doing my homework, practicing the violin, washing dishes or running errands. I just *had* to do it because everyone had to do things he really didn't feel like doing—even big people. I had a strong suspicion my father didn't like working twelve hours a day in a sweatshop.

—Sam Levenson, *Everything But Money* (1949), 15, 16.

The Humanities

(*See also* Language)

363. Let us be clear about the role of the classics: they are worth studying as examples of *how* to think, not *what* to think. We shall be acting most like Dante or Newton or Pascal if we think thoughts very different from theirs but having the same potency for our times that their thoughts had for their times. This does not exclude adoption and adaptation of former wisdom, it merely stresses the need for rethinking against rehashing. The intellectual life justifies itself when, having embraced the common facts, it asks and answers the question, What does it all mean? There lies the true responsibility of the scholar—not to a ritual but to the reality of a subject.

—Jacques Barzun, *Teacher in America* (1943), 316.

364. The average schoolmaster [in England, *circa* late 1500s] did not understand the principle upon which a study of Greek and Roman literature was based. He did not realize that it was a liberating force, not a confining one, and he conducted his classroom in the same way that his medieval ancestors had done before him. He made no attempt to awaken the curiosity or interest of his pupils, since he had none of his own, and he walked through the mighty landscapes of Greece and Rome with his eyes closed to everything but grammar and discipline. If his charges did not learn he beat them, and if they still refused to learn he merely beat them harder.

—Marchette Chute, *Ben Jonson of Westminster* (1953), 28.

365. In an age [eighteenth century] when only a minority of the population was to receive any education at all, an easy way of drawing a clear line of demarcation between those who were and those who were not educated was to have all such education as was to carry with it any social prestige in education in Latin and to make Latin an essential qualification for all the most desirable jobs in the land, whether the knowledge of it was in reality of any value for the performance of those jobs or not.

—Christopher Hollis, *Eton: A History* (1960), 56.

366. At Yale I was introduced to the perennial American debate that might be entitled, "What are the humanities, and why do they mean anything to us here in the last decades of the twentieth century?" The debate has been going on for at least thirty years, becoming more agitated and abstract as it steadily loses its meaning. Nobody wants to say, at least not for publication, that we live in a society that cares as much about the humanities as it cares about the color of the rain in Tashkent. The study of the liberal arts is one of those appearances that must be kept up, like the belief in the rule of law and the devout observances offered to the doctrines of free enterprise and equal opportunity. By advocating the tepid ideals of "the graceful amateur" and "the well-rounded man" the universities make of humanism a pious and wax-faced thing. Works of art and literature become ornaments preserved, like bank notes or trust funds, in the vaults of an intellectual museum. The society doesn't expect its "best people" (i.e., the Hotchkiss students who grow up to become investment bankers and corporation presidents) to have read William Shakespeare or Dante. Nor does anyone imagine that the secretary of state will know much more history than the rudiments of chronology expounded in a sixth-grade synopsis. If it becomes necessary to display the finery of learning, the corporation can hire a speechwriter or send its chairman to the intellectual haberdashers at the Aspen Institute. Education is a commodity, like Pepsi-Cola or alligator shoes.

—Lewis H. Lapham, *Money and Class in America* (1988), 20.

367. I do not mind confessing that for a long time past I have been very sceptical about the classics. I was myself trained as a classical scholar. . . .

But I never got any pleasure from it. . . .

So . . . I began to lie about the classics. I said to people who knew no Greek that there was a sublimity, a majesty about Homer which they could never hope to grasp. I said it was like the sound of the sea beating against the granite cliffs of Ionian Esophagus: or words to that effect. As for the truth of it, I might as well have said that it was like the sound of a rum distillery running a night shift on half time. . . . I managed to suffuse my face with an animation which made it almost beautiful. . . . I believe all scholars lie like this. . . . I know there are solid arguments advanced in favour of the classics. I often hear them from my colleagues. My friend the professor of Greek tells me that he truly believes the classics have made him what he is. This is a very grave statement, if well founded. Indeed I have heard the same argument from a great many Latin and Greek scholars. They all claim, with some heat, that Latin and Greek have practically made them what they are. This damaging charge against the classics should not be too readily accepted. In my opinion some of these men would have been what they are, no matter what they were. . . .

This is what I should like to do. I'd like to take a large stone and write on it in very plain writing—

"The classics are only primitive literature. They belong in the same class as primitive machinery and primitive music and primitive medicine"—and then throw it through the windows of a University and hide behind a fence to see the professors buzz!!

—Stephen Leacock, *Laugh With Leacock:*
"Homer and Humbug, an Academic Discussion" (1930).

368. [*Circa* 1500] Latin grammar was necessary to everything else, especially to the study of English. The notion that people should be able both to read and to write English caught on during the fifteenth century, but students studied English only as they needed it to translate Latin. English-Latin grammars and English-Latin dictionaries appeared in the fifteenth century for the first time, so that as young people learned Latin, they invariably learned something about their mother tongue. It has been frequently noted that men like Thomas More who were among the first able to write a wide-ranging, flexible, and accurate English prose had all been schooled carefully in Latin.

—Richard Marius, *Thomas More* (1984), 15.

369. As there is now nothing new to be learned from the dead languages, all the useful books being already translated, the languages are becoming useless, and the time expended in teaching and learning them is wasted. So far as the study of languages may contribute to the progress of communication of knowledge, (for it has nothing to do with the creation of knowledge) it is only in the living languages that new knowledge is to be found; and certain it is that, in general, a youth will learn more of a living language in one year, than a dead language in seven, and it is but seldom that the teacher knows much of it himself.

—Thomas Paine, *The Age of Reason* (1794), I.48.

370. That vast advantages, then, may be derived from classical learning, there can be no doubt. . . .

[A] misfortune of classical learning, as taught in England, is, that scholars have come, in process of time, and from the effects of association, to love the instrument better than the end;—not the luxury which the difficulty incloses, but the difficulty;—not the filbert, but the shell;—not what may be read in Greek, but Greek itself. It is not so much the man who has mastered the wisdom of the ancients, that is valued, as he who displays his knowledge of the vehicle in which that wisdom is conveyed. The glory is to show I am a scholar. The good sense and ingenuity I may gain by my acquaintance with ancient authors is matter of opinion; but if I bestow an immensity of pains upon a point of accent or quantity, this is something positive; I establish my pretensions to the name of Scholar, and gain the credit of learning, while I sacrifice all its utility.

—Sydney Smith,
"Too Much Latin and Greek," 1809, in W.H. Auden,
ed., *Selected Writings of Sydney Smith* (1956), 263, 265.

371. The conflict between the so-called cultural and the scientific type of higher education cuts to the very core of human nature, because man belongs to two worlds—the world of things and the world of experience, the world of fact and the world of faith, the world of matter and the world of mind, the world of sense and the world of spirit. The primary business is the unification of the two worlds in each individual.

—John Duncan Spaeth, "Science and Humanism in University Education," commencement address at Washington University, St. Louis, June 10, 1930.

Ignorance

(*See also* Stupidity)

372. Ignoramus, *n.* A person unacquainted with certain kinds of knowledge familiar to yourself, and having certain other kinds that you know nothing about.

—Ambrose Bierce, *The Devil's Dictionary* (1911).

373. Mr. Kremlin was distinguished for ignorance; for he had only one idea, and that was wrong.

—Benjamin Disraeli, *Sybil* (1845), IV.v.

374. Ignorance, Madam, pure ignorance.

—Samuel Johnson, when asked why he defined "pastern" as the "knee" of a horse in his *Dictionary,* 1755, in James Boswell, *Life of Samuel Johnson* (1791), ix.

375. Even his ignorance is encyclopedic.

—Stanislaw J. Lec, *Unkempt Thoughts,* tr. Jacek Galazka (1962).

376. Ignorance must have a great fascination for you, since you fight so valiantly for it.

—Molière, *Les Femmes savantes* (1672), IV.iii.

377. Alike in ignorance, his reason such,
Whether he thinks too little or too much.

—Alexander Pope, *An Essay on Man* (1733), II.i.11.

378. From ignorance our comfort flows:
The only wretched are the wise.

—Matthew Prior, "To the Honorable Charles Montague, Esq." (1692), ln.35.

379. This ignorance is not confined to any one part of the Union; it is universal.... Why, a person who is reputed to know any thing of geography, of philosophy, or astronomy, is looked upon with as much abhorrence by the great masses of people, as if he were in league with the devil.... Why ... do they grovel in the dark? Why don't they seek to have their minds enlightened, which is their only security against the oppression and encroachments of the wealthy? In a country like this, where the freedom of elections bestows public honors and public offices on every man alike, how can he discharge the duties of his office with honor to himself, or benefit to his country, who is ignorant of the principles of the very foundation of his government? or how can he tell when the government is administered correctly by others, when he is destitute of the knowledge by which he is to ascertain the fact?... The great mass of people are just the same; not one step do they advance in knowledge. Is there not something wrong in our system of education? If there be, where does the defect lie?... Man is a reasonable being, reason is improved by observation and study, and, as we see, hear, and understand from the cradle to the grave, we are learning from the first dawn of understanding. Man's education, therefore, begins with his life, and ends at his death.... How necessary it is then to impress the young mind with justice and humanity.... But when parents are ignorant themselves, deplorable indeed must be the state of their offspring.... Here lies the misfortune, and here I fear it is long to rest: most parents not only being ignorant but highly prejudiced against learning.

—Anne Newport Royall, ostensibly written to "Matt," a young lawyer friend, Feb. 8, 1818, in Lucille Griffith, ed., *Letters From Alabama: 1817–1822* (1969), 177–178.

380. Ignorance is the curse of God,
Knowledge the wing wherewith we fly to heaven.

—William Shakespeare, *II Henry VI* (1590–91), IV.vii.78.

381. Blind and naked Ignorance
Delivers brawling judgments, unashamed,
On all things all day long.

—Alfred, Lord Tennyson, *Idylls of the King:* "Merlin and Vivien" (1859), ln.662.

Intellectual

(*See also* Educated Person; Scholar)

382. An intellectual is simply a man in whom is writ large what makes you and me specifically human—an interest in the rational mind and an ability to use it. As such he is nothing more or less than the most important kind of person the human race can produce. One early intellectual figured out the use of fire. A recent one figured out how the universe hangs together. Between Ugug and Einstein stretches a long line of intellectuals, great and small, able to supply nothing but ideas. These ideas, however, make everything else possible—including attacks on intellectuals—for these very attacks depend on a series of ideas dreamed up by such visionaries as the inventors of the alphabet or those nineteenth-century lunatics who worked out the equations that have made radio and television possible. In a way the rest of us, no matter how industrious or transiently useful, are parasites living on the work of a handful of superior minds....

An ideologue may be defined as a mad intellectual. He is not interested in ideas, but—almost the exact contrary—in one idea. When he erects this idea into a system and forces the system to give birth to a way of life, confusion often results, usually to his great surprise. Two examples are Robespierre and Lenin....

Like the low-brow, the high-brow is limited in his conversation. He will stick to Sartre or Stravinsky or Picasso because they are what his temperament permits him to enjoy. The low-brow will stick to Yogi Berra or Jackie Gleason for exactly the same reason. The high-brow may also be an intellectual; he is more often simply an appreciator. Asked what books he would take to a desert island George Bernard Shaw replied: "Some blank notebooks." There spoke the true intellectual. Equipped only with blank notebooks the high-brow would go crazy—though less rapidly than would the non-high-brow.

—Clifton Fadiman, *Any Number Can Play:* "Eggheads, Intellectuals, Ideologues, High-Brows" (1957), 81–83.

383. The intellectual is constantly betrayed by his own vanity. God-like, he blandly assumes that he can express everything in words; whereas the things one loves, lives, and dies for are not, in the last analysis, completely expressible in words.

—Anne Morrow Lindbergh, *The Wave of the Future* (1940), 6.

384. 'Intellectuals,' no doubt, are often tiresome enough, because they are often pseudo-intellectuals—ingenious fools, too clever to be wise, though brilliant at inventing the most ingenious reasons for their fatuous beliefs. But, tiresome as intellectuals can be, even they are probably less menacing and pernicious to the world than anti-intellectuals.

—F.L. Lucas, *The Search for Good Sense* (1958), 127.

385. Swollen in head, weak in legs, sharp in tongue but empty in belly.

—Mao Zedong, description of intellectuals,
The Wilting of the Hundred Flowers (1963).

Intelligence

(*See also* Genius; Ignorance; Intellectual; Stupidity; Wisdom; Wise Person)

386. The brain is wider than the sky,
For, put them side by side,
The one the other will include
With ease, and you beside.

—Emily Dickinson, *Complete Poems*,
no.632 (c. 1862), ed. Thomas H. Johnson (1960).

387. There are many whom nature itself has left so deficient in intelligence that they are scarcely able to grasp intellectually even those things which are easy, and of these, it seems, there are two sorts. For there are some who, although they are not ignorant of their dullness, nevertheless strive eagerly for knowledge, with all the effort of which they are capable. And they incessantly sweat in study, so that what they might have less as a result of labour, they seem to achieve by an act of will. But there are others who, since they feel themselves unable by any means to comprehend the most difficult things, neglect the least; and as if resting secure in their own torpor, the more they avoid learning those lesser things which they can understand, the more they lose sight of truth in the greatest things. As the psalmist says, "They do not wish to know so that they may do well." For not to know something is far different from not wanting to know something, since not to know is weakness, but to detest knowledge is a perversion of will.

—Hugh of St. Victor, *Didascalicon*
(12th cent.), ed. C.H. Buttimer, tr. M.M.M. (1939).

388. All manifestations of intelligence remained suspect, as if they were contraband for which a man could be arrested if they were found in his possession.

—Lewis H. Lapham, *Money and Class in America* (1988), 15.

389. There are three scales of intelligence, one which understands by itself, a second which understands what is shown to it by others, and a third which understands neither by itself nor on the showing of others, the first of which is most excellent, the second good, but the third worthless.

—Niccolo Machiavelli, *The Prince* (1532), xxii.

390. Sir, your wit ambles well; it goes easily.

—William Shakespeare,
Much Ado About Nothing (1598–99), V.i.162.

Knowledge

(*See also* Learning; Studies; Wisdom)

391. I have taken all knowledge to be my province.

—Francis Bacon (1561–1626), letter
to his uncle, Lord Burleigh, asking for an appointment, 1592.

392. Knowledge and Wisdom, far from being one,
Have oft-time no connexion. Knowledge dwells
In heads replete with thoughts of other men;
Wisdom in minds attentive to their own. . . .
Knowledge is proud that he has learn'd so much
Wisdom is humble that he knows no more.

—William Cowper, *The Task,* VI:
"The Winter Walk at Noon" (1785), *The Poetical Works of William Cowper,* ed. H.F. Cary (no date), II.151.88.

393. All concrete knowledge whatever is on a par with historical judgment, bound to life—that is, to action—of which it marks a pause or an anticipation having for its function to break down . . . any obstacles barring a clear view of the situation from which it must specifically and with determination emerge. Knowledge for the sake of knowledge, so far from having anything aristocratic or sublime about it (as some believe), would be an idiotic pastime for idiots, or for the idiotic moments which we all have in us; in reality there is no such thing, it is intrinsically impossible, and the stimulus ceases with the failure of the material itself and of the end of knowledge.

—Benedetto Croce, *History as the Story of Liberty* (1941), 32. *See* Lewis, **#401,** and Newman, **#404.**

394. He said that he should prefer not to know the sources of the Nile, and that there should be some unknown regions preserved as hunting-grounds for the poetic imagination.

—George Eliot, *Middlemarch* (1872), ix.

395. The Arabians say that Abul Khain, the mystic, and Abu Ali Seena, the philosopher, conferred together, and on parting, the philosopher said, "All that he sees I know"; and the mystic said, "All that he knows I see."

—Ralph Waldo Emerson, *Representative Men:* "Swedenborg" (1850).

396. If you did not learn your lesson to display it in action, what did you learn it for?

—Epictetus, *Discourses* (c. A.D. 100), I. xxix. *See Tibetan Doctrine,* **#410.**

397. Knowledge and understanding are life's faithful companions who will never prove untrue to you. For knowledge is your crown, and understanding your staff; and when they are with you, you possess no greater treasures.

—Kahlil Gibran, *The Voice of the Master:* "Wisdom," viii, in *The Treasured Writings of Kahlil Gibran* (1980), 488.

398. The tree of knowledge is your garden grows
Not single, but at every humble door;
Its branches lend you their immortal food,
That fills you with the sense of what ye are.

—Oliver Wendell Holmes, Sr., "Manhood," ln. 46, *Wind-Clouds and Star-Drifts* (1872).

399. If it rained knowledge, I'd hold out my hand; but I would not give myself the trouble to go in quest of it.

—Samuel Johnson, in James Boswell, *The Life of Samuel Johnson,* May 12, 1778 (1791), xliii.

400. Wonderful little, when all is said,
Wonderful little our fathers knew.
Half their remedies cured you dead—
Most of their teaching was untrue.

—Rudyard Kipling, (1865–1936), "Our Fathers of Old," st.iii, *Rudyard Kipling's Verse* (1950), 565.

401. Interest in truth for its own sake—the pure and undistracted purpose to know—is not the characteristic final purpose of knowing. Knowledge for its own sake, and the contemplative life, represent an esthetic or near-esthetic ideal rather than one normally attributable to cognition. It is merely a professional fallacy of the scholar to impute his own peculiar interest in finding out the truth to human cognizing in general, as if that were the aim which rules or should rule it. He who is disinterestedly interested in finding out and knowing; who subordinates the desires and interests of action to discovery of the truth, and to contemplation of it; likewise divests knowledge of its natural and pragmatic significance. By the same token, the ideal of the contemplative life is mildly abnormal, however valid and indubitable the values to which it is addressed. The Ivory tower is characteristically the refuge of the practically defeated and of those who become disillusioned of the utilities of action.

—Clarence Irving Lewis, *An Analysis of Knowledge and Valuation* (1945), 442. *See* Croce, **#393**, and Newman, **#404.**

402. We shall not have much reason to complain of the narrowness of our minds, if we will but employ them about what may be of use to us; for of that they are capable: And it will be an unpardonable, as well as childish peevishness, if we undervalue the advantages of our knowledge, and neglect to improve it to the ends for which it was given us, because there are some things that are set out of the reach of it.

—John Locke, *An Essay concerning Human Understanding* (1690), introduction, sec.5.

403. The hunger and thirst for knowledge, the keen delight in the chase, the good-natured willingness to admit that the scent was false, the eager desire to get on with the work, the cheerful resolution to go back and begin again, the broad good sense, the unaffected modesty, the imperturbable temper, the gratitude for any little help that was given—all these will remain in my memory, though I cannot paint them for others.

—F.W. Maitland, *The Collected Papers of Frederic William Maitland:* "Memoir on Mary Bateson" (1911), III.541.

404. Knowledge is capable of being its own end. Such is the constitution of the human mind, that any kind of knowledge, if it be really such, is its own reward. And if this is true of all knowledge, it is true also of that special Philosophy, which I have made to consist in a comprehensive view of truth in all its branches, of the relations of science to science, of their mutual bearings, and their respective values. What the worth of such an acquirement is, compared with other objects which we seek, —wealth or power or honour or the conveniences and comforts of life, I do not profess here to discuss; but I would maintain . . . that it is an object, in its own nature so really and undeniably good, as to be the compensation of a great deal of thought in the compassing, and a great deal of thought in the attaining.

—John Henry Newman, *The Idea of a University,*
Discourse V (1873). *See* Croce, **#393,** and Lewis, **#401.**

405. The truth is, the more the mind acquires, the more it is capable of acquiring. On the mole-hill, in the valley, the vision of man is limited; if led from this position to some eminence on the surrounding hills, no difficulty is felt; and if transported to the chief summit of the loftiest mountain on earth, no injurious consequences result; the eye is found to be equally well adapted to this large sphere of observation; and the depth of emotion felt, and the pleasurable sensations excited, are proportionate to this enlargement of view. So it is with the mind. A desire for knowledge is one of its original, innate elements.

—John D. Pierce, first annual report of the first Superintendent of Public Instruction of the State of Michigan, 1837.

406. The Dictates and Opinions of the ancient Champions of Learning are slighted and misconstrued by some modern Innovators; whereas we are but children in understanding, and ought to be directed by those Fathers of knowledge: We are but Dwarfs and Pigmies compared to those Giants of Wisdom, on whose shoulders we stand, yet we cannot see so far as they without them. I deny not but we may and ought to strive for further knowledge, which we shall hardly reach without their supportation. I disswade no man from inventing new; but I would not have him therefore to forget the old, nor lose the substance whilst he catches the shadow.

—Alexander Ross (1590–1654),
in Gale E. Christianson, *In the Presence of the Creator: Isaac Newton and His Times* (1984), 43.

407. Our happiness as thinking beings must depend on our being content to accept only partial knowledge, even in those matters which chiefly concern us. If we insist on perfect intelligibility and complete declaration in every moral subject, we shall instantly fall into misery of unbelief. Our whole happiness and power of energetic action depend on our being able to breathe and live in the cloud; content to see it opening here and closing there; rejoicing to catch, through the thinnest films of it, glimpses of stable and substantial things; but yet perceiving a nobleness even in the concealment, and rejoicing that the kindly veil is spread where the untempered light might have scorched us, or the infinite clearness wearied.

—John Ruskin, in *Precious Thoughts: Moral and Religious,* gathered by Mrs. L.C. Tuthill (1890), 29. *See* Kyokai, **#1079**, under "Truth."

408. There are many paths to knowledge already discovered; and no enlightened man doubts that there are many more waiting to be discovered. Indeed, all paths lead to knowledge; because even the vilest and stupidest action teaches us something about vileness and stupidity, and may accidentally teach us a great deal more.

—George Bernard Shaw, *The Doctor's Dilemma,* preface (1911).

409. The knowledge of an unlearned man is living and luxuriant like a forest, but covered with mosses and lichens and for the most part inaccessible and going to waste; the knowledge of the man of science is like timber collected in yards for public works, which still supports a green sprout here and there, but even this is liable to dry rot.

—Henry David Thoreau, *Journal,* Jan. 7, 1851.

410. He who knoweth the precepts by heart, but faileth to practise them,
Is like unto one who lighteth a lamp and then shutteth his eyes.

—*Tibetan Doctrine* (Buddhist): "'Elegant Sayings' of the Lamas" (c. 500 B.C.), in Robert O. Ballou, ed., *The Viking Portable Library World Bible* (1944), 159. *See* Epictetus, **#396.**

411. Prince, I know all things: fat and spare:
Ruddy and pale, to me are known:
And Death that endeth all our care:
I know all save myself alone.

—*The Testaments of François Villon* (1456, 1461), tr. John Heron Lepper (1924), 277.

412. It is scarcely possible to reduce an enlightened people to civil or ecclesiastical tyranny. Deprive them of knowledge, and they sink almost insensibly in vassalage. Ignorance cramps the powers of the mind at the same time that it blinds men to all their natural rights. Knowledge enlarges the understanding, and at the same time it gives a spring to all the intellectual faculties which direct the deliberations of the cabinet and the enterprises of the field. A general diffusion of science is our best guard against the approaches of corruption, the prevalence of religious error, the intrigues of ambition, and against the open assaults of external foes.

—Noah Webster, *Sketches of American Policy* (1785).

413. *The Attorney-General:* The labour of two days, then, is that for which you ask two hundred guineas!

Mr. Whistler: No—I ask it for the knowledge of a lifetime.

—James McNeil Whistler,
The Gentle Art of Making Enemies (1890), 5.
Cross-examination during his suit against John Ruskin
for slander, 1878, because of Ruskin's criticism of one
of his paintings. Whistler won and was awarded one farthing
in damages. He wore the coin thereafter as a watch charm.

Language

(*See also* Grammar; The Humanities; Meaning; Word)

414. "I zeenck you are expecting too much of your scheeldren," said my French houseguest, Michelle, as she helped me set the table for a luncheon I was giving in her honor.

"What do you mean?" I asked, and she replied:

"Zjust now, you told zem to go 'peeck up' zee living room. How can anyone 'peeck up' a room? And even eef zay could, why would you want zem to? And where would zay put eet? Why do you say zees 'peeck up'?"

I explained to her that 'picking up' a room meant 'to straighten' it.

"Straighten eet?" she asked. "Why? Eez it crooked?"

"Not crooked," I said. "Messy. I want them to pick up their books and record albums or whatever, and put them away."

"You have a funny way of zaying zat," she said. "Americans, I zeenck, have a funny way of saying many zeengs."

"Like what?" I asked her as we set a water goblet at each place.

"Like what we are doing now," said Michelle. "You say we are 'setteeng" zee table. But you see zee table eet ees already setting. We are zjust putteeng zings on eet."

—Teresa Bloomingdale, *Sense and Momsense:*
"Watch Your Language" (1986), 68.

415. I looked at her and asked, "Do you remember the day you and I were in the park? She answered, "What park?" I reminded her one day she and I went to a park near her home. While we were sitting on a bench, she asked me, "Bejee, how is the English language? How long was it before you spoke English to be understood?" I said, "Day after day I learn English and still can't speak very well. For example, today I learned one new word from you and you asked 'What was that?' I said 'daddy-longfeet,' and you laughed and said, 'Bejee! daddy long-legs. Not daddy-longfeet.' You see, when I learn, I might say it backward."

She said, "But you learned, didn't you? You will learn the same way."

—Bejee Designer,
Adventurous Girl from Iran (1976), 21.

416. The language of the street is always strong. What can describe the folly and emptiness of scolding like the word *jawing?* I feel too the force of the double negative, though clean contrary to our grammar rules. And I confess to some pleasure from the stinging rhetoric of a rattling oath in the mouths of truckmen and teamsters. How laconic and brisk is it by the side of a page of the *North American Review.* Cut these words and they would bleed; they are vascular and alive; they walk and run. Moreover they who speak them have this elegancy, that they do not trip in their speech. It is a shower of bullets, whilst Cambridge men and Yale men correct themselves and begin again at every half sentence.

—Ralph Waldo Emerson, *Journals,* June 24, 1840.

417. What a pity that we cannot curse and swear in good society. . . . My page about "Consistency" would be better written thus; Damn Consistency.

—Ralph Waldo Emerson, *Journals,* Oct. 25, 1840.
Reference is to: "A foolish consistency is the hobgoblin of little minds, adored by little statesmen and philosophers and divines. With consistency a great soul has simply nothing to do."—Emerson, *Essays, First Series:* "Self-Reliance" (1841).

418. His slang . . . was always a little out of date, as though he had studied in a dictionary of popular usage, but not in the latest edition.

—Graham Greene, *The Comedians,* (1965), I.i.1.

419. The devil take what nowadays passes for language! This language in drama is the counterpart of "How beautifully put!" in conversation. Chintz, chintz, and more chintz! It may glitter but it gives no heat.

—Christian Friedrich Hebbel, *Journals,* 1836,
in Toby Cole, *Playwrights on Playwriting* (1961), 285.

420. I have seldom found much good result from hyper-critical severity, in examining the distinct force of words. Language is essentially defective in precision; more so, than those are aware of, who are not in the habit of subjecting it to philological analysis.

—William Johnson, Associate Justice
of U.S. Supreme Court, *Martin v Hunter,* 1816.

421. *Afternoon tea*—Detention after three o'clock....
Ancient mariner—A rowing Don....
Biddy—A bath in college (from French *bidet*)....
Bum curtain—A short, scant academic gown....
Bunny grub—Green vegetables....
Cathedral—A silk hat....
Clean straw—Clean sheets. Worth recording because the shift to proper bedding was put into effect by someone named Dean Fleshmonger....
Dolphin—A leading swimmer and diver....
Gold hatband—A nobleman undergraduate....
Mud student—A student at an agricultural college....
Vaseline—Butter.

—Louis Kronenberger,
Animal, Vegetable, Mineral: "English Public School Lingo (Early Twentieth Century)" (1972), 65. *See* Mencken, **#422.**

422. If an English boy goes to a *public school,* it is not a sign that he is getting his education free, but that his father is paying a good round sum for it and is accepted as a gentleman. A *public school* over there corresponds to the more swagger sort of American *prep school;* it is a place maintained chiefly by endowments, wherein boys of the upper classes are prepared for the universities. What we know as a *public school* is called a *council-school* in England, because it is in the hands of the education committee of the County Council.... The boys in a *public* (i.e., private) *school* are divided not into *classes,* or *grades,* but into *forms,* which are numbered, the highest usually being the *sixth*.... A *grammar-school,* in England, always means a place for the sons of the relatively rich. *Grade-schools* are unknown. The principal of an English *public* (i.e., private) *school* or *elementary-school* is a *head-master* or *head-mistress,* but in a secondary school he or she may be a *principal*.... The lower pedagogues used to be *ushers,* but are now *masters* or *assistant masters* (or *mistresses*). The titular head of a university is a *chancellor;* he is commonly a bigwig elected by the resident graduates for ornamental purposes only, and the *vice-chancellor* does the work.... Most English universities have *deans* of faculties much like our own.... They have minor dignitaries of kinds unknown in the United States, e.g.,

proctors, orators, and *high stewards.* In Scotland the universities have *rectors,* who are chosen by election, and like the chancellors are mainly only ornaments. The head of a mere college may be a *president, principal, master, warden, rector, dean,* or *provost*. . . . The students are not divided into *freshmen, sophomores, juniors,* and *seniors,* as with us, but simply *first-year men, second-year men,* and so on, though a *first-year man* is sometimes a *freshman* or *fresher*. . . . The American hierarchy of *assistant instructors, instructors, assistant professors, associate professors, adjunct professors* and *full professors* is unknown in the English universities; they have only *readers* or *lecturers* and *professors*. . . . [These] do not constitute a *faculty,* but a *staff,* and they are called, collectively, its *dons,* though all teachers are not, necessarily *dons* (i.e., fellows). An English university student does not *study;* he *reads*—whether for a *pass-degree* . . . or for *honours*. . . . He knows nothing of *frats, class-days, rushes, credits, points, majors, semesters, senior-proms* and other such things; save at Cambridge and Dublin he does not even speak of *commencement;* elsewhere he calls it *degree-day* or *speech-day.* On the other hand, his speech is full of terms unintelligible to an American student, e.g., *wrangler, tripos, head, greats,* and *mods.* If he is expelled he is said to be *sent down.* There are no college boys in England, but only *university men.* Alumni are *graduates,* and the graduates of what we would call a prep-school are *old-boys.*

—H.L. Mencken, *The American Language,*
4th ed. (1936), 240. *See* Kronenberger, **#421.**

423. If thought corrupts language, language can also corrupt thought. A bad usage can spread by tradition and initiation, even among people who should and do know better. . . . Phrases like *a not unjustifiable assumption, leaves much to be desired, would serve no good purpose, a consideration which we should do well to bear in mind,* are a continuous temptation, a packet of aspirins always at one's elbow.

—George Orwell, *Shooting an Elephant:*
"Politics and the English Language" (1950), 155.

424. The English language is not the King's English, or the grammarian's English, but the English-speaking world's English—to be fought for and fought over by all who find joy in the world of words.

—William Safire, "Word Watchers at Work,"
The New York Times Book Review, May 10, 1981.

425. You taught me language and my profit on't
Is, I know how to curse! The red plague rid you
For learning me your language!

—William Shakespeare, *The Tempest* (1611), I.ii.364.

426. The English have no respect for their language, and will not teach their children to speak it. They spell it so abominably that no man can teach himself what it sounds like. It is impossible for an Englishman to open his mouth without making some other Englishman hate or despise him. German and Spanish are accessible to foreigners: English is not accessible even to Englishmen. The reformer England needs to-day is an energetic phonetic enthusiast: that is why I have made such a one the hero of a popular play.

—George Bernard Shaw, preface to *Pygmalion* (1913).

427. As for your use of language: Remember that two great masters of our language, William Shakespeare and James Joyce, wrote sentences which were almost childlike when their subjects were most profound. "To be or not to be?" asks Shakespeare's Hamlet. The longest word is three letters long. Joyce, when he was frisky, could put together a sentence as intricate and glittering as a necklace for Cleopatra, but my favorite sentence in his short story "Eveline" is this one: "She was tired." At that point in the story, no other words could break the heart of the reader as those words do.

Simplicity of language is not only reputable, but perhaps even sacred. The Bible opens with a sentence well within the writing skills of a lively fourteen-year-old: "In the beginning God created the heavens and the earth."

—Kurt Vonnegut, *Palm Sunday* (1981), 78.

428. Language, be it remember'd, is not an abstrct construction of the learn'd, or of dictionary-makers, but is something arising out of the work, needs, ties, joys, affections, tastes, of long generations of humanity, and has its bases broad and low, close to the ground. Its final decisions are made by the masses, people nearest the concrete, having most to do with actual land and sea. It impermeates all, the Past as well as the Present, and is the grandest triumph of the human intellect.

—Walt Whitman, *November Boughs:* "Slang in America" (1888).

Learning

(*See also* Knowledge; Teaching; Teaching Method)

429. I'd like to learn a lot of things;
With curiosity I'm cursed.
But teacher tells me that I must
Complete my education first.

—Anonymous.

430. "Learn while you're young," he often said,
"There is much to enjoy down here below;
Life for the living, and rest for the dead!"
Said the jolly old pedagogue, long ago.

—George Arnold, "The Jolly Old Pedagogue" (1867), ii.

431. Am glad to learn my cousins Ralph Wormeley and John Wormeley thrive so fast in their learning [in England]; no doubt the continuance of careful education will render them accomplished men qualified to preserve the character of their father, and fit for the service of their country, which, to my sorrow I will complain to you, having drawn your first breath here, does at this time labor under a very thick cloud of ignorance. Pray God that in the next generation it may flourish under a set of better polished patriots.

—Robert Carter of Corotoman, letter to Francis Lee,
a Virginia merchant in London, 1702, in Louis B. Wright,
The First Gentlemen of Virginia (1940), 285.

432. Learning itself, received into the mind
By nature weak, or viciously inclined,
Serves but to lead philosophers astray,
Where children would with ease discern the way.

—William Cowper (1731–1800),
"The Progress of Error," *The Poetical Works
of William Cowper* ed. H.F. Cary (no date), I.57.

433. Books are good only as far as a boy is ready for them. He sometimes gets ready very slowly. You send your child to the schoolmaster, but 't is the schoolboys who educate him. You send him to the Latin class, but much of his tuition comes, on his way to school, from the shop-windows. You like the strict rules and the long terms; and he finds his best learning in a by-way of his own, and refuses any companions but by his own choosing. He hates grammar and Gradus, and loves guns, fishing-rods, horses, and boats. Well, the boy is right.

—Ralph Waldo Emerson, *The Conduct of Life:*
"Culture" (1860). [Gradus=*a dictionary of prosody,
intended to aid students in the writing of Latin and Greek verse*].

434. The parents of a child are but his enemies when they fail to educate him properly in his boyhood. An illiterate boy, like a heron amid swans, cannot shine in the assembly of the learned. Learning imparts a heightened charm to a homely face. Knowledge is the best treasure that a man can secretly hoard up in life. Learning is the revered of the revered. Knowledge makes a man honest, virtuous and endearing to the society. It is learning alone that enables a man to better the conditions of his friends and relations. Knowledge is the holiest of holies, the god of the gods, and commands the respect of crowned heads; shorn of it a man is an animal. The fixtures and furniture of one's house may be stolen by thieves; but knowledge, the highest treasure, is above all stealing.

—*Garuda Purana* (Hindu Scriptures)
(c. A.D. 300–750), in Robert O. Ballou, ed.,
The Viking Portable Library World Bible (1944), 72.

435. "But we don't want to teach 'em," replied the Badger. "We want to learn 'em."

—Kenneth Grahame, *The Wind in the Willows* (1908), xi.
See Nock, **#441;** and Levenson, **#1022,** under "Teaching Method."

436. There is no lack of opportunity for learning among us. What is lacking is a respect for it . . . an honest respect such as we now have for technical competence or business success. . . . We reward it with lengthy obituaries and a wretched living wage. Rather than submit it to ourselves, we hire substitutes; rather than cultivate our own brains, we pick theirs. We spend as much time and energy on short-cuts to learning and imitations of learning as we do on learning itself.

—A. Whitney Griswold, address to American and National
Institute of Arts and Letters, *New York Times,* May 22, 1958.

437. Classwork should be passionately interesting. Of course for this we should have to have passionately interested teachers, people convinced of the beauty of their mission—and not poor crocks whose chief characteristics are their mediocrity and commonplaceness. What is more, classes should not be held in cold unfriendly rooms. What is wanted is an immense library—and the right to roam among the shelves at will should be the highest prize awarded to a pupil. I dream of the time when a master will be able to say to a pupil, "You behaved badly, and I shall punish you. You will not be allowed to attend class."

—Sacha Guitry, *If Memory Serves* (1936), 64.

438. There are some things which cannot be learned quickly and time, which is all we have, must be paid heavily for their acquiring. They are the very simplest things and because it takes a man's life to know them the little new that each man gets from life is very costly and the only heritage he has to leave.

—Ernest Hemingway, *Death in the Afternoon* (1932), 192.

439. The pleasures of learning are indeed pleasures. But in fact the word should be changed. The true name is happiness. There are three other types of happiness, superior to that of learning: the happiness of love fulfilled; the happiness of serving mankind; and the happiness of creation. Though it is beneath these, learning is still a great happiness, and can be a help toward the attainment of those others; and it is an essential part of a complete life. No learner has ever found that he ran short of subjects to explore. But many people who avoided learning, or abandoned it, find that life is drained dry. They spend thirty years in a club chair looking glumly out at the sand and ocean; in a hotel lounge gossiping about the other inmates; in a porch swing awaiting for somebody to drive down the road. But that is not how to live. The chief aim of education is to show you, *after* you make a livelihood, how to enjoy living; and you can live longest and best and most rewardingly by attaining and preserving the happiness of learning.

—Gilbert Highet, *The Immortal Profession:* "The Pleasures of Learning," (1976), 19.

440. The most beautiful thing in the world is, precisely, the conjunction of learning and inspiration. Oh, the passion for research and the joy of discovery!

—Wanda Landowska, letter to a former music student, in Denise Resout, ed., *Landowska on Music* (1964)

441. My able and distinguished friend Mr. Charles A. Beard long ago remarked to me how sorry he was that the word *l'arn,* so well and truly seasoned by hard service in New England, should have gone completely out of currency as a transitive verb. "You can't *teach* a person anything," he said, "and certainly you can't *learn* him anything, but maybe you can *l'arn* him something." There is a nice distinction here, and one so highly valuable as to seem especially well worth preserving for the sake of those whose concern with pedagogy is professional; and yet I suppose it is a dynasty of doctrinaire schoolmarms of both sexes which has done most to wipe it out.

—Albert Jay Nock, *The Memoirs of a Superfluous Man* (1943), 49. *See* Grahame, **#435;** and Levenson, **#1022,** under "Teaching Method."

442. You will find the greater number of men both ready in conceiving and quick in learning; since such quickness is natural to man; and as birds are born to fly, horses to run, and wild beasts to show fierceness, so to us peculiarly belong activity and sagacity of understanding. . . . Dull and unteachable persons are no more produced in the course of nature than are persons marked by monstrosity and deformities; such are certainly but few. It will be a proof of this assertion, that, among boys, good promise is shown in the far greater number; and if it passes off in the progress of time, it is manifest that it was not natural ability, but care, that was wanting.

—Quintilian, *Institutio Oratoria* (A.D. 95 or 96), I.

443. No child . . . fails to learn from school. Those who never get in, learn that the good things of life are not for them. Those who drop out early, learn that they do not deserve the good things of life. The later dropouts learn that the system can be beat, but not by them. All of them learn that school is the path to secular salvation, and resolve that their children shall climb higher on the ladder than they did.

—Everett Reimer, *School Is Dead: Alternatives in Education* (1971), 21.

444. Learn young, learn fair;
Learn auld, learn mair.

—Scottish rhyme. Contrast *Talmud,* **#447.**

445. It is generally stated that general education is good in proportion as it serves to broaden or deepen a student's understanding of life as a whole. Our experience has taught us that this criterion is misleading. It is not that the concepts are wrong but that they are wrong in tense. After all, even in college, students are young and have a long life ahead of them. In this changing, perplexing, and indoctrination-ridden world, they must learn much more after graduation than they can possibly learn in school or college and for the most part they must be their own teachers. What is important in any program of general education, therefore, is less what the students learn at the time than how well their education fits them to go on learning in the future.

—Elliott Dunlap Smith, "General Education in Practice," *Journal of Higher Education,* October 1951.

446. He not only overflowed with learning, but stood in the slop.

—Sydney Smith (1771–1845), describing Thomas Babington Macaulay. Quoted by Peter Quennell in *New Statesman,* Aug. 25, 1934.

447. He who learns when a child, unto what is he to be compared?—Unto ink written upon a new writing sheet; and he who learns when an old man, unto what is he like?—Unto ink written on a rubbed writing sheet.

—*Talmud: Aboth,* 4.20
(before A.D. 500). *Constrast* Scottish rhyme, **#444.**

448. Learning stamps you with its moments. Childhood's learning is made up of moments. It isn't steady. It's a pulse.

—Eudora Welty, *One Writer's Beginnings* (1984), 9.

Lecture

(*See also* Teaching)

449. Could discourses teach the world, The Sermon on the Mount would have been realized long ago.

—Georges Clemenceau, debate with
Jean Jaurès, Chamber of Deputies, June 1906.

450. A sitting body will protest
When lectures are obscure,
And the weary mind can just digest
What the tired bottom can endure.

—Abbot Copeland,
in a letter to *Sarasota Herald-Tribune,* Nov. 24, 1985.

451. My Continental Fiction course included the great Russian novels of Turgenev, Tolstoy, and Doestoevsky. In preparing the students for their reading of these writers, I worked up a lecture on the characteristics of the Russian people, and hoped to explain why they were like what they were and why they wrote such long-winded novels. I had some ten characteristics, all neatly numbered.

As I delivered the lecture the students took notes solemnly and religiously. But one student in the back row laughed at everything I said, and didn't write a word. When the session was over, I signaled for her to speak to me after class.

"What's so funny about this lecture I've just been giving on the Russians?" I asked belligerently.

She smiled sweetly and replied, "I'm Russian!"

—Carl Glick, *I'm a Busybody* (1949), 158.

452. I'm not going back [to Trinity College] next term. If I have to look at those decrepit old men in their dirty gowns droning on about Shakespeare once more, I'll go potty. Drone, drone. We just sit there, hundreds of us writing down their boring words or sleeping, and they drone on, like bees in the distance. They don't care whether we're interested or not. Oh God.

—Jennifer Johnston, *The Christmas Tree* (1982), 31.

453. In the colleges of Canada and the United States the lectures are supposed to be a really necessary and useful part of the student's training. Again and again I have heard the graduates of my own college assert that they got as much, or nearly as much, out of the lectures at college as out of athletics or the Greek letter society or the Banjo and Mandolin Club. In short, with us the lectures form a real part of the college life. At Oxford it is not so. The lectures, I understand, are given and may even be taken. . . .

If the lectures are called for they give them; if not, the professor's feelings are not hurt. He merely waits and rests his brain until in some later year the students call for his lectures. There are men at Oxford who have rested their brains this way for over thirty years; the accumulated brain power thus dammed up is said to be colossal.

—Stephen Leacock, *The Leacock Roundabout:* "Oxford As I See It" (1946), 304.

Library

(*See also* Book)

454. In that great maze of books I sighed and said,—
It is a grave-yard, and each tome a tombe;
Shrouded in hempen rags, behold the dead,
Coffined and ranged in crypts of dismal gloom,
Food for the worm and redolent of mold,
Traced with brief epitaph in tarnished gold—
Ah, golden lettered hope!—ah, dolorous doom!
Yet 'mid common death, where all is cold,
And mildewed pride in desolation dwells,
A few great immortalities of old
Stand brightly forth—not tombes but living shrines,
Where from high sainte or martyr virtue wells,

Which on the living yet work miracles,
Spreading a relic wealth richer than golden mines.

—Anonymous "J.M.",
"In the Librarie at Cambridge," from *A Collection of Recente and Witty Pieces by Several Eminente Hands* (1628), in James O'Donnell Bennett, *Much Loved Books* (1927), frontispiece.

455. In Newton's day [c. 1661] the [Trinity] College library was not open for extended periods on a regular basis. Fellows had their own keys and could come and go as they pleased, a privilege denied their students. Nor could students use the collection without being accompanied by a Fellow.

—Gale E. Christianson, *In the Presence of the Creator: Isaac Newton and His Times* (1984), 57.

456. Libries niver encouraged lithrachoor anny more thin tombstones encourage livin'. No wan iver wrote annythin' because he was tol' that a hundherd years fr'm now his books might be taken down fr'm the shelf in a granite sepulcher an' some wan wud write "Good" or "This man is crazy" in th' margin. What lithrachoor needs is fillin' food.

—Finley Peter Dunne, *Dissertations by Mr. Dooley:* "The Carnegie Libraries" (1906).

457. Consider what you have in the smallest chosen library. A company of the wisest and wittiest men that could be picked out of all civil countries in a thousand years have set in best order the results of their learning and wisdom. The men themselves were hid and inaccessible, solitary, impatient of interruption, fenced by etiquette; but the thought which they did not uncover to their bosom friend is here written out in transparent words to us, the strangers of another age.

—Ralph Waldo Emerson, *Society and Solitude:* "Books" (1870).

458. Libraries and library facilities were pitiful. [In 1736,] After Harvard had been in existence one hundred years the first catalogue of the library showed that it contained 3500 volumes, two-thirds of which were theological, and though Dryden, Johnson, Pope and Swift had done their work, their names were conspicuously absent. In the ten years from 1743 to 1753, the total accessions to Yale Library numbered thirty-one volumes, "mostly sermons." At Hampden-Sidney, in the South—founded 1776—by 1821 the library consisted of only 500 volumes. It was estimated in 1782 that at Rhode Island College, later Brown University, the number of books was between two and three hundred, mostly theological and not well chosen, as the president wistfully adds, "being such as our friends could best spare." Because of this inadequacy of library facilities, college students there had to be denied access to English classics like Chaucer, Shakespeare, Pope and Dryden. There was no library building, and for lack of attendants it was possible to keep the room open only one day a week, from one to three o'clock in the afternoon.

—Christian Gauss, "The Good Old Times,"
in A.C. Spectorsky, ed., *The College Years* (1958), 85.

459. Two institutions turned millions of immigrants into Americans within a single generation—the greatest miracle of human relations in the past century. These two institutions were the free public school and the free public library. It's hard to communicate to a present-day audience what the public library meant to immigrants. The librarian was a sexless saint. I remember in the ghetto branch of the New York Public Library there was a washstand in a booth off the main entrance. You washed your hands before you went to the shelves. This was no insult. Indeed it was a compliment, a tribute to the men and women who came out of their sweatshops to stop at the library on the way home, a tribute to boys and girls who sold newspapers or played in the street and who went to the library to spend an hour before supper. If you were under fifteen years of age, the librarian would actually ask you to show your hands and you turned them over and she either said, "Go ahead," or "Go wash them." Immigrant mothers like my mother, who couldn't speak a word of English, went into that library, held up their fingers to indicate the number of children at home. The librarian issued cards, and the mother handed them out to her children. She said, "Go, learn, study, read." This was part of the process of becoming an American. If we draw up a balance sheet of America's fixed assets, we would say that the public library is one of our most precious possessions.

—Harry Golden, *So Long as
You're Healthy:* "The library" (1962), 184.

460. Whenever the shelves in the Library of Heaven were entirely full, and a new, worthy book appeared, all the books in the celestial collection pressed themselves closer together, and made room.

—Hebrew legend, in Leo Rosten, *Infinite Riches* (1979).

461. Were I not king, I would be a university man; and, if it were so that I must be made a prisoner, I could have no other prison than this library, and be chained together with all these goodly authors.

—James I of Great Britain and VI of Scotland, on visiting
the Bodlein Library at Oxford University in 1604.

462. You know my collection, its condition and extent. I have been fifty years in making it, and have spared no pains, opportunity or expense, to make it what it is. While residing in Paris, I devoted every afternoon I was disengaged, for a summer or two, in examining all the principal bookstores, turning over every book with my own hand, and putting by everything which related to America, and indeed whatever was rare and valuable in every science. Besides this, I had standing orders during the whole time I was in Europe, on its principal book-marts, particularly Amsterdam, Frankfort, Madrid and London, for such works relating to America as could not be found in Paris. So that in that department particularly, such a collection was made as probably can never again be effected, because it is hardly probable that the same opportunities, the same time, industry, perseverance and expense, with some knowledge of the bibliography of the subject, would again happen to be in concurrence. During the same period, and after my return to America, I was led to procure, also, whatever related to the duties of those in the high concerns of the nation. So that the collection, which I suppose is of between nine and ten thousand volumes, while it includes what is chiefly valuable in science and literature generally, extends more particularly to whatever belongs to the American statesman. In the diplomatic and parliamentary branches, it is particularly full. It is long since I have been sensible it ought not to continue private property, and had provided that at my death, Congress should have the refusal of it at their own price.

—Thomas Jefferson, letter to Samuel Harrison Smith, a newspaper publisher, September 21, 1814, in Saul K. Padover, *A Jefferson Profile as Revealed in His Letters* (1956), 244. Congress accepted Jefferson's offer and paid him $25,000 for his book collection, which became the nucleus of the Library of Congress.

463. If a man can keep ten thousand volumes of rare books, have them bound in precious brocade, and perfumed with rare incense, while he himself lives in a mud house with a screen of reed, paper windows and mud walls, and lives all of his life in simple cotton dress, that one might be called an extraordinary person on this earth.

—Lin Yutang, ed., *The Wisdom of China and India:* "One Hundred Proverbs" (1942), 1098.

464. This must be taken into consideration by all who earnestly desire to see such schools established and the languages preserved in the German States; that no cost nor pains should be spared to procure good libraries in suitable buildings, especially in the large cities that are able to afford it.

For if a knowledge of the Gospel and of every kind of learning is to be preserved, it must be embodied in books, as the prophets and apostles did. . . . This should be done, not only that our spiritual and civil leaders may have something to read and study, but also that good books may not be lost, and that the arts and languages may be preserved, with which God has graciously favored us.

—Martin Luther, *Letter to the Mayors and Aldermen* (1524), tr. F.V. Painter (1928).

465. If these writings of the Greeks agree with the book of God [The Koran], they are useless and need not be preserved; if they disagree, they are pernicious, and ought to be destroyed.

—Attributed to Omar I ('Umar ibn-al-Khattab), ordering the destruction of the Alexandrian Library, the largest in the ancient world, after the Arabs captured Alexandria in A.D. 640. This quotation is based on the authority of the Syrian churchman, Bar-Hebraeus (Abulfaraj) (1226–86), and is generally agreed to be a fabrication.

Literature

(*See also* Book; The Humanities; Library)

466. Milton seems to the colleges profound because he wrote of hell, a great place, and is dead.

—Stephen Leacock, *Charles Dickens* (1933). *See* Lewis, **#467.**

467. Our American professors like their literature clear and cold and pure and very dead.

—Sinclair Lewis, "The American Fear of Literature," address on accepting the Nobel Prize for Literature, Dec. 12, 1930. *See* Leacock, **#466.**

468. At least for the purposes of this collection, *essay* will mean a short piece of writing, from one to twenty or thirty pages, dealing with almost any subject, but in a personal, informal and unpretentious way. It will be reflective but not solemn. It will be on the edge of philosophy but not at all systematic. It will have a kind of loose unity but will often be delightfully digressive. It may lure us into agreement but it will not push us into concessions. Whatever else an essayist may be, he is our friend and an artist in words.

—Houston Peterson, introduction to *Great Essays* (1954).

469. A classic, according to the usual definition, is an old author canonized by admiration, and an authority in his particular style. The word *classic* was first used in this sense by the Romans. With them not all citizens of the different classes were properly called *classici*, but only those of the chief class, those who possessed an income of a certain fixed sum. Those who possessed a smaller income were described by the term *infra classem*, below the pre-eminent class. The word *classicus* was used in a figurative sense by Aulus Gellius, and applied to writers: a writer of worth and distinction, *classicus assiduusque scriptor*, a writer who is of account, has real property, and is not lost in the proletarian crowd. Such an expression implies an age sufficiently advanced to have already made some sort of valuation and classification of literature.

—Charles Augustin Sainte-Beuve, "What Is a Classic?," in Houston Peterson, ed., *Great Essays* (1954), 228.

470. A novel is a large diffused picture, comprehending the characters of life, disposed in different groups and exhibited in various attitudes, for the purpose of a uniform plan. This plan cannot be executed with propriety, probability, or success, without a principal personage to attract the attention, unite the incidents, unwind the clue of the labyrinth, and at last close the scene, by virtue of his own importance.

—Tobias Smollett, *The Adventures of Ferdinand Count Fathom* (1753), dedication.

Manners

471. Even though you be a Socrates, if you have rude manners, you are a ditch-digger.... Light-minded talk is unseemly at table; so is presumption and constant contention. It is rude to be ungrateful or cruel towards the poor. It is reprehensible to be haughty towards your dear friends; if you reject good advice, you are a fool; and lack the light of reason if you fly in the face of God....

You will be courteous if you perform the following works of mercy: if at night you give beds to the poor, if you heal the sick, if you clothe the freezing, give food to the beggar, console the afflicted, and offer drink to the thirsty....

Be not a fornicator, O student, a robber, a murderer, a deceitful merchant, a champion at dice. In the choirstalls a cleric should chant without noise and commotion.... Do not constantly urge your horse on with the spur, which should be used only on rare occasions.... Select beautiful equestrian trappings suitable to your clerical station. Ride erect unless you are bent with age. If you are of the elect you should have a rich saddle cloth.... Avoid drunkards, those who indulge in secret sin, those who like to beat and strike, those who love lewdness, evil games, and quarrels. Passing a cemetery, if you are well-bred, and if you hope for salvation, you pause to pray that the dead may rest in peace. Have nothing to do with the prostitute, but love your wife; all wives should be honoured but especially those who are distinguished by virtue. A person who is well should not recline at table in the fashion of the ancients. When you walk after dinner keep on frequented streets. Avoid insincere speeches. Unless you wish to be considered a fool learn to keep your mouth shut in season. Stand and sit upright, do not scratch yourself....

Do not be noisy, rash in your actions, odious because of your insulting words, wrathful about little annoyances.... Be a good debtor and hasten to pay your debts lest you be condemned by your burden of sin and the peasant bewailing his losses....

Learn how to entertain at table, to provide food and the sauces that go with various dishes, and to serve seasonable wine in modest quantity.... According to good custom you should place the sauce on the right, the service plate on the left.... Take hold of the base of the goblet so that unsightly finger marks may not show on the side. Polite diners pause over their wine, but gluttons, who live like mules and weevils, empty it with one draught. Pour wine properly with both hands so as not spill any.... If you wish to regain your strength as a convalescent, and keep your health when you are well, drink moderately. All Epicureans live unpure lives; they lose their eyesight, they are rude, unclean, and are doomed to die a sudden death.

—John of Garland (c. 1195–c. 1272, a professor at the University of Paris, *Morale Scolarium*, tr. L.J. Paetow (1927).

Mathematics

472. The arithmetic of 1900 differed materially from the arithmetic we now include in the elementary curriculum.... Two of its characteristics stand out prominently: (a) it was hard, and (b) it was little related to practical living.... Teachers, relying pretty much upon what was in the textbook, showed pupils what to do and then relied upon abundant practice to produce mastery. Homework assignments were heavy, and many parents were called upon to revive, temporarily at least, skills that they had forgotten. The children who survived this demanding regimen, aided often by two one-hour periods in arithmetic a day, were capable of arithmetical feats far beyond the capabilities of eighth-graders today, whether or not they ever put them to effective use.

—William A. Brownell, "The Revolution in Arithmetic," *The Arithmetic Teacher,* February 1954.

473. "My daughter," and his voice was stern,
"You must set this matter right;
What time did the Sophomore leave,
Who sent in his card last night?"

"His work was pressing, father dear,
And his love for it was great;
He took his leave and went away
Before a quarter of eight."

Then a twinkle came to her bright blue eye,
And her dimple deeper grew.
"'Tis surely no sin to tell him that,
For a quarter of eight is two."

—Lehigh Burr, "Applied Mathematics," in Frederic Lawrence Knowles, ed., *Poetry of American Wit and Humor* (1899), 302.

474. Mathematics contains much that will neither hurt one if one does not know it nor help one if one does know it.

—Johann Burkhard Mencke, *De Charlataneria Eruditorum* (1715).

475. I have hardly ever known a mathematician who was capable of reasoning.

—Plato, *Republic,* VII (c. 375 B.C.).

476. If you ask your mother for one fried egg for breakfast and she gives you two fried eggs and you eat both of them, who is better in arithmetic, you or your mother?

—Carl Sandburg, *Complete Poems:* "Arithmetic" (1950).

477. What would life be without arithmetic, but a scene of horrors?

—Sydney Smith, letter to Miss ________, July 22, 1835, *Letters.*

Meaning

(*See also* Orthography)

478. [Multiple meanings for the simple little word *bay:*] The portly gentleman with a slight *bay* window of his own stood in the *bay* window watching a ship beating up the *bay*. His thoughts turned back to his suffering in the sick *bay* of a cruiser after the accident in the bomb *bay* of the airplane. He knew that to yearn for a return to active duty at his age was idly to *bay* the moon. He could ride his new *bay* hunter, however, and listen again to the *bay* of the hounds as they brought a fox to *bay*. Putting a drop of *bay* rum on his thinning hair, he set forth.

—Anonymous, in William H. Burton, *Readings in Child Development* (1956), 295. *See* Haney, **#486,** and Horn, **#487.**

479. *I hit him in the eye yesterday.*

When the word *only* is added in any of the eight possible positions, the sentence takes on eight entirely different meanings:

Only I hit him in the eye yesterday.
I only hit him in the eye yesterday.
I hit only him in the eye yesterday.
I hit him only in the eye yesterday.
I hit him in the only eye yesterday.
I hit him in the eye only yesterday.
I hit him in the eye yesterday only.

—Sentence originated by Dr. Ernst Brennecke of Columbia University, in *U&lc.*, March 1981, published by International Typeface Corporation.

480. "When *I* use a word," Humpty Dumpty said, in rather a scornful tone, "it means just what I choose it to mean—neither more nor less."

"The question is," said Alice, "whether you *can* make words mean so many different things."

"The question is," said Humpty Dumpty, "which is to be master—that's all."

—Lewis Carroll, *Through the Looking Glass* (1872), vi.

481. "Then you should say what you mean," the March Hare went on.

"I do," Alice hastily replied; "at least—at least I mean what I say—that's the same thing, you know."

"Not the same thing a bit!" said the Hatter. "Why, you might just as well say 'I see what I eat' is the same thing as 'I eat what I see'!"

—Lewis Carroll, *Alice's Adventures in Wonderland* (1865), vii.

482. In due course the Master returned.

'Have you learnt it?' he asked.

'I think I can say it, sir,' I replied; and I gabbled it off.

He seemed so satisfied with this that I was emboldened to ask a question.

'What does it mean, sir?' 'It means what it says. Mensa, a table. Mensa is a noun of the First Declension. There are five declensions. You have learnt the singular of the first Declension.'

'But,' I repeated, 'what does it mean?'

'Mensa means table,' he answered.

'Then why does mensa also mean O table,' I enquired, 'and what does O table mean?'

'Mensa, O table is the vocative case,' he replied.

'But why O table?' I persisted in genuine curiosity.

'O table,—you would use that in addressing a table, in invoking a table.' And then seeing he was not carrying me with him, 'You would use it in speaking to a table.'

'But I never do,' I blurted out in honest amazement.

'If you are impertinent, you will be punished, and punished, let me tell you, very severely,' was his conclusive rejoinder.

Such was my first introduction to the classics from which, I have been told, many of our cleverest men have derived so much solace and profit.

—Winston Churchill,
My Early Life: A Roving Commission (1930), 11.

483. If crockery is a collection of crocks, then flattery is a collection of flats, scullery is a collection of skulls, sorcery a collection of sources, and monastery a collection of monsters. . . . [And] if jewelry is a collection of jewels, then husbandry is a collection of husbands, infantry is a collection of infants, vestry a collection of vests, and pantry a collection of pants.

—Evan Esar, *Humorous English* (1961), 69.

484. If you're anxious for to shine in the high aesthetic line as a man of
culture rare,

You must get up all the germs of the transcendental terms, and plant them everywhere.
You must lie upon the daisies and discourse in novel phrases of your complicated state of mind,
The meaning doesn't matter if it's only idle chatter of a transcendental kind.

—W.S. Gilbert (and Arthur Sullivan), *Patience* (1881), I.

485. An eminent Logician who can make it clear to you
That black is white—when looked at from the proper point of view;
A marvellous Philologist who'll undertake to show
That 'yes' is but another and neater form of 'no.'

—W.S. Gilbert (and Arthur Sullivan), *Utopia, Limited* (1893), I.

486. [Multiple meanings for the simple little word fast:]
A person is *fast* when he can run rapidly.
But he is also *fast* when he is tied down and cannot run at all.
And colors are *fast* when they do not run.
One is *fast* when he moves in suspect company.
But it is not quite the same as playing *fast* and loose.
A racetrack is *fast* when it is in good running condition.
A friend is *fast* when he is loyal.
A watch is *fast* when it is ahead of time.
To be *fast* asleep is to be deep in sleep.
To be *fast* by is to be near.
To *fast* is to refrain from eating.
A *fast* may be a period of non-eating—or a ship's mooring line.
Photographic film is *fast* when it is *sensitive* (to light).
But bacteria are *fast* when they are *insensitive* (to antiseptics).

—William V. Haney,
Communication: Patterns and Incidents
(1960), 48. See Anonymous, **#478**, and Horn, **#487**.

487. [Multiple meanings for the simple little word *run:*] The disease has *run* its course. The fence *runs* east and west. To *run* to seed. To *run* a garage. To *run* a splinter in a finger. To *run* out of money. To *run* to ruin. To *run* a risk. To *run* a bill. To *run* across a friend. To knock a home*run.* A *run* on the bank. The common *run* of persons. [Here are a few more: To *run* a fever. A *run* in a stocking. To *run* for office. Colors *run.* To *run* dry. To *run* a blockade. To *run* water for a bath. A ferry *run.* The play will *run* for two weeks. The tune has *run* through my head. Traits *run* in the family. To *run* afoul of the law. To *run* off and elope. To *run* one's eyes over a page.

His speech has *run* on and on. His writing has *run* from poor to excellent. To *run* down with an automobile. – Ed.]

– Ernest Horn, "Language and Meaning,"
National Society for the Study of Education, *41st Yearbook*
(1942), 398. *See* Anonymous, **#478**, and Haney, **#486.**

488. To question all things; – never to turn away from any difficulty; to accept no doctrine either from ourselves or from other people without a rigid scrutiny by negative criticism; letting no fallacy, or incoherence, or confusion of thought, step up unperceived; above all, to insist upon having the meaning of a word clearly understood before using it, and the meaning of a proposition before assenting to it; – these are the lessons we learn from ancient dialecticians.

– John Stuart Mill, inaugural address
as Rector of University of St. Andrews, Feb. 1, 1867.

489. *Fluellen:* Auncient Pistol, I do partly understand your meaning.
Pistol: Why, then, rejoice therefore.

– William Shakespeare, *King Henry V* (1600), III.v.

490. "Good Morning!" said Bilbo, and he meant it. The sun was shining, and the grass was very green. But Gandalf looked at him from under long busy eyebrows that stuck out further than the brim of his shady hat.

"What do you mean?" he said. "Do you wish me a good morning, or mean that it is a good morning whether I want it or not; or that you feel good this morning; or that it is a morning to be good on?"

"All of them at once," said Bilbo. "And a very fine morning for a pipe of tobacco out of doors, into the bargain. If you have a pipe about you, sit down and have a fill of mine! There's no hurry, we have all the day before us!" Then Bilbo sat down on a seat by his door, crossed his legs, and blew out a beautiful grey ring of smoke that sailed into the air without breaking and floated away over The Hill.

"Very pretty! said Gandalf. But I have no time to blow smoke-rings this morning. I am looking for someone to share in an adventure that I am arranging, and it's difficult to find anyone."

"I should think so – in these parts! We are plain quiet folk and have no use for adventures. Nasty disturbing uncomfortable things! Make you late for dinner! I can't think what anyone sees in them," said our Mr. Baggins, and stuck one thumb behind his braces, and blew out another even bigger smoke-ring. Then he took out his morning letters, pretending to take no more notice of the old man. He had decided that he was not quite his sort, and wanted him to go away. But the old man did not move. He stood leaning on his stick and gazing at the hobbit without saying anything, till Bilbo got quite uncomfortable and even a little cross.

"Good morning!" he said at last. "We don't want any adventures here, thank you! You might try over the Hill or across The Water." By this he meant that the conversation was at an end.

"What a lot of things you do use *Good morning* for!" said Gandalf. "Now you mean that you want to get rid of me, and that it won't be good until I move off."

—J.R.R. Tolkien, *The Hobbit* (1937), 17.

Negroes, Education of

491. And *whereas*, the having of slaves taught to write, or suffering them to be employed in writing, may be attended with great inconveniences; *Be it, therefore enacted* by the authority aforesaid, That all and every person and persons whatsoever, who shall hereafter teach, or cause any slave or slaves to be taught, to write, or shall use or employ any slave as a scribe in any manner of writing whatsoever, hereafter taught to write, every such person and persons shall for every such offence, forfeit the sum of one hundred pounds current money.

—Act prohibiting teaching slaves to write,
South Carolina, 1740, in Thomas Cooper and
David McCord, eds., *The Statutes at Large of South Carolina*
(1836–41), VII.413.

492. Very soon after I went to live with Mr. and Mrs. Auld, she kindly commenced to teach me the A, B, C. After I had learned this, she assisted me in learning to spell words of three or four letters. Just at this point in my progress, Mr. Auld forbade Mrs. Auld to instruct me further, telling her, among other things, that it was unlawful, as well as unsafe, to teach a slave to read. To use his own words, further, he said, "If you give a nigger an inch, he will take an ell. A nigger should know nothing but to obey his master—to do as he is told to do. Learning would spoil the best nigger in the world. . . . As to himself, it could do him no good, but a great deal of harm. It would make him discontented and unhappy."

—Frederick Douglass,
Narrative of the Life of Frederick Douglass (1845), 36.

493. EDUCATIONAL LAWS OF VIRGINIA

. . . .

THE
PERSONAL NARRATIVE
of
MRS. MARGARET DOUGLASS
A SOUTHERN WOMAN
WHO WAS IMPRISONED FOR ONE MONTH
in the
COMMON JAIL OF NORFOLK
UNDER THE LAWS OF VIRGINIA
FOR THE CRIME OF
TEACHING FREE COLORED CHILDREN TO READ

. . . .

"Search the Scriptures!"
"How can one read unless he be taught?"
HOLY BIBLE

—Title page of her book (1854).
Margaret Douglass was a white woman.
In Langston Hughes and Milton Meltzer,
A Pictorial History of the Negro in America (1956), 109.
See Crandall, #695, under "School, Advertisements for."

494. If ignorance, poverty and degradation have hitherto been our unhappy lot; has the Eternal decree gone forth, that our [Negro] race alone are to remain in this state, while knowledge and civilization are shedding their enlivening rays over the rest of the human family?

—Editorial in *Freedom's Journal,* first Negro newspaper
in the United States, Mar. 16, 1827, in Milton Meltzer,
The Black Americans: A History in Their Own Words (1984), 13.

495. I beg Mr. [Thomas] Jefferson that in case I should die without will or testament he should buy out of my money so many Negroes and free them, and that the restant [remaining] sum should be sufficient to give them education and provide for their maintenance.

—Thaddeus Kosciuszko,
American last will and testament, *circa* Apr. 20, 1798,
in Miecislaus Haiman, *Kosciuszko: Leader and Exile* (1946), 76.
The estate of Kosciuszko, the Polish general and patriot who
fought for the colonists in the American Revolution, was used in
1836 to found the Colored School at Newark, New Jersey.

496. You called yesterday for the tax upon my property in the Township, which I shall pay, excepting the "School Tax." I object to the payment of this tax, on the ground that my rights as citizen, and my feelings as a man and parent, have been grossly outraged in depriving me, in violation of law and justice, of the benefits of the school system which this tax was designed to sustain.

—Robert Purvis, letter to the tax collector
objecting to separate schools for Negroes,
The Liberator, Dec. 16, 1853, in Milton Meltzer,
The Black Americans: A History in Their Own Words (1984), 58.

497. I was born under the slave law in Georgia.... [When I was about seven years of age my younger brother and I] were sent to a friend of my grandmother, Mrs. Woodhouse, a widow, to learn to read and write. She was a free woman and lived on Bay Lane, about a half a mile from my house.

We went there every day about nine o'clock, with our books wrapped in paper to prevent the police or white persons from seeing them. We went in, one at a time, through the gate, into the yard to the L kitchen, which was the schoolroom. She had twenty-five or thirty children whom she taught, assisted by her daughter, Mary Jane. The neighbors would see us going in sometimes, but they supposed we were there learning trades, as it was the custom to give children a trade of some kind.

After school we left the same way we entered, one by one, when we would go to a square, about a block from the school, and wait for each other. We would gather laurel leaves and pop them in our hands, on the way home.

I remained at her school for two years more, when I was sent to a Mrs. Mary Beasley, where I continued until May, 1860, when she told my grandmother she had taught me all she knew, and grandmother had better get some one else who could teach me more, so I stopped my studies for a while.

I had a white playmate about this time, named Katie O'Connor, who lived on the next corner of the street from my house, and who attended a convent. One day she told me, if I would promise not to tell her father, she would give me some lessons. On my promise not to do so, and getting her mother's consent, she gave me lessons about four months, every evening. At the end of this time she was put into the convent permanently, and I have never seen her since.

—Susie King Taylor, *Reminiscences of My Life in Camp* (1902).

498. It is lamentable, that many of our children go to school, from four until they are eight or ten, and sometimes fifteen years of age, and leave school knowing but a little more about grammar of their language than a horse does about handling a musket—and not a few of them are really so ignorant, that they are unable to answer a person correctly, general questions in geography, and to hear them read would only be to disgust a man who has a taste for reading; which, to do well, as trifling as it may appear to some, (to the ignorant in particular) is a great part of learning.

—David Walker, *Appeal . . . to the Colored Citizens of the World* (1829), II, in George Ducas, ed., *Great Documents in Black American History* (1970).

Orthography

(*See also* Grammar; Language; Meaning)

499. We'll begin with a box, and the plural is boxes,
But the plural of ox should be oxes.
Then one fowl is a goose, but two are called geese,
Yet the plural of mouse should never be meese.
You may find a lone mouse or a whole nest of mice,
But the plural of house is houses, not hice.
If the plural of man is always called men,
Why shouldn't the plural of pan be called pen?
The cows in the plural may be cows or kine,
But a bow if repeated is never called bine,
And the plural of vow is vows, never vine.
If I speak of a foot and you show me your feet,
And I give you a boot, would a pair be called beet?
If the singular's this and the plural is these,
Should the plural of kiss ever be nicknamed kese?
We speak of a brother, and also of brethren,
But though we say mother, we never say methren.
The masculine pronouns are he, his, and him,
But imagine the feminine she, shis, shim.
So the English, I think, you all will agree,
Is the queerest language you ever did see.

—Anonymous.

500. I said, "This horse, sir, will you shoe?"
And soon the horse was shod.
I said, "This deed, sir, will you do?"
And soon the deed was dod!

I said, "This stick, sir, will you break?"
  At once the stick he broke.
I said, "This coat, sir, will you make?"
  And soon the coat he moke!

—Anonymous

501. Said a zealous young student named Coles,
"As we always term Poland folks 'Poles,'
  I'm more than inclined,
  With my logical mind,
To designate Hollanders 'Holes'."

—Anonymous

502. There once were some people called Sioux
Who spent all their time making shioux
Which they colored in various hioux;
Don't think that they made them to ioux
Oh, no! they just sold them for bioux.

—Anonymous, "The American Indian,
in Russell Baker, ed., *The Norton Book of Light Verse* (1986), 104.

503. A pretty deer is dear to me,
  A hare with downy hair,
A hart I love with all my heart
  But barely bear a bear.

—Anonymous, *The Beauties of English Orthography* (c. 1850).

504. I take it you already know
Of tough and bough and cough and dough!
  Others may stumble, but not you
On hiccough, thorough, bough, and through.
And cork and work and card and ward,
And font and front and word and sword.
  Well done! And now, if you wish, perhaps,
To learn of less familiar traps?

Reward of heard, a dreadful word—
That looks like beard and sounds like bird.
  And dead: it's said like bed, not bead—
For goodness sake don't call it "deed".
Watch out for meat and great and threat.

(They rhyme with suite and straight and debt).
A moth is not a moth in mother
Nor both in bother, broth in brother.

And here is not a match for there,
Nor dear and fear for bear and peer;
And then there's dose and rose and lose—
Just look them up—and goose and choose.
And cork and work and card and ward,
And do and go: then thwart and cart.

Come, come, I've hardly made a start!
A dreadful language? Man alive,
I'd mastered it when I was five!

—Anonymous,
"A Rhyming Word," in *Manchester [Neb.] Guardian.*

505. A boy who swims may say he swum,
But milk is skimmed and seldom skum,
And nails you trim, they are not trum.
When words you speak, these words are spoken,
But a nose is tweaked and can't be twoken,
And what you seek is seldom soken.
If we forget, then we've forgotten,
But things we wet are never wotten,
And houses let cannot be lotten.
The goods one sells are always sold,
But fears dispelled are never dispold,
And what you smell is never smold.
When young, a top you oft saw spun,
But did you see a grin e'er grun,
Or a potato nearly skun.

—Anonymous, in Martha Lupton, ed.,
The Treasury of Modern Humor (1938), 930.

506. The wind was rough
And cold and blough
She kept her hands inside her mough.
It chilled her through,
Her nose turned blough,
And still the squall the faster flough.
And yet although

There was no snough,
The weather was a cruel fough.
It made her cough
(Please do not scough);
She coughed until her hat blough ough.

—Attributed to a visiting European college student.

507. When the English tongue we speak
Why is *break* not rhymed with *freak?*
Will you tell me why it's true
We say *sew* but likewise *Jew?*

—Evelyn Baring, 1st Earl of Cromer,
in *London Spectator*, Aug. 9, 1902.

508. My first setback was the discovery that English is not a phonetic language.... Reason and logic are all against the orthographical antics of our language, and all in favour of the wholesale confiscations which a military despotism will no doubt levy on our speech when all else that belongs to us has been confiscated. As a man of reason and logic, I am all for reform; but as the unworthy inheritor of a great tradition, I am unalterably against it. I am forever with [2nd Viscount] Falkland [1610?–43], true martyr of the Civil War, —one of the very greatest among the great spirits of whom England has ever been so notoriously unworthy, —as he stood facing Hampden and Pym. "Mr. Speaker," he said, "when it is not necessary to change, it is necessary not to change."

—Albert Jay Nock, *Memoirs of a Superfluous Man* (1943), 6.

Parent

(*See also* Child Rearing; Discipline, Punishment)

509. Dear Sir:

My son writes me that he has to study too hard. He says he has to translate fifty hexameters of Latin a day. I looked 'hexameter' up in the dictionary and find it is a poetic verse of six feet. Now that makes 300 feet or 100 yards of poetry for my poor son to translate each day. I think about half a hexameter, or six inches, of this Latin is enough for a boy of this age.

—Anonymous, letter from an indignant mother
to the principal of an academy, in G.B.F. Hallock,
Five Thousand Best Modern Illustrations (1927), 237.

510. "Where's the maternal parent of
This boy that stands in need of beating,
And of this babe that pines for love?"
"Oh, she's at a Mothers' Meeting!"

"Fair daughter, why these young tears shed,
For passion's tale, too sweet and fleeting,
Lonely and mute, uncomforted?"
"My mother's at a Mothers' Meeting."

"Man, whom misfortunes jeer and taunt,
Whom frauds forsake, and hope is cheating,
Fly to your mother's arms." "I can't—
You see, she's at a Mothers' Meeting."

Alas, what next will women do?
Love, duty, children, home, maltreating,
The while she, smiling, rallies to
The roll-call of a Mothers' Meeting!

—Madeline Bridges,
"A Mothers' Meeting," *Lippincott's Magazine*, c. 1900.

511. Likewise, ye parents, it devolves on you,
That have your children, though but one or two,
To keep them in your charge, and give them schooling
For the full time they stay beneath your ruling.
Look then, that by the lives that ye present,
Or by your negligence in chastisement,
They perish not. For I tell you clearly
That if they do, then it will cost you dearly.

—Geoffrey Chaucer, *The Canterbury Tales:*
"The Physician's Tale" (1386–89), tr. Frank Ernest Hill (1935), 246.

512. I am greatly delighted that you are desirous to go on with your Greek; and shall finish this Letter with a short Lesson of Greek.

P.S. I find that I cannot write in this space what I wished—therefore I will send you, my dear Child! a whole Sheet of Greek Lessons in a few days.

—Samuel Taylor Coleridge, letter to his son
Derwent, age 7, Feb. 8, 1807, in Earl Leslie Griggs,
Collected Letters of Samuel Taylor Coleridge (1959), III.1.

513. Mark you, it is significant that the kind of man who is addicted to philosophy is often unhappy in his children; I suppose because Nature was determined that the taint of wisdom should not be congenital and so become widespread. Cicero's son is known to have been degenerate; and the children of Socrates were more like the mother than the father—as some historian prettily said, meaning, of course, that they were fools.

—Desiderius Erasmus, *The Praise of Folly* (1501).

514. Why do not parents league themselves against the way children are treated in schools? Is it because they forget that they were once children themselves? Or is it, on the contrary, because they do remember, and they want their children to be as unhappy as they were?

—Sacha Guitry, *If Memory Serves* (1936), 35. *See* Huxley, **#516**; and Avery, **#222**, under "Education."

515. The beggerly question of parentage—what is it after all? What does it matter, when you come to think of it, whether a child is yours by blood or not? All the little ones of our time are collectively the children of us adults of the time, and entitled to our general care. The excessive regard of parents for their children, and their dislike of other people's is, like class-feeling, patriotism, save-your-own-soul-ism, and other virtues, a mean exclusiveness at bottom.

—Thomas Hardy, *Jude the Obscure* (1895), 324.

516. Why did fathers persist in sending their sons to the same, unregenerate schools from which they themselves suffered? And why didn't these fathers do anything to get the schools reformed? Because what was good enough for me is good enough for Johnny, and it's salutary for the boy to undergo a little hardship.

—Aldous Huxley, letter to Dr. Humphry Osmond, Feb. 22, 1957, in Grover Smith, ed., *Letters of Aldous Huxley* (1969), 818. *See* Guitry, **#514**; and Avery, **#222**, under "Education."

517. Convinced that our teachers made no effort to teach us the meaning of respect, my father distrusted American schools even more than the police. He held them responsible for promoting such shocking customs as that of young boys and girls dating without a chaperone or young people marrying without their parents' consent. The American school system, for him, symbolized everything that outraged him about his adopted country. His diatribes on the subject were of such eloquence as to make us feel guilty for daring to like any of our teachers. Beneath his fury was the conviction that they were encouraging immorality, disrupting family life, and undermining his position as the head of the family. . . .

As much as my father ranted against American schools, he and my mother yearned to send one of their sons to college, something which, they reminded each other, only the rich could do in Sicily.

—Jerre Mangione, *An Ethnic at Large: A Memoir of America in the Thirties and Forties* (1978), 18–19.

518. It was the greatest fun seeing you, and I really had a satisfactory time with you, and came away with the feeling that you were doing well. I am entirely satisfied with your standing, both in your studies and in athletics. I want you to do well in your sports, and I want even more to have you do well with your books; but I do not expect you to stand first in either, if so to stand could cause you overwork and hurt your health. I always believe in going hard at everything, whether it is Latin or mathematics, boxing or football, but at the same time I want to keep the sense of proportion. It is never worth while to absolutely exhaust one's self or to take big chances unless for an adequate object. I want you to keep in training the faculties which would make you, if the need arose, able to put your last ounce of pluck and strength into a contest. But I do not want you to squander these qualities. To have to play football as well as you do, and make a good name in boxing and wrestling, and be cox of your second crew, and stand second or third in your class in the studies, is all right. I should be rather sorry to see you drop too near the middle of your class, because, as you cannot enter college until you are nineteen, and will therefore be a year later in entering life, I want you to be prepared in the best possible way, so as to make up for the delay. But I know that all you can do you will do to keep substantially the position in the class that you have so far kept, and I have entire trust in you, for you have always deserved it.

—Theodore Roosevelt, letter to his son Ted, May 7, 1901, in Joseph Bucklin Bishop, ed., *Theodore Roosevelt's Letters to His Children* (1919), 25.

519. I have no sympathy with the old idea that children owe such immense gratitude to their parents that they can never fulfill their obligations to them. I think the obligation is all on the other side. Parents can never do too much for their children to repay them for the injustice of having brought them into the world, unless they have insured them high moral and intellectual gifts, fine physical health, and enough money and education to render life something more than one ceaseless struggle for necessities.

—Elizabeth Cady Stanton, diary entry, Nov. 12, 1880, in Theodore Stanton and Harriot Stanton Blatch, eds., *Elizabeth Cady Stanton* (1922), II.

520. What unjust judges fathers are, when in regard to us they hold
That even in our boyish days we ought in conduct to be old,
Nor taste at all the very things that youth and only youth requires;
They rule us by their present wants, not by their past long-lost desires.

—Terence, *The Self-Tormentor* (163 B.C.), I.iii.i. *See* Busch, **#1184**, under "Youth and Age."

Philosopher

(*See also* Philosophy)

521. I have tried . . . in my time to be a philosopher; but I don't know how, cheerfulness was always breaking in.

—Oliver Edwards, to Samuel Johnson, in James Boswell, *Life of Samuel Johnson*, Apr. 17, 1778 (1791).

522. Do but observe our grim Philosophers that are perpetually beating their brains on knotty Subjects, and for the most part you'll find 'em grown old before they are scarce young.

—Desiderius Erasmus, *The Praise of Folly* (1509). *See* Emerson, **#678**, and Erasmus, **#679**, under "Scholar."

523. True philosophers, who are only eager for truth and knowledge, never regard themselves as already so thoroughly informed, but that they welcome further information from whomsoever and from whencesoever it may come; nor are they so narrow-minded as to imagine any of the arts or sciences transmitted to us by the ancients, in such a state of forwardness or completeness, that nothing is left for the ingenuity and industry of others. Very many, on the contrary, maintain that all we know is still infinitely less than all that still remains unknown; nor do philosophers pin their faith to others' precepts in such wise that they lose their liberty, and cease to give credence to the conclusions of their proper senses. Neither do they swear such fealty to their mistress Antiquity, that they openly, and in sight of all, deny and desert their friend Truth.

—William Harvey, "Essay on the Motion of the Heart and Blood," addressed to the Royal College of Physicians, 1628.

524. The public would suffer less present inconvenience from the banishment of philosophers than from the extinction of any common trade.

—Samuel Johnson, *The Rambler*, Aug. 6, 1751.

525. The man who is his own lawyer or physician, will be poorly served; but everyone can and must be his own philosopher. He must be, because philosophy deals with ends, not means. It includes the questions, What is good? What is right? What is valid? Since finally the responsibility for his own life must rest squarely upon the shoulders of each, no one can delegate the business of answering such questions to another . . . [but] concerning the means whereby the valid ends of life may be attained, we seek expert advice.

—Clarence I. Lewis, *Mind and the World-Order* (1929).

526. I am far from holding that philosophy is a guide to life or that it furthers happiness; rather I believe that no one is more in need of instruction in living than the majority of those engaged in teaching it. I have noticed that most of those in schools who formulate the subtlest precepts of moderation and self-mastery themselves indulge in every kind of unbridled passion.

—Cornelius Nepos
(c. 100 B.C.–c. 25 B.C.), *Ad Ciceronem Epistulae,* XVI.3.

Philosophy

(*See also* Philosopher)

527. Philosophy, *n.* A route of many roads leading from nowhere to nothing.

—Ambrose Bierce, *The Devil's Dictionary* (1911).

528. You think perhaps of philosophy as dwelling in the clouds. I hope you may see that she is able to descend to earth. You think that in stopping to pay court to her, when you should be hastening forward on your journey, you are loitering in the bypaths and wasting precious hours. . . . Here you will find the key for the unlocking of bolts and combinations that shall never be pried open by clumsier or grosser tools. You think there is nothing practical in a theory that is concerned with ultimate conceptions. That is true, perhaps while you are doing the journeyman's work of your profession. You may find in the end, when you pass to higher problems, that instead of its being true that the study of the ultimate is profitless, there is little that is profitable in the study of anything else.

—Benjamin N. Cardozo, *Growth of the Law* (1924), 23.

529. Philosophical subjects should never be taught with authority. They are not established sciences; they are full of disputed matters, open

questions, and bottomless speculations. It is not the function of the teacher to settle philosophical and political controversies for the pupil, or even to recommend to him any one set of opinions as better than another. Exposition, not imposition, of opinions is the professor's part. . . . The very word education is a standing protest against dogmatic teaching.

—Charles W. Eliot, inaugural address,
Harvard University, Oct. 19, 1869,
Educational Reform: Essays and Addresses (1898), 7.

530. Here you see the beginning of Philosophy, in the discovery of the conflict of men's minds with one another, and the attempt to seek for the reason of this conflict, and the condemnation of mere opinion, as a thing not to be trusted; and a search to determine whether your opinion is true, and an attempt to discover a standard, just as we discover the balance to deal with weights and the rule to deal with things straight and crooked.

—Epictetus, *Discourses* (c. A.D. 100), II.xi.

531. Philosophy is at once the most sublime and the most trivial of human pursuits. It works in the minutest crannies and it opens out the widest vistas. It 'bakes no bread,' as has been said, but it can inspire our souls with courage; and repugnant as its manners, its doubting and challenging, its quibbling and dialectics, often are to common people, no one of us can get along without the far-flashing beams of light it sends over the world's perspectives.

—William James, *Pragmatism* (1907), 6.

532. I hardly know wherein philosophy and wine are alike unless it be in this, that the philosophers exchange their ware for money, like the wine-merchants; some of them with a mixture of water or worse, or giving short measure.

—Walter Pater, *Marius the Epicurean* (1885), xxiv.

533. Until philosophers are kings, or the kings and princes of this world have the spirit and power of philosophy, and political greatness and wisdom meet in one, . . . cities will never have rest from their evils,—no, nor the human race.

—Plato, *Republic* (c. 375 B.C.), V.

534. The value of philosophy is, in fact, to be sought largely in its very uncertainty. The man who has no tincture of philosophy goes through life imprisoned in the prejudices derived from common sense, from the habitual beliefs of his age or his nation, and from convictions which have grown up in his mind without the co-operation or consent of his deliberate reason. To such a man the world tends to become definite, finite, obvious; common objects arouse no questions, and familiar possibilities are contemptuously rejected.

—Bertrand Russell, *Problems of Philosophy* (1912), xv.

535. *Romeo.* O, thou wilt speak again of banishment.
Friar Lawrence. I'll give thee armour to keep off that word;
Adversity's sweet milk, philosophy,
To comfort thee, though thou art banished.
Romeo. Yet banished?—Hang up philosophy!
Unless philosophy can make a Juliet,
Displant a town, reverse a prince's doom,
It helps not, it prevails not,—talk no more.

—William Shakespeare, *Romeo and Juliet* (1594–95), III.iii.53.

Poet

(*See also* Criticism, Artistic; Poetry; Writer)

536. There was a young poet of Kew,
Who failed to emerge into view.
So he said, "I'll dispense
With rhyme, meter, and sense,"
And he did, and he's now in "Who's Who."

—Anonymous.

537. "Give me a theme," the little poet cried,
"And I will do my part."
"'Tis not a theme you need," the world replied;
"You need a heart."

—Richard Watson Gilder, "A Theme,"
Poems of Richard Watson Gilder (1908), 126.

538. What does it mean, then to be a poet? It was a long time before I realized that to be a poet means essentially to see, but mark well, to see in such a way that whatever is seen is perceived by the audience just as the poet saw it. But only what has been lived through can be seen in that way

and accepted in that way. And the secret of modern literature lies precisely in this matter of experiences that are lived through. All that I have written these last ten years, I have lived through spiritually. But no poet lives through anything isolated. What he lives through all of his countrymen live through with him. If that were not so, what would bridge the gap between the producing and the receiving minds?

—Henrik Ibsen, "Speech to the Norwegian Students, September 10, 1874," *Speeches and New Letters*, tr. Arne Kildal (1910), in Toby Cole, *Playwrights on Playwriting* (1961), 285.

539. Zimron, poet, makes his will,
Orders with his last breath,
That the offspring of his quill
Shall be published after death.
A gloomy prospect 'tis for all, we say
We hope he'll live for ever and a day.

—Isaac ben Jacob (1801–63), in Lore and Maurice Cowan, *The Wit of the Jews* (1970).

540. In this nadir of poetic repute, when the only verse that most people read from one year's end to the next is what appears on greeting cards, it is well for us to stop and consider our poets. . . . Poets are the leaven in the lump of civilization.

—Elizabeth Janeway, in Helen Hull, ed., *The Writer's Book* (1950), i.

541. A poet, any real poet, is simply an alchemist who transmutes his cynicism regarding human beings into an optimism regarding the moon, the stars, the heavens, and the flowers, to say nothing of Spring, love and dogs. Was Leopardi less a writer of deathless verse because he was one of the darkest pessimists who ever lived? Show me an optimist, and, almost without exception, I'll show you a bad poet.

—George Jean Nathan, *Monks Are Monks* (1929), 163.

542. Sir, I admit your gen'ral Rule
That every Poet is a Fool;
But you yourself may serve to show it,
That every Fool is not a Poet.

—Alexander Pope, "Epigram from the French," *Miscellanies* (1732).

543. 'Tis a fine thing for children to learn to make verse; but when they come to be men, they must speak like other men, or else they will be laughed at.

—John Selden, *Table Talk* (1689).

544. Vex not thou the poet's mind
With thy shallow wit:
Vex not thou the poet's mind;
For thou canst not fathom it.
Clear and bright it should be ever,
Flowing like a crystal river;
Bright as light, and clear as wind.

—Alfred, Lord Tennyson, "The Poet's Mind" (1830), *The Poetical Works of Tennyson* (1886).

545. The poet is he that hath fat enough, like bears and marmots, to suck his claws all winter. He hibernates in this world, and feeds on his own marrow. Alas, the poet too is, in one sense, a sort of dormouse gone into winter quarters of deep and serene thoughts, insensible to surrounding circumstances; his words are the relation of his oldest and finest memory, a wisdom drawn from the remotest experience. Other men lead a starved existence, meanwhile, like hawks that would fain keep on the wing and trust to pick up a sparrow now and then.

—Henry David Thoreau, *A Week on the Concord and Merrimack Rivers:* "Sunday" (1849).

546. 'I wish poets could be clearer!' shouted my wife angrily from the next room.

Hers is a universal longing. We would all like it if the bards would make themselves plain, or we think we would. The poets, however, are not easily diverted from their high mysterious ways. A poet dares to be just so clear and no clearer; he approaches lucid ground warily, like a mariner who is determined not to scrape his bottom on anything solid. A poet's pleasure is to withhold a little of his meaning, to intensify by multiplication. He unzips the veil from beauty, but does not remove it. A poet utterly clear is a trifle glaring.

—E.B. White, *One Man's Meat* (1944), 143.

Poetry

(*See also* Criticism, Artistic; Poet, Writing)

547. BOSWELL: "Then, Sir, what is poetry?"
DR. JOHNSON: "Why, Sir, it is much easier to say what it is not."

Boswell must have chosen an off day to ask the question. The answers are always plentiful. Everybody knows what poetry is, and says so, especially in our time:

R.P. BLACKMUR: "Poetry is life framed and identified."
JOHN HALL WHEELOCK: "A poem is a way of knowing."
RICHARD WILBUR: "The poem is an effort to make or discover some pattern in the world. . . . It is conflict with disorder."
PAUL ENGLE: "Poetry is ordinary language raised to the Nth power."
RAINER MARIA RILKE: "Verses are not, as people imagine, simply feelings. They are experiences."
CARL SANDBURG: "Poetry is hyacinths and biscuits."
T.S. ELIOT: "We must learn what poetry is — if we ever learn — from reading it."
WALLACE STEVENS: "Poetry is the supreme fiction, madame."
MARIANNE MOORE: ". . . imaginary gardens with real toads in them."
DYLAN THOMAS: "Poetry is what in a poem makes you laugh, cry, twist your toes, twinkle, prickle, be silent, know you are alone and not alone in an unknown world."

— Helen Bevington, *When Found, Make a Verse Of:* "What Is Poetry?" (1961), 84. *See* Sandburg, **#558.**
[For additional definitions and descriptions of poetry see my *Teacher's Treasury of Quotations* (1985), 221–23. — Ed.]

548. People who speak disparagingly of minor poetry are either stockbrokers and lawyers and rich practical people who don't understand, or reviewers in the Press, who are always young men fresh from a university with souls so stuffed full of intellectual pride that they might as lightly speak of minor roses or minor sunsets.

— Rupert Brooke, in Christopher Hassall, *Rupert Brooke: A Biography* (1964), 92.

549. Poetry, sir, in my judgment, is like a tender virgin in her bloom, beautiful and charming to amazement: all other sciences are so many virgins, whose care it is to enrich, polish, and adorn her; as she is to make use of them all, so are they all to have from her a grateful acknowledgment. But this virgin must not be roughly handled, nor dragged along the streets, nor exposed to every marketplace, and corner of great men's houses. A good poet is a kind of alchymist, who can turn the matter he prepares into the purest gold and an inestimable treasure. But he must keep his muse within the rules of decency, and not let her prostitute her excellency in lewd satires and lampoons, nor in licentious sonnets.

—Miguel de Cervantes, *Don Quixote* (1615), II.II.xvi.

550. Jem writes his verse with more speed
Than the printer's boy can set 'em;
Quite as fast as we can read,
And only not so fast as we forget 'em.

—Samuel Taylor Coleridge, ["Dear Brother Jem"] (1799), *The Complete Poetical Works of Samuel Taylor Coleridge*, ed. Ernest Hartley Coleridge (1912), II.956.

551. The great easiness of blank verse renders the poet too luxuriant; he is tempted to say many things which might better be omitted, or at least shut up in fewer words; but when the difficulty of artful rhyming is interposed, where the poet commonly confines his sense to his couplet, and must contrive that sense into such words that the rhyme shall naturally follow them, not they the rhyme; the fancy then gives leisure to the judgment to come in, which, seeing so heavy a tax imposed, is ready to cut off all unnecessary expenses.

—John Dryden, *The Rival Ladies* (1664), preface.

552. A poem ... begins as a lump in the throat, a sense of wrong, a homesickness, a lovesickness. It is never a thought to begin with. It is at its best when it is a tantalizing vagueness. It finds its thought and succeeds, or doesn't find it and comes to nothing. It finds its thought or makes its thought. I suppose it finds it lying around with others not so much to its purpose in a more or less full find. That's why it oftener comes to nothing in youth before experience has filled the mind with thoughts. It may be a big emotion then and yet finds nothing it can embody in. It finds the thought and the thought finds the words. Let's say it again: A poem particularly must not begin with thought first.

—Robert Frost, letter to Louis Untermeyer, Jan. 1, 1916, in Lawrance Thompson, *Robert Frost: The Years of Triumph, 1915–1938* (1970), 65.

553. We hate poetry that has a palpable design upon us—and if we do not agree, seems to put its hand in its breeches pocket. Poetry should be grand

& unobtrusive, a thing which enters into one's soul, and does not startle or amaze it with itself but with its subject.

—John Keats, letter to John Reynolds,
Feb. 3, 1818, in Hyder Edward Rollins, ed.,
The Letters of John Keats, 1814–1821 (1958), I.224.

554. The moon . . . isn't just a moon to a poet. Sometimes it's a "dying lady, lean and pale, Who totters forth in a gauzy veil." Again it is "a pearly apple caught in a tree of night," "a ghostly galleon," "a clown-faced jester," "A little prairie dog" that "shivers through the night." At other times it is a "gong hung in the wind," "the North Wind's cooky," and in a poet's most imaginative moments

"... It is a griffin's egg,
Hatching tomorrow night,
And how the little boys will watch
With shouting and delight..."

—Bernice E. Leary, *The World Leaps Forth to Life* (1941), 4.

555. Poetry is uncouth, unshaven, boisterous prose afflicted with a crying drunk. Through its empty prose head there flows suddenly unsteady visions of its boyhood home, the little red schoolhouse, its first sweetheart, and the first kiss in the field of daisies back of the old circus lot, and, passing its hand over its prosy, stubby face, it has a moment of alcoholic self-disesteem and of melancholy repentance for what it thinks it might have been and might have had—had things been other than they are—of an almost unreal happiness. It idiotically and boozily wants something it cannot have, something that, once gone, it can never recapture, and in this mood it sings its futile, groggy and sometimes very beautiful song.

—George Jean Nathan, *Materia Critica* (1924).

556. A poem, in my opinion, is opposed to a work of science by having, for its immediate object, pleasure, not truth; to romance, by having, for its object, an indefinite instead of a definite pleasure, being a poem only so far as this object is attained; romance presenting perceptible images with definite, poetry with indefinite sensations, to which end music is an essential, since the comprehension of sweet sound is our most indefinite conception. Music, when combined with a pleasurable idea, is poetry; music, without the idea, is prose, from its very definiteness.

—Edgar Allan Poe, *Works:* "Letter to Mr. B----" (1831).

557. Among the Haida Indians of the Pacific Northwest, the verb for "making poetry" is the same as the verb "to breathe."

—Tom Robbins, *Another Roadside Attraction* (1971), 168.

558. Poetry is the journal of a sea animal living on land, wanting to fly in the air. Poetry is a search for syllables to shoot at the barriers of the unknown and the unknowable. Poetry is a phantom script telling how rainbows are made and why they go away.

—Carl Sandburg, "Poetry Considered," *Atlantic Monthly,* March 1923. In his *Complete Poems* (1950), Sandburg gives 38 definitions of poetry. *See also* Bevington, **#547.**

559. I would rather have written that poem, gentlemen, than take Quebec to-morrow.

—Major-General James Wolfe, referring to Thomas Gray's *Elegy Written in a Country Churchyard* the night before he was killed on the Plains of Abraham, Sept. 13, 1759.

Principal

560. If he looks around, he's snooping; if he doesn't, he's lazy.

If he tries to settle all complaints, he's a fool; if he doesn't, he's not earning his pay.

If he confers with an experienced teacher, she is his pet; if he doesn't, he's a bull-headed dictator.

If he talks with young teachers, he's a Romeo; if he doesn't, he shuns their problems.

If he insists on rules, he's a stickler; if he doesn't, he's a lax administrator.

He's expected to be cunning as a cat, as blind as a bat, as patient as Job, and as wise as Solomon. . . But isn't that asking a bit too much?

—Anonymous, "What Is a School Principal?" *See* Wilson, **#919,** under "Teacher."

561. Doctor Strong's was an excellent school; as different from Mr. Creakle's as good is from evil. It was very gravely and decorously ordered, and on a sound system; with an appeal, in everything, to the honour and good faith of the boys, and an avowed intention to rely on their possession of those qualities unless they proved themselves unworthy of it, which worked wonders. . . .

But the doctor himself was the idol of the whole school: and it must have been a badly-composed school if he had been anything else, for he was the kindest of men; with a simple faith in him that might have touched the stone hearts of the very urns upon the wall. As he walked up and down that part of the court-yard which was at the side of the house, with the stray rooks and jackdaws looking after him with their heads cocked slyly, as if they knew how much more knowing they were in worldly affairs than he, if any sort of vagabond could only get near enough to his creaking shoes to attract his attention to one sentence of a tale of distress, that vagabond was made for the next two days. It was so notorious in the house, that the masters and headboys took pains to cut these marauders off at angles, and to get out windows, and turn them out of the court-yard, before they could make the Doctor aware of their presence; which was sometimes happily affected within a few yards of him, without his knowing anything of the matter, as he jogged to and fro. Outside his own domain, and unprotected, he was a very sheep for the shearers. He would have taken his gaiters off his legs, to give way.

—Charles Dickens, *David Copperfield* (1849–50), 225, 226.

562. There is a particular monopoly of uninterrupted speech reserved for headmasters, judges and generals.

—Abba Eban, *An Autobiography* (1977), 5.

563. A slight noise from the doorway caught her attention. She saw the burnished knob turn and watched the door swing open slowly and silently on its well-oiled hinges. Her heart leaped in her breast as she recognized him. Softly he stepped into the room and, careful to make no disturbance, made his way noiselessly along the left wall. He chose his vantage-point carefully, and from it his eyes seemed to miss no detail. She watched him tensely, trying to pull her scattered thoughts together, but was shaken anew as his hand went to his pocket and withdrew the black, flat object he habitually carried there. With a great effort of will she tore her eyes from him. . . .

An episode from a mystery thriller? No; simply a description of a principal making a routine supervisory visit in the manner recommended by some authorities a decade and a half ago.

—Willard S. Elsbree and Harold McNally, *Elementary School Administration and Supervision* (1951), 397.

564. [The headmaster's name] was Mr. High, but in fact he was very short, and also very stout. His stomach protruded like a balloon blown up to the bursting point. It was commonly said that if you could tap his navel, you would turn on undiluted cider. He was never actually sober nor ever completely drunk.

If he was a walking cider barrel, his wife [also a teacher] was a tall vinegar bottle. They hated each other with a cold, polite venom. They had no children, which may have been the root of the matter. It was a matter of opinion whether she had driven him to drink by her sour nature, or had acquired her sourness because of his drinking. . . .

Mostly he treated us all with good-natured sarcasm, but now and again, when he was taking a class, he went into one of his tantrums. When he felt a tantrum coming on, the slightest misdemeanour, real or unintended, would set him off. Forms and desks toppled over as he dragged us out, clouting us round the ears with one hand, wielding his stick with the other. He threw our exercise books in the air, and pages came flying all over the classroom. It always gave me a fit of the giggles; I knew he would be likely to bring a chair down on my head if he noticed, so I always bent down to tie up my bootlaces during the hurricane. That way I got my whacks along my back. He never favoured anyone; we all got a hiding when he was in the mood. It did him the world of good—he was well-behaved for a long time afterwards.

—Winifred Foley, *As the Twig Is Bent* (1978), 48.

565. The junior form, or class [of St. Edward's School, 1868], was in session, so to speak, and I was modestly occupying that position, at the very bottom, which seemed to me natural enough, when the then Headmaster entered—a man who had somehow formed an erroneous idea of my possibilities. Catching sight of me, he asked, sternly, 'What's that thing doing down there?' The master in charge could only reply that whether it was crass ignorance or invincible stupidity, he wotted not, but there it was. The Headmaster could not really have studied that immortal work, the *Republic* of Plato, in which the principles of ideal justice are patiently sought out, merely remarked that if the thing—meaning me—was not up there or near it, pointing to the head of the form, before the close of work, it was to be severely caned; and left the room.

—Kenneth Grahame, prize-giving speech, 1906?,
in Peter Green, *Kenneth Grahame: A Biography* (1959), 34.

566. That headmaster with his odious attitude. . . . I can see him now, acting his part so badly, the part of the man who is severe because he must be, and is just because it is his duty to be. Just! As if I had been guilty of something! Idiotic gravity; stupid authority; and what an antipathetic face! And for what reason? To terrify a child of seven? How clever! Do they understand nothing? They surely cannot understand that their profession could become the most wonderful in the world. They prefer being feared to being loved. It's more quickly done; obviously easier. But school ought to be a synonym for paradise. The very idea of gathering children together in order to educate them and make social beings of them is a beautiful idea. Why, then, should all *lycées* give off the atmosphere of prisons? To begin with, it should not be possible to build whatever one chooses. People should be forbidden to dishonor cities. The architects who put up such horrors should be punished. And how does it happen that in all these years the teachers have never found the means to make it impossible that children hate them and make fun of them?

—Sacha Guitry, *If Memory Serves* (1936), 32.

567. Probably the most forbidding figure throughout our entire public or private school career was the principal or headmaster. Whether it was a man or woman, we always sensed a pervading air of ultimate authority. Everyone in the school was responsible to this person. When our problems could not be handled within the classroom, it was to the principal we were sent. This was the final stopping place before expulsion. Instinctively we knew that no matter who ran the school system or the school board, the autonomy and control of our school was under the rule of the principal, administrator, or headmaster. Most of us simultaneously feared and respected him, but we never really understood his functions. What were his responsibilities? He simply seemed always to be there, always omnipotent, and always the final arbiter in the decisions and problems affecting our lives at school.

—Murray M. Kappelman and
Paul R. Ackerman, *Between Parent and School* (1977), 11.

568. I find myself utterly unable to adopt the indurating policy which seems to be the refuge of all schoolteachers. I must be interested and discharge my conscience of the 80 souls that are waiting on me for instruction and example. These are a terrible weight upon me: I dream for them, I labor for them, I suffer for the thousand brutalities and derelictions of their parents, which it requires all my patience, all my labor, all my ingenuity, all my art and culture and poverty and religion to withstand it all.

—Sidney Lanier (1842–81), in Myron C. Tuman,
"Prometheus Bound: The Brief Teaching Careers
of Great Writers," *Phi Delta Kappan* Magazine, December 1980.
Lanier was the principal of a school in Prattville, Alabama.

569. In the year 1809 George III appointed as Headmaster of Eton, Dr. Keate, a terrible little man who considered the flogging-block a necessary station on the road to perfection, and who ended a sermon on the Sixth Beatitude by saying, "Now, boys, be pure in heart! For if not, I'll flog you until you are!"

—André Maurois,
Ariel: The Life of Shelley (1924), opening sentence.

570. A headmaster has to pretend to know everything, and the pretense soon becomes a conviction.

—George Santayana, *Persons and Places* (1944), 152.

571. The headmaster [of the Dutch school was] a tight-lipped, sallow-complexioned old fundamentalist. . . . He inspired me with so much more terror than respect that I still see his ghost at times. There was not a spark of humor in that man. Not once in all those years did I see his face soften into a smile. He had come to the teaching profession much in the same spirit as an Inquisitor approaches a victim in the torture chamber. His conception of his task was not to guide and shepherd, but to correct a crowd of hopelessly bad children, who were inclined from birth—as that lovely Catechism specified—"to do evil and hate God." In fact, the whole system of "Schools with the Bible" in Holland was set up to counteract the rational mode of thought which swept over Europe in the wake of the French Revolution. Against the spirit of inquiry and free thought of the nineteenth century, which was deemed to have poisoned two or three generations of Dutchmen, these schools were to provide an antidote by instilling respect for the ancient verities.

The "instilling" was frequently done (in our case) with the aid of a brass-edged ruler of ebony wood, which the principal, in spite of his reputed shortsightedness, manipulated with uncanny precision. He never missed. Upon the slightest provocation: a mere whisper in the classroom or a giggle, he advanced upon you without a word, seized hold of your wrist, and brought down his stick on your knuckles, not in anger, but with calm deliberation. If you wept in pain and humiliation after one of these punitive ministrations, he locked you up for the rest of the day in a small dark room where the coal was kept and which swarmed with rats and mice.

—Pierre van Paassen, *Days of Our Years* (1939), 5.

Professor

(*See also* College; College, American; College, British; Scholar; Teacher)

572. There once was a scholar named Fressor
Whose knowledge grew lessor and lessor.
It at last grew so small
He knew nothing at all,
And today he's a college professor!

—Anonymous, in Bennett Cerf, *The Life of the Party* (1956), 191.

573. The most impressive of all the kinds of Professors is the Full Professor. It is not apparent at first glance precisely what it is full of, but there is an obvious fullness. In fact it is so full that it seems ready to burst. It may, however, only be bursting with pride. At a closer look or, better, upon dissection, it will be seen that the Full Professor is full of such things as Information, Experience, and Authority. There may also be bites and pieces of Instructors, Assistant Professors, and Associate Professors it has chewed out or devoured because of its insatiable appetite to rise to the Top Rank and they got in the way.

—Richard Armour, *The Academic Bestiary* (1974), 70.

574. Dr. Spooner, who could still be seen in the streets of Oxford when I was an undergraduate, did not himself, it seems, make any spoonerisms. His conversation, however, could be very odd. In his *Memories* Sir Maurice Bowra reports the following snatch of dialogue.

Dr. Spooner: I want you to come to tea next Thursday to meet Mr. Casson.

Mr. Casson: But I am Mr. Casson.

Dr. Spooner: Come all the same.

—W.H. Auden, *A Certain World: A Commonplace Book* (1970), 118.

575. These were the days of the genial President [John Thornton] Kirkland [of Harvard College, 1810–28], who, after conducting an examination, regaled the boys with a fine dish of pears. He was an easy-going man, a Unitarian minister, like most of the professors, sympathetic and of the gentlest temper, naturally frank and cordial, with all the delicate feeling for human behaviour that characterized the best New Englanders. It was said that he threw his sermons into a barrel, as the farmers threw their corn into the silo, and that on Sunday morning he fished out enough for a discourse and patched the leaves together. . . . He never took the narrow view. Hearing that flip at the Porter House had proved to be too attractive to the students, he dropped in to see the proprietor. "And so, Mr. Porter," he said, "the young gentlemen come to drink your flip, do they?"—"Yes, sir," said

Mr. Porter, "sometimes." —"Well, I should think they would," the president said. "Good day, Mr. Porter."

—Van Wyck Brooks, *The Flowering of New England* (1936), 36.

576. The professors of that day [c. 1898] were taskmasters and looked their part. Some of them still survived in our expansive period, bearded men, a little dusty, whose clothes and faces were emphatically different from the world's, as were the old-time clergymen's. Men sure of themselves, severe, arid, uncompromising, uninventive, uninterested in the constantly new things which we call life, yet often unexpectedly wise and serene. Or so they seemed in the decay of the age of discipline. . . .

It seemed to me incredible that a mature and civilized person, who in private life had an impeccable character and often geniality and charm, should be willing to earn a living (and usually a meager living) by asking trivial questions day after day of young men who had either memorized the answers as the easiest way of getting on with college life and their real education or constructed a system of bluff so transparent that only a defeatist who did not believe in education would have stood for it. I understand more now how hard it was for a scholar to get enough to live on in those days. Even so I wonder when I think of men who persisted in this rigamarole for forty years.

—Henry Seidel Canby, *American Memoir* (1947), 162.

577. The professor who taught a single subject in which he had specialized did not appear even at Harvard until the arrival of the 19th century, and in most colleges until almost the end of the century faculty members were expected to teach over the whole expanse of the curriculum—and most of them did. For example, Professor Oliver March, a member of the faculty and an important administrator at Northwestern University beginning in 1862, at one time or other during his 27 years there taught mathematics, geology, mineralogy, zoology, botany, chemistry, physics, logic, and Greek.

—W.H. Cowley, *An Appraisal of American Higher Education* (1956). (Stanford University, mimeographed and unpublished.)

578. Every college and university in the land possesses some odd faculty member whose behavior makes legends. At Exeter I remember hearing tales about an extremely cross-eyed Latin master, whom we called "Squint" among ourselves. Enraged in class one time, Squint glared at a squirming student and roared, "Look out, I've got my eye on you!" "Which eye?" the student asked innocently. In another irate mood Squint commanded, "You

in the back row, stand up," transfixing a malefactor with his wrathful gaze. Thereupon six students stood up. I always accepted these stories as gospel until recently, when I began to investigate the ways of college folklore.

—Richard M. Dorson, "Folklore,"
The American Mercury Magazine, 1949.

579. Gee but this man [Nathaniel] Griffin is terrible. I sit here bored to death and hear him pick English poetry to pieces. Small man, small mind. Snotty, disagreeable. Damn him. "Neat" is his favorite word. Imagine Shakespeare being neat. Yesterday I counted and found that he used the expression "Isn't that so" fifty four times. Oh what a disagreeable silly ass he is. He's going to get married. God help his wife. Poor girl. Shes [sic] in for a bad time. They say Griffin has made more men leave the English department than any other praeceptor in [Princeton] College. The slovenly old fool! I have the most terrible *praeceptors.*

—F. Scott Fitzgerald, 1916,
written in his textbook edition of Sir Philip Sidney's
Defense of Poesie, in Matthew J. Bruccoli, *Some Sort of Epic Grandeur: The Life of F. Scott Fitzgerald* (1981), 68.

580. Not long after my arrival at the University of Colorado I received a note from the dean asking that I drop into his office. I had no idea what he wanted....

So that morning I dropped into his office, smiling and at ease, for it was always a great pleasure to chat with Dean Hellems.

But he wasn't smiling as he motioned me to a seat and said abruptly, "I hear you've been drinking with the students."

"Yes, sir," I replied truthfully. "But it's pretty bad stuff, and I don't recommend it."

Now, this was during prohibition, and bootleggers were thicker on the campus than faculty wives.

Dean Hellems glared at me a moment, then asked, "Don't you know that faculty members aren't supposed to drink with students?"

"I've heard rumors that it isn't common practice," I replied.

"Then why do you do it?"

"I was told in New York that if a man in Colorado offered me a drink and I refused—I'd be shot. I've been acting in self-defense."

"A mistaken notion," he mumbled. "Possibly true in the old, untamed days of the Wild West. But the custom—while a good one—has long since been abolished."

Then he softened a bit and added, "I like a glass of sherry myself, now and then. And should you want a drink occasionally, who am I to deny you the privilege? However, in the future, please drink only with members of the faculty."

"Which faculty members?" I asked.

He dismissed me with a gesture.

—Carl Glick, *I'm a Busybody* (1949), 150.

581. This pedagogue deserves the highest heaven;
He never diced or drank or went with the wenches.
His listeners are a small but loyal seven:
The four walls of his school and three old benches.

—From *The Greek Anthology.*

582. For thirty five years I have been suffering the exigencies of being a teacher, the pretension and the duty, namely, of meeting the mental needs and difficulties of other persons, needs that I couldn't possibly understand; and now that I have shuffled off the professional coil, the sense of freedom that comes to me is as surprising as it is exquisite. I wake up every morning with it: "What! not to have to accommodate myself to this mass of alien and recalcitrant humanity, not to think under resistance, not to have to square myself with others at every step I make—hurrah, it is too good to be true!"

—William James, upon his retirement from teaching,
in Jacques Barzun, *A Stroll With William James* (1983), 278.

583. Dear Young Ladies,—

I am deeply touched by your remembrance. It is the first time anyone ever treated me so kindly, so you may well believe that the impression on the heart of the lonely sufferer will be even more durable than the impression on your minds of all the teachings of Philosophy 2A. I now perceive one immense omission in my Psychology,—the deepest principle of Human Nature is the craving to be appreciated, and I left it out altogether from the book, because I had never had it gratified until now. I fear that you have let loose a demon in me, and that all my actions will now be for the sake of such rewards.

—William James,
letter to his students for the gift of an azalea tree,
Apr. 6, 1896. *See* Leacock's acceptance of a gift, **#584.**

584. May I say that I appreciate more than I can tell you your gift of a set of my works to the college library and another set to my son. I am told that you were in some doubt whether to let it be Shakespeare's works, or my own. You have chosen wisely. I have not only written more than Shakespeare, but what I have written is worth more. Shakespeare's books can be had anywhere at fifteen cents each, while mine run from a dollar up.

—Stephen Leacock, response on May 4, 1936
upon accepting two red morocco-bound sets
from former students upon his retirement
from McGill University, in David M. Legate, *Stephen Leacock*
(1970), 210. *See* James, #583.

585. It is from [the tutor], or rather with him, that the students learn all they know.... Yet it is a little odd to know just how he does it. "We go over to his rooms ... and he just lights a pipe and talks to us. We sit round with him ... and he simply smokes and goes over exercises with us." From this and other evidence I gather that what an Oxford tutor does is to get a little group of students together and smoke at them. Men who have been systematically smoked at for four years turn into ripe scholars.... A well-smoked man speaks and writes English with a grace that can be acquired in no other way.

—Stephen Leacock, *The Leacock*
Roundabout: "Oxford As I See It" (1946), 304.

586. I went to Frankfurt, and got drunk
With that most learn'd professor, Brunck;
I went to Wortz, and got more drunken,
With that more learn'd professor, Ruhnken.

—Richard Porson (1759–1808), "Facetiae Cantabrigienses."

587. No one shall lecture in the arts at Paris before he is twenty-one years of age, and he shall have heard lectures for at least six years before he begins to lecture, and he shall promise to lecture at least two years, unless a reasonable cause prevents, which he ought to prove publicly or before examiners. He shall not be stained by any infamy, and when he is ready to lecture, he shall be examined according to the form which is contained in the writing of the lord bishop of Paris....

In the principia and meetings of the masters and in the responsions or oppositions of the boys and youths there shall be no drinking.... None of the masters lecturing in arts shall have a cope except one round, black, and reaching to the ankles, at least while it is new. Use of the pallium is permitted. No one shall wear with the round cope shoes that are ornamented or with elongated pointed toes. If any scholar in arts or theology dies, half of the masters of arts shall attend the funeral at one time, the other half the next time....

Each master shall have jurisdiction over his scholar. No one shall occupy a classroom or house without asking the consent of the tenant, provided one has a chance to ask for it. No one shall receive the licentiate from the chancellor or another for money given or promise made or other condition agreed upon. Also, the masters and scholars can make both between themselves and with other persons obligations and constitutions supported by faith or penalty or oath in these cases: namely, the murder or mutilation of a scholar or atrocious injury done a scholar, if justice should not be forthcoming, arranging the prices of lodgings, costume, burial, lectures and disputations, so, however, that the university be not thereby dissolved or destroyed. As to the status of the theologians, we decree that no one shall lecture at Paris before his thirty-fifth year and unless he has studied for eight years at least, and has heard the books faithfully and in classrooms, and has attended lectures in theology for five years before he gives lectures himself publicly. . . .

Moreover, that these decrees may be observed inviolate, we by virtue of our legatine authority have bound by the knot of excommunication all who shall contumaciously presume to go against these our statutes, unless within fifteen days after the offence they have taken care to emend their presumption before the university of masters and scholars or other persons constituted by the university. Done in the year of Grace 1215, the month of August.

—Robert de Courçon, in *Chartulary of the University of Paris* (13th cent.), I.78, in Lynn Thorndike, ed., *University Records and Life in the Middle Ages:* "Rules of the University of Paris, 1215" (1944), 27. [cope=*long mantle worn by ecclesiastics;* pallium=*draped rectangular cloth worn by men of ancient Greece and Rome as a cloak*].

588. After teaching homiletics (the study of writing and preaching sermons) for over 20 years, I am certain no purgatory can exist for me, as I have already listened to thousands of students' sermons.

—Rev. Craig P. Skinner, professor, Golden Gate Baptist Theological Seminary, *Sarasota Herald-Tribune,* May 2, 1987.

589. The advantage of being one's master, which the fellow of an Oxford or Cambridge enjoys, was outweighed, for me, by some disadvantages in the university don's career that, according to my reckoning, were grave.

The gravest was one that is intrinsic to the educator's job at all levels. The rhythm of educational work is, and seems bound to be, cyclic. Each year the conveyor-belt brings to a teacher, for him to educate, a new annual batch of pupils of the same age as the batches that have passed and the batches that are still to come; and the teacher has to give to each successive batch the same instruction. For each generation of pupils in turn, it inevitably becomes staler and staler with each accumulating year. In my second year as a don I was already catching myself repeating the same form of words in discussing with my pupils an essay or some stock subject; and there were some subjects that were so essential that one could not avoid setting essays on them to every pupil who passed through one's hands. I now made a count; and I found that, if I were to stay at the college as long as the present Master had been there already (he was turned seventy, while I was still only twenty-four), the number of times that, by then, I should have set, listened to, and criticized the unavoidable essay on, say, Solon or on Peisistratus would run into four figures. This disconcerted me.

—Arnold Toynbee, *Experiences* (1969), 66.

590. The only reason I took philosophy at Harvard was because of my admiration for William James. How could you help listening to a college professor who denied that his could be the best of all possible worlds as long as there was a "single cockroach suffering the pangs of unrequited love."

—Arthur Train, *Yankee Lawyer* (1943), 4.

591. Entering university work as a life career is very much like entering matrimony: everybody agrees that it is an important event but so many intangibles are involved that nobody knows exactly how it happens. The candidate must choose and be chosen, and despite the indeterministic beliefs of a democratic society, chance and the pressure of circumstances are just as decisive as sentiment and rational choice.

—Logan Wilson, *The Academic Man: A Study in the Sociology of a Profession* (1942), 15.

Punishment, Corporal

(*See also* Discipline; Punishment, Corporal [Con]; Punishment, Corporal [Pro]; Punishment, Corporal [by Students])

592. *Boys.* Master, we children ask you to teach us to speak correctly for we are unlearned and speak corruptly.

Master. What do you want to say?

Boys. What do we care what we say so long as we speak correctly and say what is useful, not old-womanish or improper.

Master. Will you be flogged while learning?

Boys. We would rather be flogged while learning than remain ignorant; but we know that you will be kind to us and not flog us unless you are obliged.

—Abbott Aelfric, colloquy written in 1005,
in A.F. Leach, *Educational Charters* (1911), 37.

593. If idle in learning, I was beaten. For this was judged right by our forefathers; and many, passing the same course before us, framed for us weary paths, through which we were fain to pass; multiplying toil and grief upon the sons of Adam.

—St. Augustine, *Confessions* (c. A.D. 400), I.

594. Ferule, *n.*
A wooden implement designed
To open up the infant mind
And make the pupil understand
The bearings of the thing in hand.

—Ambrose Bierce, *The Enlarged
Devil's Dictionary*, ed. E.R. Hopkins (1967).

595. The Form Master's observations about punishment were by no means without their warrant at St. James's School. Flogging with the birch in accordance with the Eton fashion was a great feature of its curriculum. But I am sure no Eton boy, and certainly no Harrow boy of my day, ever received such a cruel flogging as this Headmaster was accustomed to inflict upon the little boys who were in his care and power. They exceeded in severity anything that would be tolerated in any of the Reformatories under the Home Office. . . . Two or three times a month the whole school was marshalled in the Library, and one or more delinquents were hauled off to an adjoining apartment by the two head boys, and there flogged until they bled freely, while the rest sat quaking, listening to their screams.

—Winston Churchill,
My Early Life: A Roving Commission (1930), 12.

596. One German schoolmaster with a Teutonic exactitude worthy of a better cause, kept a record of what punishments he had used during his fifty-one years of teaching. The totals were:

blows with a cane	911,527
blows with a rod	124,010
blows with a ruler	20,989

blows with the hand	136,715
blows with a book	22,763
blows over the mouth	10,235
blows over the ears	7,905
raps on the head	1,115,800

The same man had punished pupils 777 times by making them kneel on peas and 613 times on small triangles of wood. On 3001 occasions he had made a pupil put on a fool's cap, and in addition he had invented a few tortures of his own. Even his scoldings were carefully recorded in a list of some 3000 abusive words or phrases that he used for minor offenses. Nothing shows the condition of elementary teaching any more clearly than the fact that such a man could hold a job for fifty-one years. Altogether, the picture of schools during the seventeenth and eighteenth centuries indicates that their reputation as being poor places for children is completely justified.

—Luella Cole, *A History of Education* (1950), 447.
Figures are from H. Barnard, ed., *Memoirs of Eminent Teachers and Educators in Germany* (1863), 509.

597. This school was on the top of a hill so that God could see everything that went on. It looked like a cross between a prison and a church and it was. . . .

One night . . . a boy descended two flights of stairs, traversed the crossbar of the "H," and climbed two flights of stairs on the other wing to keep a tryst [with another schoolboy]. . . .

His sin was the occasion of the only public beating that I ever witnessed. The entire school was assembled in the big hall and seated on benches on either side of the room. In the open space in the middle the modern Romeo bent over and the headmaster ran down the room to administer the blows. . . . What made this exhibition so disgusting was not the pain inflicted. Today a go-ahead schoolmaster would say, "This delights me more than it delights you." In many parts of London, such goings-on are just another way of making a party go with a swing. What was almost insufferable was that a simple form of self-gratification should be put forward as a moral duty. Before that day I had disliked the head; afterward I hated him.

—Quentin Crisp, *The Naked Civil Servant* (1968), 11, 12.

598. A strong Scots background, and thirty years at Carlyle Rural, had made her an expert disciplinarian. A short, fat implacable woman, she ruled her three groups—for Carlyle Rural had only two rooms and she took the most advanced classes—not with a rod of iron, but with the leather strap that was issued by the school board as the ultimate instrument of justice. She did not use if often; she had only to take it from a drawer and lay it across her desk to quell any ordinary disobedience. When she did use it, she displayed a strength that even the biggest, most loutish boy dreaded, for not only did she flail his hands until they swelled to red, aching paws, but she tongue-lashed him with a virtuosity that threw her classes into an ecstasy of silent delight.

—Robertson Davies, *What's Bred in the Bone* (1985), 78.

599. [The school head,] Mr. Creakle came to where I sat, and told me that if I were famous for biting, he was famous for biting, too. He then showed me the cane, and asked me what I thought of *that*, for a tooth? Was it a sharp tooth, hey? Was it a double tooth, hey? Had it a deep prong, hey? Did it bite, hey? Did it bite? At every question he gave me a fleshly cut with it that made me writhe....

A large majority of the boys (especially the smaller ones) were visited with similar instances of notice, as Mr. Creakle made the round of the schoolroom. Half the establishment was writhing and crying before the day's work began, and how much of it had writhed and cried before the day's work was over I am really afraid to recollect, lest I should seem to exaggerate.

I should think there never can have been a man who enjoyed his profession more than Mr. Creakle did. He had a delight in cutting at the boys, which was like the satisfaction of a craving appetite. I am confident that he couldn't resist a chubby boy, especially; that there was a fascination in such a subject, which made him restless in his mind, until he scored and marked him for the day. I was chubby myself, and ought to know. I am sure when I think of the fellow now, my blood rises hotly, because I know him to have been an incapable brute, who had no more right to be possessed of the great trust he held, than to be Lord High Admiral, or Commander-in-Chief—in either of which capacities it is probable that he would have done infinitely less mischief.

—Charles Dickens, *David Copperfield* (1849–50), 89.

600. "Let any boy speak a word without leave," said Mr. Squeers mildly, "and I'll take the skin off his back."

—Charles Dickens,
Nicholas Nickleby (1838–39), viii. *See* Twain, **#614.**

601. The rod of correction is a rule of God necessary sometimes to be used upon children. The schoolmaster shall have full power to punish all or any of his scholars, no matter who they are. No parent or other person living in the place shall go about to hinder the master in this. But if any parent or other shall think there is just cause for complaint against the master for too much severity, they shall have liberty to tell him so in friendly and loving way.

—Dorchester, Massachusetts,
school rules, 1645, in Clifton Johnson,
Old-time Schools and School-books (1904), 11.

602. "I dhropped in on Cassidy's daughter, Mary Ellen, an' see her kindygatnin'. Th' childher was settin' ar-round on th' flure an' some was moldin' dachshunds out iv mud an' wipin' their hands on their hair, an' some was carvin' figures iv a goat out iv paste-board an' some was singin' an' some was sleepin' an' a few was dancin' an' wan la-ad was pullin' another la-ad's hair. 'Why don't ye take th' shovel to that little barbaryan, Mary Ellen?' says I. 'We don't belive in corporeal punishment,' says she. 'School shud be made pleasant f'r the childher,' she says. 'Th' child who's hair is bein' pulled is larnin' patience,' she says, 'an' th' child that's pullin' th' hair is discoverin' th' futility iv human indeavor,' says she. . . . 'Mary Ellen,' says I, 'Don't ye niver feel like bastin' th' seeraphims?' 'Th' teachin's iv Freebull and Pitzotly is conthrary to that,' she says. 'But I'm goin' to be marrid an' lave th' school on Choosdah, th' twinty-sicond iv Janooary,' she says, 'an' on Mondah, th' twinty-first, I'm goin' to ask a few iv th' little darlin's to th' house an,' she says, 'stew thim over a slow fire,' she says."

—Finley Peter Dunne, *Mr. Dooley's Philosophy:* "What I Larned in Colledge" (1900).

603. Corporal punishment, often in the presence of the student body, continued at Harvard until the middle of the eighteenth century, though to the receiver it may have been mitigated by the thought that its infliction had been preceded and followed by prayers from the president.

—Christian Gauss,
"How Good Were the Good Old Times?"
in A.C. Spectorsky, ed., *The College Years* (1958).

604. [In 1781, when Edward John Trelawny was nine years old, his father,] Charles Trelawny halted in front of a "walled and dreary buliding" and knocked "at a prison-looking gate."

The place was a school, and the headmaster, a Mr. Sayer, was a dapper little man with a precise and pedantic manner that was "most fearful to a boy." Charles immediately enrolled his sons as boarding students, and particularly warned Sayer about the younger [Edward], saying he "would come to the gallows if the devil were not scourged out of him." . . . .

Edward John lived through a nightmare at the school, although it must be admitted that Mr. Sayer's treatment of his pupils was no worse than that found at other, similar institutions for the sons of the gentry. . . . [Edward's] own description of his situation is graphic:

> I was flogged seldom more than once a day, or caned more than once an hour. I became callous and was considered by the master the most obdurate and violent rascal that had ever come into his hands. Every kind and gentle feeling of my naturally affectionate nature seemed subdued by this savage treatment, and I became sullen and vindictive. I vented my rage on the boys and, as I grew bodily in strength, I gained respect by fear, and became the ringleader in all sports and mischief. I thus learned my first lesson as to the necessity of depending on myself, and the spirit in me was gaining strength, in spite of every effort to destroy it, like a young pine flourishing in the cleft of a bed of granite.

—Noel B. Gerson, *Trelawny's World: A Biography of Edward John Trelawny* (1977), 8.

605. I had once been whipped in school [in France]. The school was nothing more than a room in our house. For the master, on my account alone, had disregarded the interests of others whom he had at times accepted. My mother, increasing his fee and bestowing this honor, had wisely required him to do so. So, when my studies were over at a certain hour in the evening, I had gone over to my mother's lap, having been punished severely and undeservedly. When she started to ask me, as she invariably did, whether I had been whipped that day, I said definitely, "No!" in order not to inform on my master. Willy-nilly, she stripped off my tunic, that they call an undergarment or rather shirt, and observed the livid ribs on my back from the lashes of the osier twigs and also my bruised skin. With all her heart she bemoaned the punishment inflicted on my tender years cruelly and unreasonably, and in frenzied agitation, her eyes filled with sorrow, she said: "You will never henceforth become a cleric nor will you pay the penalty for another just to learn your letters."

—Guibert of Nogent (1053–1124), *De Vita Sua*, tr. Harry Ezekiel Wedeck. Nonetheless, he became a Benedictine theologian and historian.

606. Fone sayes, those mighty whiskers he do's weare,
Are twigs of Birch, and willow, growing there:
If so, we'll think too, (when he do's condemne
Boyes to the lash) that he do's whip with them.

—Robert Herrick, "Upon Fone a School-master. Epig," *Hesperides* (1648).

607. From some boyish, but mischievous pranks of mine, this reverend gentleman, Mr. Robert Lloyd, though himself far from a saint, took a strong and rooted dislike of me, which he had many opportunities of betraying; and in consequence of his prejudice he let no occasion pass of what is there termed "showing me up," that is, conducting me to his father the doctor, to procure me a flogging, the ushers having no authority to use the birch; that tremendous instrument of schoolboys, the rod, being within the peculiar province of the two Masters only. The culprit thus "shown up" is never heard in the way of defence, the charge, as exhibited by the usher, is conclusive, and the posteriors of the unhappy delinquent undergo a castigation. This is a ceremony the frequency of its occurrence in no degree reconciled me to; and, as I imagined I was often unjustly punished, I took a violent dislike to the school, and everything appertaining to it. . . .

The disgust at the harsh treatment I met with produced an indifference as to all school exercises. I falsely argued that, as I was to be flogged, it had better be for some offence, than without cause; instead, therefore, of preparing my theme, verses, or constructing Virgil, I loitered away my time in Tothil Fields, and St. James's Park, or if I could muster cash, hired a boat to cruise about Chelsea Reach.

—William Hickey, *The Prodigal Rake: Memoirs of William Hickey*, ed. Peter Quennell (1962), 28.

608. The master [at Christ Hospital (School), London] was in the habit of "spiting" C----; that is to say, of taking every opportunity to be severe with him, nobody knew why. One day he comes into the school, and finds him placed in the middle of it with three other boys. He was not in one of his worst humours, and did not seem inclined to punish them, till he saw his antagonist. "Oh, oh, sir," said he: "what! you among them, are you?" and gave him an exclusive thump on the face. He then turned to one of the Grecians [the three head boys], and said, "I have not time to flog all those boys; make them draw lots, and I'll punish one." The lots were drawn, and C----'s was favorable. "Oh, oh! returned the master, when he saw them, "you have escaped have you, sir?" and pulling out his watch, and turning again to the Grecian, observed, that he found he *had* time to punish the whole three; "and, sir," added he to C----, with another slap, "I'll begin with *you*." He then took the boy into the library and flogged him; and, on issuing forth again, had the face to say, with an air of indifference, "I have not time, after all, to punish these two other boys; let them take care how they provoke me another time."

—Leigh Hunt, *The Autobiography of Leigh Hunt* (1859), 77.

609. In his gentler moods, when the *rabidus furor* was assuaged, he had resort to an ingenious method, peculiar, of what I have heard, to himself, of whipping the boy, and reading the Debates, at the same time; a paragraph and a lash between; which . . . was not calculated to impress the patient with a veneration for the diffuser graces of rhetoric.

—Charles Lamb: *The Essays of Elia:*
"Christ's Hospital [School] Five-and-Thirty Years Ago" (1823).

610. I chastise thee, not because I hate thee, but because I love thee.

—Latin saying of medieval schoolmasters flogging their pupils.

611. Many explorers have commented on the gentleness of various primitive peoples with their children. It is unusual to find a primitive society in which an adult, after the deed has been done and tempers have cooled down, will deliberately get out a whip or a switch and actually beat a child. Punishment of this kind is one of the unfortunate concomitants of great civilizations, as are the rack and the screw, the dungeon, the gallows and the electric chair. But in occasional outbursts of anger, all the primitive peoples with whom I have ever worked will express their annoyance physically by slapping a child, dragging it suddenly by one arm, even occasionally picking up a stick to reinforce the lesson. Shaking, cuffing, dragging—even, on occasion, throwing a bit of stinging pepper into the child's eyes—all these are expressions of momentary irritation and anger. What one seldom finds in a primitive society is the systematic moralistic philosophy of "spare the rod and spoil the child" or "never strike the child in anger." . . .

It is necessary to distinguish between deliberate beating—a moralistic, cold-blooded and usually cruel and sadistic proceeding—and a good hearty shake, slap or cuff that is not heavy enough to damage the child and yet is convincing enough to be remembered. Failure to make this distinction is responsible for much of the confusion about discipline in the United States. Deliberate corporal punishment, administered self-righteously, tends to beget not a healthy avoidance of the next smack but a deep and often murderous hatred of all authority—and often produces a child who in later life must be "disciplined" by that odious invention, legal corporal punishment.

—*Margaret Mead: Some Personal Views,* ed. Rhoda Metraux
(1979), 122. *See* Erikson, **#68,** under "Child Rearing."

612. Professor Knapp . . . was a virtuoso with the rattan, and chose his tool for a given caning with apparent care. He had an arsenal as large as a golfer's bag of clubs, and carried it with him from class to class. But the routine of the operation was always the same, and every boy knew it as familiarly as he knew the rules of run-a-mile or catty. The condemned would be beckoned politely to the place of execution beside the teacher's desk, and at the word *Eins* from the professor he would hold up his hands. At *Zwei* he would lower them until they stuck out straight from his shoulders, and at *Drei* he would bend over until his finger-tips touched his ankles. The punitive swooshes *a posteriori* would follow – sometimes two, three or even four, but more often only one. As I have said, it was etiquette for the condemned to make an outcry. He was allowed and even expected to massage his *gluteus maximus* violently as he pranced back to his bench. This always led the professor to remark sagely: "You can't rub it out." Criminal girls were punished more gently, with smacks from a ruler on the open palm. They consoled themselves by hugging the insulted hand under the opposite arm.

– H.L. Mencken, *Happy Days: 1880–1892:* "The Caves of Learning" (1940), 29.

613. [At St. George's School, c. 1884] The hapless schoolboy who had committed an insignificant crime was hauled off to the headmaster's study where a wooden box covered with rough black cloth served as the execution block. Two senior boys forced the victim down and pulled off his trousers. The headmaster, fortified with a glass of Marsala, then attacked the boy's bare buttocks with a birch rod, inflicting fifteen or twenty cuts, until the flesh was streaming with blood. Roger Fry . . . wrote:

> Generally of course the boys endured it with fortitude but sometimes there were scenes of screaming, howling and struggling which made me almost sick with disgust. . . . There was a wild red-haired Irish boy, . . . who whether deliberately or as a result of pain or whether he had diarrhoea, let fly. The irate clergyman instead of stopping at once simply went on with increased fury until the whole ceiling and walls of his study were spattered with filth. I suppose he was afterwards somewhat ashamed of this for he did not call in the servants to clean up but spent hours doing it himself with the assistance of a boy who was his special favorite.

– Robert Payne, *The Great Man: A Portrait of Winston Churchill* (1974), 57.

614. It used to take me all vacation to grow a new hide in place of the one they flogged off me during school term.

– Mark Twain, letter to the *Alta Californian,* May 28, 1867. *See* Dickens, **#600.**

615. Although school teaching was one of the few occupations open to women in the nineteenth century, I had but one woman teacher in the score of years that I spent in school. In the [one-room] Stony Creek [Michigan] school a man teacher was always employed on the grounds that it was necessary to have a teacher physically able to punish the large boys. Having seen no corporal punishment (Father never allowed even the animals to be whipped), many times I grew faint watching the teacher snatch a hulking farm boy by the coat collar, swing him out of his seat to his knees in the center of the room, and with a strong leather strap belabor him till he regained his feet, only to be thrown on his knees again and again.

The girls weren't flogged, but they were punished by being forced to extend a hand while a ferule was brought down upon it until they no longer drew the hand away.

—Bertha Van Hoosen, *Petticoat Surgeon* (1947), 33.

616. Either learn, or depart; a third course is open to you, and that is, submit to be flogged.

—Winchester College (England), motto of the schoolroom.

Punishment, Corporal (Con)

(*See also* Discipline; Corporal Punishment [Pro])

617. I experienced a great deal of physical punishment both at home and at school but never became resigned to it or regarded it quite as casually as did some of my contemporaries. In my case it was aggravated by the appalling fact that tears came easily to my eyes—not from the pain which I regarded as nothing—but from the embarrassment and indignity of the whole miserable proceedings. I have been involved in outbursts of violence in my own life but I have always regretted it afterwards. I have yet to see the occasion when physical punishment achieved a really worthwhile result even under the best of motivation. Maybe there are occasions when as a last resort it is better than nothing, but generally it indicates an inability to handle the problem by more constructive means.

—Sir Edmund Hillary, *Nothing Venture, Nothing Win* (1975), 20.

618. The public seems to cling to the despotism in the government of schools which has been discounted everywhere else. The husband can no longer chastise his wife nor the master his servant or apprentice. Even the degrading cruelties of the naval service have been arrested. Why the person

of the schoolboy should be less sacred in the eyes of the law than that of the apprentice or the sailor is not easily explained.

—Indiana Supreme Court, *Cooper v McJunkin*, 1853.

619. 47. The usual lazy and short way by chastisement and the rod, which is the only instrument of government that tutors generally know or even think of, is the most unfit of any to be used in education. . . .

49.2. This sort of correction naturally breeds an aversion to that which 'tis the tutor's business to create a liking to. How obvious is it to observe that children come to hate things which were at first acceptable to them, when they find themselves whipped, and chid, and teased about them? And it is not to be wondered at in them, when grown men would not be able to be reconciled to anything by such ways. . . .

50.3. Such a sort of slavish discipline makes a slavish temper. The child submits, and dissembles obedience, whilst the fear of the rod hangs over him; but when that is removed, and by being out of sight, he can promise himself impunity, he gives the greater scope to his natural inclination; which by way this way is not at all altered, but, on the contrary, heightened and increased in him; and after such restraint, breaks out usually with the more violence; or. . . .

51.4. If the severity carried to the highest pitch does prevail, and works a cure upon the present unruly distemper, it often brings in the room of it a worse and more dangerous disease, by breaking the mind; and then, in the place of a disorderly fellow, you have a low-spirited moping creature, who, however with his unnatural sobriety he may please silly people, who commend tame unactive children, because they make no noise, nor give them any trouble; yet at last, will probably prove as uncomfortable a thing to his friends, as he will be all his life an useless thing to himself and others. . . .

60. Frequent beating or chiding is therefore carefully to be avoided: because this sort of correction never produces any good, farther than it serves to raise shame and abhorrence of the miscarriage that brought it on them.

—John Locke, *Some Thoughts concerning Education* (1693).

620. I condemn all harsh measures in the bringing-up of a tender soul that is being trained for honour and freedom. There is something that savours of slavishness in severity and compulsion; and I hold that what cannot be done by reason, by wisdom and tact, can never be done by force. . . . I have never known any other effect of the rod but to render the soul more cowardly and more deceitfully obstinate.

—Michel de Montaigne, *Essays:*
"Of the Affection of Fathers for Their Children" (1580), II.viii.

621. I am by no means in favor of whipping boys, though I know it to be a general practice. In the first place, whipping is unseemly, and if you suppose the boys to be somewhat grown up, it is an affront in the highest degree. In the next place, if a boy's ability is so poor as to be proof against reproach he will, like a worthless slave, become insensible to blows. Lastly, if a teacher is assiduous and careful, there is no need to use force. I shall observe further that while a boy is under the rod he experiences pain and fear. The shame of this experience dejects and discourages many pupils, makes them shun being seen, and may even weary them of their lives.

—Quintilian, *Institutio Oratoria* (A.D. 95 or 96), I.iii.13.

Punishment, Corporal (Pro)

(*See also* Discipline; Punishment, Corporal [Con])

622. And if thy children be rebel, and will not them bow,
If any of them misdo, neither curse them nor blow,
But take a smart rod and beat them on a row
Till they cry mercy, and be of their guilt aknow.

—Anonymous, in Derek Brewer, *Chaucer in His Time* (1963), 119. [be of their guilt aknow=*acknowledge their guilt*].

623. For betere is child vnboren thenne vnbeten.

—Anonymous, *Proverbs of Alfred* (c. 1275).

624. When you are to correct any stubborne or unbroken boy, you [should] make sure with him to hold him fast.... To this end to appoint 3 or 4 of your Schollers, whom you know to be honest, and strong enough, or moe if neede be, to lay hands on him together, to hold him fast, over some fourme, so that he cannot stirre hand nor foot; or else if no other remedy will serve, to hold him to some post (which is farre the safest and free from inconvenience) so as he cannot any way hurt himselfe or others, be he never so peevish. Neither can he hope by any device or turning, or by his apparell, or any other meanes to escape....

To be very wary for smiting them over the backes, in any case, or in such sort as in any way to hurt or indanger them:—And withall, to avoid for these causes, all smiting them upon the head, with hand, rod, or ferula.... That the Master do not in any case abase himselfe to strive or struggle with any boy to wake him up; but to appoint other of the strongest to do it, where such need is and the rather for feare of hurting them in his anger, and for the evils which may come there of, of which some schoolmasters have lamented after.

That the Masters and Ushers also do by all means avoid furious anger, threatening, chafing, fretting, revilling: for these things will diminish authoritie and do much hurt, and much indanger many waies.

—John Brinsley,
Ludus Literarius, or the Grammar School (1622).

625. Discipline by force is not direct education; but it is, at times, and with a minority of children, a condition of education. Such discipline in school is precisely what the policeman and the jail are in the community. You must have your policeman and jailer to protect the community against the two per cent of its citizens who lack the normal domestic, economic, social, and civic interests in life. In the same way, there must be a policeman and jailer quality in every teacher; and figuratively speaking, there must be a billy, a pair of hand-cuffs, and a cell in every school. No school is any more safe without them, than a community. They are essential to the prosecution of its work; and they check bad habits, and induce good habits in the obstreperous individual.

Furthermore, this background is inexorable, impartial discipline must win on every issue it joins, and fight every battle, if need be, to the bitter end.

—William D. Hyde, *The Teacher's Philosophy* (1910), 10.

626. He who does not beat his child will later beat his own breast.

—Turkish proverb.

627. If it was like others, the Henrys [William and Patrick] learned little more at their "common English school" than how to read, write, "cyfer," and endure a deal of switching, paddling, and even flogging. Corporal punishment at the time was not merely incidental, but quite systematic, being highly regarded as the very essence of learning. Almost everybody agreed that "ye wretched boys"* had quite literally to have the hell beaten out of them if they were ever to come to any good.

*They were "young vipers!" hissed that great breather of hell fire, the Reverend Jonathan Edwards, a long-suffering schoolmaster and later a college president. "Yea!" he exclaimed, "infinitely more hateful than vipers to God."

—George F. Willison,
Patrick Henry and His World (1969), 20.

Punishment, Corporal (By Students)

628. The oppressions of these young brutes [senior boys who were appointed monitors] are heart-sickening to call to recollection. I have been called out of my bed, and *waked for the purpose,* in the coldest winter nights—and this not once, but night after night—in my shirt, to receive the discipline of a leathern thong, with eleven other sufferers, because it pleased my callous overseer.

—Charles Lamb, *The Essays of Elia:*
"Christ's Hospital [School] Five-and-Thirty Years Ago" (1823).

629. [At Eton, *circa* 1809] Barbarous customs reigned amongst the boys themselves. The little boys were the slaves or "fags" of the big boys. The fag made his master's bed, fetched from the pump outside and carried up his water in the mornings, brushed his clothes and cleaned his shoes. Disobedience was punished by torments to fit the crime. A boy writing home, not to complain, but to describe his life, says: "Rolls, whose fag I am, put on spurs to force me to jump a ditch which was too wide for me. Each time I funked it he dug them into me, and of course my legs are bleeding, my "Greek Poets" reduced to pulp, and my new clothes torn to tatters."

—André Maurois, *Ariel: The Life of Shelley* (1924), 8.
See Amis, **#706,** under "School British";
and Waugh, **#760,** under "School Rules."

630. 'Justice' in [Westminster] College [c. 1893] was administered by monitors to Juniors and Second Elections under a show of legality. The slamming of Seniors' Room door was the signal for a 'case,' or, as one might call it, a session. The captain and the three other monitors sat in council within; the Under Elections, all potential victims, clustered together without. The chosen victim was summoned. He entered nervously, shuffled along the wall, step by step, until he faced his judges. The dialogue might go like this:

Captain: You were ragging up-Fields to-day.

Junior (swallowing): No, I wasn't.

Captain (negligently): Have you any other excuse to make?

Junior (at a loss): No.

Captain (formally and without interest): Do you wish to appeal to the Headmaster?

Junior (wishing to): No.

The Captain hands the cane to the monitor whose turn it is. The monitor takes off his coat, and judging his distance points to the place of execution. The Junior bends down and gets four. He shuffles out with an air of indifference, hurries into 'prayer room' (the Under Elections' common-room), and rushes around in circles rubbing himself. The 'offence' and the names of victim and executioner are entered by the Captain in the Black Book.

—A.A. Milne, *Autobiography* (1939), 121.

631. Torture in a public school is as much licensed as the knout in Russia.

—William Makepeace Thackeray, *Vanity Fair* (1847), 31.

Reader

(*See also* Book; Reading)

632. A bookworm of Kennebunk, Me.,
Found pleasure in reading Monte.,
He also liked Poe,
And Daniel Defoe,
But the telephone book caused him pe.

—Anonymous.

633. At a famous meeting of the Free Religious Association of America held in Boston during the last half of the nineteenth century, a somewhat zealous minister quoted certain passages from the Christian Gospels, adding that these could not be matched in the sacred books of any other religion. At this point Ralph Waldo Emerson, who was in the audience, rose and said quietly, "The gentleman's remark proves only how narrowly he has read."

—Robert O. Ballou, ed.,
The Viking Portable Library World Bible (1944), 13.

634. The vast difference in attention strata appealed to by a visual dramatization on television and the words on a page is well known to us all. How absurd to think them competitive. The poet or storyteller who feels he is competing with a superb double play in the World Series is a lost man. One would not want as a reader a man who did not appreciate the finesse of a double play.

—John Cheever, "In Praise
of Readers," *Parade* Magazine, Dec. 28, 1980.

635. There are four kinds of readers. The first is like an hourglass; and their reading being as sand, it runs out, and leaves not a vestige behind.

A second is like the sponge, which imbibes everything, and returns it in nearly the same state, only a little dirtier.

A third is like a jelly bag, allowing all that is pure to pass away, and retaining only the refuse and dregs.

And the fourth is like the slaves in the diamond mines of Golanda, who, casting aside all that is worthless, retain only pure gems.

—Samuel Taylor Coleridge,
Notebooks (1794–1834). Compare *Mishnah*, **#641.**

636. The great books of the world will not unbosom themselves to slovenly, incurious, inartistic readers. The page of a great book does not differ mechanically from the page of a worthless book—it is merely a sheet of paper with some black odd-looking specks on it. It remains that, or it is transformed into wisdom, beauty, joy. But the transformation depends finally upon the reader—upon the reader's ability *to read.*

—Lee Wilson Dodd,
"On Learning to Read," *Atlantic Monthly*, July 1932.

637. 'Tis the good reader that makes the good book; a good book cannot be read amiss, in every book he finds passages which seem confidences or asides hidden from all else and unmistakably meant for his ear.

—Ralph Waldo Emerson, *Society and Solitude:* "Success" (1870).

638. Thou say'st my lines are hard;
And I the truth will tell;
They are both hard, and marr'd,
If thou not read'st them well.

—Robert Herrick, "To My Ill Reader," *Hesperides* (1648).

639. Stupid men read a book and do not understand it; second-rate minds think that they understand it perfectly; master spirits sometimes do not understand it entirely: that appears to them obscure which is obscure, as that seems clear which is clear. Witlings try to look upon that as obscure which is not so, and not to understand what is perfectly intelligible.

—Jean de La Bruyère, *Les Caractères* (1688), i.

640. To read my Booke the Virgin shie
May blush, (while Brutus standeth by:)

But when he's gone, read through what's writ,
And never staine a cheeke for it.

—Martial, epigram (A.D. 93),
tr. Robert Herrick as "Another," *Hesperides* (1648).

641. There are two kinds of readers of serious books. The first is like unto a man who squeezes grapes with his finger tips, extracting from them mere watery juice. When the stuff fails to ferment, he forthwith blames the grapes. The second is like unto a man who crushes grapes thoroughly, extracting from them all their richness. Such a one is never moved to complain, for the stuff he lays down will readily ferment, and he is left with the most excellent wine.

—*Mishnah: Ribesh Tov* (c. A.D. 200). *Compare* Coleridge, **#635.**

642. How well he's read, to reason against reading!

—William Shakespeare, *Love's Labour's Lost* (1594), I.i.94.

643. *Apemantus.* Canst not read?
Page. No.
Apemantus. There will little learning die, then, that day thou art hanged.

—William Shakespeare, *Timon of Athens* (1607–08), II.ii.84.

644. These are the Men, who pretend to understand a Book, by scouting thro' the *Index* as if a Traveller should go about to describe a *Palace,* when he had seen nothing but the *Privy.*

—Jonathan Swift,
"A Discourse Concerning the Mechanical
Operation of the Spirit," in Ricardo Quintana, ed.,
Gulliver's Travels and Other Writings (1958), 406.
See Swift, **#658,** under "Reading."

645. I have sometimes dreamt . . . that when the Day of Judgment dawns and the great conquerors and lawyers and statesmen come to receive their rewards—their crowns, their laurels, their names carved indelibly upon imperishable marble—the Almighty will turn to Peter and say, not without a certain envy when he sees us coming with our books under our arms, "Look, these need no reward. We have nothing to give them here. They have loved reading."

—Virginia Woolf, *The Second Common Reader:*
"How Should One Read a Book?" (1932), 245.

Reading

(*See also* Book; Reader)

646. Of considerable interest is the origin of the word *reading*, which is derived from the Anglo-Saxon *roed*, which meant "counsel," and *roedan*, which meant "to counsel, to advise."

—Fay Adams, Lillian Gray
and Dora Reese, *Teaching Children to Read* (1949), 91.

647. If we consider men and women generally, and apart from their professions and occupations, there is only one situation I can think of in which they almost pull themselves by their bootstraps, making an effort to read better than they usually do. When they are in love and are reading a love letter, they read for all they are worth. They read every word three ways; they read between the lines and in the margins; they read the whole in terms of the parts, and each part in terms of the whole; they grow sensitive to context and ambiguity, to insinuation and implication; they perceive the color of words, the odor of phrases, and the weight of sentences. They may even take the punctuation into account. Then, as never before or after, they read.

—Mortimer J. Adler, *How to Read a Book* (1940), i.4.

648. No, I only read for pleasure or profit.

—Winston Churchill,
reply when asked by an author whether Churchill had read
his latest book, in Bill Adler, *The Churchill Wit* (1965), 41.

649. Read, read, Sirrah, and refine your Appetite; learn to live upon Instruction; feast your Mind, and mortifie your Flesh; Read, and take up Nourishment in at your Eyes; shut up your Mouth, and chew the Cud of Understanding. So Epictetus advises.

—William Congreve, *Love for Love* (1695), I.i.12.

650. He tears into a book for a sentence as a woodpecker grubs into a tree for a worm.

—Ralph Waldo Emerson, *Journals*,
1863. *See* Churchill, **#784**, under "Speech."

651. The privy [of the village school] was my seat of learning. There I could stay for long sessions of undisturbed reading, and escape into fantasy.

—Winifred Foley, *As the Twig Is Bent* (1978), 52.

652. A great obstacle to good [women's] education is the inordinate passion prevalent for novels, and the time lost in that reading which should be instructively employed. When this poison infects the mind, it destroys its tone and revolts against wholesome reading. Reason and fact, plain and unadorned, are rejected. Nothing can engage attention unless dressed in all the figments of fancy, and nothing so bedecked comes amiss. The result is a bloated imagination, sickly judgment, and disgust towards all the real business of life.

—Thomas Jefferson, letter to Nathaniel Burwell,
Mar. 14, 1818, in Adrienne Koch and William Peden, eds.,
The Life and Selected Writings
of Thomas Jefferson (1944), 688.

653. I would put a child into a library (where no unfit books are) and let him read at his choice. A child should not be discouraged from reading anything that he takes a liking to, from a notion that it is above his reach. If that be the case, the child will soon find it out and desist; if not, he of course gains the instruction; which is so much the more likely to come, from the inclination with which he takes up the study.

—Samuel Johnson, in James Boswell,
Life of Samuel Johnson, 1780 (1791), xlvii.

654. Reading was the primal member of the traditional "three R's" of learning—Reading, 'Riting, 'Rithmetic. To be able to read the Bible was sufficient motivation for parents and pupils to support a school. A minimum social literacy test in writing was the ability to "sign" one's name. But the canons for reading were somewhat more extensive.

"Reading" then meant to read aloud to an audience—even an imagined one. The bases for judging a student's ability in the art were clean, clear enunciation and pronunciation, a sense for the rise and fall of the dramatic cadence of a sentence, and all the many techniques of what we now call public speaking. Reading in unison (so-called)—the whole class or even the entire school more or less in harmony and time (but in every pitch)—

served to "develop" the aural senses; it certainly materially helped the poor reader to "learn" the selection.

—W.W. Livengood, ed., *Americana as Taught to the Tune of a Hickory Stick* (1954), 1.

655. I see no point in reading.

—Louis XIV, in Louis, Duc de Saint-Simon (1675–1755), *Mémoires.*

656. Have you ever rightly considered what the mere ability to read means? That it is the key which admits us to the whole world of thought and fancy and imagination? to the company of saint and sage, of the wisest and the wittiest at their wisest and wittiest moment? That it enables us to see with the keenest eyes, hear with the finest ears, and listen to the sweetest voices of all time? More than that, it annihilates time and space for us.

—James Russell Lowell, *Democracy and Other Addresses:* "Books and Libraries" (1887).

657. [At Carclaze Elementary School in the early 1900s] There was a lot of Silent Reading, it was called, during which our harassed teachers with forty or fifty children on their hands would get on with their mark-books or attendance registers, while we read more or less silently. How well I remember those somnolent afternoons: the hard benches without any backs, the difficulty of finding a comfortable posture, and at length finding one, propping your head up with elbows on the desk, hand over your ears so as not to be interrupted in your self-regarding pleasure; occasionally looking up in a dream, to hear the rustling of leaves being turned, boots scraping the floor, the sparrows chittering or saying their rich 'gulge-gulge' in the eaves. Yes, that is the sound which I associate always with Silent Reading at the elementary school—an automatic mnemonic: if I hear it to-day, my mind goes back thirty years to myself as a child with those other children, when life and hope were new, when there never seemed any end to one's vitality or any diminution of the spirits, when everything came fresh and full of savour to the eager appetite, when one did not know what life had in store for one, and the experience of the moment was its own satisfaction.

—A.L. Rowse, *A Cornish Childhood* (1942), 114.

658. We of this age have discovered a shorter, and a more prudent method to become scholars and wits, without the fatigue of reading or of thinking. The most accomplished way of using books at present, is two-fold: either,

first, to serve them as some men do lords, learn their titles exactly, and then brag of their acquaintance. Or, secondly, which is indeed the choicer, the profounder, the politer method, to get a thorough insight into the index, by which the whole book is governed and turned, like fishes by the tail. . . . Thus men catch knowledge, by throwing their wit on the posteriors of a book, as boys do sparrows with flinging salt upon their tails.

—Jonathan Swift, *A Tale of a Tub* (1704), vii. *See* Swift, **#644**, under "Reader."

659. My attention span is not what it was, since the thoughts of middle age are short thoughts. One grows dreamy, reading, the eye has a tendency to slip from the relentless line of text to the cool white or the margin, and there bathe indefinitely.

—Gore Vidal, *Two Sisters* (1970).

Report, School

660. To be sure, not all its parts fulfill my wishes and expectations, but with Albert I got used a long time ago to finding not-so-good grades along with very good ones.

—Hermann Einstein, letter to Jost Winteler, head of his son Albert's public school, returning Albert's report card, *Sarasota Herald-Tribune*, May 3, 1987.

661. Pushkin's supreme and ultimate ambition is to excel in the field of poetry; but it seems unlikely that this ambition will ever be fulfilled, for he has an aversion to serious study and his intelligence, being neither profound nor penetrating, is superficial and, one might say, French. And this is the most indulgent judgment that can be passed upon him. His heart is cold and empty. There is neither love nor religious conviction in him. Never, it may well be, was a young man's heart as devoid of feeling as his. The tender sentiments characteristic of adolescence are cheapened and debased in his imagination by his reading of erotic works of French literature—which he knew almost by heart when he first entered the school, as though they were the proper content of a primary education.

—Report on Alexander Pushkin, age 16, by Headmaster Egor Engelhardt, March 22, 1816, in Henri Troyat, *Pushkin* (1970), 49.

662. Moses is a Learning the Mat[hemat]ecks at Mr. Mallcoms whoe tells me he will Goe thro' it with abundance of Ease, and be perfect in a Very

Little time[.] Phila Learns french Spanish hebrew and writting in the morning and in the Afternoon She goers at Mrs. Brownells[.] She makes a Quick advance in whatever She Learns[.] Mr. Lopas Tells me he is Surprised at her advancement in ye Spanish, I intend to Send for Some patterons for her to work opon next Summer.

—Abigail Franks, letter to Naphtali Franks, Oct. 7, 1733, in Leo Hershkowitz and Isadore S. Meyer, eds., *The Letters of the Franks Family: (1733–1748)* (1968), 12.

663. Dear Sir:

The Faculty last evening voted "that Lincoln, Junior, be publicly admonished for smoking in Harvard Square after being privately admonished for the same offence." The word "publicly" simply makes it my duty to inform you of the admonition, and I trust, Sir, that you will impress upon him the necessity not only of attention to matters of decorum, but of giving heed to the private admonitions of his instructors.

—Thomas Hill, letter to President Lincoln from the president of Harvard, Dec. 9, 1862.

664. Boston, Sept 29th 1851

To

E.S. Dixwell Esq.

Dear Sir,

O.W. Holmes, jr., the bearer, whom . . . I take delight in calling my young friend, has been for four years under my charge as a pupil. He has been uniformly docile, thoughtful, amiable and affectionate. Young as he is, his habits of application are confirmed, while his proficiency in all the English branches, and his love of study are remarkable for his age.

Yours respectfully,

T.R. Sullivan

—Letter of introduction given to ten-year-old Holmes to be delivered to the headmaster of the Private Latin School, in Mark DeWolfe Howe, *Justice Oliver Wendell Holmes* (1957), I.5.

665. Respectable but desultory in habits of reading—& not sufficiently attentive to the rules of the College.

Respectable, but not uniformly regular or so satisfactory as might be expected.

Improved in diligence & attention but still deficient in both. In part, concerning his studies good; in other parts irregular. Amiable & respectable but far from regular.

—Reports on Matthew Arnold from Dr. Richard Jenkyns, Master of Balliol College, in Park Honan, *Matthew Arnold: A Life* (1981), 52.

666. The best time to see Protestantism in full flower is not in Church but on report-card day in a Wasp home. When Gail Parent's hero David Meyer brought home all A's, he was praised as "a regular Einstein." When the Wasp child brings home all A's, he is paid off in cold cash, so much for each A. The Jewish parent cares about what his child has actually learned. The Wasp parent is concerned with how hard his child worked. Therefore, report-card day is really payday.

Comparing our loot was standard practice for my classmates and me on day-after-report-card day. I got a dollar for every B and three dollars for every A, and considered myself gainfully employed; school was my "job".

Praise was something else. My parents said, 'That's nice," and Granny said, "A studious woman and a crowing hen always come to a tragic end." Nobody ever spent the proverbial "week on the telephone" bragging about me, and I was never nagged about my grades unless you want to count my mother's admonition the day I entered kindergarten: "I don't care if you're not the smartest one in the class as long as you're not the dumbest."

—Florence King, *Wasp, Where Is Thy Sting?:* "Anti-Intellectualism" (1977), 117. *Compare* Levenson, **#667.**

667. A "B" in conduct was the equivalent of a scarlet letter. It meant I had offended God, man, and country. I was guilty of high treason. Mama would wring her hands in grief: "What have we come to? Look at me, bum, son of Cain, thug. Better to look at me than at a judge." Brother Joe joined in, "Whatsamatta? You a wise guy or something?" And Brother Jack, "Making trouble for the teacher? Papa works all day in the shop so you can be a hoodlum or something?" And Mike: "Swear on your pinkie you'll never be bad again."

—Sam Levenson, *Everything But Money* (1949), 62. *Compare* King, **#666.**

668. I am greatly pleased with your rational and parental affection for your Son's welfare, not only because such an affection is amiable in itself, but because from this I am persuaded that you will be disposed to give your Son such Directions and Injunctions, both with Regard to his Behavior and his application to his studies, as may be of use to him and render him obedient to the Directions which he receives from us. . . .

Your Son's conduct and application to his studies is unexceptional, but as every young man is exposed to bad Example, your frequent writing him and putting him in Mind of his Duty and of your Affections and Expectations, will be one of the best means of preserving him from their Infection, and our Admonitions shall not be wanting.

—Letter from Dr. Charles Nesbit, president of Dickinson College, to the father of (later Chief Justice of U.S. Supreme Court) Roger Brooke Taney, Feb. 6, 1793, in Walker Lewis, *Without Fear or Favor*, (1965), 18. Taney's name is usually associated with the Dred Scott Case, 1857.

669. I do not hesitate to express my opinion that he possesses, along with other and natural endowments, a very uncommon share of genius. Gentle and cheerful in his intercourse with others, playful and ready in conversation, he is capable of acquirements and knowledge far beyond his years, while his reason is so clear and so jealous of error, that he will not rest satisfied without a most exact solution of whatever appears to him obscure.... You must not entrust your son with a full knowledge of his superiority over other boys. Let him discover this as he proceeds. The love of excellence is far beyond the love of excelling; and if he should once be bewitched into a mere ambition to surpass others I need not urge that the very quality of his knowledge would receive a stain of a more serious description still.

—Letter from James Tate II, headmaster of Richmond School, to the parents of Charles Dodgson (Lewis Carroll) at the end of Charles's first term at the school, 1845, in Anne Clark, *Lewis Carroll* (1979), 39.

Schedule, Daily Study

670. Before it is light I wake up, and sitting on the edge of my bed, I put on my shoes and leg-wraps because it is cold. Then I take a clean towel. A slave brings a jar of water which I pour over my hands and face and fill my mouth with it. After rubbing my teeth and gums I then spit it out and dry myself properly.

Taking off my nightshirt I put on my tunic and belt; I put oil on my hair, comb it, wrap a scarf around my neck and put on my white cloak. Followed by my school attendant and my nurse I go to say good morning to daddy and mummy and I kiss them both. I find my writing things and exercise book and give them to a slave. I set off to school followed by my school attendant. I say good morning to the school friends whom I meet and they say good morning to me. Arriving at the entrance I climb the stairs without making a noise. I leave my cloak in the hall and quietly comb my hair.

I go into the schoolroom and say 'Good morning master'. He kisses me and returns my greeting. The slave gives me my wax tablets, my writing things and ruler.

'Hello fellows, let me get to my place, squeeze up there. Come out! That's my place, I had it before you.' Then I sit down and begin to work. When I finish learning my lesson I ask the master to let me go home to lunch. As he lets me go I wish him well as he does me. Reaching home I change, take some white bread, olives, cheese, dried figs, and nuts and drink some cold water. After lunch I go back to school where the master is beginning to read. He says, 'Let's begin work.'

At the end of the afternoon I'm off to the Baths with some towels with my slave. I run to meet the people going to the Baths and we all say to each other 'Have a good bathe and a good supper.'

—School exercise describing a schoolboy's day
in Imperial Rome, in F.R. Cowell, *Everyday Life in Ancient Rome* (1961), 40. *See* Lucan, **#674,**
for a description of a schoolboy's day in ancient Athens.
See also Juvenal, **#804,** under "Student."

671. I will tell you my order of time for the day. . . . At 6 o'clock, we all rise. We breakfast at 7. Our study hours begin at 8. At 9 we all meet in Seminary Hall for devotions. At $10\frac{1}{4}$ I recite a review of Ancient History in connection with which we read Goldsmith and Grimshaw. At 11, I recite a lesson in Pope's Essay on Man, which is merely transposition. At 12 I practise calisthenics and at $12\frac{1}{4}$ read until dinner which is at $12\frac{1}{2}$, and after dinner, from $1\frac{1}{2}$ until 2, I sing in Seminary Hall. From $2\frac{1}{4}$ until $3\frac{3}{4}$ I practise upon the piano. At $3\frac{3}{4}$ I go to Sections, where we give in all our accounts for the day, including absence, tardiness, communications, breaking silent study hours, receiving company in our rooms, and ten thousand other things which I will not take time or place to mention. At $4\frac{1}{2}$ we go into Seminary Hall and receive advice from Miss Lyon in the form of a lecture. We have supper at 6, and silent study hours from then until the retiring bell, which rings at $8\frac{3}{4}$ but the tardy bell does not ring until $9\frac{3}{4}$, so that we don't often obey the first warning to retire.

—Emily Dickinson, describing her day's activities
at Mount Holyoke Seminary, in a letter to Abiah Root,
Nov. 6, 1847, in Robert N. Linscott, ed., *Selected Poems and Letters of Emily Dickinson* (1959), 220.

672. I Observe You Give me an Acc[oun]t how you Spend your time[.] I find noe fault in it but your not takeing more time for your Studying of books for If You dont doe it now you will hardly fallow it when you grow oulder and will have an Excuse that buissness is a hindrance[.] My advice Should be that two mornings in a Week Should be intirly Untill dinner time Dedicated to Some Usefull book besides and hour Every morning throughout the Year to the Same Purpose[.] pray Let me know wether you have forgot Versifying.

—Abigail Franks, letter to Naphtali Franks, June 9, 1734, in Leo Hershkowitz and Isadore S. Meyer, eds., *The Letters of the Franks Family: 1733–1748* (1968), 27.

673. With respect to the distribution of your time the following is what I should approve.

from 8. to 10 o'clock practise music.
from 10 to 1. dance one day and draw another.
from 1. to 2. draw on the day you dance, and write a letter the next day.
from 3. to 4. read French.
from 4. to 5. exercise yourself in music.
from 5. till bedtime read English, write, &c.

—Thomas Jefferson, letter to his eldest daughter Martha, age eleven, Nov. 28, 1783, in Sarah Randolph, *The Domestic Life of Thomas Jefferson* (1871).

674. [An Athenian schoolboy] gets up at dawn, washes the sleep from his eyes, and puts on his cloak. Then he goes out from his father's house, with his eyes fixed upon the ground, not looking at any one who meets him. Behind him follow attendants and paidagogoi, bearing in their hands the implements of virtue, writing-tablets or books containing the great deeds of old; if he is going to a musical school, the well-tuned lyre. When he has laboured diligently at his intellectual studies, and his mind is sated with the benefits of the school curriculum, he exercises his body in liberal pursuits, riding or hurling the javelin or spear. Then the wrestling-school with its sleek, oiled pupils, labours under the mid-day sun, and sweats in the regular athletic contests. Then a bath, not too prolonged; then a meal, not too large, in view of afternoon school. For the schoolmasters are waiting for him again, and the books which openly or by allegory teach him who was a great hero, who was a lover of justice and purity. With the contemplation of such virtues he waters the garden of his young soul. When evening sets a limit to his work, he pays the necessary tribute to his stomach and retires to rest, to sleep sweetly after his busy day.

—Lucan (A.D. 39–65), *Loves*, 44.
[paidagogoi=*slaves who accompanied a Greek boy wherever he went*]. *See* Cowell, **#670**, for a schoolboy's day in Imperial Rome. *See also* Juvenal, **#804**, under "Student."

675. Up at four o'clock for the morning office, followed by a lecture at six, when Mass was said. After Mass came breakfast, and then from eight until ten, the *grand classe* with a discussion for the ensuing hour. Eleven o'clock brought dinner, which was accompanied by readings from the Bible or the life of a saint and followed by prayers and college notices. At twelve the students were questioned about their morning's work, but from one to two was a rest period with a public reading. Here our sources skip an hour, and it may be that the students were left free until the afternoon class claimed them from three to five. Now vespers were said, and after vespers a discussion on the afternoon class took place. Between supper, with its attendant readings, and bed-time at eight in winter or nine in summer there was time for further interrogation and for chapel. On two days a week opportunity was given for recreation.

—T.H.L. Parker, *John Calvin* (1975), 8.
Description of a student's daily schedule
at Le Collège de Montaigu (France), c. 1521.

676. DAILY TIME—TABLE FOR MY DAUGHTER LAURE

Monday	*Notes*
Rise at 7	Clean teeth; wash hands and face; tidy bedroom.
7–8, cleanliness	
8–9, breakfast and recreation	
9–10, writing	
10–12, useful work	By useful work I mean dress-making, knitting, hemming, embroidery. Clothes for her dolls are recreation.

—Sophie Sallambier, rules for her daughter,
in André Maurois, *Prometheus* (1965), 21.
Laure Sallambier was Honoré Balzac's mother.

Scholar

(*See also* Educated Person; Professor)

677. We ordain that doctors, grammarians and other professors of letters, and the goods they possess in their cities, shall be exempt from taxation and shall have the honors due to their functions. We forbid their citation to court, or the infliction of any injury upon them. . . . We order that their goods and salaries be duly paid. And since like parents, masters and tutors they ought not be loaded with onerous offices, we permit them to fulfill public offices if they are willing, but we do not compel them to do so contrary to their inclination.

—Constantine the Great (288?–337),
Roman emperor. Edict issued in A.D. 321.

678. The studious class are their own victims; they are thin and pale, their feet are cold, their heads are hot, the night is without sleep, the day a fear of interruption,—pallor, squalor, hunger, and egotism.

—Ralph Waldo Emerson, *Representative Men:*
"Montaigne" (1850). *See* Erasmus, **#679**, and also Erasmus' description of philosophers under "Philosopher," **#522.**

679. Those few who write for a small learned public are pitiable to my mind rather than amusing, for they lead a life of torment. They must puzzle out every obscure classical text, even Persius and Laelius, and spend a lifetime adding glosses and emendations. Their days are wasted in detecting spuria, restoring readings, expounding, copying, correcting, never to their own satisfaction. The prize, if they get it, is no more than praise from one or two critics. Think of the price they pay—loss of the greatest of all blessings—sleep, with waste of money and sweat, and all manner of vexation. Think what the scholar endures in the way of ill-health, wasting away, eyestrain or even blindness, poverty, jealousy, abstinence from pleasure, premature old age, untimely death. What is the reward that these wiseacres think compensates them for all that? The approval of one or two other blind old bookworms!

—Desiderius Erasmus,
The Praise of Folly (1509), 76. tr. Harry Carter. *See* Emerson, **#678,** and also Erasmus under "Philosopher," **#522.**

680. He was a man of great learning, and of reputation for learning greater even than the learning itself.

—John Chipman Gray, referring to Justice
Joseph Story, *The Nature and Sources of the Law* (1909).

681. Deign on the passing World to turn thine Eyes
And pause awhile from Letters to be wise;

There mark what Ills the Scholar's Life assail,
Toil, Envy, Want, the Patron, and the Jail.

—Samuel Johnson, *The Vanity of Human Wishes* (1749), ln.157.

682. When you talk with famous scholars, the best thing is to pretend that occasionally you do not quite understand them. If you understand too little, you will be despised; if you understand too much, you will be disliked; if you just fail occasionally to understand them, you will suit each other very well.

—Lusin (Chou Shujen), in Lin Yutang, ed., *The Wisdom of China and India:* "The Epigrams of Lusin" (1942), 1087.

683. I hate and scorn that Kestrell kind
Of bastard scholars that subordinate
The precious choice of inducements of the mind
To wealth or worldly good.

—Henry Moore (1614–87), *Minor Poems:* "Cupid's Conflicts." [Kestrell=*kestrel, a small falcon, notable for hovering in the air with its head to the wind*].

684. As far as Pa was concerned, anybody who lifted a hand in anger or violence against a stranger was committing a shameful sin.... Even to fight back in self-defense was sinful....

Pa was a Talmudic scholar, he had been a teacher of religious law, and he was a *cohain*—a descendent of the original sect of high priests who administered the religious law and acted as chief judges in the ancient days of Israel....

"The religious man, Beryl, prizes learning above everything else," Pa often told me. "Let the atheists be the fighters, the *trumbeniks*, the murderers—*we* are the scholars."

—Barney Ross and Martin Abramson, *No Man Stands Alone* (1957), 21, 22.
Ross was later to become the welterweight boxing champion of the world. [trumbeniks=*bums, ne'er-do-wells, fakers*].

685. If a man and his father and his teacher were in captivity he takes precedence [in procuring ransom] over his teacher and his teacher takes precedence over his father, while his mother takes precedence over all of them. A scholar takes precedence over a king of Israel, for if a scholar dies there is none to replace him while if a king of Israel dies, all Israel are eligible for kingship.

—*Talmud: Horayoth* 13a (before A.D. 500).
See Maimonides, #959, under "Teacher, Praise for."

686. Having begun his apprenticeship with a teacher when he was twelve years of age, Svetaketu returned to his father when he was twenty-four, having then studied all the Vedas—conceited, considering himself well-read, and stern.

—*The Upanishads* (c. 800–600 B.C.),
in Robert O. Ballou, ed., *The Viking Portable Library World Bible* (1944), 54. [Veda ("Knowledge")=*the holy books of Hinduism*].

School

(*See also* School, Advertisements for; School, American; School, British; School, Establishment of; School, Remembrances of; Schoolhouse; Student, First Day of School)

687. Near me, under an awning, a boys' school is already at work. No history, geography, literature, religion, or rhetoric taught here! It's reading, writing, arithmetic all the year round, from dawn to noon, without a break; except for summer holidays, and one day off in eight. The schoolmaster, a ferocious wretch in a rickety chair, sits waggling his birch rod. Frightened pupils huddle together on benches. He distributes bead-frames among them, one to every group of three and, while I am waiting, sets them a problem. 'Add seventeen, two thousand, and one hundred and fifty-four. Hurry, villains! And no prompting!' Each boy moves beads along the wires for his third-share of the problem, and when everyone has finished, the tyrant checks results. There follow heavy blows of the rod, dealt out by groups—he never bothers to find out which boy has miscalculated.

—Robert Graves, *Collected Short Stories:*
"The Tenement: A Vision of Imperial Rome" (1968), 139.

688. *Class* has its origin in *classis*, the Latin word for fleet. At first the Romans applied the word to a group of ships only, but gradually they extended its application to a group of people, and this meaning has come down to our times. . . .

School, believe it or not, originally meant leisure, spare time, ease. It comes from the Greek *skhote,* which is also the root of scheme.

—Francis Griffith, *Phi Delta Kappan* Magazine.

689. A synagogue may be turned into a house of study, but a house of study may not be turned into a synagogue, because the holiness of a house of study is greater than that of a synagogue: objects may be raised to holier use but not lowered to less holy use.

—Maimonides, *Mishneh Torah (Repetition of the Law)* (1180), in Harry Gersh, *The Sacred Books of the Jews* (1968), 165.

690. We may picture to ourselves a group of lads seated on the floor [c.800], which was strewn with clean straw, their waxen tablets in their hands, and busily engaged in noting down the words read by the scholasticus from the manuscript volume. So rarely did the pupil in those days gain access to a book that "to read" (legere) became synonymous with "to teach." The scholars traced the words on their tablets, and afterwards, when their notes had been corrected by the master, transferred them to a little parchment volume, the treasured depository of nearly all the learning they managed to acquire in life.

—James B. Mullinger, *The Schools of Charles the Great* (Charlemagne) (1877), 131.

School, Advertisements for

691. AT THE HOUSE formerly Sir Charles Hobby's are taught Grammar, Writing after a free and easy manner, in all the hands usually practiced, Arithmetick Vulgar and Decimal in a concise and Practical Method, Merchants Accompts, Geometry, Algebra, Mensuration, Geography, Trigonometry, Astronomy, Navigation and other parts of Mathematicks, with the use of Globes and other Mathematical Instruments, by Samuel Grainger.

They whose Business won't permit 'em to attend the usual School Hours, shall be carefully attended and instructed in the Evenings.

—Advertisement in the *Boston Gazette,* Mar. 21–22, 1720, in Robert F. Seybolt, *The Private Schools of Colonial Boston* (1935), 15.

692. Any Gentlemen (Members of the Church of England) that are desirous of having their Sons Educated after the Method of Westminster

School, may be further inform'd by applying to J. Boydell. Conditions, To find their own Bed, Bedding, etc. and to bring as Entrance, one pair of Sheets, Six Towels, six napkins, one Silver Spoon value 10s. Sterling, one knife, Fork, and Pewter Porringer; which Entrance on their leaving the School is not to be returned. None to be admitted but such as can read and write; nor the Number of six to be exceeded.

—Boarding school advertisement which appeared in the *Boston Gazette*, Oct. 24-31, 1737, in George Francis Dow, *Every Day Life in Massachusetts Bay Colony* (1935), 124.

693. MISS BYERLEYS
BEG leave respectfully to acquaint their
Friends and Public, that their School
for YOUNG LADIES, in WARWICK, will be opened on
the 29th inst.

The charges for Board, exclusive of Washing, and for instruction in English Reading, Spelling, Grammar and Composition, in Geography, and the Use of the Globes, and in Ancient and Modern History, are, Thirty Guineas for Entrance.

The terms for Instruction in the French Language, Music, Drawing, Dancing, and Writing and Arithmetic, and for Washing, are inserted in a printed Paper, which will be delivered to any Person who will do Miss Byerleys the Honour to ask for it.

To Day-Scholars the annual Charges for the general course of Instruction, will be Eight Guineas, but they are not required to pay any Entrance, and they will be instructed in French, Drawing, Music, Dancing, Writing and Arithmetic, upon the same Terms which are proposed for Boarders.

—Miss Byerleys, prospectus in the Warwickshire (England) press, Jan. 15, 1810, in Winifred Gérin, *Elizabeth Gaskell* (1976), 24.

694. On the Plains of Hesitation bleach the bones of countless millions who, at the Dawn of Victory, sat down to wait—and waiting, died.

—George W. Cecil, advertisement titled "The Warning of the Desert," written for the International Correspondence Schools, *American Magazine*, March 1923.

695. PRUDENCE CRANDALL
PRINCIPAL OF THE CANTERBURY, (CONN.)
FEMALE BOARDING SCHOOL

RETURNS her most sincere thanks to those who have patronized her School, and would give information that on the first Monday of April next, her School will be opened for the reception of young Ladies and little Misses of color. The branches taught are as follows: – Reading, Writing, Arithmetic, English Grammar, Geography, History, Natural and Moral Philosophy, Chemistry, Astronomy, Drawing and Painting, Music on the Piano, together with the French language.

The terms, including board, washing, and tuition, are $25 per quarter, one half paid in advance.

Books and Stationery will be furnished on the most reasonable terms.

For information respecting the School, reference may be made of the following gentlemen, viz. – [followed by a long list of names].

– Prudence Crandall, advertisement in the *Liberator*, 1833. She was a white Quaker who opened a school expressly for Negro girls. For this she was arrested and convicted.
– Langston Hughes and Milton Meltzer, *A Pictorial History of the Negro in America* (1956), 109. *See* M. Douglass, **#493**, under "Negroes, Education of."

696. Mr. Ralph Nickleby took a newspaper from his pocket, and after unfolding it, and looking for a short time among the advertisements, read as follows:

"EDUCATION. – At Mr. Wackford Squeer's Academy, Dotheboys Hall, at the delightful village of Dotheboys, near Greta Bridge in Yorkshire, Youth are boarded, clothed, booked, furnished with pocket-money, provided with all necessaries, instructed in all languages, living and dead, mathematics, orthography, geometry, astronomy, trigonometry, the use of the globes, algebra, single stick (if required) writing, arithmetic, fortification, and every other branch of classical literature. Terms, twenty guineas per annum. No extras, no vacations, and diet unparalleled. Mr. Squeers is in town, and attends daily, from one till four, at the Saracen's Head, Snow Hill.

N.B. An able assistant wanted. Annual salary £5. A Master of Arts would be preferred."

– Charles Dickens, *Nicholas Nickleby* (1838–39), 29.

697. Mr. Pelham's Writing and Arithmetick School, near the Town House (during the Winter Season) will be open from Candle-Light 'till Nine in the Evening as usual, for the Benefit of those employed in Business all the Day; and at his Dwelling House near the Quaker's Meeting in Lindell's Row.

All persons may be supply'd with the best Virginia Tobacco cut, spun into the very best pigtail, and all other Sorts; also Snuff, at the cheapest Rates.

—Evening school advertisement,
Boston Evening Post, Sept. 12, 1748,
in Robert F. Seybolt, ed., *The Evening School in Colonial America* (1925).

698. In addition to the usual elements of education comprising English Reading, Writing, Grammar, and Composition, Arithmetic, Mathematics, Geography, Drawing, Ancient and Modern Languages, Mr M. will make it his endeavour, to impart to his Pupils, both Male and Female, the leading principles of Moral Science, Political Economy, History, Natural Science, Human Physiology, and the other Branches of Knowledge which must form an important part of every Enlightened System of Education.

—James A.H. Murray, announcement placed
in the *Advertiser* (Scotland), Sept. 12, 1857,
in K.M. Elisabeth Murray, *Caught in the Web of Words*
(1977), 30. He became the editor of the *New English Dictionary*
(later known as the *Oxford English Dictionary*).

699. Pencey Prep is this school that's in Agerstown, Pennsylvania. You probably heard of it. You've probably seen the ads, anyway. They advertise in about a thousand magazines, always showing some hot-shot guy on a horse jumping over a fence. Like as if all you ever did at Pencey was play polo all the time. I never even once saw a horse anywhere near the place. And underneath the guy on the horse's picture, it always says: "Since 1888 we have been molding boys into splendid, clear-thinking young men." Strictly for the birds. They don't do any damn more molding at Pencey than they do at any other school. And I didn't know anybody there that was splendid and clear-thinking at all. Maybe two guys. If that many. And they probably came to Pencey that way.

—J.D. Salinger, *The Catcher in the Rye* (1951), 4.

School, American

(*See also* College; Punishment, Corporal; School, Advertisements for; School, Remembrances of; Schoolhouse; Teacher, Remembrances of; Textbook)

700. Reliable clocks remained relatively expensive until the nineteenth century. As late as 1786 so few people in Salem, Massachusetts, owned clocks or watches that public notice of the time was given throughout the town at one in the afternoon. At that hour, it was proposed, school should start, which would prevent the children from going swimming when they were "too crammed with animal food."

—*The American Heritage History of Colonial Antiques* (1967), 283.

701. I was about six years old when I first went to school. My teacher was "Aunt Delight," a maiden lady of fifty, short and bent, of sallow complexion and solemn aspect. We were all seated upon benches made of slabs—boards having the exterior or rounded part of the log on one side. As they were useless for other purposes, they were converted into school benches, the rounded part down. They had each four supports, consisting of straddling wooden legs set into auger holes. The children were called up one by one to Aunt Delight, who sat on a low chair, and required each, as a preliminary, "to make his manners," which consisted of a small, sudden nod. She then placed the spelling-book before the pupil, and with a penknife pointed, one by one, to the letters of the alphabet, saying, "What's that?"

—Anonymous, description of an elementary school in the period following the Revolution, in Newton Edwards and Herman Richey, *The School in the American Social Order* (1947), 117.

702. [In America] After a child's love of learning, his aptitude for reflection, and his independent thinking have been thoroughly stifled by several years of eternally deadening spelling, he is crammed full of a mass of names, from geography, history, and grammar. These remain only words, are never understood, never take on flesh and blood meanings. The child absorbs nothing but words. For assistance he has the textbook, which the poor student must learn without comprehending. The mind is in this manner exercised and overtaxed for six or eight years at the expense of the higher intellectual capacities, and nine times out of ten the scholar forgets, since it is all absorbed without reflection, in one year what he has learned in six.

—Israel Joseph Benjamin, *Drei Jahre in Amerika 1859–1862 (Three Years in America)* (1862), in Oscar Handlin, *This Was America* (1949), 280. Benjamin was born in Romania.

703. To my mind, Hinnissy, we're wastin' too much time thinkin' iv the future iv our young, an' thryin' to larn thim early what they oughtn't to know till they've growed up. We sind th' childher to school as if 'twas a summer garden where they go to be amused instead iv a pinitinchry where they're sint f'r th' original sin. Whin I was a la-ad I was put at me ah-bee-abs, th' first day I set fut in th' school behind th' hedge an' me head was sore inside an' out befure ai wint home. Now th' first thing we larn th' future Mark Hannas an' Jawn D. Gateses iv our naytion is waltzin', singin', an' cuttin' pitchers out iv a book. We'd be much better teachin' thim the sthrangle hold, f'r that's what they need in life.

—Finley Peter Dunne, *Mr. Dooley's Philosophy:* "What I Larned in Colledge" (1900).

704. During the period immediately after the Revolution our schools were incredibly meager and poor. Since there were few highways and no transportation except by horseback, coach or boat, the intellectual life of the country was feeble and local. Teachers were untrained, and there was not a town, city, county, or state superintendent in the land. There were no publishers of textbooks, no makers of school furniture, and no one skilled in the art of designing healthful school buildings. During this period the school became poorer rather than better. Wealthier parents depended on private schools and had little interest in the common schools.

—Joy Elmer Morgan, *The School That Built a Nation* (1954), 30.

705. The dame school was a necessity of the times. Boys were not generally admitted to the master's school until they could "stand up and read words of two syllables and keep their places"; girls were not admitted at all. . . . The floor was scoured to whiteness and covered with fine sand. Here instruction in arithmetic was oral, Miss Betty making figures on the sanded floor with her rod, . . . and her pupils, with their square pieces of birch bark and bits of charcoal, copying the sums she gave them. . . . Their dinners were many times frozen, and sometimes their food required cooking. Miss Betty was devoted in her care for them in preparing their frugal repast. Apples were roasted and nuts were cracked in profusion, and then with their old fashioned games they had an enjoyable time.

—W.H. Small, *Early American Schools* (1914), 162–164.

School, British

(*See also* College; Principal; Punishment, Corporal; School, Remembrances of; Schoolhouse; Teacher, Remembrances of; Textbook)

706. 'What I don't quite see is why these Victorians of yours were so keen on the idea of an after-life when they were so eaten up with guilt about what they'd been doing in this one. They'd have thought they'd be much more likely to end up in hell than in any sort of—'

'Oh, but, my dear, that's the whole *point*, do you see. They were mad about hell—it was going to be just like their public school, where they'd had the only really intense emotional experiences they were capable of. Caning and flogging and fagging and cold baths and rowing and slip-practice and the terrifying all-powerful old man always telling you what an utter shit you were and how you were polluting yourself. They were off their heads about it, I promise you. You don't imagine it's a coincidence, do you, that this was the great age of masochism, chiefly in England but by no means confined to here?'

—Kingsley Amis, *The Green Man* (1969), 179. [fagging: *see* Maurois, **#629**, under "Punishment, Corporal (by Students)," and Waugh, **#760**, under "School Rules"]

707. I don't know precisely when it was first introduced (1840?), but I know more or less when it came to an end. When I was young, not only was every boy at a boarding school compelled to take a cold bath every morning, a rule based on the entirely erroneous theory that cold water subdued the carnal passions, but also most adult males of the upper and middle classes took one of their free will. I believe I belong to the first generation which resolved, once we left school and got to the university, that we would never take a cold bath in our lives again. Today, inquiries lead me to think that there are a few schools now where cold baths are obligatory, and I am sure no adult ever takes one except during a heat wave.

—W.H. Auden, *A Certain World: A Commonplace Book* (1970), 31.

708. William soon discovered that life at an English public school [Winchester College, 1735] was hard indeed. It was to be nearly a hundred years before [Thomas] Arnold (himself a Winchester boy) was to bring some humanity and understanding to the education of schoolboys. Left to their own devices, boys often developed a rough and even brutal way of life in which the weak and the sensitive were made to suffer misery, fear and degradation. The danger from all this was that any defects which existed in a boy's character when he arrived at the school were likely to be accentuated whilst he was there. A bully grew worse and encouraged others to bully; a homosexual was given unlimited scope for his activities and was able to initiate others. There were no organised games, and in their recreation hours boys were free to roam the local countryside, stealing from farmers or stoning birds and dogs.

Winchester at this period was as good a school as any in England, but this is not to say very much. It was overcrowded, ill-equipped and insanitary. Living conditions for the masters, as well as for the boys, were bad.... The teaching was of a low standard ... a few odd facts were flogged into them....

There were no school terms as such, and new boys might arrive at any time. Holidays were very short.

—Henry Blyth, *Old Q: The Rake of Piccadilly: A Biography of the Fourth Duke of Queensberry* (1967), 11.

709. Would you your son should be a sot or dunce
Lascivious, headstrong; or all these at once;
That, in good time, the stripling's finish'd taste
For loose expense and fashionable waste
Should prove your ruin and his own at last;
Train him in public with a mob of boys,
Childish in mischief only and in noise,
Else of a mannish growth, and five in ten
In infidelity and lewdness men.
There shall he learn, ere sixteen winters old,
That authors are most useful pawn'd or sold;
That pedantry is all that schools impart.

—William Cowper, "recommending private tuition," *Tirocinium or, a Review of Schools* (1785), ln. 201.

710. I found my first Ragged School in an obscene place called West Street, Saffron Hill, pitifully struggling for life under every disadvantage. It had no means; it had no suitable rooms; it derived no power or protection from being recognized by any authority; it attracted within its walls a fluctuating swarm of faces—young in years, but youthful in nothing else—that scowled Hope out of countenance. It was held in a low-roofed den, in a sickening atmosphere, in the midst of taint, dirt and pestilence; with all the deadly sins let loose, howling and shrieking at the doors. Zeal did not supply the place of method and training; the teachers knew little of their office; the pupils, with an evil sharpness, found them out, got the better of them, made blasphemous answers to Scriptural questions, sang, fought, danced, and robbed each other—seemed possessed by a legion of devils. The place was stormed and carried over and over again; the lights were blown out,

the books strewn in the gutters, and the female scholars carried off triumphantly to their old wickedness.

—Charles Dickens,
in Alvin Redman, *The House of Hanover* (1960), 355.

711. Mr. Wopsle's great-aunt kept an evening school in the village; that is to say, she was a ridiculous old woman of limited means and unlimited infirmity, who used to go to sleep from six to seven every evening, in the society of youth who paid twopence per week each, for the improving opportunity of seeing her do it. . . .

The Educational scheme or Course . . . may be resolved into the following synopsis. The pupils ate apples and put straws down one another's backs, until Mr. Wopsle's great-aunt collected her energies, and made an indiscriminate totter at them with a birch rod. After receiving the charge with every mark of derision, the pupils formed in line and buzzingly passed a ragged book from hand to hand. The book had an alphabet in it, some figures and tables, and a little spelling—that is to say, it had had once. As soon as this volume began to circulate, Mr. Wopsle's great-aunt fell into a state of coma; arising either from sleep or a rheumatic paroxysm. The pupils then entered among themselves upon a competitive examination on the subject of Boots, with a view of ascertaining who could tread the hardest upon whose toes. This mental exercise lasted until Biddy [Mr. Wopsle's great-aunt's granddaughter] made a rush at them and distributed three defaced Bibles (shaped as if they had been unskillfully cut off the chump-end of something), more illegibly printed at the best than any curiosities of literature I have since met with, speckled all over with ironmould, and having various specimens of the insect world smashed between their leaves. This part of the Course was usually lightened by several single combats between Biddy and refractory students. When the fights were over, Biddy gave out the number of a page, and then we all read aloud what we could—or what we couldn't—in a frightful chorus; Biddy leading with a high shrill monotonous voice, and none of us having the least notion of, or reverence for, what we were reading about. When this horrible din had lasted a certain time, it mechanically awoke Mr. Wopsle's great-aunt, who staggered at a boy fortuitously, and pulled his ears. This was understood to terminate the Course for the evening, and we emerged into the air with shrieks of intellectual victory.

—Charles Dickens, *Great Expectations* (1860–61), 50, 76.

712. Our breakfast [at Christ Hospital (School), London] was bread and water, for the beer was too bad to drink. The bread consisted of the half of a three-penny loaf, according to the prices then current. This was not much for growing boys, who had nothing to eat from six to seven o'clock the preceding evening. For dinner we had the same quantity of bread, with meat only every other day, and that consisting of a small slice, such as would be given an infant three or four years old. Yet even that, with all our hunger, we very often left half-eaten — the meat was so tough. On the other days we had a milk-porridge, ludicrously thin; or rice-milk, which was better. There were no vegetables or puddings. Once a month we had roast beef; and twice a year . . . a dinner of pork. One was roast, and the other boiled; and on the latter occasion we had our only pudding, which was of peas. . . . For supper we had a like piece of bread, with butter or cheese; and then to bed, "with what appetite we might."

Our routine of life was this. We rose to the call of a bell, at six in summer, and seven in winter; and after combing ourselves, and washing our hands and faces, went, at the call of another bell, to breakfast. All this took up about an hour. From breakfast we proceeded to school, where we remained till eleven, winter and summer, and then had an hour's play. Dinner took place at twelve. Afterwards was a little play till one, when we again went to school, and remained until five in summer and four in winter. At six was the supper. We used to play after it in summer till eight. In winter, we proceeded from supper to bed. On Sundays, the school-time of the other days was occupied in church, both morning and evening; and as the Bible was read to us every day before meal, and on going to bed, beside prayers and grace, we rivalled the monks in the religious part of our duties.

—Leigh Hunt, *The Autobiography of Leigh Hunt* (1859), 67.

713. It was a room on the ground floor, up a dark entry, and about 12 ft. square. Here 43 boys and girls were assembled, of all ages from 5 to 14. Patches of paper were pasted over the broken panes of one small window, before which also sat the master intercepting the few rays of light which would otherwise have crept into the gloom. . . . [He had] laid aside his coat. In this undress he was the better able to wield three canes, two of which, like weapons of an old soldier, hung conspicuously on the wall, while the third was on the table ready for service. When questioned as to the necessity of this triple instrumentality, he assured us that the children were "abrupt and rash."

—Report on an English school, 1840–41,
in Mary Sturt, *The Education of the People* (1967), 39.

714. [For Mrs Jones, wife of the headmaster of The Downs School, c.1917,] Character building was her obsession, and for her this meant punctuality and cleanliness. The price of these, she believed, was eternal vigilance. . . .

When one of the junior matrons woke us up first thing in the morning, she noted the precise time. We were allowed ten minutes in which to take a cold bath, wash and dress. If we took longer, we missed porridge at breakfast. Instead we had to change back into pyjamas and dressing gown, report to Mrs Jones in the dining room and dress again. The slow dresser missed his breakfast altogether. If we got ready in the prescribed ten minutes, we lined up before Mrs Jones who inspected our hands, teeth and ears, ruthlessly sending us back at the slightest sign of dirt.

After breakfast we made our beds. These were inspected three times – bottom sheet on, top blanket tucked in, and finally coverlet on. It was particularly important that the foot of the bed should be made like a parcel. If anything was wrong, the bed was stripped and we had to start again. If all went well, Mrs Jones or a matron uttered a strange cry which I thought was Turnip and Co. It was in fact Turn Up and Go. There was much the same routine with shoe cleaning: one when the polish was put on and one when the shoes had been polished.

–A.J.P. Taylor, *A Personal History* (1983), 32.

715. Any one who has been to an English public school will always feel comparatively at home in prison.

–Evelyn Waugh, *Decline and Fall* (1928), III.iv.

716. [At Eton, in the 1700s] A wide gulf separated the aristocracy from the lower ranks. For example, sons of the nobility usually (and sons of the gentry often) brought their own private tutors with them to school. The aristocracy ate and lodged in the town, not on campus. . . . Peers "occupied the stalls in chapel" . . . . Furthermore, by the eighteenth century the nobility and gentry were unquestionably of higher social standing than the persons who taught them. . . . The assistant masters, who bore much of the drudgery, were clearly regarded as inferior beings. Not only did they have to buy their posts, but also, since the nobility and gentry brought along their own tutors, they ended by teaching only the poor (and socially inferior). . . . The aristocrat, receiving instruction from "a master whom he did not consider a gentleman," knowing that his success in a future career would not "in any way" depend on his school record, needed little inducement to flout discipline and challenge authority. . . .

The school taught the sanctity of the ranks, but it also taught that within each rank the strongest and the bravest survived. Etonians were never "coddled." Punishments were corporal, sports were often brutal, fights frequent and occasionally fatal. Classical education at Eton had been utterly dehumanized and had been reduced to grammar and parsing. Woe to the boy who missed his assignment, for the rod awaited him. The lucky student who escaped a beating within the classroom was unlikely to avoid one outside it. Sooner or later he would fight with one of his classmates or take a thrashing from one of the older boys. When the headmaster Henry Bland (1719 to 1728) set up a system of declamations, he intended for students to present opposite sides of an argument. But in typical Eton fashion two senior collegers translated their words into deeds: one of them knocked the other's head against the chapel wall. In 1730 a student named Edward Cockburn died after one of his schoolmates stabbed him with a penknife.

—Franklin and Mary Wickwire,
Cornwallis: The American Adventure (1970), 19, 22.

717. [William Penn entered Chigwell Free Grammar School in 1655 at age eleven.] A safely Anglican institution, Chigwell held as its chief goal the "stirring up of the buds of virtue" in its students; its two-man faculty, both men over twenty-seven who neither smoked nor drank, were "poets [i.e., university graduates] . . . of grave behavior." . . .

Life at Chigwell was not easy. Classes began early and ran on for ten straight hours in summer and eight in winter, broken only by a brief lunch period and by a psalm-reading in the afternoon. Recitations were in Latin, with the masters instructed to whip or slap any boy who inadvertently let drop a word of English; the instructors were also to reprove in the same way any lad who swore or lied or used any word the masters considered filthy. The Chigwell boys had one consolation, however; the master who struck more than thrice or who punched anyone in the face paid forty shillings fine for each illegal blow. The fine was heavy for the times and the school retained the money. The rules had been laid down in 1629 by Chigwell's founder, Archbishop Samuel Harsnett.

—Harry Emerson Wildes, *William Penn* (1974), 15, 16.

School, Establishment of

(*See also* Education, Government Support of)

718. After God had carried us safe to *New-England,* and wee had builded our houses, provided necessaries for our livelihood, rear'd convenient places for Gods worship, and settled the Civill Government: One of the next things we longed for, and looked after was to advance *Learning* and perpetuate it to Posterity; dreading to leave an illiterate Ministry to the Churches, when our present Ministers shall lie in the Dust. . . . It pleased God to stir up the heart of one Mr. Harvard . . . to give the one halfe of his Estate (it being about 1700. l.) towards the erecting of a Colledge, and all his Library: after his mother gave him 300. l. others after them cast in more, and the publique hand of the State added the rest.

—Anonymous, *New Englands First Fruits; with Diverse Other Special Matters Concerning That Country* (1643).

719. We are therefore about to establish a school of the Lord's service in which we hope to introduce nothing harsh or burdensome.

—St. Benedict of Nursia (A.D. 480?–543?), *Rule of St. Benedict*, prologue. He founded the first Benedictine monastery (c. 529) on Monte Cassino.

720. Lord, for schools everywhere among us! That our schools may flourish! That every member of this assembly may go home, and procure a good school to be encouraged in the town where he lives! That before we die, we may be so happy as to see a good school encouraged in every plantation in the country.

—John Eliot (1604–90), a Massachusetts Bay Puritan, in Lawrence A. Cremin, *American Education: The Colonial Experience, 1607–1783* (1970), 167.

721. At this time, after Redwald's successor Erpwald, his brother Sigebert presided over the kingdom of the East Angles, a good and religious man; who some time before, while on exile in Gaul, flying from the enmity of Redwald, received baptism. After his return home, as soon as he obtained the throne, wishing to imitate what he had seen well ordered among the Gauls, he set up a school in which boys might be taught grammar. He was assisted therein by bishop Felix, who came to him from Kent, and provided them with pedagogues and masters after the fashion of the Canterbury men.

—"Foundation of East Anglican Grammar School, on the Model of Canterbury School," A.D. 631, in Arthur F. Leach, ed., *Educational Charters and Documents, 598 to 1909* (1911), 3.

722. At a town meeting held at Plymouth [Massachusetts] in the court house on the fifteenth day of February 1724/25 . . . there was a long debate about a school or schools, and after some time there was a vote called whether they would have three schools. And there being a great assembly, it was sometime difficult to distinguish the vote by holding up the hand; and it was thereupon ordered by the moderator that the assembly should withdraw out of the house and then to come in and pass by the clerk and declare whether or not they were for one or three schools. And it was voted by a majority of the votes that there should be one school. And there being a great tumult in the meeting and the people difficult to be settled, the moderator therefore adjourned the present meeting to the first day of March next to meet at ten o'clock in the forenoon at the usual place of meeting.

—*Foundations of Colonial America: A Documentary History*, ed. W. Keith Kavenagh (1973), I. 565.

723. It is proposed,

That some persons of leisure and public spirit apply for a charter . . . to erect an academy for the education of youth. . . .

That the members of the corporation make it their pleasure, and in some degree their business, to visit the academy often. . . .

That a house be provided for the academy, if not in the town, not many miles from it; the situation high and dry, and if it may be, not far from a river, having a garden, orchard, meadow, and a field or two. . . .

That the house be furnished with a library . . . with maps of all countries, globes, some mathematical instruments, an apparatus for experiments in natural philosophy, and for mechanics; prints, of all kinds, prospects, buildings, machines, etc. . . . .

That the rector be a man of good understanding, good morals, diligent and patient, learned in the languages and sciences, and a correct pure speaker and writer of the English tongue: to have such tutors under him as shall be necessary. . . .

That the boarding scholars diet together, plainly, temperately, and frugally. . . .

That, to keep them in health, and to strengthen and render active their bodies, they be frequently exercised in running, leaping, wrestling, and swimming, etc. . . . .

That they have peculiar habits to distinguish them from other youth, for this, and among other reasons, that their behavior may be better observed.

—Benjamin Franklin, "Proposals Relating to the Education of Youth in Pennsylvania," 1749, in Nathan A Goodman, *A Benjamin Franklin Reader* (1945), 323. The academy later became the University of Pennsylvania.

724. It is well that in all towns and villages good primary schools should be established out of which could be picked and chosen those who are fit for the universities, out of which then the men can be taken who are to serve your land and people. If the towns or their citizens cannot do this, then it would be well to establish new stipends for the few bright fellows in the deserted monasteries, so that every town might have one or two students. In the course of time, when the common people see that their sons can be pastors and preachers, and get other offices, many of those who now think that a scholar cannot get a living will again keep their sons in school.

—Martin Luther (1483–1546),
letter to Margrave George of Brandenburg,
Luther's Correspondence and Other Contemporary Letters,
tr. Preserved Smith (1913–18), II.487.

725. It being one chiefe project of ye ould deluder, Satan, to keepe men from the knowledge of ye Scriptures. . . .

It is therefore ord^{r}ed, y^{t} evry towneship in this iurisdiction, aft^{r} ye Lord hath increased y^{m} number to 50 household^{rs}, shall then forthwth appoint one wth in their towne to teach all such children as shall resort to him to write & reade, whose wages shall be paid eith^{r} by ye parents or mastrs of such children, or by ye inhabitants in gen^{r}all, by way of supply, as ye maior pt of those y^{t} ord^{r} ye prudentials of ye towne shall appoint; provided, those y^{t} send their children be not oppressed by paying much more y^{m} they can have y^{m} taught for in oth^{r} townes; & it is furth^{r} ordered, y^{t} where any towne shall increase to ye numb^{r} of 100 families or househould^{rs}, they shall set up a grammar schoole, ye m^{r} thereof being able to instruct youth so farr as they shall be fitted for ye university, provided, y^{t} if any towne neglect ye performance hereof above one yeare, y^{t} every such towne shall pay 5 pounds to ye next schoole till they shall perform this order.

—Massachusetts Bay Colony school law of 1647,
in Henry Steele Commager, ed., *Documents of American History*, 8th ed. (1968), 29. Five years earlier
Massachusetts enacted the first known law on education
in the American colonies. The "old deluder Satan" law
established the first system of public education.

726. My first school yar was opened in 1829 in a house on Tradd Street occupied by one Caesar Wright. It consisted of his three children, for each of whom he paid me fifty cents a month. I also taught three adult slaves at night, at the same price, thus making my monthly income from teaching only three dollars.

—Daniel A. Payne, *Recollections of Seventy Years* (1888). Payne, a free Negro born
in Charleston, South Carolina, in 1811, was the first
Negro to become a college president (Wilberforce College).

727. After trying vainly almost every school in the Union that he could hear of as entertaining views at all liberal toward the colored race, he was compelled to give up the attempt. He then conceived the idea of establishing an academy for colored men.

—R.C. Smedley, *History of the Underground Railroad in Chester and the Neighboring Counties of Pennsylvania* (1883), 65. John Miller Dickey founded Ashmun Institute (now Lincoln University) in 1854 after he tried without success to find a school where John Amos, a Negro, could be educated.

728. In the name of God Amen this Twelfth day of Febry Anno Domini one thousand Six hundred and thirty four I Benjamin Syms being of perfect health, & memory praised by God make & ordain this my last Will and textament in manner & forme following Viz

I commend my soul into the hands of God my Creator and Redeemer and my body to the Earth whence it came to have a Christian burial whereas there is due to me two hundred acres of land lying in the old Poquoson River and Eight Milch cows—I bequeath it as follows Viz The use of the said land with the milk and Increase Male of the said cattle to be for mantaynance of an honest & learned man to keep upon said Ground a free School to Educate & teach the Children of the adjoining Parishes of Elizb City & Poquoton from Mary's Mount downwards to the Poquoson River.

Item My will and desire is that the Worshipful the Commander and ye rest of the Commissioners of this liberty with the ministers and Church Wardens of said Parish where the said School is founded to see it from time to time justly & truly performed.

Item My Will and Desire is that when it please God there is sufficient Increase of the said cattle yt some part of them be saved for the erecting a very sufficient School house and the Rest of the Increase that are left to be disposed of before nominated and in Repairing the said School. . . .

—Benjamin Syms (of Virginia), last will and testament, 1634, in Edgar W. Knight and Clifton L. Hall, eds., *Readings in American Educational History* (1951), 58.

729. On the morning [in 1881] that the [Tuskegee] school opened, thirty students reported for admission. I was the only teacher. The students were about equally divided between the sexes. Most of them lived in Macon County, the county in which Tuskegee is situated, and of which it is the county-seat. A great many more students wanted to enter the school, but it had been decided to receive only those who were above fifteen years of age, and who had previously received some education. The greater part of

the thirty were public-school teachers, and some of them were nearly forty years of age. With the teachers came some of their former pupils, and when they were examined it was amusing to note that in several cases the pupil entered a higher class than did his former teacher. It was also interesting to note how many big books some of them had studied, and how many high-sounding subjects some of them claimed to have mastered. The bigger the book and the longer the name of the subject, the prouder they felt of their accomplishment. Some had studied Latin, and one or two Greek. This they thought entitled them to special distinction.

—Booker T. Washington, *Up From Slavery* (1901), 87.

730. I have heretofore proposed to the consideration of Congress the expediency of establishing a national university, and also a military academy. The desirableness of both these institutions has so constantly increased with every new view I have taken of the subject that I cannot omit the opportunity of once for all recalling your attention to them.

—George Washington, message to Congress, Dec. 7, 1796.
In his last will and testament, signed July 9, 1799, five months before his sudden death, Washington bequeathed 50 shares of Potomac Company stock toward the establishment of a university in the District of Columbia, a stipulation that was never fulfilled. —*The Writings of George Washington*, ed. Worthington C.Ford (1889–93), XIV.271–98.

School, Remembrances of

(*See also* Schoolhouse; Student, First Day of School; Student Pranks; Teacher, Remembrances of)

731. It was a little, square pine building, blazing in the sun, upon the highway, without a tree for shade or sight near it; without bush, yard, fence or circumstance to take off its bare, cold, hard, hateful look. . . . In winter we were squeezed into the recess of the furthest corner, among little boys, who seemed to be sent to school merely to fill up the chinks between the bigger boys. Certainly we were never sent for any such absurd purpose as an education. There were the great scholars; the school in winter was for them, not for us piccaninnies. We were read and spelt twice a day, unless something happened to prevent, which did happen about every other day. For the rest of the time we were busy in keeping still. . . . Our shoes would always be scraping on the floor. . . . All of our little legs together (poor, tired, nervous, restless legs, with nothing to do!) would fill up the corner

with such a noise, that every ten or fifteen minutes the master would bring down his two-foot hickory ferule on the desk with a clap that sent shivers through our hearts to think how that would have felt if it had fallen somewhere else; and then, with a look that swept us all into utter extremity of stillness, he would cry, 'Silence in that corner!' Stillness would last for a few minutes....

A women kept the [summer] school, sharp, precise, unsympathetic, keen and untiring. Of all the ingenious ways of fretting little boys doubtless her ways were the most expert.... The benches were slabs with legs in them. The desks were slabs at an angle, cut, hacked, scratched ... until [they] then wore cuttings and carvings two or three inches deep. But if we cut a morsel ... or pinched off splinters, the little sharp-eyed mistress was on hand, and one look of her eye was worse than a sliver in our foot, and one nip of her fingers was equal to a jab of a pin; for we had tried both....

I have not a single pleasant recollection in connection with my schoolboy days. The woods were full of temptations, the trees called me, the birds wanted me.... It seemed cruel to be shut up. The brooks, birds, flowers, sunshine, and breezes were free; why not I?

—Henry Ward Beecher, *Star Papers:* "School Reminiscence" (1855), 189–93.

732. Our schoolboy days are looked back to by all with fondness. Oppressed with the cares of life, we contrast our worn and harassed existence with that sweet prime, free from anxiety and fragrant with innocence. I can not share these feelings. I was a most miserable child; and school I detested more than ever I abhorred the world in the darkest moments of my experienced manhood.

—Benjamin Disraeli, *Contarini Fleming* (1832), 103.

733. Aunt Lucy was teaching school at that time.... I had said something about one of the girls which hurt her feelings deeply.... My words sent her to my teacher-aunt who listened to the report and then called me to her.

"You will have to apologize," she ruled, once she had made certain of my guilt in the matter.

I knew the voice of authority when I heard it. "All right," I agreed. "Call her over and I'll do it."

I didn't sound very repentant, even to my own ears.

"Oh, no," my aunt said. "You must go to her."

"But she's with a whole bunch of kids," I protested. "I can't apologize with all of them listening."

"You said it before them, didn't you?" she reminded me.

I pondered her words. I looked at the inflexible face of authority. I looked at the children—the big ones, the little ones, and those between, the ones who were my own age. They were watching me, knowing something out of the ordinary was in the air. I swallowed two or three times.

"Might as well get it over with," my aunt advised sensibly.

I hesitated only a moment longer. Then I turned and marched over to where the injured girl stood. I do not remember what I said to her, but it must have been adequate, for she mumbled something which sounded like, "Oh, that's all right." Those who heard her must have shared her sentiments, for they got out of the little tight knot into which they had been bound and started a baseball game. I was chosen third or fourth instead of the usual well-toward-the-last, for at baseball I was no good at all. I never seemed to see the ball until it was well past me.

—Loula Grace Erdman, *Life Was Simpler Then* (1963), 112.

734. If the impossible ever happens and I am asked to help break up a school what I shall say is this: 'Ladies and gentlemen, boys and bies. School was the unhappiest time of my life, and the worst trick it ever played on me was to pretend that it was the world in miniature. For it hindered me from discovering how lovely and delightful and kind the world can be, and how much of it is intelligible. From this platform of middle age, this throne of experience, this altar of wisdom, this scaffold of character, this beacon of hope, this threshold of decay, my last words to you are: There's a better time coming.'

—E.M. Forster, "Breaking Up," *Spectator*, July 28, 1933, in P.N. Furbank, *E.M. Forster: A Life* (1977), I.48.

735. My twelfth and last school . . . was run by Monsieur Prax, who was a very nice person. He had given up his room to me, and I enjoyed a certain measure of freedom in his house—which I used and even abused. I was seventeen! I took many a meal out, many a class not at all, and I often came in late at night or early in the morning.

Monsieur Prax bore with me for several months, but in the end he thought it his duty to inform my father. . . . Monsieur Prax knocked on my father's dressing-room door, walked in, and said:

"Sir, I have made up my mind to expel your son; but unfortunately I cannot do it."

"Why not?" asked my father. "If you won't keep him, I'm sorry. I suppose you'll have to send him away."

"That is impossible, sir. I can't put him out—because he hasn't come home these past five days."

—Sacha Guitry, *If Memory Serves* (1936), 62.

736. I got out of bed to see what had happened in the night. I had fallen asleep watching the snow falling through the half-frosted window. . . . The world had changed. All the houses, fences, and barren trees had new shapes. Everything was round and white and unfamiliar. . . .

I headed for the school, jumping like a clumsy rabbit in and out of snowbanks. It seemed wrong to spoil the smooth outlines of these snowdrifts and I hoped that nobody else would pass this way after me. . . .

When eventually, encased in snow, I arrived at the school, I found scores of white-covered figures already there. The girls had taken shelter inside, but the boys stayed in the storm. . . .

Passing through the halls during recess we whispered to one another about the snowstorm, guessing how deep the snowdrifts must be by this time. We looked nervously at our teachers who stood in the classroom doorways stiff and far removed from the secret whispers about the snow.

I felt sorry for these teachers. . . .

As for my own teacher, a tall, thin woman with a man's face, by afternoon I had become so happy I could no longer hear what she was saying. I sat looking at the large clock over her head. My feeling on the way to school that it would never be light again and that the snowstorm would keep on forever had increased so that it was something I now knew rather than hoped. My eagerness to get out into the world of wind, gloom, and perpetual snow, kept lifting me out of my seat.

At three o'clock we rushed into the storm. Our screams died as we reached the school entrance. What we saw silenced us. Under the dark sky the street lay piled in an unbroken bank of snow. And above it the snowfall still hung in a thick and moving cloud. Nothing was visible but snow. Everything else had disappeared. Even the sky was gone.

I saw the teachers come out and look around them, frowning. The children of the lower grades stood chattering and frightened near the teachers. I waited until the teacher with the two black braids saw me and then, paying no attention to her warning, spoken in a gentle voice, I plunged into the storm. I felt brave but slightly regretful that Miss Wheeler could no longer see me as I pushed into the head-high piles of snow and vanished fearlessly into the storm. But I was certain that she was still thinking of me and worrying about my safety.

—Ben Hecht, "Snowfall in Childhood,"
Esquire Magazine, November 1934.

737. One divine spring day the windows [of the Greek school] were open. A tangerine tree was in bloom across the street, and its perfume entered the classroom. Each of our minds had turned into a blossoming tangerine tree; we could not bear to hear anything more about acute and circumflex

accents [from the unpopular third grade teacher]. A bird came just then, perched on a plane tree in the schoolyard and began to sing. At that point a pale redheaded student who had arrived that year from his village, Nikoliós by name, was unable to control himself. He raised his finger.

"Be quiet, sir," he cried. "Be quiet and let us hear the bird."

—Nikos Kazantzakis, *Report to Greco* (1965), 57. *See* Kazantzakis, #977, under "Teacher, Remembrances of" for a description of this teacher.

738. It was never learning I associated with that school: only the necessity to succeed, to get ahead of the others in the daily struggle to "make a good impression" on our teachers. . . . The white, cool, thinly ruled record book sat over us from their desks all day long, and had remorselessly entered into it each day . . . our attendance, our conduct, our "effort," our merits and demerits; and to the last possible decimal point in calculation, our standing in an unending series of "tests"—surprise tests, daily tests, weekly tests, formal mid-term tests, final tests.

—Alfred Kazin, *A Walker in the City* (1951).

739. The Columbian School . . . [had not] been planned for safety; it was two-storied, and a bell tower, with a real bell in it, rose higher than that. The janitor rang the bell every morning and following our one-hour lunch break. We needed the hour; most of us went home for the meal, and our district was not a small one.

The bell was rung to call us all to line up at one of the doors. . . . We stood in line until we were quiet enough to satisfy the teacher, and she then gave us permission to "pass" into the building and to our room.

The bell was rung a second time a few minutes later. If you came in after that tardy bell, it usually meant a corresponding stay after school. One morning I had dawdled along on my return trip following lunch, and suddenly I realized I was in danger of being tardy—there were no children left on the playground. I tore into the building at top speed, to find the janitor, who was our neighbor, standing by the bell rope. "I saw you coming," he said. "Hurry! I won't ring it until you're in the room!"

—Beth R. Kiteley, "The School on Second Street," *Yesterday's* Magazine, March/April 1989.

740. A few months later [in kindergarten] a[n] . . . urge wells up and overmasters me. This time it is in drill. March, march, round and round the schoolroom to a rollicking tune from Miss Davis at the piano. *Halt!* The music breaks off. I call out: 'Miss Davis!' on a reckless note.

'Yes, what is it?'

'I don't like being in the middle.'

'What do you mean, dear?' Puzzle for Miss Davis. I have in fact been top of the class this week and in consequence I lead the march.

"Well . . . I'm not the oldest . . . and I'm not the youngest. . . .' Now I have qualms. 'Helen's older and Baby (my sister Beatrix) is—'

'Ah yes, I see.' She breaks into a soft chuckle. 'Well, I'm the middle one too, in my family. I think it's rather nice. Like jam in the middle of a sandwich. Attention children, forward march! Heads up! Swing your arms!'

Forward I march, leading a Band of Hope, to the tune of *John Brown's Body*. When it comes to *glory glory Allelujah!* we belt it out with a will, I loudest of all for once, and most rejoicing. For lo! I am absolutely on the map, the sweet surprise of it!—I am linked with Miss Davis, middle one of the family, I am the jam between the bread slices, given status and protection.

—Rosamond Lehmann, *The Swan in the Evening* (1967), 10.

741. I disliked school [in Wyre, the Orkney Islands, Scotland] from the start. The classroom which had to serve us all, with its smell of ink, chalk, slate pencils, corduroy, and varnish, made me feel as if my head were stuffed with hot cotton-wool, and I realized quite clearly that I was caught and there was no escape. A map of the world covered one of the walls, a small, drab world, smaller even than the classroom; the light brown benches with the inkpots let into them seemed too hard and new; the windows showing nothing but the high clouds floating past. Time moved by minute degrees there; I would sit for a long time invisibly pushing the hands of the clock on with my will, and waken to realize that they had scarcely moved. . . .

I had to leave for Edinburgh by the morning train a few years ago—I was living at St. Andrews at the time—and as I walked to the station I passed children going to school. It was a dismal morning draped with discoloured rags of clouds like a great washing; a few drops of rain splashed down at meaningless intervals; sodden leaves were plastered to the pavements and low walls. I watched the children, their satchels on their backs, walking through the school gate and trudging towards a door in the high wall; there was little sound anywhere, for it was an unfrequented street; everything had an air of secrecy. I can give no idea of the dreariness of the scene; the earth bleared and wet; the dejected children. I seemed to see an enormous school, higher even than this one, and millions of children all over the world creeping towards it and disappearing into it. The picture rose of itself, and it brought back a still Sunday evening in Wyre, when my mother and I had gone for a walk. The walk took us past the school, which, being shut, had a clean, forsaken look. My heart beat faster as we drew near, and I looked with dread at the ragged grass of the playground, not pounded now by the boots of the other boys, but lying peaceful and lost. I lingered to glance at the classroom windows, and my head grew hot and tight, as if I had been shut in a clothes cupboard. That was the feeling which my first year at school gave me, a feeling of being shut in some narrow, clean, wooden place: it must be known to every one who has attended a school, and the volume of misery it has caused will not bear thinking of.

—Edwin Muir, *An Autobiography* (1954), 41.

742. It appears to me now that the most unusual and salutary thing about our life in that [boarding] school [at age fourteen] was its atmosphere of freedom. Within our hours of work the discipline was strict enough to keep things going as they should, but it was not unkind, unreasonable, or on a proper occasion, inflexible. Out of hours we had all the range there was, free to wander in the fields, row on the river, hob-nob with the townspeople, and strike up acquaintances where we chose. The policy worked well enough. We were never cautioned against putting beans up our noses, or subjected to any snivelling talk about being on our honour, or keeping up the credit of the dear old school, or any such odious balderdash. Nevertheless we somehow managed to behave decently, no doubt because we had no overweening inducements to behave otherwise. I do not recall any pranks serious enough to come in for more than a good-natured reprimand. Yet we were not holding any brief for Condorcet's or Rousseau's views on the essential goodness of human nature. There was always plenty to do that was legitimate and more interesting than anything likely to land us in trouble, so why get in trouble? This was all there was to it; this was the sum of our ethical imperative. Not so long afterwards I began to suspect that this might also be the sum of the ethical imperative affecting the conduct of mankind-at-large.

—Albert Jay Kock,
The Memoirs of a Superfluous Man (1943), 69.

743. "I was fired from . . . [the school operated by nuns from the Blessed Sacrament Convent], finally, for a lot of things," she told an interviewer many years later, "among them my insistence that the Immaculate Conception was spontaneous combustion."

"Convents," she said," do the same things that progressive schools do, only they don't know it. They don't teach you how to read; you have to find out for yourself. At my convent we did have a textbook, one that devoted a page and a half to Adelaide Ann Proctor; but we couldn't read Dickens; he was vulgar, you know. But I read him and Thackeray, and I'm the only woman you'll ever know who's read every word of Charles Reade, the author of *The Cloister and the Hearth.* But as for helping me in the outside world, the convent taught me only that if you spit on a pencil eraser it will erase ink. And I remember the smell of oilcloth, the smell of nuns' garb.

"All those writers who talk about their childhood!" she said bitterly. "Gentle God, if I ever wrote about mine, you wouldn't sit in the same room with me."

—Dorothy Parker, in John Keats, *You Might as Well Live: The Life and Times of Dorothy Parker* (1970), 20.

744. I made him stay with me till 11 at night, talking of old school stories, and very pleasing ones, and truly I find that we did spend our time and thoughts then otherwise than I think boys do now, and I think as well as methinks that the best are now.

—Samuel Pepys, *Diary,* July 25, 1664.

745. By the midway in the first year I had been jumped to the third grade. This helped one problem but created another. I was now in a class with children older than I, and at that age a difference of even a year or two is a chasm in terms of both physical and psychological maturity. I only saw my real contemporaries briefly at recess, while I didn't fit in with my classroom companions. The consequences of that were to haunt me the rest of my school days.

That's a perennial educational dilemma for which I know no good solution. It's criminal, I think, to hold back children when they are ready to read, or at any other educational level. Yet the psychologists are right that a young child among older ones, like the ugly duckling of that childhood story, does risk becoming a social misfit. I don't wish to exaggerate, but I certainly became so, at least in part.

—Vermont Royster, *My Own, My Country's Time* (1983), 18.

746. Full well I remembered the morning . . . [the schoolmaster] called me into his study to feel the pulse of my intellect, in order that he might know in what class to place me.

—Mary Martha Sherwood, *Memoirs* (1854).

747. Finally, I . . . was permitted to go to school in the day for a few months, with the understanding that I was to rise early in the morning and work in the furnace till nine o'clock, and return immediately after school closed in the afternoon for at least two more hours of work.

The schoolhouse was some distance from the furnace, and as I had to work till nine o'clock, and the school opened at nine, I found myself in a difficulty. School would always be begun before I reached it, and sometimes my class had recited. To get around this difficulty, I yielded to a temptation for which most people, I suppose, will condemn me but since it is a fact, I might as well state it. . . . There was a large clock in a little office in the furnace. This clock, of course, all the hundred or more workmen depended upon to regulate their hours of beginning and ending the day's work. I got the idea that the way for me to reach school on time was to move the clock hands from half-past eight up to the nine o'clock mark. This I found myself doing morning after morning, till the furnace "boss" discovered that something was wrong and locked the clock in a case. I did not mean to inconvenience anybody; I simply meant to reach that schoolhouse in time.

—Booker T. Washington, *Up From Slavery* (1901), 23. Charles S. Brooks considers the idea of moving the classroom clock ahead to shorten the teaching period (*see* **#1016** under "Teaching Method"), and Katherine Brush advances the clock hands to reduce her piano practicing time (*see* **#1115** under "Women, Education of").

748. In September 1910, when I was rising seven years of age, I was sent for the first time to [Heath Mount] school . . . [where] I gladly remained for the next six years. . . .

The day began with the school assembled by forms round the walls of the gymnasium; 'toeing the line' under the orders of the prefects, who had a pretty free hand in cuffing us. . . . [The headmaster,] Mr. Grenfell bounded up the three brass-bound steps and said 'Good morning, gentlemen.' We in chorus cried: 'Good morning, sir.' We then recited the Lord's Prayer . . .; any necessary announcements were made and we dispersed to our classes; except on Saturday mornings, when an alarming ceremony occurred.

Mr. Grenfell then appeared with a ledger in which were recorded the results of the masters' meeting on the preceding afternoon. First he read the names of those commended. 'Geoghegan minor, plus three for Latin. Where is Geoghegan minor? Let me see him. Fine boy, Geoghegan minor . . . Mackenzie, plus five for Mathematics and French. Keep it up, Mackenzie. I am very pleased with you.'

Then with a dramatic change in tone: 'We will now turn to the other side. What is this I find? *Fletcher.* Fletcher has been idle. Stand out, Fletcher.' Mr. Grenfell glared and bristled. Fletcher cringed. 'What does this mean? Idle? We had better understand one another, young man. You do not come here to be idle. And I am going to see that you work. Any idling, Fletcher, and'—with great vehemence and a blow of his fist on the table—'I'll be down on you like a ton of bricks.' Then he would turn to the assistant masters grouped behind him. 'Keep your eyes on Fletcher, gentlemen. Any more trouble, send him to me, and he knows what he'll get.'

His rage, I now realise, was simulated. . . .

Mr. Grenfell seldom beat anyone and then only for outrageous behaviour; lying and cheating were considered by him and by all of us the extremity of wickedness.

—Evelyn Waugh, *A Little Learning: An Autobiography* (1964), 80–83.

749. It was in P.S. 2 [in New York City] that I contracted the fear of platforms that has dogged me all my life and caused me to decline every invitation to speak in public. For the assembly performances, pupils were picked in alphabetical order, and since there were a great many pupils and my name began with W, I spent the entire term dreading the ordeal of making a public appearance. I suffered from severe anticipatory sickness. Usually the term ended before my name came up, and then the new term started again at the top of the alphabet. I mounted the platform only once in my whole career, but I suffered tortures every day of the school year, thinking about the awesome—if improbable—event.

—E.B. White, in Scott Elledge, *E.B. White: A Biography* (1984), 22.

750. It was a mild benevolent school, boys and girls, two big rooms with crayons and blocks, a-b-c frames with battered beads, slates to be breathed on hotly, oleographs of Bible catastrophes—the Flood, Lot's Wife, and Moses looking like our bearded neighbor Ishmael Jones angry in a nightgown. At noon we would file out, lift our tins off the stove and settle in corners; the tea tasted tinny, but it was different from home and that was good. I learnt to write English, while not yet speaking it, by copying words printed in exquisite copperplate: "Silence is golden," "Virtue is its own reward."

—Emlyn Williams, *George: An Early Autobiography* (1961), 30. He was born in Wales.

School Rules

751. All students of this school [Academy for Establishing Virtue] must observe closely the following regulations.

1. *Ceremonies held on the 1st and 15th of every month.* At daybreak, the student on duty for that day will sound his clappers. At the first round of the clappers, you should rise, wash your face, comb your hair, and put on proper clothing. By the second round of the clappers, you should be dressed either in ceremonial robes or in summer robes and gather in the main hall. The teachers will lead you to the image of Confucius, to which you will bow twice. After incense has been lit, you will make two more bows.

Afterwards, the teachers walk over to the southwestern corner, and you line up in order of your ages in the northeast. Then you pay respect to the teachers by making two bows to them, while the teachers accept the salutation, standing erect. An older student then comes forward and delivers a short speech; this is followed by two more bows to the teachers. Afterwards, the teachers retire into a room, and you form a circle and bow to each other twice. When this is done, you go to your seats.

2. *Daily salutations held in the morning and in the evening.* On ordinary days, . . . at the second round of the clappers you will enter the hall and line up to wait for the teachers to come out. Then the teachers and you bow to each other with hands folded in front. Next, you divide into two groups and bow to each other, after which you begin your daily studies. . . .

3. *Daily behavior* . . . . When sitting, you must straighten your backs and sit squarely in the chair. You should not squat, lean to one side, cross your legs, or dangle your feet . . . .

4. *Gait and posture.* You should walk slowly. When standing, keep your hands folded in front. Never walk or stand in front of an elder. Never turn your back on those who are your superiors in age or status . . . .

5. *Looking and listening.* Do not gape. Do not eavesdrop.

6. *Discourse.* Statements should always be verifiable . . . . Your manners should be serious . . . .

7. *Appearance.* Be dignified and serious . . . . Do not reveal your joy or anger.

8. *Attire.* Do not wear unusual or extravagant clothing. Yet do not go to the other extreme and appear in clothes that are ragged, dirty, or in bad taste. Even in your private quarters you should never expose your body or take off your cap . . . .

9. *Eating.* Do not fill yourself . . . . Never drink unless on a holiday or unless you are ordered to do so by your elders . . . .

10. *Travel* . . . . You are not allowed to leave the campus at will. Before your departure and after your return you should report to your teacher . . . .

11. *Reading* . . . . You should count the number of times you read an assigned piece. If, upon completion of the assigned number, you still have not memorized the piece, you should continue until you are able to recite it. On the other hand, if you have memorized the piece quickly, you should still go on to complete the assigned number of readings.

12. *Writing.* Do not scribble. Do not write slanted or sloppy characters.

13. *Keep your desk tidy*. . . .

14. *Keep the lecture halls and private rooms clean.* Each day one student is on duty. . . . He should sprinkle water on the floor of the lecture hall. Then after an appropriate wait, he should sweep the floor and wipe the desks. The other cleaning jobs should be assigned to the pages. . . .

15. *Terms of address.* You should address those who are twice your age as 'elder," those who are ten years older than you as "older brothers," and those who are about your age by their polite names. Never address one another as "you.". . .

16. *Visits*. . . . Only when the teacher orders them [visitors] to retire they may leave. If the guest should wish to speak to a student privately, he should, after seeing the teacher, approach the student at his seat. If the student finds the visitor incompatible, he is not obliged to be congenial.

17. *Recreation*. . . . Gambling and chess games are lowly pastimes and should be avoided by our students.

18. *Servants*. . . . Treat them with dignity and forbearance. When they make mistakes, scold them or report to the teacher. If they do not approve after being punished, report to the teacher to have them discharged. A student should not expel his page at will.

—Ch'eng Tuan-li, *A Schedule for Learning* (1315), in Patricia Buckley Ebrey, ed., *Chinese Civilization and Society: A Sourcebook* (1981), 114–16.

752. A general laxity of student discipline further plagued the [Cambridge] University throughout the seventeenth century and beyond. So serious had matters become by the 1630s that Charles I felt constrained to draft a series of ordinances aimed at curbing the more flagrant aspects of student carousing. Among other things, the ordinances included prohibitions against student liaisons with "women of mean estate and no good fame" (whore was too indelicate a word) and the excessive frequenting of taverns "to eat or drink or play or to take tobacco." . . . Further regulations, handed down in 1636 . . . forbid *[sic]* the wearing of long hair over the forehead or ears, absence outside the college walls after eight o'clock in the evening, or "venturing into town or country" without the express permission of a tutor or other college official. Finally, in an attempt to curb sexual promiscuity within the University itself, female bedmakers under the age of fifty were no longer to be employed.

—Gale E. Christianson, *In the Presence of the Creator: Isaac Newton and His Times* (1984), 31.

753. Since the carrying India Teas into the Hall is found to be a source of uneasiness and grief to many of the Students, and as the use of it is disagreeable to the People of this Country in general . . . be advised not to carry it in for the future . . . so peace and happiness may be preserved within the Walls of the College whatever convulsions may unhappily distract the State abroad.

—Harvard faculty resolution, 1775,
in *Life* Magazine, September 1986.
The British tax on tea led to the Boston Tea Party, 1773.

754. [At School Field, Rugby, c. 1900,] A new boy must have been a little perplexed at first by the numerous regulations and niceties of difference in degree of seniority. There was a roll call three times a day, and, for the first year, at the shout of 'fag' you rushed to the spot and, if the last to arrive, got down to cleaning the shoes or tidying the cell of the privileged youth who had issued the summons. You must not have your hands in your pockets while walking between the house and the school, but at a later stage you might put one hand in a pocket, then both, but with your books tucked under each arm, then under one arm, according to your place in the scheme of things; and you mustn't walk on the opposite side of the road from your house, nor walk anywhere with a boy from another house . . .; and your straw hat, obligatory of course when down town, was plain or speckled, straight or tilted, according to status. A plain straw hat, cocked to an angle, both hands in the pockets, and all books under one arm, denoted a senior swell beyond all shadow of cavil.

—Christopher Hassall, *Rupert Brooke: A Biography* (1964), 35.

755. Gentlemen:

Permit me to call to your attention a peculiarly humorous state of affairs. At the present time men of the Dean's List are allowed to cut chapel as often as they like. The natural inference is that excellence in scholarship makes religious education unnecessary. I can see no mention made of this inducement in "Student Life at Brown," the naive propaganda publication of that university. I have no doubt that prospective students would be interested in knowing that a grade of B or better excuses them from worshipping the Creator in Brown University. Does this rather fantastic ruling represent a departure from the old fear-God days?

—S.J. Perelman, letter to
Brown [University] Daily Herald, Mar. 18, 1925,
in Dorothy Hermann, *S.J. Perelman: A Life* (1986), 42.

756. 1st Mind to have your Hands and faces washed and Heads Combed every morning before you come to school and be careful to be there by the time appointed.

2nd Come into School quietly and Soberly, and when there be Quiet and still at your proper business; and mind the instructions of the Teacher, move not from seat to seat, or go out unnecessarily, and but one at a time.

3rd Do not scribble in your own, or one anothers Speling *[sic]*, reading, writing or Cyphering Books; nor use one anothers pens etc without leave.

4th In coming to or going from School, behave with decency and sobriety, not differing with or purposly *(sic)* hurting or offending each other; mock not nor insult any person, neither stop on the road to play, or make a great and unbecoming noise....

—Regulations governing student conduct
in a common school in Pennsylvania, 1798.

757. I wish that the custom which was instituted from the beginning in this house by the counsel of good men may be kept, and if anyone ever has transgressed it, that henceforth he shall not presume to do so.

No one therefore shall eat meat in the house on Advent, nor on Monday or Tuesday of Lent, nor from Ascension Day to Pentecost....

Also, all shall wear closed outer garments, nor shall they have trimmings of vair or grise or of red or green silk on the outer garment or hood.

Also, no one shall be received in the house unless he shall be willing to leave off such and to observe the aforesaid rules.

Also, no one shall be received in the house unless he pledges faith that, if he happens to receive books from the common store, he will treat them carefully as if his own and on no condition remove or lend them out of the house, and return them in good condition whenever required or whenever he leaves town.

Also, let every fellow have his own mark on his clothes and one only and different from the others. And let all the marks be written on a schedule and over each mark the name of whose it is. And let that schedule be given to the servant so that he may learn to recognize the mark of each one....

Also, no one shall form the habit of talking too loudly at table. Whoever after he has been warned about this by the prior shall have offended by speaking too loudly, provided this is established afterwards by testimony of several fellows to the prior, shall be held to the usual house penalty, namely two quarts of wine.

The penalty for transgression of statutes which do not fall under an oath is twopence, if the offenders are not reported by someone, or if they were, the penalty becomes sixpence in the case of fines. I understand "not reported" to mean that, if before the matter has come to the attention of the prior, the offender accuses himself to the prior or has told the clerk to write down twopence against him for such an offence, for it is not enough to say to the fellows, "I accuse myself."

—Robert de Sorbonne, in *Chartulary of the University of Paris* (13th cent.), I.505–14, in Lynn Thorndike, ed., *University Records and Life in the Middle Ages:* "Early Statutes of the Sorbonne" (1944), 88–92.

758. 1. No freshman shall wear his hat in the College except when it rains, snows, or hails, or he be on horse back or hath both hands full.

2. No freshman shall wear his hat in his senior's chamber or in his own if his senior be there.

3. No freshman shall go by his senior, without taking his hat off if it be on.

4. No freshman shall intrude into his senior's company.

5. No freshman shall laugh in his senior's face.

6. No freshman shall talk saucily to his senior or speak to him with his hat on.

7. No freshman shall ask his senior an impertinent question. . . .

—Rules for freshmen entering Harvard College as recorded by Richard Waldron, a freshman, in June 1735.

759. It is the duty of every school child:

To rise as the teacher or director enters or leaves the classroom.

To rise and stand erect while reciting; to sit down only on permission of the teacher; to raise the hand when desiring to answer or ask a question.

To be respectful to the school director and the teachers, to greet them on the street with a polite bow, boys removing their hats.

—From *Rules for Small Children,* Soviet of People's Commissars, U.S.S.R., 1943.

760. It was the custom at Lancing [School in 1917] that during one's first three weeks an 'underschool,' as Lower boys were dubbed, was deputed to take charge of one and instruct one in the habits of the place. In theory—although I do not remember it ever put into practice—any punishment incurred during this time was visited on him. The code inculcated was elaborate, trivial but not particularly irksome, and related chiefly to dress and to the places where one might set the feet. Costume was entirely subfusc for the first two years; then coloured socks were permissible; in the Sixth Form coloured ties. For the first year hands must be kept from the trouser pockets, for the second year they could be inserted but with the jacket raised, not drawn back. A two-year man might link arms with a one-year man, not vice versa. Grass, in which the grounds abounded, was in general forbidden territory; every plot was the preserve of some privileged caste, the most sacred being the Lower Quad, where only the school prefects might tread. . . . On the third Sunday of term one stood on the table in the House Room and sang a song, after which one was an initiated member of the tribe and subject to fagging and beating.

—Evelyn Waugh, *A Little Learning: An Autobiography* (1964), 102. [fagging=*to do menial chores for an older student.*] *See* Amis, **#706,** under "School, British"; and Maurois, **#629,** under "Punishment, Corporal (by Students)."

Schoolhouse

(*See also* School; School, American; School, British)

761. The [school] hut was low built, the walls not more than six feet high with clapboard roof, only a door opening—no window—light entering the room through a space made by cutting out a part of one of the side logs and placing therein panes of 8×10 glass side by side and just above the split-out puncheon [a split log or heavy slab with the face smoothed], which was fastened at a convenient inclination inside the wall for writing on. The bench on which the children sat to write was high enough from the floor for grown persons to rest their feet on the floor, but the greater number of pupils when sitting on the bench could not touch the floor with a foot by 4 to 12 inches. This arrangement was beneficial to the children in some respects as it tended to prevent their growing bow-legged, or knock-kneed—their lower extremities swinging so much upon a straight stretch; and to the school, as it prevented the shuffling of the feet upon the sounding floor.

—Daniel Harmon Brush, *Growing Up with Southern Illinois: 1820 to 1861* (1944), 28.

762. I gazed upon the schoolroom into which he took me, as the most forlorn and desolate place I had ever seen. I see it now. A long room, with three long rows of desks, and six forms [benches], and bristling all round with pegs for hats and slates. Scraps of old copy-books and exercises litter the dirty floor. Some silkworms' houses, made of the same materials, are scattered over the desks. Two miserable little white mice, left behind by their owner, are running up and down in a fusty castle made of pasteboard and wire, looking in all the corners with their red eyes for anything to eat. A bird, in a cage very little bigger than himself, makes a mournful rattle now and then in hopping on his perch, two inches high, or dropping from it; but neither sings nor chirps. There is a strange unwholesome smell upon the room, like mildewed corduroys, sweet apples wanting air, and rotten books. There could not well be more ink splashed about it, if it had been roofless from its first construction, and the skies had rained, snowed, hailed, and blown ink through the varying seasons of the year.

—Charles Dickens, *David Copperfield* (1849–50), 78.

763. The schoolhouse chimney was of stone, and the fireplace was six feet wide and four feet deep. The flue was so ample and so perpendicular that the rain, sleet, and snow fell directly to the hearth. In winter the battle for life with green fizzling fuel, which was brought in lengths and cut up by the scholars, was a stern one. Not unfrequently the wood, gushing up with sap as it was, chanced to let the fire go out, and as there was no living without fire, the school was dismissed, whereat all the scholars rejoiced.

—Samuel G. Goodrich (1793–1860),
describing his school in Connecticut in the period
after the Revolution, in Newton Edwards and Herman Richey,
The School in the American Social Order (1947), 116.

764. According to the town reports available [to Horace Mann in 1835–39], most of the school buildings [in Massachusetts] were small and shabby. In Westport a teacher held class for fifteen children in a room fourteen by sixteen. Tyringham boasted of its "good" school, where seventeen pupils were closeted in a fourteen by eighteen space. Great Barrington reported sixteen students in a building sixteen by twenty-four whose condition was described as "bad . . . stands in road." Other towns complained of equally depressing conditions. Out of seven schoolhouses in Ashburnham, the Town Committee declared five as "bad," one "decent," and one "good." And little more could be said for the furnishings inside these. To the question, "What is the furniture of the School House, and the apparatus including maps?" the Lanesborough Committee responded with a sense of hard-won accomplishment, "All the schools are provided with stoves, tables, pails and dippers." Wilmington simply answered, "None," while Taunton officials gave the more descriptive response, "Inconvenient benches, a clumsy desk, chair for the master,—bare walls,—no maps,—nor other apparatus, save school books, and the switch or ferule." Many town and country folk even tolerated the absence of that all-important convenience, the outhouse; but when a school in Kingston even lacked its substitute, "the shades of the surrounding forest," one school board member finally erupted in righteous indignation, "What sort of a place is this, to send your sons and daughters to learn the most desirable of all virtues, Modesty?" In terms of comforts and conveniences, much less the simple amenities, the rural and townfolk of Massachusetts provided better shelter for their livestock than for their children.

—Jonathan Messerli, *Horace Mann* (1972), 252.

765. Of conveniences [in the schoolhouse] I shall mention no other but the confused and shattered and nastie posture that it is in, not fitting for to reside in, the glass broke, and thereupon very raw and cold; the floor very much broken and torn up to kindle fires, the hearth spoiled, the seats some burned and others out of kilter, that one had well-nigh as goods keep school in a hog stie as in it.

—Roxbury [New England] schoolmaster, 1681, in Alice Morse Earle, *Customs and Fashions in Old New England* (1893), 32.

766. Although most wooden schoolhouses in the United States are now painted white, a few generations ago it was customary, especially in New England and other northeastern sections of the country, to paint frame schoolhouses red, not because that color was preferred, but because red paint was cheaper than any other kind obtainable. Thus the little red schoolhouse became a symbol of popular education in general.

—George Stimpson, *A Book About a Thousand Things* (1946), 113.

767. In a green lane that from the village street
Diverges, stands the school-house; long and low
The frame, and blackened with the hues of Time.
Around it spreads the green with scattered trees;
Fenced fields and orchards stretching either hand,
And fronting. When the strawberry ripe and red
Is nestling at the roots of the deep grass,
And when the autumn sun has decked with gold
And crimson and gnarled apple-bough, light paths
Stretch from the play-ground, worn by urchin feet,
To the forbidden treasures; forays sad!
For fingers stained, or bulging pockets oft
Betrayed what the faint sobbing voice denied.
A picture of soft beauty shines the scene

When painted by the sinking summer sun
In tints of light and shade; but winter's gloom
Shows nothing but a waste, with one broad track
Stamped to the humble door-post from the lane;
The snow-capped wood-pile stretching near the walls;
And half-severed log with axe that leans
Within the gaping notch.

The room displays
Long rows of desk and bench; the former stained
And streaked with blots and trickles of dried ink,
Lumbered with maps and slates and well-thumbed books,
And carved with rude initials; while the knife
Has hacked and sliced the latter. In the midst
Stands the dread throne whence breathes supreme command,
And in a locked recess well known, is laid
The dread regalia, gifted with a charm
Potent to the rebellious. When the bell
Tinkles the school-hour, inward streams the crowd,
And bending heads proclaim the task begun.
Upon his throne, with magisterial brow,
The teacher sits, round casting frowning looks
As the low giggle and the shuffling foot
Betray the covert jest, or idleness.
Oft does he call, with deep and pompous voice,
The class before him; and shrill, chattering tones
In pert or blundering answers, break the soft
And dreamy hum of study, heretofore
Like beehive sounds prevailing. Now, perchance,
Some luckless urchin stands before the throne,
With features swoln as scarce to keep the tears,
And shoulders raised, while the detected fault
Is forth paraded, and the broken law
Learnedly dwelt on: then with staring sight,
Face all awry, and chattering teeth, he sees
The sceptre taken slowly from its nook,
A whip with thongs: pursues with blinking gaze
Its upward motion, then, with hideous yell,
Tells that the whizzing blow falls not in vain.
Now rising from his seat, the teacher strides
Athwart the room; as treads he past, each desk
Starts into industry: white figures grow
Upon the slate; black, spattering pothooks sprawl

Upon the blotted, dog-eared copy-book;
And eyes are glued upon the letters huge
And pictures of the primer: as he wheels,
The wandering glance has scarcely time to sink,
The queer grimace, and the replying grin
To vanish; each regaining its mute sway
As turns the back upon them. But bright noon
Now through the casement streams in quivering haze,
And gushes on the floor: the word is given,
And, bursting from the thraldom, rush without
The merry throngs, and breaking into groups,
Drive their loud pastime on the sunny green.
Here flies the ball, – there shoots the marble, – now
The racers seek the goal, – each sinew now
Is straining in the leap, – while heartfelt mirth
Echoes upon the soft and balmy air:
The clouds that float and wreathe upon the breeze
Not more restrainless than those happy hearts.
The glee, bright contrast to the sullen looks
And lingering steps with which each urchin seeks,
At the sad summons of the morning bell,
The hated porch. Yet is the school-house rude,
As is the chrysalis to the butterfly,
To the rich flower the seed. The dusky walls
Hold the fair germs of knowledge; and the tree,
Glorious in beauty, golden with its fruits,
To the low school-house traces back its life.

– Alfred B. Street, "The School-House,"
The Poems of Alfred B. Street (1867), I.55.
[pothooks = *S-shaped strokes in writing (from the S-shaped hooks for hanging pots and kettles over an open fire)*].

768. [In the classrooms of Mount Vernon (New York) High School in 1914] the desks were bolted to the floor. Whatever the furniture lacked in comfort and charm, you could be sure of one thing: It would be right there in the morning, in the exact same spot. Furthermore, the desk of one scholar was an integral part of the seat of the one scholar in front of him. Communication was maintained by sticking your toe through the slot between desk and seat and boring into the behind of your friend or enemy. The ferocity of the thrust was tempered to the state of the relationship. Desks were of black cast iron and dark-brown wood, and every desk had a distinct character of its own – the nicks and challenges of former occupants defacing it and creating a link between generations, the cuneiform record of the interminable hours. Every desk had a pencil groove, a sunken inkwell surrounded by a Devil's half acre of blue-black stain, and a book well.

—E.B. White, in Scott Elledge,
E.B. White: A Biography (1984), 33.

769. Still sits the school-house by the road,
A ragged beggar sleeping;
Around it still the sumachs grow,
And blackberry-vines are creeping.

Within, the master's desk is seen,
Deep scarred by raps official;
The warping floor, the battered seats,
The jack-knife's carved initial;

The charcoal frescoes on its wall;
Its door's worn sill, betraying
The feet that, creeping slow to school
Went storming out to playing!

—John Greenleaf Whittier, "In School-Days"
(1870), st.i–iii, *Complete Poetical Works* (1891).

Schoolmaster

See Teacher

Science

770. If you live you have to be going somewhere. You have to choose a direction. And science is completely impartial. It doesn't give a damn which way you go. It can invent the atom bomb but can't tell whether to use it or not. Science is like—well, it's like a flashlight in a totally dark room measuring two billion light-years across—and with walls that shift away from you as you go towards them. The flash can show you where your feet are on the floor; it can show you the furniture or the people close by; but as for which direction you should take in that endless room it can tell you nothing.

—Maxwell Anderson, *Joan of
Lorraine* (1946), II, "Rehearsal Preface."

771. Of course, there is only one [culture]. Of course, the natural sciences are just as "humane" as letters. There are, however, two languages, the spoken verbal language of literature, and the written sign language of mathematics, which is the language of science. This puts the scientist at a great advantage, for, since like all of us he has learned to read and write, he can understand a poem or a novel, whereas there are very few men of letters who can understand a scientific paper once they come to the mathematical parts.

—W.H. Auden, *A Certain World: A Commonplace Book* (1970), 92.

772. I am the last person to question the importance of genuine literary education, or to suppose that intellectual culture can be complete without it. An exclusively scientific training will bring about a mental twist as surely as an exclusively literary training. The value of the cargo does not compensate for a ship's being out of trim; and I should be very sorry to think that the Scientific College would turn out none but lopsided men.

—Thomas Henry Huxley, address in 1880 at the opening of Mason College (now University of Birmingham), *Collected Essays:* "Science and Culture" (1894). *See* Rabi, #775.

773. The phrase "popular science" has in itself a touch of absurdity. That knowledge which is popular is not scientific.

—Maria Mitchell, *Life, Letters and Journals,* compiled by Phebe Mitchell Kendall (1898).

774. Does science leave no mystery? On the contrary it proclaims mystery where others profess knowledge. There is mystery enough in the universe of sensation and in its capacity for containing those little corners of consciousness which project their own products, of order and law and reason, into an unknown and unknowable world. There is mystery enough here, only let us clearly distinguish it from ignorance within the field of possible knowledge. The one is inpenetrable, the other we are daily subduing.

—Karl Pearson, *The Grammar of Science* (1899).

775. What the world needs is a fusion of the sciences and the humanities. The humanities express the symbolic, poetic, and prophetic qualities of the human spirit. Without them we would not be conscious of our history; we would lose our aspirations and the graces of expression that move men's

hearts. The sciences express the creative urge in man to construct a universe which is comprehensible in terms of the human intellect. Without them, mankind would find itself bewildered in a world of natural forces beyond comprehension, victims of ignorance, superstition and fear.

—Isador I. Rabi, "Engineering and Science," commencement address at California Institute of Technology, June 1954. *See* Huxley, #772.

776. Our scientific world is our world of reasoning. It has its greatness and uses and attractions. We are ready to pay homage due to it. But when it claims to have discovered the real world for us and laughs at the worlds of all simple-minded men, then we must say it is like a general grown intoxicated with his power, usurping the throne of his king.

—Rabindranath Tagore, *Personality* (1917).

777. I passed all the other courses that I took at my University, but I never could pass botany. This was because all botany students had to spend several hours a week in a laboratory looking through a microscope at plant cells, and I could never see through a microscope. This used to enrage my instructor. He would wander around the laboratory pleased with the progress all the students were making in drawing the involved and, so I am told, interesting structure of flower cells, until it came to me. I would just be standing there. "I can't see anything," I would say. He would begin patiently enough, explaining how anybody can see through a microscope, but he would always end up in a fury, claiming that I could *too* see through a microscope but just pretended that I couldn't. "It takes away from the beauty of the flowers anyway," I used to tell him. "We are not concerned with beauty in this course," he would say. "We are concerned solely with what I may call the *mechanics* of flars." "Try it just once again," he'd say, and I would put my eye to the microscope and see nothing at all, except now and again a nebulous milky substance—a phenomenon of maladjustment. You were supposed to see a vivid, restless clockwork of sharply defined plant cells. "I see what looks like a lot of milk," I would tell him. This, he claimed, was the result of not having adjusted the microscope properly, so he would readjust it for me, or rather, for himself. And I would look again and see milk.

—James Thurber, "University Days," *The New Yorker* Magazine, 1933.

Sex

778. I think the test of obscenity is this: whether the tendency of the matter charged as obscenity is to deprave and corrupt those whose minds are open to such immoral influences, and into whose hands a publication of this sort may fall.

—Sir Alexander Cockburn, *Regina v Hicklin*, 1868; known as the Hicklin Rule. *Compare* Woolsey, **#782.**

779. The teacher in their one-room schoolhouse (c. 1865) . . . was constantly dismayed by the free and easy attitude of her farm-bred pupils toward sex. From the age of eight on they were busy experimenting, happily poking and feeling and rolling in the grass. It was shocking. And, occasionally, it was alarming. She always had to keep an eye on the outhouse door because that four-holer the local citizens had so generously built with their own hands was, she knew, a Mecca for her experimental biologists.

On several occasions, she had to interrupt the desk work she did during recess or lunch to go out, drive away the children waiting in line at the knot-holes and pound at the door until it was opened by one of the flush-faced children within.

—John S. Crosbie, *The Incredible Mrs. Chadwick* (1975), 7.

780. In English preparatory and public schools, romance is necessarily homo-sexual. The opposite sex is despised and hated, treated as something obscene. Many boys will never recover from this perversion. . . . For every born homo-sexual, there are at least ten permanent pseudo-homo-sexuals made by the public school system. And nine of these ten as honourably chaste and sentimental as I was.

—Robert Graves, *Goodbye to All That* (1929), 27.

781. The word vulgar, appearing promiscuously in American criticism, is the emptiest word in the critical vocabulary. Indiscriminately and with a supercilious snoot visited upon the writings of some of our best artists, its users betray simply their own fastidiousness, to say nothing of their ignorance of the platitudinous fact that some of the grantedly greatest art that the world has known has been as vulgar as pigs' feet. What, may one ask, would these critics say today of an artist whose characters expectorated all over the place, talked of whores and intimate biological functions and discoursed on human sex indulgence in terms of animals; who treated of incest, named certain of his women characters after the social diseases and their consequences and descended to the lowest form of gutter speech; whose characters were Christened after the more esoteric portions of the human anatomy and after the act of copulation, drank themselves into a state of stomach sickness, indulged in a prodigious belching, never failed to speak of disgusting odors, and swore like bohunks? That is, conceiving a second coming, of an artist like Shakespeare?

—George Jean Nathan,
American Mercury Magazine, July 1928.

782. The meaning of the word "obscene" as legally defined by the Courts is: tendency to stir the sex impulses or to lead to sexually impure and lustful thoughts. . . . Whether a particular book would tend to excite such impulses and thoughts must be tested by the Court's opinion as to its effect on a person with average sex instincts. . . . It is only with normal persons that the law is concerned.

—Justice John M. Woolsey,
Federal District Court decision, *United States v One Book Called "Ulysses,"* Dec. 6, 1933. *Compare* Cockburn, **#778.**

Speech

783. You ain't learnin' nothing when you're talking.

—Anonymous, motto that hung in the office of Lyndon B. Johnson during his years in the United States Senate, in Henry A. Zeiger, *Lyndon B. Johnson: Man and President* (1963), 67.

784. He mouths a sentence, as curs mouth a bone.

—Charles Churchill, *The Rosciad* (1761), ln. 332. *See* Emerson, **#650,** under "Reading."

785. An unnamed Alabama public school pupil told his teacher he didn't join in a classroom discussion because: "I think I will learn more by listening. Anything I would say, I already know."

—*Detroit Free Press,* Jan. 7, 1981.

786. A sophistical rhetorician, inebriated with the exuberance of his own verbosity.

—Benjamin Disraeli, referring to William E. Gladstone in a speech at the Riding School, London, July 27, 1878.

787. Gobbledygook: Talk or writing which is long, pompous, vague, involved, usually with Latinized words. It is also talk or writing which is merely long, even though the words are fairly simple, with repetition over and over again, all of which could have been said in a few words.

—Maury Maverick, *New York Times Magazine*, May 21, 1944.

788. Msimangu opened the book, and read to them first from the book. And Kumalo had not known that his friend had such a voice. For the voice was of gold, and the voice had love for the words it was reading. The voice shook and beat and trembled, not as the voice of an old man shakes and beats and trembles, nor as a leaf shakes and trembles, but as a deep bell when it is struck. For it was not only a voice of gold, but it was the voice of a man whose heart was golden, reading from a book of golden words. And the people were silent, and Kumalo was silent, for when are three such things found in one place together?

—Alan Paton, *Cry, the Beloved Country* (1948), 89.

789. Besides, as is usually the case, we are much more affected by the words which we hear, for though what we read in books may be more pointed, yet there is something in the voice, the look, the carriage, and even the gesture of the speaker, that makes a deeper impression on the mind.

—Pliny the Younger, *Letters*, II.iii (c. A.D. 98).

790. Spare me all superfluity of words.

—Sophocles, *Electra* (c. 410 B.C.), ln. 1288.

791. The arts babblative and scribblative.

—Robert Southey, *Colloquies on the Progress and Prospects of Society* (1829), X.ii.

792. I had by [the third grade] . . . picked up the notion that there was not necessarily much connection between the way teachers [in the Missouri Ozarks] expected you to pronounce words in oral reading and the way they were pronounced in real life.

Teacher speech in general struck me as a special lingo, lying somewhere between book language and normal speech. I was willing to adopt it myself for use in the schoolroom, but I had no reason to believe that it was ever spoken elsewhere. In fact I felt so strongly that it was inappropriate for everyday use that when one of my step-uncles brought his ex-schoolteacher wife back to the hills from Colorado, I helpfully taught their three children to abandon some of their teacherish speech habits.

I remember one puzzling episode in Aunt Elda's kitchen when I was visiting there shortly after I had started to school. Aunt Elda was fixing her children and me a snack, and she handed Marjorie two pieces of bread and jelly, asking her to take one to her brother.

Marjorie said, "He doesn't want any."

I said, "What do you say it like that for? That ain't the way people says it."

"That isn't the way people say it," Aunt Elda, who had resumed her chores, said distractedly.

"That's what I told her," I said.

—Ethel Strainchamps, *Don't Never Say Cain't* (1965), 10.

793. Who does not know that eloquence and all other arts have declined from their ancient glory, not from dearth of men, but from the indolence of the young, the carelessness of parents, the ignorance of teachers, and the neglect of the old discipline?

—Tacitus, *A Dialogue on Oratory* (c. A.D. 81), xxviii.

794. Would you repeat that again, sir, for it soun's sae sonorous that the words droon the ideas?

—John Wilson (*pseud.* Christopher North), *Noctes Ambrosianiae* (1822–35), xxvii.

Student

(*See also* Student, College; Student, First day at School; Student Pranks; Student Songs)

795. The college president: "Such rawness in a student, 'tis a shame,/ But lack of preparation is to blame."

The high school principal: "What crudity! The boy's a fool./ The fault, of course, is with the grammar school."

The grammar school principal: "O that from such a dunce I might be spared./ They send them up to me so unprepared."

The primary principal: "Poor kindergarten blockhead! And they call/ That preparation—worse than none at all."

The kindergarten teacher: "Such lack of training I ne'er did see;/ What sort of person can the mother be?"

The mother: "You stupid child! But you're not to blame;/ Your father's family are all the same!"

—Anonymous, "Passing the Buck," quoted by Merton E. Hill at a principals' convention in 1929, in *Phi Delta Kappan* Magazine, March 1979.

796. In the annals of medical science, no virus has given doctors as much trouble as the *Scholastis Adolescum,* otherwise known as school sickness.

The *Scholastis Adolescum* has been known to attack children of all ages and on every economic and social level. The symptoms are always the same. The child wakes up in the morning and says he has a "pain in the stomach," a "headache," a "sore throat" or he "just doesn't feel well." In rare cases he might also have a "slight" fever.

What has puzzled scientists for years is that the virus only attacks on weekdays and never on weekends or during summer vacations. It lasts only 24 hours, and while it has no serious after-effects, it keeps returning during the school year and even builds up in intensity just before test time.

Very little was known about the *Scholastis Adolescum* until Professor Heinrich Applebaum, in charge of virology at the Dropout Institute of Technology, did some unbelievable experiments in his laboratory.

Professor Applebaum used white mice for his experiment. . . .

On the basis of these experiments Professor Applebaum concluded the *Scholastis Adolescum* was connected with the nervous system, and would attack at any time the mice had to go to "school," do "homework" or face "tests." It would only disappear if the mice were assured they could play or watch television.

The mice in his experiment have by now all had offspring, and the offspring have all suffered from *Scholastis Adolescum,* showing conclusively that school sickness is inherited and passed on from one generation to another.

—Art Buchwald, *Son of the Great Society:* "Scholastis Adolescum" (1965), 188.

797. He who wishes to be a good pupil, besides performing his tasks well, must put forth every effort to resemble his master, and, if it were possible, to transform himself into his master. And when he feels that he has made some progress, it will be very profitable to observe different men of the same calling, and governing himself with that good judgment which must ever be his guide, to go about selecting now this thing from one and that thing from another.

—Baldassare Castiglione, *Il Libro del Cortegiano* (1528); tr. *The Courtyer* (1561).

798. I said: "You know, you are boring the hell out of me. You're supposed to be art students. Art students talk about art and books and movies and ideas. You're not talking about anything."

Dead silence. I thought: "Already the first day and I, with my big mouth, have blown it." Then I heard a soft voice saying: "Well, maybe the reason we don't talk about anything is that nobody ever asked us what we thought." I was very moved. I realized that no one had ever demanded of these women that they reach their potential.

—Judy Chicago, *Through the Flower* (1982), 74.

799. The schoolboys still their morning rambles take
To neighbouring village school with playing speed,
Loitering with pastime's leisure till they quake,
Oft looking up the wild-geese droves to heed,
Watching the letters which their journeys make;
Or plucking haws on which the fieldfares feed,
And hips, and sloes; and on each shallow lake
Making glib slides, where they like shadows go
Till some fresh pastimes in their minds awake.
Then off they start anew and hasty blow
Their numbed and clumpsing fingers till they glow;
Then races with their shadows wildly run
That stride huge giants o'er the shining snow
In the pale splendour of the winter sun.

—John Clare, "Schoolboys in Winter" (1824–32), in Donald J. Gray and G.B. Tennyson, eds., *Victorian Literature: Poetry* (1976), 18. [haws=*hawthorn berries;* hips=*the false fruit of roses;* sloes=*the fruit of the blackthorn tree;* glib=*smooth;* clumpsing=*benumbed*].

800. "You are oncommon in some things. You're oncommon small. Likewise you're a oncommon scholar."

"No, I am ignorant and backward, Joe."

"Why, see that letter you wrote last night! Wrote in print even! I've seen letters—Ah! and from gentlefolks!—that I'll swear weren't wrote in print," said Joe.

"I have learnt next to nothing, Joe. You think much of me. It's only that."

"Well, Pip," said Joe, "be it so, or be it son't, you must be a common scholar afore you can be a oncommon one, I should hope! The king upon his throne, with his crown upon his 'ed, can't sit and write his acts of Parliament in print, without having begun, when he were a unpromoted Prince, with the alphabet—Ah!" added Joe, with a shake of the head that was full of meaning, "and begun at A too, and worked his way to Z. And I know what that is to do, though I can't say I've exactly done it."

There was some hope in this piece of wisdom, and it rather encouraged me.

—Charles Dickens, *Great Expectations* (1860–61), ix.

801. At school, friendship is a passion. It entrances the being; it tears the soul. All loves of after life can never bring its rapture, or its wretchedness; no bliss so absorbing, no pangs of jealousy or despair so crushing and so keen! What tenderness and what devotion; what illimitable confidence; infinite revelations of inmost thoughts; what ecstatic present and romantic future; what bitter estrangements and what melting reconciliations; what scenes of wild recrimination, agitating explanations, passionate correspondence; what insane sensitiveness, and what frantic sensibility; what earthquakes of the heart, and whirlwinds of the soul, are confined in that simple phrase—a schoolboy's friendship! 'Tis some indefinite recollection of these mystic passages of their young emotion that makes gray-haired men mourn over the memory of their schoolboy days. It is a spell that can soften the acerbity of political warfare, and with its witchery can call forth a sigh even amid the callous bustle of fashionable saloons.

—Benjamin Disraeli, *Coningsby* (1844), 43. *See* Stekel, **#92,** under "Childhood."

802. When I think of the life-history of my schoolfellows [of the Scottish Foundation in Austria, 1888], I am struck by the comparatively few of our prize pupils who rose to later prominence. How easily our teachers may err in their judgment is shown by the abuse addressed by a master at the Schotten-gymnasium to Prince Conrad Hohenlohe: "Be glad you are a prince. With your Greek you'd never be more than a cobbler!" Yet Conrad Hohenlohe, later known as "the Red Prince" on account of his active sympathy with the workers, became a provincial governor, afterwards prime minister, and one of Austria's most brilliant sons.

—George Franckenstein, *Diplomat of Destiny* (1940), 9.

803. *Student* goes back to Latin *studium,* zeal or eagerness—a misnomer if there ever was one.

—Francis Griffith, *Phi Delta Kappan* Magazine.

804. Your poor little scholar
Paying his penny tuition, with one slave guarding his schoolbag.

—Juvenal, *Satires* (c. A.D. 125), IV.x.115. *See* Cowell, **#670,** and Lucan, **#674,** both under "Schedule, Daily Study."

805. A child may be transferred from one teacher to another who is more competent in reading and grammar, only, however, if both the teacher and the pupil live in the same town and are not separated by a river. But we must not take the child to a school in another town or even across a river in the same town, unless it is spanned by a firm bridge, not likely soon to collapse.

—Maimonides, *Mishneh Torah (Repetition of the Law* (1180), I.ii, in J.S. Minkin, *The World of Moses Maimonides* (1957), 287.

806. The notion that schoolboys are generally content with their lot seems to me to be a sad delusion. They are, in the main, able to bear it, but they like it no more than a soldier enjoys life in a foxhole. The need to endure it makes actors of them; they learn how to lie—perhaps the most valuable thing, to a citizen of Christendom, that they learn in school. No boy genuinely loves and admires his teacher; the farthest he can go, assuming him to have all of his wits, is to tolerate her as he tolerates castor oil. She may be the loveliest flower in the whole pedagogical garden, but the most he can ever see in her is a jailer who might conceivably be worse.

School-days, I believe, are the unhappiest in the whole span of human existence. They are full of dull, unintelligible tasks, new and unpleasant ordinances, brutal violations of common sense and common decency. It doesn't take a reasonably bright boy long to discover that most of what is rammed into him is nonsense, and that no one really cares very much whether he learns it or not. His parents, unless they are infantile in mind, tend to be bored by his lessons and labors, and are unable to conceal the fact from his sharp eyes. His first teachers he views simply as disagreeable policemen. His later ones he usually sets down quite accurately as asses. . . .

There should be more sympathy for school-children. The idea that they are happy is of a piece with the idea that the lobster in the pot is happy. They are, in more ways than one, the worst and most pathetic victims of the complex of inanities and cruelties called civilization. The human race is so stupid that it has never managed to teach them its necessary tricks and delusions in a painless and pleasant manner. The cats and dogs do better by their young, and so, in fact, do savages.

—H.L. Mencken, *New York American*, Jan. 20, 1936, in *A Mencken Chrestomathy* (1949), 308, 310.

807. It is different, somehow with boys to teach. Of course, there are not yet many pupils in the high school, thirty-odd this year [1875]. And most of them are boys who are ambitious and are preparing themselves for college. They actually want to learn. . . . Besides, boys are pleasanter to teach than girls: they don't dodge and squirm down devious paths in their minds. If you ask them questions they can't answer, they say they don't know.... They have intellectual curiosity: they want to find out. And girls after all, when and if you have taught them, what do they do? Get married!... Out of a lifetime's teaching of boys, there will be a few who will become great and famous men, and one will have the satisfaction of having helped them at the start.

—Helen Hoover Santmyer,
"...*And Ladies of the Club*" (1982), 200.

808. Rockwell [Kent's] stubbornness ... led to conflicts with teachers [of Episcopal Academy, 1893]. Though an adequate student, he did not see any value in learning Latin, and therefore decided that he would not. The teacher, having another opinion, forced Kent to spend every evening in his presence with the Latin book open to the day's lesson. Night after night went by with the teacher and student locked in a test of wills. "It got to be like a sporting event, a kind of marathon. Who'd last the longest." The teacher, finally deciding that victory would not be worth the cost of his evenings, gave up the struggle.

—David Traxel, *An American Saga: The Life and Times of Rockwell Kent* (1980), 10.

Student, College (University)

(*See also* College; Manners; Student Pranks; Student Songs)

809. [In 1099] I arrived at last in Paris where for a long time dialectics had specially flourished under William of Champeaux, rightly reckoned the first of my masters in that branch of study. I stayed some time in this school, but, though well received at first, I soon got to be an annoyance to him because I persisted in refuting certain ideas of his, and because, not being afraid to enter into argument against him, I sometimes got the better. This boldness, too, roused the wrath of those fellow-students who were classed higher, because I was the youngest and the last comer. This was the beginning of my series of misfortunes which still last; my renown every day increasing, envy was kindled against me in every direction.

—Peter Abelard, at 20 years of age, in Henry Brooks Adams, *Mont Saint-Michel and Chartres* (1904). Because his fame as a dialectician attracted so many students, Abelard is usually regarded as the founder of the University of Paris.

810. I knew three undergraduates [of Edinburgh University] who lodged together in a dreary house at the top of a dreary street; two of them used to study until two in the morning, while the third slept. When they shut up their books they woke number three, who arose, dressed, and studied until breakfast time. Among the many advantages of the arrangement the chief was that, as they were dreadfully poor, one bed did for the three. Two of them occupied it at the one time, and third another. Terrible privations? Frightful destitution? Not a bit of it. The Millennium was in those days. If life was at the top of a hundred steps, if students occasionally died of hunger and hard work combined, if the midnight oil only burned to show a ghastly face "weary and worn," if lodgings were cheap and dirty, and dinners few and far between, life was still real and earnest; in many cases it did not turn out an empty dream.

—J.M. Barrie, c. 1878–82, in Janet Dunbar,
J.M. Barrie: The Man Behind the Image (1970), 39.

811. When I went away to college, a generation ago, I took a steamer trunk to hold my clothes and a shopping bag for miscellaneous items such as an alarm clock, an umbrella, a radio, and a tennis racket. I remember my father teasing me about "taking all that stuff to school," and my arguing that these were all "absolute necessities," though I suppose it was a bit much, especially since I was also toting a typewriter, an extra coat, and a huge stuffed animal to which I was not particularly devoted but which was definitely *de rigueur* in a girl's dorm room in that era.

A generation later, when our son John went off to college, things were a bit different. John took a shopping bag to hold his clothes (his entire wardrobe consisting of two pairs of jeans, a couple of T-shirts, and twelve sweat bands) and a U-Haul for his miscellaneous items: refrigerator, recliner, hot plate, sunlamp, television set, full component stereo system, typewriter, tape recorder, ten-speed bike, and numerous boxes of records and books, some of which were expensive college texts that he had managed to purchase secondhand during summer.

"You can't take all that stuff to school!" I admonished John, with much less humor than my father had shown me twenty-five years before.

To my surprise, John agreed.

"You're right," he said. "I'll never be able to store all this stuff in my room. I'll have to sacrifice something."

And he did. He gave up the textbooks.

—Teresa Bloomingdale,
Up a Family Tree: "Off to College" (1981), 145.

812. Why did they go to college [c. 1898], those thousands upon mounting thousands that crowded the campuses in those decades? . . .

They came for the best of reasons. They swarmed from the drab experiences of small town or commercial city, direct or via the boarding schools, because they had heard of college life, where, instead of the monotony of school discipline or the bourgeois experience which had succeeded their confident childhood, there was singing, cheering, drinking, and the keenest competition for honor and prestige, a life rich in the motives which were being stifled in the struggle for power in the adult world outside. They desired romance, they sought distinction, and were not unwilling to spend some bookish labor in order to win the opportunities of a class that called itself educated.

—Henry Seidel Canby, *American Memoir* (1947).

813. A Clerk[1] ther was of Oxenford also,
That un-to logik hadde longe y-go[2].
As lene was his hors as is a rake,
And he nas nat[3] right fat, I undertake;
But loked holwe[4], and there-to soberly.
Ful thredbar was his overest courtepy[5];
For he had geten[6] him yet no benefice,
Ne was so worldly for to have office[7].
For him was levere[8] have at his beddes heed
Twenty bokes, clad in blak or reed
Of Aristotle and his philosophye,
Than robes riche, or fithele[9], or gay sautrye[10].
But al be that he was a philosophre,
Yet hadde he but litel gold in cofre;
But al that he mighte of his frendes hente[11],
On bokes and on lerninge he spente
And bisily gan for the soules preye
Of hem that yaf[12] him where-with to scholeye[13].
Of studie took he most cure[14] and most hede.
Noght o[15] word spak he more than was nede,
And that was seyd in forme and reverence,
And short and quik, and ful of hy sentence[16].
Sowninge in[17] moral vertu was his speche,
And gladly wolde he lerne, and gladly teche.

—Geoffrey Chaucer, *Canterbury Tales:* "Prologue," (c. 1386).
[1. student; 2. gone, devoted himself; 3. was not; 4. hollow; 5. outer short coat; 6. gotten; 7. secular employment; 8. rather; 9. fiddle; 10. psaltery; 11. obtain; 12. gave; 13. go to school; 14. care; 15. not one; 16. meaning; 17. tending to.]

814. When she comes tripping by, stone lions will bark. A Revolutionary War cannon will fire out. Two facing statues will solemnly dismount from their pedestals, walk to the center of the courtyard, and clasp hands in congratulation. A series of boulders, delicately balanced atop each other by nature's art, will suddenly collapse. When she gazes their way, the Flattop Mountains will turn purple with rage.

On these college campuses throughout the country these various signs will greet her achievement. For she will be the first virgin to graduate from the University. One report states that the teetering rocks on the University of Alabama campus did once topple to the earth, when an undefiled soul passed by. It belonged to a young man.

—Richard M. Dorson, "Folklore,"
The American Mercury Magazine, 1949.

815. On entering the [Erfurt] university [in 1501] the new student was subjected to 'deposition,' an old custom, carried out pretty roughly, that consisted of 'deposing' the 'brutish' non-student, symbolized by a cap surmounted with horns and asses' ears which was torn off him, and 'christening' him as a new-born undergraduate by ducking him in the water-butt.... The uniform resembled that of a priest, and this in any case was what most of the students were going to be; at the side of the gown, however, each student carried a short sword, and it was not worn merely for decoration. Despite the strict daily schedule, brawls were frequent.... The official drink at meals, which were copious, was beer, but we may be certain that not everyone contented himself with this.... Among the professors were some very gay spirits, though not, of course, among those of the older and more devout school.... The humanist professors, who called themselves proudly 'the poets' and turned out their Latin verses, had found precedents among the ancients to justify a somewhat freer life.

—Richard Friedenthal, *Luther: His Life and Times* (1970), 19.

816. When James A. Garfield was president of Hiram College, in Ohio, he was approached by the father of a prospective pupil.

"Can't you simplify the course?" he asked. "My boy will never take all that in. He wants to get through by a shorter route."

"Certainly," answered Garfield, "I can arrange that. It depends, of course, on what you want to make of him. When God wants an oak, he takes a hundred years; but when he wants to make a squash, he requires only two months."

—James A. Garfield, in Martha Lupton, ed.,
The Treasury of Modern Humor, (1938), 872.

817. Sir, I was at Colonel Peter Randolph's about a fortnight ago, and my schooling falling into discourse, he said he thought it would be to my advantage to go to college, and was desirous I should go, as indeed I am myself for several reasons. In the first place as long as I stay at the mountains the loss of one-fourth of my time is inevitable, by company's coming here and detaining me from school. And likewise my absence will in a great measure put a stop to so much company, and by that means lessen the expenses of the estate in house-keeping. And on the other hand by going to college I shall get a more universal acquaintance, which may hereafter be serviceable to me; and I suppose I can pursue my studies in the Greek and Latin as well there as here, and likewise learn something of the mathematics. I shall be glad of your opinion, and remain, sir, your most humble servant.

—Thomas Jefferson, age 17,
letter to John Harvey, Jan. 14, 1760, in Saul K. Padover,
A Jefferson Profile as Revealed in His Letters (1956), 3.

818. Digamma Phi was housed in a residence built in the expansive days of 1885. The living room suggested a recent cyclone. Knife-gashed tables, broken Morris chairs, and torn rugs were flung about the room, and covered with backless books, hockey shoes, caps, and cigarette stubs. Above, there were four men to a bedroom, and the beds were iron double-deckers, like a steerage.

For ash-trays the Digams used sawed skulls, and on the bedroom walls were anatomical charts, to be studied while dressing. In Martin's room was a complete skeleton. He and his roommates had trustingly bought it from a salesman who came out from a Zenith surgical supply house.

—Sinclair Lewis, *Arrowsmith* (1925), 15.

819. The students [of Le Collège de Montaigu, c. 1521] fell into three groups: the rich *pensionnaires* or *portionnistes* who ate at a common table; the also rich *caméristes* who lived *en chambre* in neighbouring homes and were fed at their own expense; and *les pauvres,* who lived in the college itself and seem to have occupied a position somewhat akin to that of sizars [students who received financial aid] in unreformed Oxford and Cambridge. They had to do housework; they worshipped in a separate chapel; the arts students among them had to enter the lecture room before *les riches* and sit apart from them. And whereas the *pensionnaires* and *caméristes* were expected to cope with their fleas and lice themselves, *les pauvres* had to undergo a regular inspection.

—T.H.L. Parker, *John Calvin* (1975), 7.

820. Madam, we guarantee results—or we return the boy.

—Francis Landey Patton,
president of Princeton University (1888–1902),
in Jacques Barzun, *The Teacher in America* (1944), 13.

821. He was sent, as usual, to a public school, where a little learning was painfully beaten into him, and from thence to the university, where it was carefully taken out of him.

—Thomas Love Peacock, *Nightmare Abbey* (1818), i.

822. We the undersigned conscious of the alarming degree to which the drinking of spiritous liquor has been carried in the Corps, and knowing full well that if continued it must prove destructive of the most valuable Institution, do set our countenances against it, and do pledge our word and honor that we will not in any wise use Wine or Spiritous liquor so long as we remain members of the Institution except when sanctioned by the Superintendent.

—Pledge signed by 49 West Point cadets,
February 1824, in Sidney Forman, *West Point* (1950).

823. Howbeit seeing that divers Chronicles do remember a very grievous discord to have hapned this year [1354] between the Scholars [of Oxford] and the Townsmen, and that divers were wounded and some slain....

On Tuesday 10 Feb. (being the feast of S. Scholastica the Virgin) came Walter de Springheuse, Roger de Chesterfield, and other Clerks, to the Tavern called Swyndlestock ... and there calling for wine, John de Croydon the Vintner brought them some, but they disliking it, as it should seem, and he avouching it to be good, several snappish words passed between them. At length the Vintner giving them stubborn and saucy language, they threw the wine and vessel at his head. The Vintner therefore receding with great passion, and aggravating the abuse to those of his family and neighborhood, several came in, encouraged him not to put up the abuse, and withal told him they would faithfully stand by him.... [They] caused the Town Bell at St. Martin's to be rung, that the Commonalty might be summoned together in a body. Which being begun they in an instant were in arms, some with bows and arrows, others with divers sorts of weapons. And then they without any more ado did in a furious and hostile manner, suddenly set upon divers Scholars, who at that time had not any offensive arms, no not so much as any thing to defend themselves.

On the next day ... the Ballives of the Town ... had given particular warning to every Townsman at his respective house in the morning that they should make themselves ready to fight with the Scholars against the time when the Town Bell should ring out, and also given notice before the country round about, and hired people to come in and assist the Townsmen in their intended conflict with the Scholars. . . .

The Scholars . . . , being unable to resist so great and fierce a company, they withdrew themselves to their lodgings. . . .

But the Townsmen finding no Scholars in the streets to make any opposition, pursued them, and that day broke open five Inns, or Hostles of Scholars with fire and sword.

—Anthony Wood, *History and Antiquities of University of Oxford* (1674). The medieval universities were self-governing communities with special grants and privileges bitterly resented by the townspeople. The riot, in which sixty students were killed, lasted three days and nights. The number of town casualties is unreported.

Student, First Day of School

824. Education was free. That subject my father had written about repeatedly, as comprising his chief hope for us children, the essence of American opportunity, the treasure that no thief could touch, nor even misfortune of poverty. It was the one thing that he was able to promise us when he sent for us; surer, safer than bread or shelter. On our second day I was thrilled with the realization of what this freedom of education meant. A little girl from across the alley came and offered to conduct us to school. My father was out, but we five between us had a few words of English by this time. We knew the word school. We understood. This child, who had never seen us until yesterday, who could not pronounce our names, who was not much better dressed than we were, was able to offer us the freedom of the schools of Boston! No application was made, no questions asked, no examinations, rulings, exclusions; no machinations, no fees. The doors stood open for every one of us. The smallest child could show us the way.

—Mary Antin, *The Promised Land* (1912), 186. She emigrated from White Russia in 1894.

825. The day came when I was to enter school. I was to go to what was called "the receiving grade," which antedated the kindergarten. But first I had to be vaccinated, and there were several unforgettable visits to the doctor's office. . . .

At last the big day arrived. I was to go to school. I remember my dress. It was of white voile, printed with tiny rosebuds. . . . Gene Glenn . . . , two houses away, was delegated to take me to school. He arrived in knickerbockers and cap, said, "Come on," and stalked ahead of me. At the schoolyard he pointed, said, "In there," and in I went.

My teacher was Miss Timmons. I will never forget her, because through her I had the greatest thrill of my life, and something happened which has enriched all my days, and will until I die.

She had a big chart, with leaves that flopped over, and a long-handled pointer. With this she showed us a letter of the alphabet (which we all knew and recognized) and taught us to make appropriate sounds. *Aaaaaa* for A. A stuttering *bbbbbb*, then a sound like K, or *kkkkkk* for C, and so on. This went on for some time, and seemed to have no reason. It was just something teachers do.

But one day she showed three letters and we sounded each one. C *(kkkkkk)* A *(aaaaaa)* T *(tttttt)*. And there, on the chart, was a picture of a cat. And we had said it! CAT! The wonderful, radiant light broke over me. This was reading! I never got over it.

—Elizabeth Borton de Treviño,
The Hearthstone of My Heart (1977), 22.

826. It was a memorable day in the records of the Frick family when the eager-eyed lad [Clay Frick] set forth [in 1857] . . . to seek an education. No more than acquaintance with the custom of the time is required to visualize accurately the pretty picture, typical of pastoral life, when, scrubbed and brushed, in a brand new suit of store clothes and brass knobbed shoes, holding fast to his mother's hand, he awaited impatiently in the doorway the arrival of his cousin Isaac Overholt to escort him to school. And no less clearly can the mind's eye dwell with smiling sympathy upon the fair countenance of [his mother] . . . as with hands folded, following a final pat upon his head, she watched her man-child march primly forward to take his place in the busy world.

Schoolmaster Voight greeted the little chap with a low bow and, taking him by the hand, led him upon the stage and announced impressively to the boys and girls:

"I present to you Mr. Henry Clay Frick."

—George Harvey, *Henry Clay Frick* (1928), 13.

827. "Now, Tom, my boy," said the Squire, "remember you are going at your own request, to be chucked into this great school, like a young bear with all your troubles before you, earlier than we should have sent you perhaps. If schools are what they were in my time, you'll see a great many cruel blackguard things done, and hear a deal of foul bad talk. But never you fear. You tell the truth, keep a brave and kind heart, and never listen to, or say anything you wouldn't have your mother or sister hear, and you'll never feel ashamed to come home, or me to see you."

—Thomas Hughes, *Tom Brown's School Days* (1857).

828. Bending over, my father touched my hair and patted me. . . .

"You're going to learn to read and write here so you can become a man," he said. "Cross yourself."

The teacher appeared in the doorway. He was holding a long switch and seemed like a savage to me, a savage with huge fangs. I pinned my eyes on the top of his head to see if he had horns. But I was unable to see, because he was wearing a hat.

"This is my son," my father said.

Untangling my hand from his own, he turned me over to the teacher.

"His bones are mine, his flesh is yours. Don't feel sorry for him. Thrash him and make a man of him."

Don't worry, Captain Michael," said the teacher, pointing to his switch. "Right here is the tool which makes men."

—Nikos Kazantzakis, on enrolling in a Greek school, *Report to Greco* (1965), 52.

829. I began life [in Scotland], and that after no pleasant fashion, as near as I can guess, about the age of six years. One glorious morning in early summer I found myself led by the ungentle hand of Mrs. Mitchell toward a little school on the outside of the village, kept by an old woman called Mrs. Shand. . . . I looked around at the shining fields and up at the blue sky, where a lark was singing as if he had just found out that he could sing, with something like despair of a man going to the gallows and bidding farewell to the world. . . . I was led to the cottage door—no such cottage as some of my readers will picture, with roses and honeysuckle hiding its walls, but a dreary little house with nothing green to cover the brown stones of which it was built. . . . Did I say there was nothing on the walls? This morning there was the loveliest sunshine, and that I was going to leave behind. . . .

Mrs. Mitchell opened the door and led me in. It was an awful experience. Dame Shand stood at her table ironing. She was as tall as Mrs. Mitchell, and that was enough to prejudice me against her at once. She wore a close-fitting widow's cap, with a black ribbon around it. Her hair was gray, and her face was as gray as her hair, and her skin was gathered in wrinkles about her mouth, where they twitched and twitched, as if she were constantly meditating something unpleasant. She looked up inquiringly.

"I've brought you a new scholar," said Mrs. Mitchell.

"Well. Very well," said the dame, in a dubious tone. "I hope he's a good boy, for he must be good if he comes here."

"Well, he's just middling. His father spares the rod, Mrs. Shand, and we know what comes of that." . . .

Meanwhile I was making what observations my terror would allow. About a dozen children were seated on benches along the walls, looking over the tops of their spelling books at the newcomer. . . . Some movement drew my eyes to the floor; there I saw a boy of my own age on all fours, fastened by a string to a leg of the table at which the dame was ironing, while—horrible to relate!—a dog, not very big, but very ugly, and big enough to be frightened at, lay under the table watching him. I gazed in utter dismay.

"Ah, you may look!" said the dame. "If you're not a good boy, that is how you shall be served. The dog shall have you to look after."

—George MacDonald, *Ranald Bannerman's Boyhood* (1871).

830. After my father's departure [on the first day of school in Lahore, India] I kicked up a terrible row, and said I would burn the place down. That evening my father came again, and I thought we would go home now, but we did not. Every day, in the morning and evening, my father came to take me for a walk, or for a carriage ride. . . . Then, one day, he did not come either in the morning or in the evening. . . . I sobbed and sobbed. Inside me, my heart was sick. . . .

About the next few months my memories are vague, except that of an intense grief which hung about my heart every hour of the day. With the passing of time I was able to divert myself to some temporary amusement, but then, suddenly in the middle of things, a wave of nostalgia would rush upon me, making me helpless and stricken, and again and again the feeling of the fear of the unknown would come upon me. Nothing could really make me forget my loss and parting from those I loved, and to this day at the time of sorrow the same sense of loss comes over me.

—Savitri Devi Nanda, *City of Two Gateways* (1950).

831. Mother took the day off to enroll me in Fernwood Elementary School. I pulled at her hand all the way. Inside the big red-brick building, I breathed in its perfume—the fragrance of chalk, of pine-smelling soap. In a small room with bright-yellow walls, a black-haired woman with soft brown eyes sat on a chair as small as mine and talked to me. How wonderful to talk to an adult without looking way, way up!

Her name, she said, was Elsa Leiser, and she was the principal. Did I want to meet my teacher? I wanted to stay right there, talking to the nice lady with eyes the color of Hershey bars. . . .

Kindergarten was only slightly disappointing. Miss Wasachek explained that *next year* I would learn to read. Meanwhile, I had other things to figure out—like how the piano worked and why the sky I painted logically at the top of the paper looked all wrong.

I was also giving some thoughts to why boys were treated less kindly than girls. Even sweet-tempered Miss Wasachek scolded them often. I noticed too that their clothes were of drab colors, whereas mine were pretty and bright. Well, boys did seem to get muddy a lot. Perhaps their mothers dressed them so that mud would not show. But even Miss Leiser spoke more sternly to the boys than to us. I felt sorry for them. Most of them were very nice. But I noticed too that, except for the janitor, there were no men in the school. Apparently, unlike in Grandfather's house, the outside world was run by women.

—Lois Mark Stalvey,
The Education of an Ordinary Woman (1982), 13.

832. When . . . I found myself at the school for the first time, . . . [a] . . . difficulty [arose] . . . with regard to my name, or rather *a* name. From the time when I could remember anything, I had been called simply "Booker." Before going to school it had never occurred to me that it was needful or appropriate to have an additional name. When I heard the school-roll called, I noticed that all of the children had at least two names, and some of them indulged in what seemed to me the extravagance of having three. I was in deep perplexity, because I knew that the teacher would demand of me at least two names, and I had only one. By the time the occasion came for the enrolling of my name, an idea occurred to me which I thought would make me equal to the situation; and so, when the teacher asked me what my full name was, I calmly told him "Booker Washington," as if I had been called by that name all my life; and by that name I have since been known. Later in my life I found that my mother had given me the name of "Booker Taliaferro" soon after I was born, . . . and [I] made my full name "Booker Taliaferro Washington." I think there are not many men in our country who have had the privilege of naming themselves in the way that I have.

—Booker T. Washington, *Up From Slavery* (1901), 24, 25.

833. I was sent to school. What a day! Ma started to take me, but Pa objected. He always objected when she coddled me. Of course I liked to be coddled, and I sided with her; but he had his way. The compromise was that he said, "I'll take him!" And so we started out. She was in the doorway, and I left her with eyes full of tears, for she knew, having taught school, that I would never come back her baby! She knew that I was gone out of her life as a child and would return that noon a middle-aged young person, out in the world for good and all. Pa took me two blocks on the way to the schoolhouse, still three blocks away, and when he was out of sight of Ma and the doorway he prodded me with his cane in pride and affection and said:

"Now, Willie, you are a man. Go to school!" and turned and left me. He could not bear the shame of bringing me into the schoolroom, shame for him and shame for me, and we both knew it. And I trudged on and was glad. And then, for the first time, I remember Albert Ewing coming along the same way, and he and I walked into the schoolroom together — my first boy friend. After that day we were inseparable for ten years.

— William Allen White, *Autobiography* (1946), 37.

Student Pranks

834. To-night, to-night,
The pillow fight,
Tomorrow's the end of school;
Break the dishes, break the chairs,
And trip the teachers on the stairs!

— Anonymous.

835. At the end of the first year of operation [of Cornell University, 1869] the Business Manager, Erastus G. Putnam, included in his report the following items under the head of Malicious Mischief:

Damages to College Furniture by wanton breakage and cutting, besides ordinary wear and tear	$ 500
Damage to buildings (not including accidental damage)	500
Tools, lumber, and combustibles consumed in the Christmas bonfire	200
Outhouse destroyed at the July vacation	255
Loss of burning of Eddy's factory near Cascadilla House	1,000
Settees and beds stored therein, all new	890
Other property known to have been burned	300
Steam engine destroyed	500
Damage to Cascadilla House	100
	$4,245

This reckoning is clearly much inflated. It is nevertheless noteworthy, at a time when the operating budget of the University was about $100,000.

— Morris Bishop, *A History of Cornell* (1962), 130.

836. [*Circa* 1800] Young [John] Tyler and other boys in the neighborhood were attending school kept by a Mr. McMurdo, a Scotchman, who imposed a Spartan discipline. His rule over his pupils was so severe that, as President Tyler afterwards said, "it was a wonder he did not whip all the sense out of his scholars." Finally his tyranny reached the point at which forbearance on the part of his pupils ceased to be a virtue, and they rose in revolt. Young Tyler headed this miniature rebellion.

The boys, after throwing McMurdo down, proceeded to tie his hands and feet. The victory having been won, the boys locked the door with their victim firmly bound within. He remained in this uncomfortable and humiliating position until late in the afternoon, when a passing traveler found and released him.

—Oliver Perry Chitwood,
John Tyler: Champion of the Old South (1939), 13.

837. Most of the teachers [of Cathedral School in Denmark] were the natural victims of our hunting instincts. . . . Throughout our school days we actually spent less time and energy on our work than in our efforts to invent new ways of torturing our teachers. I remember I took my turn in heating the handle of our classroom door with an alcohol lamp just before the arrival of one man we detested.

Once we locked up a rooster in the teacher's desk. When he opened it to get out his papers, the bird flew straight into his face. He ran to the headmaster's office, far enough from our classroom to give us time to throw the poor bird out the window and to close it again. When the headmaster arrived there was no rooster and no boy had seen any bird in the room. Unfortunately the rooster was returned to the school by a man who had caught it coming out of the window. Although the matter was never cleared up, I was taken to be the culprit. The headmaster told me I ought to be expelled, but since he suspected that Jonathan, the bishop's son, was my accomplice, he dropped the matter.

—Peter Freuchen, *Vagrant Viking*, tr. Johan Hambro (1953), 21.

838. Most of the hostility the students [of Brown University, c. 1816] had for their professors was siphoned off in the form of good-natured horseplay. . . .

Pranks . . . forced the faculty and neighbors ever to be on alert. Nearby henhouses were raided when portions became diminished at commons, and the plunder was picked, cleaned, and then roasted in the open fireplace in the students' rooms. One cold December night the entire student body was roused from its sleep by the smell of smoke and shouts of fire.

The steward's outhouse was going up in flames, and from there the fire spread to several haystacks in the college yard. [President] Asa Messer's letter to more than one parent the following week made it plain that he did not believe the blaze had been caused by spontaneous combustion. Samuel Gridley Howe, later to become Mann's closest coworker in many reforms, was involved in a number of escapades. Once he filled his tutor's bed with ashes. He also performed the more remarkable feat of leading President Messer's horse up the stairs of University Hall. At the appropriate time, the bewildered animal stuck its head out of a window and whinnied at its surprised master who happened by. At another time a farmer's wood sled was dismantled, carried to the roof of University Hall, and reassembled. Messer's horse also put in an impromptu appearance at a junior exhibition sporting the freshly painted letters "A.M." on its flanks. All these seasoned an otherwise monotonous fare. . . .

However, by comparison with other colleges, Brown was a model of decorum.

—Jonathan Messerli, *Horace Mann* (1972), 36–38.

839. [*Circa* 1917] The toilets were at the rear of the school; the girls' outhouse was of brick and the boys' was of wood. (Talk about Women's Lib!). . . .

The girls' brick outhouse was a challenge to the boys. They would sneak up to it and listen to the doorlatch to hear all the secrets the girls were chattering and giggling about; sometimes about them. We would jeer loudly when he heard something we were not supposed to. We threatened to tell the teacher what a certain little miss thought about her. Or we would pepper the privy door with stones, just to hear the girls holler. Sometimes one of them would use some bad language, and we catcalled, "We're gonna tell teacher! We're gonna tell teacher!" We grew quiet when a girl would remind us that we had said nasty words and drawn dirty pictures of female organs on the walls of a shed across the road where milk was picked up. Often, we boys would dare each other to invade the girls' privy while they entered it during recess, but no one quite succeeded. One of us came close when he followed a squealing girl through the open door, but he was shoved out by some of the girls already inside. I suspect they enjoyed the thrill of this game as much as we did.

—Charles A. Root, Jr., *The House on Ann Street* (1986), 33.

840. The only exciting event which occurred while I was at this [log cabin] school [in the 1780s] was barring out the school-master. It was the custom to have a fortnight's holiday at Christmas; and the day it was to commence was always announced by the school-master a week beforehand. The object of barring him out was to compel him to begin the holidays some days sooner. But it was not so much for the purpose of gaining a few more days of idleness, as for the pleasure and excitement of the feat. And, strange as it may appear at this day, the parents of the scholars all knew of the plan, and were ready to advise as to the best mode of defence, and encouraged the children to fight bravely and conquer the master, if he should prove obstinate and break in.

The barring-out to which I was a party, was carefully planned among the boys some days before it was executed. It was the custom of the schoolmaster to give us recess every day from twelve o'clock until one, to give us an opportunity of eating our dinners (which we all brought with us) and for recreation. This hour was technically called in the school, playtime, during which the teacher always went to his own house, distant a few hundred yards, for his own dinner. When the hour was out, he appeared at the door and shouted with a loud voice, "Come to books." The boys determined that on the appointed day the barring-out should take place at playtime. Accordingly, as soon as the recess commenced, and the schoolmaster was out of hearing, the benches were heaped against the door, and the window nailed up, and a strong fire made, to prevent him from ascending the low roof of the cabin and coming down the chimney; and after eating our frugal dinners, we awaited with some anxiety his return. The girls who belonged to the school were of course excluded from the garrison.

He returned at the usual hour, and appeared surprised when he found the door closed against him. He ordered us to open it. We refused unless he agreed that the holidays should commence on that day. He seemed offended, and threatened us; and after trying to force the door by his own strength, and failing, he took a rail from a fence at hand and began striking the door with considerable force, as if he was determined to break in. We began to think there would be a real fight. But after thumping the door for some time, and trying the window, and threatening to keep us confined there all the ensuing night unless we surrendered, he finally yielded to our demands, and we unbarred the door and let him in. After some good-natured conversation on both sides, we took leave of him in our usual respectful manner, calling him "Master," as was the usage of the time, and returned to our homes in triumph. But I doubt whether he intended to do more than he supposed to be necessary for the purpose of showing that he did not connive in our attempts to gain an addition to the customary holiday, by which he would, in truth, profit as well as ourselves.

—Roger Brooke Taney, unfinished autobiography,
in Walker Lewis, *Without Fear or Favor* (1965), 10.

841. Mr. Graves [a teacher at Harvard], not having his name for nought, lost the love of the undergraduates by his too much austerity, whereupon they used to strike a nail above the hall door-catch while we were reciting to him, and so nail him in the hall. At which disorder I was troubled, whereupon being desired by him to go into the buttery privily and watch who did it, one morning I did so; but being spied by the scholars I was fain to haste out and make haste to Boston before I spake to Mr. Graves, the better to cloak over the business that so the scholars might conclude it was accidental and not *ex proposito* (for I was fearful of incensing them against me), for which, notwithstanding the hazard I was in of setting them against me and the love I expressed to Mr. Graves in putting myself for his sake into such a hazard, I was checked by him when I came up again.

—Edward Taylor (1642?–1729), diary,
in *Proceedings of the Massachusetts Historical Society*, 1881.

842. Above the entrance [of the Dutch school] hung a signboard with its inscription painted in vivid letters of black on white: HERE IS A SCHOOL WITH THE BIBLE, THE FEAR OF THE LORD IS THE BEGINNING OF WISDOM....

Not a single detail of the school's interior arrangement has faded from memory.... I still see the long line of wooden shoes in the hallway and the austere whitewashed classrooms where our eyes smarted from the clouds of acrid smoke which poured from the potbellied stoves when the wind blew from the northwest.... Back of the principal's desk hung a rack for his collection of long clay pipes which he used in rotation. Occasionally, when we judged the reprisals were in order for some measure of collective punishment the master had meted out, we secretly smeared the mouthpieces of his pipes with a certain invisible and unmentionable concoction. We then sat back to watch his grimaces of disgust when he placed the stem in his mouth.

—Pierre van Paassen, *Days of Our Years* (1939), 4.

Student Songs

843. No more lessons, no more books,
No more teacher's sassy looks,
No more Latin, no more French,
No more sitting on a hard board bench.

—Anonymous, schoolchildren's song, c. 1850.

844. Many's the night I spent with Minnie the Mermaid,
Down at the bottom of the sea.
She forgot her morals, down among the corals,
Gee but she was good to me.

Many's the night when the pale moon was shining,
Down on her bungalow.
Ashes to ashes, dust to dust,
Two twin beds and only one of them mussed.

Oh it's easy to see she's not my mother,
'Cause my mother's forty-nine.
And it's easy to see she's not my sister,
'Cause I'd never give my sister such a helluva good time.

And it's easy to see she's not my sweetie,
'Cause my sweetie's too refined.
She's just a cute little kid who never knew what she did,
She's just a personal friend of mine.

—Anonymous, in Richard M. Dorson, "Folklore," *The American Mercury* Magazine, 1949.

845. Old Eleazor Wheelock was a very pious man,
He went into the wilderness to teach the Indi-an,
With a Gradus and Parnassus,
A bible and a drum
And five hundred gallons of New England rum!

Chorus
Fill the bowl up, fill the bowl up,
Drink to Eleazor—
And his primitive Alcazar,
Where he mixed drinks for the heathen
In the goodness of his so-ul!

—Richard Hovey (1864–1900), "Eleazor Wheelock," Dartmouth College drinking song, toasting its founder. [Gradus=*a dictionary used as an aid in writing Greek or Latin poetry;* Parnassus=*a collection of poems or elegant literature;* Alcazar=*a castle or fortress of the Spanish Moors*].

Studies

(*See also* Study)

846. P. What is writing?
A. The custodian of history.
P. What is speech?
A. The interpreter of the soul.
P. What produces speech?
A. The tongue.
P. What is the tongue?
A. The whip of the air.
P. What is air?
A. The guardian of life.
P. What is life?
A. The joy of the good, the sorrow of the evil, the expectation of death.
P. What is death?
A. An inevitable event, an uncertain journey, a subject of weeping to the living, the fulfillment of wills, the thief of men.

—Alcuin (A.D. 735?–804),
from *Disputation of Pepin,* syllabus prepared
for the instruction of Pepin, son of Charlemagne.

847. I must go back to my charming occupation of hearing students give lessons. Here is my programme for this afternoon: Avalanches—The Steam Engine—The Thames—India Rubber—Bricks—The Battle of Poictiers—Subtraction—The Reindeer—The Gunpowder Plot—The Jordan. Alluring, is it not? Twenty minutes each, and the days of one's life are threescore years and ten.

—Matthew Arnold (1822–88), letter to Lady de Rothschild,
in Louis Kronenberger, *Animal, Vegetable, Mineral* (1972), 138.

848. And I do not mean by all this my talk that young gentlemen should always be poring on a book, and by using good studies should leave honest pleasure and haunt no good pastime. . . .

Therefore, to ride comely; to run fair at the tilt or ring; to play at all weapons; to shoot fair in bow or surely in gun; to vault lustily; to run, to leap, to wrestle, to swim; to dance comely; to sing and play of instruments cunningly; to hawk, to hunt, to play at tennis, and all pastimes generally, which be joined with labour, used in open place, and on the daylight containing either some fit exercise for war, or some pleasant pastime for peace, be not only comely and decent, but also very necessary, for a courtly gentleman to use.

—Roger Ascham, *The Schoolmaster* (1570), I.61–63, ed. Henry Morley (1888).

849. Studies serve for delight, for ornament, and for ability. Their chief use for delight, is in privateness and retiring; for ornament, is in discourse; and for ability, is in the judgment, and disposition of business. For expert men can execute, and perhaps judge of particulars, one by one; but the general counsels, and the plots and marshalling of affairs, come best, from those that are learned. To spend too much time in studies is sloth; to use them too much for ornament, is affection; to make judgment wholly by their rules, is the humor of a scholar. They perfect nature, and are perfected by experience: for natural abilities are like natural plants, that need proyning, by study; and studies themselves, do give forth directions too much at large, except they be bounded by experience. Crafty men contemn studies, simple men admire them, and wise men use them; for they teach not their own use; but that is a wisdom without them, and above them, won by observation. Read not to contradict and confute; nor to believe and take for granted; nor to find talk and discourse; but to weigh and consider. Some books are to be tasted, others to be swallowed, and some few to be chewed and digested; that is, some books are to be read only in parts; others to be read, but not curiously; and some few to be read wholly, and with diligence and attention.... Reading maketh a full man; conference a ready man; and writing an exact man.... Histories make men wise; poets witty; the mathematics subtile; natural philosophy deep; moral grave; logic and rhetoric able to contend.... Nay, there is no stond or impediment in the wit, but may be wrought out by fit studies.

—Francis Bacon, *Essays:* "Of Studies" (1597).
[ability=*to make able;* expert men=*who have learned from experience, not study;* proyning=*pruning, cultivating;* curiously=*with great care;* conference=*discussion;* writing=*taking notes;* stond=*stand*].

850. He learn'd the arts of riding, fencing, gunnery,
And how to scale a fortress—or a nunnery.

—Lord Byron, *Don Juan* (1819), I.xxxviii.303.

851. What object is there in learning subjects that are of no use to those who know them and the lack of which is not felt by those who do not know

them? Subjects that are certain to be forgotten as time passes on and the business of life becomes more engrossing? This short life of ours has more than enough to accompany it, even if we do not waste it on worthless studies. Schools must therefore be organized in such a way that the scholars learn nothing but what is of value.[a]

Truly it has been said, that nothing is more useless than to learn and to know much, if such knowledge be of no avail for practical purposes; and again, that not he who knows much is wise, but he who knows what is useful.[b]

Whatever is taught should be taught as being of practical application in everyday life and of some definite use. That is to say, the pupil should understand that what he learns is not taken out of some Utopia or borrowed from Platonic ideas, but is one of the facts which surround us, and that a fitting acquaintance with it will be of great value in life.[c]

—John Amos Comenius,
The Great Didactic (1628–32), a. 144; b. 180; c. 189.

852. As to their studies, it would be well if they could be taught everything that is useful, and everything that is ornamental. But art is long, and their time is short. It is therefore proposed that they learn those things that are likely to be most useful and most ornamental, regard being had to the several professions for which they are intended.

—Benjamin Franklin, "Proposals Relating to the Education of Youth in Pennsylvania," 1749, in Nathan G. Goodman, ed., *A Benjamin Franklin Reader* (1945), 325.

853. *Curriculum* originally meant a race course, from Latin *currere*, to run, and there are still many today who believe, with good reason, that a curriculum is a run-around.

—Francis Griffith, *Phi Delta Kappan* Magazine.

854. [In America *circa* early 1900s] Always on the alert for the mischief the young devils [of the *heder*, or Hebrew elementary school] might invent, and with a stick in hand for admonitory persuasion, the *melamed* [teacher] begins his class. First he drill his pupils, through mass repetitive chanting in the *alef-bet*, or Hebrew alphabet, sometimes writing the letters on the blackboard or, if that luxury is lacking, on the wall. After the alphabet come the recital of prayers from the Pentateuch, meant to prepare the child for the liturgy of the synagogue, though only a small number of pupils ever learn to read Hebrew passably well and fewer still to understand it. On occasion the *melamed* paces the youngsters through the *kaddish*, or prayer for the dead, though it is rare for any effort to be made that might bring all this into a living relation with either the Jewish tradition or the American experience. Restless after a day in public school, where discipline has to be taken seriously, and bored by the rasping drone of the *melamed*, the pupils resent the *heder* as a theft of time that might better be used in playing stickball; soon they come to see it as a theatre of war in which their aim is to torment the *melamed* as ingeniously as possible.

—Irving Howe, *World of Our Fathers* (1976), 201.

855. Until a few years back, a boy might have passed through any one of the great public schools [of England] with the greatest distinction and credit and might never so much as heard of modern geography, modern history and modern literature, of the English language as a language, or of the whole circle of sciences, physical, moral and social; might never have heard that the earth goes around the sun; that England underwent a great revolution in 1688 and France in 1789; that there once lived certain notable men called Chaucer, Shakespeare, Milton, Voltaire, Goethe, Schiller.

—Thomas Henry Huxley, 1893, in Stephen Leacock, *The Leacock Roundabout:* "Education Eating Up Life" (1945), 293.

856. Having been a college professor, I agree fervently with the dictum that a student has no sense. But neither has a bee, yet the hive is a marvel of organized efficiency. The fact that an individual student subordinates classroom work to other things means precisely nothing, but when half a million students do so it means a great deal. If American students are going in for things not prescribed in the catalogue, the chances are that there is a flaw in the catalogue. The condition indicates that the things they need most are not in the catalogue.

—Gerald Johnson, "Should Our Colleges Educate?" *Harper's Magazine*, 1927.

857. Strangely enough there is nowhere the average person can go to learn how to live his daily life. Children are taught Latin and astronomy, but no school or college tells them how to clear their mind for a decision, how to tell certain psychological, or even psychopathic types, and how to deal with them; how, for any individual, to draw the line between idleness and serenity, between over-work and fullness of life, between sweet charity and being everyone's dupe. Everybody needs such instruction.

—Alice Duer Miller, *Green Isle* (1930). *See* Newton, #859.

858. Few have heard of Fra Luca Parioli, the inventor of double-entry bookkeeping; but he has probably had much more influence on human life than has Dante or Michelangelo.

—Herbert J. Muller, *The Uses of the Past* (1952), viii.

859. I wish that some one would give a course in how to live. It can't be taught in the colleges: that's perfectly obvious, for college professors don't know any better than the rest of us.

—A. Edward Newton, *The Book-Collecting Game*(1928), x. *See* Miller, #857.

860. We press their memory too soon, and puzzle, strain, and load them with words and rules to know grammar and rhetorick, and a strange tongue or two, that it is ten to one may never be useful to them; leaving all their natural genius to mechanical, and physical or natural knowledge uncultivated and neglected; which would be of exceeding use and pleasure to them thro' the whole course of their lives.

—William Penn, *Some Fruits of Solitude* (1693), I. no.6.

861. Action or language, it's all the same: great sticky honey-balls of phrases, every sentence looking as though it had been plopped and rolled in popyseed and sesame. A boy gorged on a diet like this can no more acquire real taste than a cook can stop stinking.

—Petronius Arbiter, *Satyricon* (c. A.D. 60), i.3, tr. William Arrowstreet.

862. Boyes, instead of reading hard Hebrew words in the Bible (where they either trample on, or play with Mysteries) or parrot-like repeating heteroclitious nounes and verbs, might read and hear the History of Faculties expounded, so that before they be bound Apprentices to any Trade, they may foreknow the good and the bad of it, what will and strength they have to it, and not spend seven years in repenting, and in swimming against the stream of their inclinations.

—Sir William Petty, *Advice of W[illiam] P[etty] to Mr. Samuel Hartlib for the Advancement of Some Particular Parts of Learning* (1648), 23.

863. Why "liberal studies" are so called is obvious: it is because they are the ones considered worthy of a free man. But there is really only one liberal study that deserves the name—because it makes a person free—and that is the pursuit of wisdom. Its high details, its steadfastness and spirit make all other studies puerile and puny in comparison.

—Lucius Annaeus Seneca (the younger),
Letters to Lucilius (c. A.D. 64), LXXXVIII.ii.

864. We were then in the midst of an exciting political campaign (Autumn, 1867), and it was for the first time that the well-known sentence was inaugurated—"Now is the time for all good men to come to the aid of the party."

—Charles E. Weller (1840–1925),
The Early History of the Typewriter (1918).

Study

(*See also* Studies)

865. A learned man came to visit a Hasidic rabbi.

"What have you done all your life?" the Master asked him.

"I have gone through the whole of the Talmud three times," answered the learned man.

"Yes, but how much of the Talmud has gone through you?" the rabbi inquired.

—Anonymous

866. In boyhood itself, however, (so much less dreaded for me than youth,) I loved not study, and hated to be forced to it. Yet I was forced; and this was well done towards me, but I did not well; for unless forced, I had not learnt. But no one doeth well against his will, even though what he doeth, be well.

—St. Augustine, *Confessions* (c. A.D. 400), I.

867. My system of studying was no less strict. In lecture courses I had my notebooks so arranged that one-half of the page could be devoted to drawings of five-pointed stars (exquisitely shaded), girls' heads, and tick-tack-toe. . . .

These notes I would take home after the lecture, together with whatever supplementary reading the course called for. Notes and textbooks would then be placed on a table under a strong lamplight. Next came the sharpening of pencils, which would take perhaps fifteen minutes. I had some of the best sharpened pencils in college. These I placed on the table beside the notes and books.

At this point it was necessary to light a pipe, which involved going to the table where the tobacco was. As it so happened, on the same table was a poker hand, all dealt, lying in front of a vacant chair. Four other chairs were oddly enough occupied by students, also preparing to study. It therefore resolved itself into something of a seminar, or group conference, on the courses under discussion. For example, the first student would say:

"I can't open."

The second student would perhaps say the same thing.

The third student would say: "I'll open for fifty cents."

And the seminar would be on.

At the end of the seminar, I would go back to my desk, pile the notes and books on top of each other, put the light out, and go to bed, tired but happy in the realization that I had not only spent the evening busily but had helped put four of my friends through college.

—Robert Benchley, *The Early Worm:* "What College Did to Me" (1927), 72.

868. There is no virtue in study itself. Study is not an end, but a means. I should blush to write down such a platitude, did I not know by experience that the majority of readers constantly ignore it. The man who pores over a manual of carpentry and does naught with it is a fool. But every book is a manual of carpentry, and every man who pores over any book whatever and does naught else with it is—deserving of an abusive epithet. What is the object of reading unless something definite comes of it? You would be better advised to play billiards. Where is the sense of reading history unless you obtain from it a clearer insight into actual politics and render yourself less liable to be duped by the rhetoric of party propaganda? What is the sense of reading morals unless your own are improved? Where is the sense of reading biography unless it is going to affect what people will say about you after your funeral? Where is the sense of reading poetry or fiction unless you see more beauty, more passion, more scope for your sympathy, than you saw before?

—Arnold Bennett, *Things That Have Interested Me:* "Translating Literature Into Life" (1921), 55.

869. Not satisfied with the vernacular, . . . [Charlemagne] even took pains to learn foreign languages; he mastered Latin so effectively that he was accustomed to pray in that language as well as in his native tongue. In Greek his understanding was better than his pronunciation. . . . He cultivated the liberal arts enthusiastically. Scholars he deeply respected and heaped great honors on them. In the study of grammar he heard the lectures of Peter

Pisanus, an elderly deacon; in other subjects he had as teacher Albinus, surnamed Alcuin, also a deacon, a man of Saxon race from Britain, the most learned man of his time. Under him he devoted a great deal of time and effort to the study of rhetoric and dialectics and particularly astronomy. He learned the art of reckoning and with keen concentration he investigated in great detail the course or the stars.

—Einhard, *Vita Karoli*
(c. A.D. 829–836), tr. Harry Ezekiel Wedeck.
For a sample of Alcuin's teaching *see* **#846**, under "Studies."

870. I've studied now Philosophy
And Jurisprudence, Medicine
And even, alas, Theology
From end to end with labor keen;
And here, poor fool; with all my lore
I stand no wiser than before.

—Johann Wolfgang von Goethe,
Faust: "Night" (1808), I, tr. Bayard Taylor.

Stupidity

(*See also* Ignorance)

871. DUNCE. A dolt; a stupid person. The word is taken from *Duns* Scotus (c. 1265–1308), so called from his birthplace, Dunse, in Scotland. Tyndal says, when they saw that their hair-splitting divinity was giving way to modern theology, 'the old barking curs raged in every pulpit' against the classics and new notions, so that the name indicated an opponent to progress, to learning, and hence a dunce.

—Ebenezer Cobham Brewer,
Dictionary of Phrase and Fable (1870).

872. Some boys are born stupid, and thou art one of them; some achieve stupidity—that's thee again, Jim—thou wast born stupid and hast greatly increased thy birthright—and some . . . have stupidity thrust upon them, which, if it please the Lord, shall not be thy case, my lad, for I will thrust stupidity from thee, though I have to box thine ears in doing so.

—Samuel Butler, *The Way of All Flesh* (1903), 3.

873. His wit invites you by his looks to come
But when you knock it never is at home.

—William Cowper, "Conversation" (1782), in H.F. Cary, ed., *The Poetical Works of William Cowper* (no date), I.168. ln.303.

874. *Sh*--- alone my perfect image bears,
Mature in dullness from his tender years;
Sh--- alone, of all my Sons, is he
Who stands confirm'd in full stupidity.
The rest to some faint meaning make pretence,
But *Sh*--- never deviates into sense.
Some Beams of Wit on other souls may fall,
Strike through and make a lucid intervall;
But *Sh*---'s genuine night admits no ray,
His rising Fogs prevail upon the Day.

—John Dryden, "Mac Flecknoe" (1682), ln.15.

875. Varnished over with good breeding, many a blockhead makes a tolerable show.

—Sir George Etherege, *The Man of Mode* (1676), III.i.

876. Why, Sir, Sherry [Thomas Sheridan] is dull, naturally dull; but it must have taken a great deal of pains to become what we now see him. Such an excess of stupidity, Sir, is not in Nature.

—Samuel Johnson, in James Boswell, *Life of Samuel Johnson*, July 28, 1763 (1791), xv.

877. I was educated some in chemistry, and in biology and physics, too, at Cornell University. I did badly, and I soon forgot all they tried to teach me. The Army sent me to Carnegie Tech and the University of Tennessee to study mechanical engineering—thermodynamics, mechanics, the actual use of machine tools, and so on. I did badly again. I am used to failure, to being at the bottom of every class.

An Indianapolis cousin of mine, who was also a high school classmate, did very badly at Cornell. His father asked him what the trouble was, and he made what I consider an admirable reply: "Don't you know, Father? I'm dumb!" It was the truth.

—Kurt Vonnegut, *Palm Sunday* (1981), 73.

878. That man is so stupid it sits on him like a halo.

—Emlyn Williams, *The Corn Is Green* (1938), II.i.

Talent

See Genius

Teacher

(*See also* Principal; Professor; Teacher, Description of; Teacher, Dispraise for; Teacher, Image of; Teacher, Praise for; Teacher, Remembrances of)

879. Run away on the 28th of last month, from his bail, Samuel Jaques, and James Marshall, of Elizabeth town, Essex county, in East New-Jersey, one Edward Kite, an English man, about 30 years of age, of middle stature, brown complexion, has a fresh colour, black eyes, and has a bold look: Had on when he went away, an old green jacket, an old bob wig, and a speckled shirt. He had some time ago broke one of his Legs, which by observing, will be found to be a little crooked, and is somewhat thicker than the other. He is a cooper by trade, but he has lately taught school, and writes a good round hand. Whoever takes up and secures said Edward Kite, so that his bail may have him again, shall have Four Pounds reward, and reasonable charges, paid by

Samuel Jaques, and James Marshall

N.B. All masters of vessels, and others, are forbid to harbour or carry him off, at their peril.

—Advertisement for a runaway schoolmaster, *Pennsylvania Gazette*, June 6, 1751, in Ellwood P. Cubberley, ed., *Readings in Public Education in the United States* (1934), 70. *See* Boucher, **#928,** under "Teacher, Dispraise for."

880. Notice is thereby given that Syme's free School, in *Elizabeth-City* County, will be vacant on the 25th *March* Inst. a Tutor of good Character, and properly qualified, may meet with good Encouragement, by applying to the Trustees of the said School.

N.B. The Land Rent of the said School is 31 £ *per Ann.* besides Perquisites.

—Advertisement in the *Virginia Gazette*, Mar. 12, 1752, in Willard S. Elsbree, *The American Teacher* (1939), 56.

881. The indentures governing the relationship of master and apprentice generally followed English precedent. Besides faithfully teaching the lad the "art and mystery" of his craft, the master was obliged to provide him with bed, board, and clothing. He was also responsible for the moral welfare of his apprentice, and usually for his instruction in reading, writing, and ciphering. At times the master was required, in addition, to send his charge to night school either at his own or the parents' expense.

—*The American Heritage History of Colonial Antiques* (1967), 94.

882. When you are a teacher you are always in the right place at the right time. There is no wrong time for learning. It may be the wrong time for what the teacher had planned to teach, but just as certainly it will be the perfect time to teach something else. Teachers learn to grasp the moment. Any time a student is there before you, the possibility is present, the moment is yours.

When you are a teacher, you, along with others on this planet, are dipping your hand into the stream. Do I understand this metaphor, and does it apply to us as truthfully as I feel it does? I think it has to do with time and with our little significance, but also with our ability to affect the flow. As teachers we live, whether we recognize it or not, by the principle of *amor, fati,* we must love what is. So we give ourselves to what is at hand, and what is at hand is life itself.

—Betty B. Anderson, "To the Teachers: Unique Breed," *Sarasota Herald-Tribune,* May 30, 1988.

883. A successful teacher needs: the education of a college president, the executive ability of a financier, the humility of a deacon, the adaptability of a chameleon, the hope of an optimist, the courage of a hero, the wisdom of a serpent, the gentleness of a dove, the patience of Job, the grace of God, and the persistence of the Devil.

—Anonymous.

884. I'd rather see a lesson than hear one any day;
I'd rather one should walk with me than merely show the way.
The eye's a better pupil and more willing than the ear;
Fine counsel is confusing, but example always clear.

—Anonymous, "To My Teacher."

885. There once lived a teacher named Dodd
With manners arresting and odd.
He said, "If you please,

Spell my name with three D's,"
Though one was sufficient for God.

—Anonymous, in Bennett Cerf,
The Life of the Party (1956), 189.

886. When schoolmasters are such as they should be, they have it in their power to new model and set right, by God's blessing, once in twenty years a whole kingdom.

—Anonymous, 1600s,
in Charles J. Finger, *A Man for A' That* (1929), 45.

887. No one feels more than I do how laborious is . . . [the schoolteachers'] work, how trying at times to the health and spirits, how full of difficulty even for the best: how much fuller for those, whom I too often see attempting the work of a schoolmaster—men of weak health and purely studious habits, who betake themselves to this profession, as affording the means to continue their favourite pursuits: not knowing, alas, that for all but men of the most singular and exceptional vigour and energy, there are no pursuits more irreconcilable than those of the student and the schoolmaster.

—Matthew Arnold, report of 1854,
in F. Sandford, ed., *Reports on Elementary Schools* (1889), 40. Arnold was a school inspector.

888. At my table looking out the windows I wonder what to say to you . . . to a young teacher. . . . I look back on fifty years, you look forward on fifty years. The world is yours, not mine. It was mine when I was young and I strongly knew it. . . . From fifty I have no advice. But from thirty I have! In the splendid authority of youth to youth I quote from those blurring pages, written in fierce swift pencil-passion: "You must be true to yourself. Strong enough to be true to yourself. Brave enough, to be strong enough, to be true to yourself. Wise enough, to be brave enough, to be strong enough, to be true enough to shape yourself from what you actually are. What big words, O my Self: true, strong, brave and wise! But that's how it is, my Self. That's how it must be for you to walk steadily in your own ways, as gracefully as you feel, as upright as you feel, a ridiculous flower on top of your head, a sentimental daisy. For therein lies your individuality, your own authentic signature, the source of others' love for you."

—Sylvia Ashton-Warner, preface to *Myself* (1967), 12.

889. Many of the pioneer teachers taught in small log or frame houses so open that the sun could enter through the crevices . . . the sod school houses were far more comfortable than the frame or log buildings. The boarding places of the teachers were, of necessity, often a mile or more away from the school house and accommodations much like camping out. A former teacher explained that the school house she taught in was made of logs and was so open where the "chinks" had been left out between the logs that a fairly good view of the outdoor landscape was possible. . . . A limited supply of green cottonwood fuel, that the teacher must use to warm the school house in time for morning classes, after walking a mile from her boarding place, did not provide an atmosphere to study. She boarded with a family whose small house was so open that everything freezable suffered from frost during the night. There was but one bed in the house and she slept with the wife in the bed while the husband slept with the children on the floor. Bread making under such environments required originality to make it a success. In such an atmosphere only dry yeast could be used. It would be started at noon and at night worked down hard and kept till morning when it would be set by the stove till it had risen enough to make into loaves and then it was baked. To keep it warm and from freezing at night the wife wrapped it up well and placed it in bed at the teacher's feet.

—Cass G. Barns, *The Sod House* (1930), in *The American Heritage History of the Confident Years* (1973), 157. *See* Shaw, **#912.**

890. The bare wooden structure [one-room school] was a circus of many rings, presided over by a pale young woman. She dispensed fundamental education and worried over glimpses of flesh and underwear that might arouse the lust lurking in the eyes of older boys.

Two facts were apparent. She taught school as a stopgap until some young farmer would propose marriage, and if too much time elapsed she would accept an older bachelor, or failing that, a widower.

—Harry J. Boyle, *Memories of a Catholic Boyhood* (1973), 9.

891. Education is, I suppose, largely a matter of the individual, both on the side of the teacher and of the scholar, and both teacher and scholar are perhaps born and not made. I would say that if a man does not want an education nothing on earth can force it down him and, conversely, that if he desires it nothing can prevent him from achieving it. In between, of course, are all the people who do not know whether they want to learn or understand anything or not, and that is where the inspired teacher comes in, the man or woman who can lend excitement to any subject and surround himself with young people whose lives may be changed by contact with the flame he represents. These of course are all too rare, for the great majority who teach are not thus blessed but are merely making a living at a task which gradually becomes more and more distasteful or maintaining toward their work an attitude of dullness and detail which turns any subject into a misery. And of course there is in the teaching profession itself an element which inevitably leads toward eventual desiccation and academic God-almightiness—the fact that a teacher sits on a throne and dictates to those with less academic knowledge and less authority.

—Louis Bromfield, *Mr. Smith* (1951), 75.

892. The little red schoolhouse in my community [c. 1920] was white. In fact, I do not recall ever seeing any red schoolhouse in rural Maine in the old days; usually they were white, or, more commonly, the color of weather-beaten shingles. It must be remembered that the reputation of town officials was measured by their reluctance to spend money on education.

Since the low salaries in rural schools kept the profession from being attractive to men, the teacher was invariably a woman. Prior to the 1920s, when teachers were paid even less, they boarded "around," living a week or two at a time with one family and then moving on to the nearest or most desirable place they could find. If some of the living conditions were less than satisfactory, at least they were free, for it was then a public duty for townspeople to take turns "boarding the teacher." After two or three years of this rather nomadic way of life, most school mistresses were ready to marry anyone who asked their hand, in order to escape. If a teacher was fortunate enough to live near the school, she might make a lifetime career of instructing the young, thereby becoming what was always called "an old maid schoolteacher."

—K.W. Carter, "I Remember . . . My Little *White* Schoolhouse," *Down East* Magazine, April 1979.

893. Teachers almost invariably take their pupils as they find them; they turn them, card them, comb them, drill them into certain forms, and expect them to become a finished and polished product; and if the result does not come up to their expectations (and I ask you how could it?) they become indignant, angry, and furious. And yet we are surprised that some men shrink and recoil from such a system. Far more is it a matter for surprise that any one can endure it at all.

—John Amos Comemius, *The Great Didactic* (1628–32).

894. To Mr. James Jeffray Greeting.

I do hereby authorize and Impower You to Keep and Teach School within the city of New York and to Instruct all children with whom you shall be intrusted in the art of Writing and Arithmetick for and During my Pleasure.

Given under my hand and Seal at ffort Anne in New Yorke this Seventeenth day of Aprill—in the fifth Year of the reign of our Sovereign Lady Anne, by the Grace of God of England, Scotland ffrance and Ireland Queen Defender of the faith, etc.—Annoque Domini 1706

Cornbury

—Teaching license granted to James Jeffray by Governor Edward Cornbury, in Willard S. Elsbree, *The American Teacher* (1939), 51.

895. To every class we have a school assign'd,
Rules for all ranks and food for every mind:
Yet one there is, that small regard to rule
Or study pays, and still is deem'd a school;
That, where a deaf, poor, patient widow sits,
And awes some thirty infants as she knits;
Infants of humble, busy wives, who pay
Some trifling price for freedom through the day.
At this good matron's hut the children meet,
Who thus becomes the mother of the street:
Her room is small, they cannot widely stray,—
Her threshold high, they cannot run away:
Though deaf, she sees the rebel-heroes shout,—
Though lame, her white rod nimbly walks about;
With band of yarn she keeps offenders in,
And to her gown the sturdiest rogue can pin:
Aided by these, and spells, and tell-tale birds,
Her power they dread and reverence her words.

—George Crabbe, *The Borough:* "Schools," (1810), st.i, *The Poetical Works of George Crabbe,* ed. A.J. and R.M. Carlyle (1932), 205.

896. I believe that

—the teacher is engaged, not simply in the training of individuals, but in the formation of the proper social life.

—every teacher should realize the dignity of his calling; that he is a social servant set apart for the maintenance of proper social order and the securing of the right social growth.

—in this way the teacher always is the prophet of the true God and the usherer in of the true kingdom of God.

—John Dewey, "My Pedagogic Creed,"
The School Journal, Jan. 16, 1897.

897. Waited on Dr. John Witherspoon [president of Princeton], about nine o'clock, to hear his proposal for my going to Virginia. He read me a letter which he received from Col. Carter [Robert Carter of Nomini Hall], & proposed the following terms—To teach his children, five daughters & three young sons, who are from five to seventeen years old. The young ladies are to be taught the English language. And the boys are to study the English language carefully & be instructed in Latin & Greek. And he proposes to give thirty-five pounds sterling, which is about sixty pounds currency, provide all accommodations, allow him the undisturbed use of a room and horse, & a servant to wait. By the advice of the Dr. & his recommendation of the gentleman & the place, I accepted the offer & agreed to go in the fall to Virginia.

—Philip Vickers Fithian,
diary entry of Aug. 9, 1773, in Hunter D. Farish, ed.,
Journal and Letters of Philip Vickers Fithian, 1773–1774:
A Plantation Tutor of the Old Dominion (1943), 39.

898. December 14, 1744
A petition of Christopher Ortman being read, wherein he greatly complains of hard dealings being used which has occasioned his being discharged by the Society from his office of schoolmaster at Ebenezer [Georgia]. The Board taking the same into consideration are of the opinion that said Christopher Ortman has been misrepresented to the said Society and by means he is reduced to great poverty, both he and his wife being uncapable by reason of their old age and infirmities for any labor, and they, never hearing any otherwise of him than that he was an honest, sober and inoffensive man, do, therefore in charity, appoint him schoolmaster for the village of Vernonburgh and Acton, the inhabitants there having often complained for want of such; and for the subsistance of himself and wife the Board does allow him at the rate of twenty shillings per month until the Trustees' pleasure is therein known. And they also think that it will be a saving to the trust for his being so placed rather than to be obliged to maintain him otherwise for doing of nothing. And whereas five pounds a year

has been the Trustees' order paid to the said Christopher Ortman as schoolmaster at Ebenezer, we think it reasonable that the said five pounds be paid toward defraying the said expenses.

—*Foundations of Colonial America: A Documentary History*, ed. W. Keith Kavenagh (1973), III.2126.

899. Whoever would be a teacher of men let him begin by teaching himself before teaching others; and let him set an example before teaching by word. For he who teaches himself and rectifies his own ways is more deserving of respect and reverence than he who would teach others and rectify their ways.

—Kahlil Gibran, in Annie Salem Otto, *The Parables of Gibran* (1963).

900. An appeal is once more made to the members of our National Legislature on behalf of the women of our country who are engaged in the duties of public education. . . . The munificent donations of public lands, given by Congress for the establishment of Agricultural Colleges, have been appropriated entirely for the benefit of young men. This may have been in accordance with the intention of the law; but if so it leaves an important act of justice to be done. . . .

By common consent in our country the office of teacher of children has come to be held as peculiarly proper for women. . . .

The profession of teacher requires . . . as thorough and special training as any of the other intellectual professions. The great majority of our teachers are deficient in this training. . . . The complaint on this head is indeed universal. And it is coupled with another complaint of the inadequate salaries almost everywhere paid to teachers, but more especially in rural districts. . . .

It is to redress these admitted and most serious evils that the national aid is now solicited. Women already compose two-thirds of the whole number of persons engaged throughout our country teaching youth. . . . It is a duty which our law-makers owe to their country to see that these educators are properly trained.

—Sarah Josepha Hale, "Appeal to the Fortieth Congress of the United States," *Godey's Lady Book*, Dec. 1868, in Ruth E. Finley, *The Lady of Godey's* (1931), 233.

901. Belvidera 14th. June 1774
My Dearest Life
. . . . I am now settled with on[e] Colonel Wm. Daingerfield Esqr. of Belvidera, on the Banks of the River Rappahannock about 160 Miles from the Capes or sea mouth, and seven Miles below the Toun of Fredericksburgh. My business is to teach his Children to read write and figure. Edwin his oldest son about 8 years of [age] Bathurest his second 6 years of age & William his youngest son 4 years of age. He has also a Daughter whose name is Hanna Basset. I came to this pleace on Thursday 26th. May and next morning I received his three sons into my charge to teach, the two youngest boys I got in A:B:C, and the oldest just begun to syllab and I have now the two youngest spelling and the oldest reading. I am obliged to teach in the English method which was a little aquard to me at first but now quite easy. I am also obliged to talk english the best I can, for Lady Daingerfield speacks nothing but high english, and the Colonel hade his Education in England and is a verry smart Man. As to my Agreement it is as follows Vizt. I am obliged to continue with Coll. Daingerfield for four years if he insists on it, and for teaching his own Children I have Bed, Board, washing and all kinds of Cloaths during the above time, and for what schoolars I can get more than his Children I have five shillings currancy per Quarter for each of them which is equall to four shillings Sterling. . . .

—John Harrower, letter to his wife, *Journal*, 1773–76, in *The American Heritage History of the Thirteen Colonies* (1967), 332. He was an impoverished Scottish merchant who sailed for Virginia as an indentured servant and found employment as a tutor.

902. At this time it is still almost axiomatic that quite a number of pedagogues are inclined to consider the whole world as their classroom and will continue to examine and give homework to any casual strangers that happen to cross their paths.

—Alexander King, *Rich Man, Poor Man, Freud and Fruit* (1965), viii. *See* Lamb, **#949**, under "Teacher, Image of."

903. Tuesday July 24th [1856] Farewell to school room and schollars for a season. I am glad to be *free* once again. I love my pupils; and think I feel some desire to do them good. I usually feel my duties to them to be but a pleasant task: but I grow weary of the *monotony* and *confinement* of the school room, and sometimes foolishly wish that I were not obligated to teach. It seems rather hard to labor day after day and week after week just to procure the necessaries and comforts of life: but I trust this is *not* my only objects for *then* poor indeed would be the compensation. I would do a little good in the world. I would leave my mark on the sands of time. I ask not I desire not that *fame* shall speak of this poor worm when it shall have run its race; and he's sleeping beneath the cloak of the valley. Then shall I be forgotten by the *world* and it matters not; but I would that my memory might live in the hearts of *those who love me.*

—Amelia Akehurst Lines,
To Raise Myself a Little: The Diaries and Letters of Jennie, a Georgia Teacher, 1851–1886, ed. Thomas Dyer (1982), 31.

904. 1. Teachers each day will fill lamps, clean chimneys and trim wicks.

2. Each teacher will bring a bucket of water and a scuttle of coal for the day's sessions.

3. Make your pens carefully. You may whittle nibs to the individual tastes of the pupils.

4. Men teachers may take one evening each week for courting purposes, or two evenings a week if they go to church regularly.

5. After ten hours of school, the teacher should spend the remaining time reading the Bible, or other good books.

6. Women teachers who marry or engage in unseemly conduct will be dismissed.

7. Every teacher should lay aside from each pay day a goodly sum of his earnings for his benefit during his declining years, so that he will not become a burden on society.

8. Any teacher who smokes, uses liquor in any form, frequents pool or public halls or gets shaved in a barber shop will give good reason to suspect his worth, intentions, integrity, and honesty.

9. The teacher who performs his labors faithfully and without fault for five years will be given an increase of twenty-five cents per week in his pay, providing the Board of Education approves.

—List of rules posted
by a principal in the City of New York, 1872.

905. 1. You will not marry during the term of your contract.

2. You are not to keep company with men.

3. You must be home between the hours of 8 p.m. and 6 a.m. unless attending a school function.

4. You may not loiter downtown in ice cream stores.

5. You may not travel beyond the city limits unless you have the permission of the chairman of the board.

6. You may not ride in a carriage or automobile with any man unless he is your father or brother.

7. You may not smoke cigarets.
8. You may not dress in bright colors.
9. You may under no circumstances dye your hair.
10. You must wear at least two petticoats.
11. Your dresses must not be any shorter than two inches above the ankle.
12. To keep the school room neat and clean, you must: sweep the floor at least once daily; scrub the floor at least once a week with hot, soapy water; clean the blackboards at least once a day; and start the fire at 7 a.m. so the room will be warm by 8 a.m.

—List of rules for teachers
which appeared in the Cabell County
(West Virginia) Board of Education school bulletin, 1915.

906. Teachers are employed for purposes "vastly great." They must teach the science of health with all the learning but without the pay of a doctor; they must inculcate the principle of morality with all the impressive sincerity but without the sectarianism of the minister; they must be altogether more patient and discreet than God Almighty himself, for He was "wroth" when He punished the wicked, whereas, if a teacher punishes in anger, he is guilty of an assault and battery; they must invest schemes to invert human nature, and make every good thing and thought enticing and every bad thing and thought abominably disgusting ... they must tenderly moderate the zeal of the too ambitious, and inspire the dullest blockhead with a manly thirst for fame and knowledge; the incorrigibly uncouth and vicious, they must endow with the tastes, the instincts, and the manners of the refined and virtuous. And in short, they must turn all from the thousand paths that lead to indolence, ignorance, and folly; and prepare them to find infallibly all the ways of pleasantness and all the paths of peace.

—A.P. Marble, 1887, in Willard S. Elsbree,
The American Teacher (1939), frontispiece.

907. In our complex civilization, teaching draws on an immense diversity of talents and skills....

Nevertheless, I believe all good teachers have some characteristics in common. The most extraordinary thing about a really good teacher is that he or she transcends accepted educational methods. Some methods are designed to help average teachers approximate the performance of good teachers.

I think, too, that good teachers want their pupils, at whatever stage, to learn what it is their task to teach. They are willing to put up with those who are brighter than they are—and there will be some; they are also patient with those who are slower. Their enjoyment of teaching affects those who are taught, so that they feel some *positive* emotion—joy, delight, achievement, relief—when they learn what their teachers teach.

Good teachers are glad when a term begins and a little sad when it ends. They remember some of their students for many years, and their students remember them. They never make assumptions about what their pupils know; they take the trouble to find out, and they are tireless in finding new ways of repeating where repetition is necessary. In a sense, good teachers always suffer fools gladly.

—*Margaret Mead: Some Personal Views,* ed. Rhoda Metraux (1979), 195.

908. When the last Friday at school [before his retirement] came . . . he felt rather sad. He knew the place so well that somehow or other he had become a part of it. His life had been lived in that dull red building, standing grimly and coldly in its piece of asphalt playground. It seemed almost incredible that he was standing for the last time in the shabby school-hall, with its stale smell, with 'Play the Game' framed over the headmaster's platform, and with insipid pictures of country scenes and battles hung round its walls; and that such inevitable parts of his life as playing the hymn and teaching standard three were finished with. He thought of his first lesson as a pupil teacher to a class of eighty boys. Now he had reached the last. All the intervening ones seemed just a grey waste in which nothing stood out as being different from anything else.

—Malcolm Muggeridge, *Things Past:* "An Elderly Teacher" (1978).

909. The elementary school is left to the lowest and the worst class of teacher, because good scholars will not abase themselves to it. The first grounding should be undertaken by the best teachers, and his reward should be the greatest, because his work demands most energy and most judgment, and competent men could easily be induced to enter these lower ranks if they found that sufficient reward were offered. . . . If the master's salary is fixed by agreement at a definite sum, then he should not be given too large numbers to deal with, nor should he be obliged to eke out his income in other ways outside his profession. It is unreasonable to demand a man's whole time, and yet make such scant payment that he has to look elsewhere, outside the school, to add to it. Among many causes that make our schools inefficient, I know none so serious as the weakness of the profession owing to the bareness of the reward. . . . Our calling creeps low, and has pain for a companion, always thrust to the wall, though always formally admitted to be worthy. . . . Why should not teachers be well provided for, so that they can continue their whole life in the school, as divines, lawyers, and physicians do in their several professions? If this were the case, judgment, knowledge, and discretion would grow in them as they get older, whereas now the school, being used for a shift, from which they will afterwards pass to some other profession, though it may send out competent men to other careers, remains itself far too bare of talent, considering the importance of the work. I consider therefore that in our universities there should be a special college for the training of teachers, inasmuch as they are the instruments to make or mar the growing generation of the country, and because the material of their studies is comparable to that of the greatest professions wherein the forming of the mind and the exercising of the body require the most careful consideration, to say nothing of the dignity of character which should be expected from them.

—Richard Mulcaster, (1530?–1611) in J. Oliphant, *The Educational Writings of Richard Mulcaster* (1903), 85–98. Mulcaster's ideas on education were well ahead of his time. Many of his educational theories were not generally accepted until at least 250 years after his death. *See* Phelps, #939, under "Teacher, Dispraise for."

910. I do swear by the contents of this book, that I will freely without exacting any money, diligently instruct and teach the children of this parish, and all others that shall resort to me, in Grammar and other humane doctrine, according to the statutes thereof made, — and I shall not read to them any corrupt or reprobate books or works set forth at any time contrary to the denomination of the universal catholique church, whereby they may be infected in their youth in any kind of heresie or corrupt doctrine, or else to be indured to insolent manner of living: And further shall observe all the statutes and ordinances of this schoole now made, or hereafter to be made which concern me, and shall doe nothing in the prejudice thereof, but help to maintain the same from time to time during my aboad herein to the best of my power — so help me God, ant the contents of this book.

—Oath of a grammar schoolmaster in England, 1566, in Nicholas Carlisle, *A Concise Description of the Endowed Grammar Schools in England and Wales* (1818), II.714.

911. SCHOOLMASTERS of good capacities and fair characters may expect to meet with encouragement in the middle and southern states. They will succeed better if they confine their instructions to reading, writing, English grammar, and the sciences of number and quantity. These branches of literature are of general necessity and utility, and of course every township will furnish scholars enough for the maintenance of a schoolmaster. Many

young men have risen by means of the connections they have formed in this useful employment to rank and consequence in the learned professions in every part of this country.

—Benjamin Rush, "To ________ ________: Information to Europeans Who Are Disposed to Migrate to the United States," Apr. 16, 1790, in L.H. Butterfield, ed., *Letters of Benjamin Rush* (1951), I.555. Written to a Quaker living in London.

912. [In 1862] When I was fifteen years old I was offered a situation as school-teacher. By this time the community was growing around us with the rapidity characteristic of these Western settlements [in Michigan], and we had nearer neighbors whose children needed instruction. I passed an examination before a school-board consisting of three nervous and self-conscious men whose certificate I still hold, and I at once began my professional career on the modest salary of two dollars a week and my board. The school was four miles from my house, so I "boarded round" with the families of my pupils, staying two weeks in each place, and often walking from three to six miles a day to and from my little log school-house in every kind of weather. During the first year I had about fourteen pupils, of varying ages, sizes, and temperaments, and there was hardly a book in the school-room except those I owned. One little girl, I remember, read from an almanac, while a second used a hymn-book. In winter the school-house was heated by a wood-stove, to which the teacher had to give close personal attention. I could not depend on my pupils to make the fires or carry in the fuel; and it was often necessary to fetch the wood myself, sometimes for long distances through the forest. Again and again, after miles of walking through winter storms, I reached the school-house with my clothing wet through, and in these soaked garments I taught during the day. In "boarding round" I often found myself in one-room cabins, with bunks at the end and the sole partition a sheet or blanket, behind which I slept with one or two of the children. It was the custom on these occasions for the man of the house to delicately retire to the barn while we women got to bed, and to disappear again in the morning while we dressed. In some places the meals were so badly cooked that I could not eat them, and often the only food my poor little pupils brought to school for their noonday meal was a piece of bread or a bit of raw pork.

—Anna Howard Shaw, with Elizabeth Jordan, *The Story of a Pioneer* (1915). *See* Barns, **#889**.

913. In ev'ry village mark'd with little spire,
Embow'r'd in trees, and hardly known to fame,

There dwells, in lowly shed, and mean attire,
A matron old, whom we school-mistress name;
Who boasts unruly brats with birch to tame.

—William Shenstone, "The School-Mistress" (1737), ln. 10.

914. [Three rabbis were sent to inspect the state of education throughout Palestine.] They came to a place where there were no teachers. They said to the inhabitants, "Bring us the protectors of the town." They brought them the military guard. The rabbis exclaimed, "These are not the protectors of the town but its destroyers!" "Who, then, are the protectors?" they were asked; and they answered, "The teachers."

—*Talmud: Chagigah* (before A.D. 500).

915. One
Discuss'd his tutor, rough to common men,
But honeying at the whisper of a lord.
And one the Master as a rogue in grain
Veneer'd with sanctimonious theory.

—Alfred, Lord Tennyson,
The Princess: "Prologue" (1847), ln.113.

916. As for the young lady's teacher, I prefer that she have a woman rather than a man. It is best that the teacher be her mother, her aunt, or her sister rather than an outsider. If she must be an outsider, however, she should be known by the family and, if possible, she should have the following qualifications: she should be advanced in years, clean in behavior, esteemed in reputation, tranquil in temperament, and skilled in learning . . . but if a lady with all the qualities cannot be obtained, the teacher must at least possess good reputation and skill in learning. If a lady with these two qualities cannot be found, select with great care an old man who has proven himelf worthy in behavior, reputation, and scholarship. If possible, he should be a married man rather than a bachelor; his wife should be sufficiently attractive and he should get on well with her, for if this is the case he will not be driven to covet any other woman, being satisfied with his own.

—Juan Luis Vives,
The Instruction of a Christian Woman (1524).

917. *Father:* Inform me, I beg, thou who art most versed in the study of letters, who in this school is the best teacher of boys?

Relative: The most learned is a certain Varro; but the most industrious and the most upright is Philoponus, whose erudition, moreover is not to be despised. Varro has the best frequented school, and in his house he has a numerous flock of boarders. Philoponus does not seem to delight in numbers, but is content with fewer boys.

Father: I should prefer him. That must be he walking into the hall of the school. Son, this is, as it were, the laboratory for the formation of men, and he is the artist-director. Christ be with you, master! Uncover your head, my boy, and bow your right knee, as you have been taught. Now, stand up!

Philoponus: May your coming be a blessing to us all! What may be your business?

Father: I bring you this boy of mine to make him a man from the beast.

Philoponus: This shall be my earnest endeavor. He shall become a man from a beast, a fruitful and good creature out of a useless one. Of that have no doubt.

Father: What is the charge for your instruction?

Philoponus: If the boy makes good progress, it will be little; if not, a good deal.

Father: That is acutely and wisely said, as is all you say. We share the responsibility then; you, to instruct zealously, I to recompense your labor richly.

—Juan Luis Vives, *Linguae Latinae Exercitatio:* "Deductio ad Ludum" (1539). Vives wrote these dialogues in Latin to help Spanish boys who were learning to speak Latin.

918. The principal defect in our plan of education in America is the want of good teachers in the academies and public schools. By good teachers I mean men of unblemished reputation and possessed of abilities competent to their stations. . . .

Yet abilities are not the sole requisites. The instructors of youth ought, of all men, to be the most prudent, accomplished, agreeable, and respectable. What avails a man's parts if, while he is the "wisest and brightest," he is the "meanest of mankind?" The pernicious effects of bad example on the minds of youth will probably be acknowledged, but with a view to improvement it is indispensably necessary that the teachers should possess good breeding and agreeable manners. In order to give full effect to instructions, it is requisite that they should proceed from a man who is loved and respected.

—Noah Webster, *A Collection of Essays and Fugitiv Writings:* "On the Education of Youth in America" (1790). Webster had spent some time teaching.

919. Condemned, each tedious day, such cares to bear
As well might drive e'en Patience to despair;

The partial's parent's taunt—the idler dull—
The blockhead's dark inpenetrable scull—
The endless round of A,B,C's whole train
Repeated o'er ten thousand times in vain.
Placed on a point, the object of each sneer,
His faults enlarge, his merits disappear;
If mild—"Our lazy master loves his ease,
The boys at school do anything they please."
If rigid—"He's a cross hard-hearted wretch,
He drives the children stupid with his birch."

—Alexander Wilson (1766–1813), "The Schoolmaster," ln.33, *The Poetical Works of Alexander Wilson* (1844). *See* Anonymous, **#560**, under "Principal."

Teacher, Description of

(*See also* Teacher, Image of; Teacher, Remembrances of)

920. This celebrated Mrs. Pipchin was a marvellous ill-favoured, ill-conditioned old lady, of a stooping figure, with a mottled face, like bad marble, a hook nose, and a hard grey eye, that looked as if it might have been hammered at on an anvil without sustaining any injury. Forty years at least had elapsed since the Peruvian mines had been the death of Mr. Pipchin; but this relict still wore black bombazeen, of such a lusterless, deep, dead, sombre shade, that gas itself couldn't light her up after dark, and her presence was a quencher to any number of candles. She was generally spoken of as "a great manager" of children; and the secret of her management was, to give them everything that they didn't like, and nothing that they did—which was found to sweeten their dispositions very much. She was such a bitter old lady, that one was tempted to believe there had been some mistake in the application of the Peruvian machinery, and that all her waters of gladness and milk of human kindness, had been pumped out dry, instead of the mines.

—Charles Dickens, *Dombey and Son* (1848), 113. [relict=*a widow;* bombazeen=*bomazine, a twill fabric, often dyed black for mourning wear*].

921. The cognomen of Crane was not inapplicable to his person. He was tall, but exceedingly lank, with narrow shoulders, long arms and legs, hands that dangled a mile out of his sleeves, feet that might have served for shovels, and his whole frame most loosely hung together. His head was small, and flat on top, with large ears, large green glassy eyes, and a long snipe nose, so that it looked like a weathercock perched upon his spindle neck, to tell which way the wind blew. To see him striding along the profile of a hill on a windy day, with his clothes bagging and fluttering about him, one might have mistaken him for the genius of famine descending upon the earth, or some scarecrow eloped from a corn-field.

—Washington Irving, *The Legend of Sleepy Hollow* (1820).

922. [The colonial schoolmaster] wore a three-cornered [hat]. His coat descended in long, square skirts, quite to the calves of his legs. He had on nankeen small-clothes, white silk stockings, paste knee and shoe buckles. His waistcoast was of yellow embossed silk with long lappels. The sleeves and skirts of his coat were garnished with rows of silver buttons. He wore ruffle cuffs; on his neck was a snow-white linen stock. Under his hat appeared a gray wig falling in rolls over the shoulders. He had on a pair of turquoise-shell spectacles. A golden-headed cane was thrust under his arm.

—Sylvester Judd, *Margaret* (1845).
[nankeen=*a firm, durable, yellow or buff fabric*].

923. [Samuel Johnson's] 'academy' failed—no doubt this uncouth eccentric, with his tics and grimaces, seemed too forbidding even to eighteenth-century parents.[1]

[1]Compare the objections raised in August 1735, . . . when Gilbert Walmesley tried to get Johnson a school at Solihull—he was, the Governors admitted, an excellent scholar; but 'he has ye Caracter of being a very haughty, ill natured Gent. & yt he has such a way of distorting his Face (wch. though he can't help) ye Gent. think it may affect some Young Ladds.'

—F.L. Lucas, *The Search for Good Sense* (1958), 38.

924. My teacher [in Lahore, India] now was Punditji; his face was like a dried brinjol, somewhat shriveled; so was all his person; his nose was very long, and I felt, when God made him, he made his nose last, and made it of a softer material, so that it drooped down with its own weight and dried just in time to remain like a nose. His color was like parchment.

—Savitri Devi Nanda, *City of Two Gateways* (1950). [brinjol=*eggplant*].

925. By far the most distinguished of his teachers this first year was Mr. Edward ("Buck") Benson, the Greek professor. Buck Benson was a little man in the middle-forties, a bachelor, somewhat dandified, but old-fashioned in his dress. He wore wing collars, large plump cravats, and suede-topped shoes. His hair was thick, heavily grayed, beautifully kept.

His face was courteously pugnacious, fierce, with large yellow bulging eyeballs, and several bulldog pleatings around the mouth. It was an altogether handsome ugliness.

His voice was low, lazy, pleasant, with an indolent drawl, but without changing its pace or its inflection he could flay a victim with as cruel a tongue as ever wagged, and in the next moment wipe out hostility, restore affection, heal all wounds by the same agency. His charm was enormous.

—Thomas Wolfe, *Look Homeward, Angel* (1929), 401.

Teacher, Dispraise for

(*See also* Teacher, Remembrances of)

926. "Why does teaching always seem to attract the intellectually flabby?"

"Perhaps because we want to seem infallible and think that little boys may find us so. How wrong we are."

—Louis Auchincloss, *The Rector of Justin* (1964), 14.

927. You had in mind to teach me the Arabian tongue, to read and write. I am much obliged, forsooth, for having me lose so much time upon a language that requires ten or twelve years to attain to its perfection; as if the son of a king should think it to be an honor to him to be a grammarian or some doctor of the law, and to learn other languages than of his neighbors when he can well be without them; he, to whom time is so precious for so many weighty things, which he ought by times to learn. As if there were any spirit that did not with some reluctancy, and even with a kind of debasement, employ itself in so sad and dry an exercise, so longsome and tedious as is that of learning words. . . .

If you had seasoned me with that philosophy which formeth the mind to ratiocination, and insensibly accustoms it to be satisfied with nothing but solid reasons; if you had given me those excellent precepts and doctrines which raise the soul above the assaults of fortune, and reduce her to an unshakable and always equal temper, and permit her not to be lifted up by prosperity nor debased by adversity; if you had taken care to give me the knowledge of what we are and what are the first principles of things, and had assigned me in forming in my mind a fit idea of the greatness of the universe, and of the admirable order and motion of the parts thereof; if, I say, you had instilled into me this kind of philosophy, I should think myself incomparably more obliged to you than Alexander was to his

Aristotle, and believe it my duty to recompense you otherwise than he did him.

—Aurangzeb (1618–1707), Mongol emperor of India, scathing letter to a boyhood tutor, probably Mullah Sahe, who had requested a sinecure and a reward, in M. Lincoln Schuster, *A Treasury of the World's Great Letters* (1940), 97.

928. Planters were accustomed to buy indentured servants [as schoolmasters]..., to the disgust of competing tutors. Jonathan Boucher, a Virginia tutor, complained in 1773 that "at least two thirds of the little education we receive are derived from instructors, who are either INDENTURED SERVANTS, OR TRANSPORTED FELONS. Not a ship arrives either with redemptioners or convicts, in which schoolmasters are not regularly advertised for sale, as weavers, tailors, or any other trade; with little difference, that I can hear of, excepting perhaps that the former do not usually fetch so good a price as the latter."

—Jonathan Boucher, in *The American Heritage History of the Thirteen Colonies* (1967), 304. *See* "Advertisement for a runaway schoolmaster," **#879**, under "Teacher."

929. Lucian ... has left the opinion, in writing, that when the gods have determined to render a man ridiculously miserable, they make a schoolmaster of him; and an experience of more than four years does not, in my own case, authorize me to contradict this assertion.... The despicable wretchedness of teaching can be known only to those who have tried it; and to Him who made the heart, and knows all.

—Thomas Carlyle, in Myron C. Tuman, "Prometheus Bound: The Brief Teaching Careers of Great Writers," *Phi Delta Kappan* Magazine, December 1980.

930. Although any man who has proved his unfitness for any other occupation of life, was free, without examination or qualification, to open a school anywhere; although preparation for the functions he undertook, was required in the surgeon..., the chemist, the attorney, the butcher, the baker, the candlestick maker; the whole round of crafts and trades, the schoolmaster excepted; and although schoolmasters, as a race, were the blockheads and imposters that might naturally be expected to spring from such a state of things, and to flourish in it; these Yorkshire schoolmasters were the lowest and most rotten round in the whole ladder.

Traders in avarice, indifference, or imbecility of parents, and the helplessness of children; ignorant, sordid, brutal men, to whom few considerate persons would have entrusted the board and lodging of a horse or a dog; they formed the worthy cornerstone of a structure, which, for absurdity and a magnificent high-minded *laissez-aller* neglect, has rarely been exceeded in the world.

We hear sometimes of an action for damages against the unqualified medical practitioner, who has deformed a broken limb in pretending to heal it. But, what of the hundreds of thousands of minds that have been deformed for ever by the incapable pettifoggers who have pretended to form them!

—Charles Dickens, *Nicholas Nickleby* (1838–39), preface. *See* Caldwell, **#943**, under "Teacher, Image of."

931. What a fool am I, and a proper butt for the satirists, to spend so much time on the manifestations of vulgar folly! Let me draw nigh to them that wear wisdom's mien and hunt the golden bough of legend. Foremost of these are the schoolmasters, a wretched tribe indeed, harried, despised and God-forsaken, did I not mitigate the miseries of their appalling vocation with a sweet insanity. To say they were cursed with that fivefold anathema that begins the "Iliad" would be nothing: five hundred would be nearer the mark. Half-starved and threadbare, they lead their lives in those so-called schools, rather penitentiaries, treadmills or slaughter-houses, amid hordes of boys, bent with the drudgery, deafened with the noise, befouled with the filth and stench, yet all the while as happy as kings. Such joy it gives them to quell the trembling flock with threatening looks and tones, to flay little wretches with ferules, rods, and whips, to tyrannise and rage at their pleasure, and generally play the ass in a lion's skin. The dirt seems ornament to them, the stink sweet to their nostrils, the squalid slavery they would not exchange for a kingdom, nor admit any Phalaris or Dionysius as joint-tyrant to share their despotism. Of late they have won new glory from the modern craze for learning; and now, however trivial their teaching, they fancy themselves more erudite than any of the fabled sages of old. Moreover, by some marvel that I cannot fathom, they succeed in persuading the silly parents of their scholars that they are what they would seem.

—Desiderius Erasmus, *The Praise of Folly* (1509), 73, tr. Harry Carter.

932. We didn't sleep any more that night, we just chatted about this and that.

"Miss Haynes."

"What's wrong with Miss Haynes?"

"Do-lally-tap. She's barmy."

"Can't be, she's a school-ma'am. You can't be a school-ma'am if you're do-lally."

"She is."

"What makes you think?"

"She says I can't know everything."

"Guess she's right."

"Why?"

"Suppose your noddle's not big enough."

"That's the outside."

"Pardon me. I forgot."

"I can know everything inside."

—Fynn *(pseud.), Mister God, this is Anna* (1974), 88.

933. The greater part of the people we assign to educate our sons we know for certain are not educated. Yet we do not doubt that they can give what they have not received, a thing which otherwise cannot be otherwise acquired.

—Giacomo Leopardi, *Pensieri* (1834–37), x.

934. [I hope] that I may soon find a tutor, now that I have rejected Theon. Yes, I too have formed a low opinion of him because he is so irresponsible by nature. When I informed Philoxemos of your opinion he agreed, saying that the city suffered from a shortage of professors, but that Didymos, who (it appears) is a friend of his, would be sailing down and holding school, and he said that Didymos would be more attentive than the others. He has also persuaded the sons of Appollonios son of Herodes to sign up with Didymos; for since the death of Philologos, whose pupils they used to be, he has now been looking with them for a more effective tutor. For my part, my prayers would be answered if I could find some worthwhile tutors and never have to lay my eyes on Didymos even from a distance. The thing that gets me down is that he's seen fit to enter into competition with other tutors [here], this man who was nothing but a country schoolmaster. So, realizing that there is no benefit to be had from [any available] tutor, just paying steep fees for nothing, I am relying on my own devices. Write me quickly what you think. There's Didymos, always ready, as Philoxenos puts it, to give me his time and do everything he can for me. But I'm sure I'll do just fine, the gods willing, just listening to the public lectures, Poseidonios amongst them.

—Letter from a young man to his home,
in Naphtali Lewis, *Life in Egypt Under Roman Rule*
(1983), 63. In Egypt, *circa* the first century, education

beyond the elementary level required a period of study in Alexandria, but often this experience proved to be somewhat disappointing, as this city had its share of mediocrities and charlatans.

935. What right have you to disturb me, abominable schoolmaster, object abhorred alike by boys and girls? Before the crested cocks have broken silence, you begin to roar out your savage scoldings and blows. Not with louder noise does the metal resound on the struck anvil, when the workman is fitting a lawyer on his horse; nor is the noise so great in the large amphitheater, when the conquering gladiator is applauded by his partisans. We, your neighbors, do not ask you to allow us to sleep for the whole night, for it is but a small matter to be occasionally awakened; but to be kept awake all night is a heavy affliction. Dismiss your scholars, brawler, and take as much for keeping quiet as you receive for making noise.

—Martial, *Epigrams* (A.D. 93), IX.68.

936. It is boasted of a schoolmaster that such a brave man had his education under him, but it is never said how many who might have been brave have been ruined by him.

—Cotton Mather, *Essays to Do Good* (1710).

937. Next to the clerk in holy orders, the fellow with the foulest job in the world is the schoolmaster. Both are underpaid, both fall steadily in authority and dignity, and both wear out their hearts trying to perform the impossible. How much the world asks of them, and how little they can actually deliver! The clergyman's business is to save the human race from Hell. If he saves one-eighth of one per cent, even within the limits of his narrow flock, he does magnificently. The schoolmaster's is to spread the enlightenment, to make the great masses of the plain people think—and thinking is precisely the thing that the great masses of the plain people are congenitally and eternally incapable of. . . . The truth is that the average schoolmaster, on all the lower levels, is and always must be essentially and next door to an idiot, for how can one imagine an intelligent man engaging is so puerile an avocation?

—H.L. Mencken, *The New York Evening Mail*, Jan. 23, 1918, in *A Mencken Chrestomathy* (1949), 301, 304.

938. Let them teach who can do nothing better, whose qualities are laborious application, sluggishness of mind, muddiness of intellect, prosiness of imagination, chill of the blood, patience to bear the body's labors,

contempt of glory, avidity for petty gains, indifference to boredom. . . . Let them watch boys' fidgety hands, their wandering eyes, their *sotto voce* whisperings who delight in that task, who enjoy dust and noise and clamor of mingled prayers and tears and whimperings under the rod's correction. Let them teach who love to return to boyhood, who are shy of dealing with men and shamed by living with equals, who are happy to be set over their inferiors, who always want someone to terrify, to afflict, to torture, to rule, someone who will hate and fear them.

—Petrarch, letter to Zanobi da Strada,
a Florentine schoolmaster and poet, Apr. 1, 1352 (or 1349?),
in Morris Bishop, tr., *Letters from Petrarch* (1966), 108.

939. [Elementary schools] are mainly in the hands of ignorant, unskilled teachers. The children are fed upon the mere husks of knowledge. They leave school for the broader theater of life without discipline; without mental power or moral stamina. . . . Poor schools and poor teachers are in a majority throughout the country. Multitudes of the schools are so poor that it would be well for the country if they were closed. . . . They afford the sad spectacle of ignorance engaged in the stupendous fraud of self-perpetuation at the public expense. . . . Hundreds of our American schools are little less than undisciplined juvenile mobs.

—William Franklin Phelps,
in National Education Association *Proceedings*, 1870. At the time
Phelps was the head of a normal school in Winona, Minnesota.
See Mulcaster, #909, under "Teacher."

940. [John] Reed found the result [of education at Portland Academy, c. 1900] deadly. "Why should I have been interested in the stupid education of our time? We take soaring young imaginations consumed with curiosity about the life they see all around and feed them with dead technique: the flawless purity of Washington, Lincoln's hum-drum chivalry, our dull and virtuous history and England's former glory; Addison's graceful style as an essayist, Goldsmith celebrating the rural clergy of the eighteenth century, Dr. Johnson at his most vapid, and George Elliott's *[sic]* 'Silas Marner'; Macaulay, and the sonorous oratings of Edmund Burke; and in Latin, Caesar's Gallic guide-book, and Cicero's mouthings about Roman politics."

Nothing was inherently wrong with the subject matter; the real problem was the teaching. Perhaps [the subjects] . . . might have come alive had not the teachers been desiccated men and women who showed no sparkle of enthusiasm, no joy in learning, no attempt to make any subject a living explanation of the world. With few exceptions, he came to despise such people "whose chief qualification is that they can plough a dull round of dates, acts, half-truths and rules for style, without questioning, without interpreting, and without seeing how ridiculously unlike the world their teachings are." . . .

Years later Reed bitterly recalled that "many fine things I have had to force myself to explore again, because school once spoiled them for me."

—Robert A. Rosenstone, *Romantic Revolutionary: A Biography of John Reed* (1975), 17.

Teacher, Image of

(*See also* Teacher, Description of)

941. To be sure, there is an age-old prejudice against teaching. Teachers must share with doctors the world's most celebrated sneers, and with them also the world's unbounded hero-worship. Always and everywhere, "He is a schoolteacher" has meant "He is an underpaid pitiable drudge." Even a politician stands higher, because power in the street seems less of a mockery than power in the classroom. But when we speak of Socrates, Jesus, Buddha, and "other great teachers of humanity," the atmosphere somehow changes and the politician's power begins to look shrunken and mean. August examples show that no limit can be set to the power of a teacher, but this is equally true in the other direction: no career can so nearly approach zero in its effects.

—Jacques Barzun, *Teacher in America* (1944), 4.

942. Last week I had for about the hundredth time an experience that always disturbs me. Riding on a train, I found myself talking with my seatmate, who asked me what I did for a living. "I teach English." Do you have any trouble predicting the response? His face fell, and he groaned, "Oh dear, I'll have to watch my language." In my experience there are only two other possible reactions. The first is even less inspiriting: "I hated English in school; it was my worst subject." The second, so rare as to make an honest English teacher almost burst into tears of gratitude when it occurs, is an animated conversation about literature, or ideas, or the American language—the kind of conversation that shows a continuing respect for "English" as something more than being sure about who and whom, lie and lay.

—Wayne C. Booth, "Boring from Within: The Art of the Freshman Essay," in Arthur M. Eastman, ed., *The Norton Reader*, 4th ed., (1977), 151.

943. The evil which is really the greatest of all is the want of qualified teachers. It may be difficult to obtain a teacher at all, but it is pretty certain, in the present state of the country, not one is property fitted for the occupation. Do we think that of all the professions in the world that a schoolmaster requires the least formation? If we do, there cannot be a more egregious mistake.... He could scarcely comprehend [the necessary teaching skills] and establish them in his habits in less than two years.... Yet in our present mode of popular education, we act upon the principle that schoolkeeping is a business to which scarcely anyone but an idiot is incompetent, if he only knows reading, writing, and arithmetic....

In the present condition of society and public opinion, the occupation of a schoolmaster, in comparison with others, is regarded with contempt. It would be wonderful were it otherwise, when we look at the manner in which it is often if not most usually filled. Is a man, constitutionally and habitually indolent, a burden upon all from whom he can extract a support? Then there is one way of shaking him off—let us make him a schoolmaster. To teach a school is, in the opinion of many, little else than sitting still and doing nothing. Has any man wasted all his property or ended in debt by indiscretion and misconduct? The business of schoolkeeping stands wide open for his reception, and here he sinks to the bottom for want of capacity to support himself.

Has anyone ruined himself, and done all he could to corrupt others, by dissipation, drinking, seduction, and a course of irregularities? Nay, has he returned from prison, after an ignominious atonement for some violation of the laws? He is destitute of character and cannot be trusted, but presently he opens a school, and the children are seen flocking into it; for if he is willing to act in that capacity, we shall all admit that as he can read and write and cipher to the square root, he will make an excellent schoolmaster. In short, it is no matter what the man is, or what his manners or principles, if he has escaped with life from the penal code, we have the satisfaction to think that he can still have credit as a schoolmaster.

—Joseph Caldwell, *Letters on Popular Education, Addressed to the People of North-Carolina* (1832), in *The Annals of America* (1968), V.557–58.
See Dickens, **#930**, under "Teacher, Dispraise for."

944. One of the discouraging views of society at the present moment is, that ... generally it seems to be thought, that any body may become a teacher. The most moderate ability is thought to be competent to the most important profession in society. Strange, too, as it may seem, on this point parents incline to be economical. They squander thousands on dress, furniture, amusements, think it hard to pay comparatively small sums to the instructer [*sic*]; and through this ruinous economy, and this ignorance of the dignity of a teacher's vocation, they rob their children of aid, for which the treasures of worlds can afford no compensation.

—William Ellery Channing (1780–1842), "Remarks on Education," *Christian Examiner*, November 1833.

945. Whatever our teacher may have lacked—adequate salary, teaching aids, approved teaching load—he certainly did possess, in full measure, standing in the community. He made his own decisions, backing them with his own authority. He was looked up to as a person of substance and worth. One of the biggest occasions in the school calendar was the time Teacher came home to spend the night with you. The dinner Mama cooked to do honor to the occasion was every bit as delectable as the one prepared for the preacher. Promptly upon arriving home from school, we put on our best clothes and helped Mama set the table with the Haviland china, the cut glass, and the good silver. Moreover, we knew only the best manners were acceptable at such times, and we'd better remember them.

—Loula Grace Erdman, *Life Was Simpler Then* (1963), 18.

946. Teachers in books, drama, magazine cartoons, and films were depicted as tyrannical, brutal, dull, awkward, queer, and depressed. The few attractive teachers remained in the profession only long enough to find a mate. Teachers had a difficult time getting and staying married. . . . [One] writer noted that "to succeed as a teacher one must fail as a man or woman."

—George Gerbner, "Teacher Image and the Hidden Curriculum." *American Scholar*, winter, 1972–73.

947. Teachers are respected; not always admired. We are praised for regularity and a sense of duty; but most people do not necessarily expect us to be bright. Doctors are held in honor, and lawyers are esteemed for their sharp intelligence; but teachers are sometimes thought of as respectable drudges—like hospital nurses, or even like attendants in an asylum for the harmless insane. Yet they have high ideals, and often suffer in pursuing them. The man in the street scarcely realizes that many forms of business, some major industries, and one or two minor professions could be completely abolished without gravely injuring American society; whereas the disappearance—or even what we see in some quarters, the continuous neglect and degradation—of the teaching profession must mean a disaster to the entire nation. If the average man can be made to understand that our careers, although ill rewarded, are not merely unsuccessful attempts to make money, but are endeavors to attain a difficult set of ideals,

ideals valuable to the whole community, perhaps he will take us, and his responsibilities to us, more seriously than he and his elected representatives now do.

—Gilbert Highet, *The Immortal Profession: The Joys of Teaching and Learning* (1976), 37.

948. Teachers are villains in Waspland. We have done everything possible to denigrate them in our literature and popular entertainment. From the ghouls in Dickens and Charlote Bronte, to Ichabod Crane, to the sexually frustrated, spindle-shanked Miss Sidney in William Inge's *Picnic,* we have drawn teachers as loathsome, utterly ridiculous, and inadequate in all ways. And, of course, skinny, should anyone miss the point of their poverty. . . .

We believe that teachers are people who wish to be important, but who fear that no one but children will find them so.

We also feel that teachers are timid people with an underlying bullying nature who must arrange matters so that their victims are certain to be physically smaller. This makes teachers offenders against fair play—an even greater sin than timidity. Today's teachers have unions and tend to be militant rather than timid, but the Wasp has an answer for that, too. Militant teachers are "on their high horse." How dare they not be timid? After all, they're only teachers. It's their duty to refuse to strike because they're supposed to be dedicated. However, the most scorned teacher is the most dedicated one because, in Waspland, dedication to lofty ideals instead of lofty salaries is proof of impracticality.

It gets even worse. Many Wasps feel there is something strange about an adult who chooses to be around children so much. Don't teachers feel confident of their ability to cope with their contemporaries, and if not, why? Are they weak? Spineless? If so, you can't trust them. In England, choosing the company of children carries even more ominous overtones. As Evelyn Waugh made plain in *Decline and Fall,* pedagogy and pedophilia go together like tea and crumpets. As the expelled hero leaves Oxford, the gatekeeper says, "Sent down for indecent behavior, were you. Expect you'll become a schoolmaster, eh wot?"

—Florence King, *Wasp, Where Is Thy Sting?:* "Anti-Intellectualism" (1977), 118, 119. The exact quotation from Waugh reads: "I expect you'll becoming a schoolmaster, sir. That's what most of the gentlemen does, sir, that gets sent down for indecent behaviour." [sent down=*expelled*].

949. Why are we never quite at our ease in the presence of a schoolmaster?—because we are conscious that he is not quite at his ease in

ours. He is awkward, and out of place, in the society of his equals. He comes like Gulliver from among his little people, and he cannot fit the stature of his understanding to yours. . . . He is so used to teaching, that he wants to be teaching you. . . . He is forlorn among his coevals; his juniors cannot be his friends.

—Charles Lamb, *The Essays of Elia:* "The Old and the New Schoolmaster" (1823). *See* King, **#902**, under "Teacher."

950. Not to be outdone by Pickle Week, Foot Care Week and Remember the Buffalo Week, some teachers' organizations have managed to promote a Teachers' Recognition Day. My parents did not need to be prodded by public-relations programs into an attitude of respect for teachers. I was raised to believe that teachers are infallible and superhuman. A teacher was not like a relative, a neighbor, or even a friend. When a teacher passed on the street the mothers stopped whatever they were doing and bowed their heads slightly in acknowledgment of her presence. The fathers, who rarely tipped their hats to anyone, did so in respectful silence to a teacher. She was above parents and just a little below God, and as such was held in the kind of awe that bordered on fear.

As a child I could never conceive of a teacher's being subject to the habits of ordinary people. We never saw her eat, or drink, or scratch, or blow her nose, or, perish the thought, go to the bathroom. Her conduct was as stainless as her stiffly starched blouse.

—Sam Levenson, *Everything But Money* (1949), 61.

951. "I ain't no enemy, Mr. Caldwell. I like you. All the kids like you."

"That's the trouble, Deifendorf. That's the worst thing can happen to a public school teacher. I don't want you to like me. All I want from you is to sit still under me for fifty-five minutes a day five days a week. When you walk into my room, Deifendorf, I want you to be stiff with fear. Caldwell the kid-killer; that's how I want you to think of me. Brrouh!"

—John Updike, *The Centaur* (1963), iv.

Teacher, Praise for

(*See also* Teacher, Remembrances of)

952. [Lady Jane Grey's] parentes, the Duke and Duches, with all the household, Gentlemen and Gentlewomen, were huntinge in the Parke: I founde her, in her Chamber, readinge *Phaedon Platonis* in Greeke. . . .

I asked hir, whie she wold leese soch pastime in the Parke? smiling she answered me: I wisse, all their sporte in the Parke is but a shadoe to that pleasure, that I find in Plato. Alas good folke, they never felt, what trewe pleasure ment. And how came you, Madame, quoth I, to this deepe knowledge of pleasure, and what did chieflie allure you unto it: seinge, not many women, but very fewe men have atteined therunto? I will tell you, quoth she, and tell you a troth, which perchance ye will mervell at. One of the greatest benefites, that God ever gave me, is that he sent me so sharpe and severe Parentes, and so jentle a scholemaster. For when I am in presence either of father or mother, whether I speake, kepe silence, sit, stand, or go, eate, drinke, be merie, or sad, be sowying, plaiyng, dauncing, or doing anie thing els, I must do it, as it were, in soch weight, mesure, and number, even so perfitelie, as God made the world, or else I am so sharplie taunted, so cruellie threatened, yea pesentlie some tymes, with pinches, nippes, and bobbes, and other waies, which I will not name, for the honor I beare them, so without measure misordered, that I thinke my selfe in hell, till tyme cum, that I must go to M. Elmer, who teacheth me so jentlie, so pleasantlie, with soch faire allurements to learning, that I thinke all the tyme nothing, whiles I am with him. And when I am called from him, I fall on weeping, because, what soever I do els, but learning, is ful of grief, trouble, feare, and whole misliking unto me: And thus my booke, hath bene to moch my pleasure, and bringeth dayly to me more pleasure and more, that in respect of it, all other pleasures, in very deede, be but trifle and troubles unto me.

—Roger Ascham, *The Scholemaster* (1570), 33.
He was tutor, and later secretary, to Queen Elizabeth.

953. There is no office higher than that of a teacher of youth, for there is nothing on earth so precious as the mind, soul, character of the child. No office should be regarded with greater respect. The first minds of the community should be encouraged to assume it. Parents should do all but impoverish themselves, to induce such to become the guardians and guides of their children.

—William Ellery Channing (1780–1842),
"Remarks on Education," *Christian Examiner*, November 1833.

954. I am not willing that this discussion should close without mention of the value of a true teacher. Give me a log hut, with only a simple bench, Mark Hopkins on one end and I on the other, and you may have all the buildings, apparatus and libraries without him.

—James A. Garfield, address in New York
to Williams College alumni, Dec. 28, 1871,
in Burke A. Hinsdale, *President Garfield and Education* (1882).

955. Beside yon straggling fence that skirts the way,
With blossom'd furze unprofitably gay,
There, in his noisy mansion, skill'd to rule,
The village master taught his little school;
A man severe was he, and stern to view;
I knew him well, and every truant knew;
Well had the boding tremblers learn'd to trace
The day's disasters in his morning face;
Full well they laugh'd, with counterfeited glee,
At all his jokes, for many a joke had he;
Full well the busy whisper, circling round
Convey'd the dismal tidings when he frown'd;
Yet he was kind: or if severe in aught
The love he bore to learning was in fault;
The village all declar'd how much he knew;
'Twas certain he could write, and cypher too;
Lands he could measure, terms and tides presage,
And even the story ran that he could gauge.
In arguing too, the parson own'd his skill,
For e'en though vanquish'd, he could argue still;
While words of learned length and thundering sound
Amaz'd the gazing rustics rang'd around,
And still they gaz'd, and still the wonder grew,
That one small head could carry all he knew.

—Oliver Goldsmith, *The Deserted Village* (1770). [fault: pronounced like *fought;* own'd=*showed*].

956. If the heavens were all parchment, and the trees of the forest all pens, and every human being were a scribe, it would still be impossible to record all that I have learned from my teachers.

—Attr. Johanan ben Zakkai (died c. A.D. 80), leader of the Pharisees of Jerusalem and, later, founder of the academy at Jabneh.

957. Good teachers have a toehold on immortality, which is only a word for little islands in the rising tide of time.

Islands remembered briefly, for time's eventual tide gets us all. But good teachers, I think, are longer remembered over the brief tick tock of decades; each man recalls his own.

Nobody can define good teachers. "Good teacher" in fact is redundant. (Bad teacher, a contradiction in terms.) Some teachers, it seems certain from here, must be remembered more than others, although the terrain of childhood is unmapped now and I cannot remember exactly where I was, or precisely what I felt.

—John Keasler, "Teaching Brings Its Special Reward," *Sarasota Herald-Tribune*, Jan. 21, 1986.

958. "One thing only," said Mr. Crantit, "prevents our established system of education from crumbling into the dust and ashes of the minds which devised it, and that is the stubborn virtue of the individual teachers. Teachers who, under-paid and over-worked in a revolting environment—breathing daily the inspissated odours of boyhood and unclean clothes—stand like missionary saints against the hypocrisy and their present employment and the barbarism of tomorrow!"

—Eric Linklater, *Laxdale Hall* (1951).

959. Just as a person is commanded to honor and revere his father, so he is under an obligation to honor and revere his teacher, even to a greater extent than his father; for his father gave him life in this world, while his teacher who instructs him in wisdom, secures for him life in the world to come. If he sees an article that his father had lost and another article that his teacher had lost, the teacher's property should be recovered first, and then the father's. If his father and his teacher are loaded with burden, he should first relieve his teacher and then his father. If his father and teacher are in captivity, he should first ransom his teacher. But if his father is a scholar, though not of the same rank as his teacher's, he should first recover his father's lost property and then his teacher's.

—Maimonides, *Mishneh Torah (Repetition of the Law)*, I.v., in J.S. Minkin, *The World of Moses Maimonides* (1957), 288. *See* Talmud, **#685**, under "Scholar."

960. Conscientious teachers of small children are destined to sit on the right hand of God.

—*Midrash: Pesikta De-Rav Kahana*, xxviii. Rabbi Kahana lived in the 3rd century.

961. When I was in high school, I admitted to my mother that I planned to become a teacher someday. That seemed to please her. But I never tried to explain that it was not the occupation of teaching I yearned for as much as it was something more elusive: I wanted to *be* like my teachers, to possess their knowledge, to assume their authority, their confidence, even to assume a teacher's persona.

—Richard Rodriguez, *Hunger of Memory: The Education of Richard Rodriguez* (1982), 55.

962. —Teachers who have plugged away at their jobs for twenty, thirty and forty years are heroes. I suspect they know in their hearts they've done a good thing, too, and are more satisfied with themselves than most people are.

—Most of us end up with no more than five or six people who remember us. Teachers have thousands of people who remember them for the rest of their lives.

—Andrew A. Rooney, *Word for Word:* "School Days" (1984), 234.

963. I sing the praise of the unknown teacher. Famous educators plan new systems of pedagogy, but it is the unknown teacher who delivers and guides the young. He lives in obscurity and contends with hardship. He keeps watch along the borders of darkness and makes the attack on the trenches of ignorance and folly. Patient in his daily duty he strives to conquer the evil powers which are the enemies of youth. He awakens sleeping spirits. He quickens the indolent, encourages the eager, and steadies the unstable. He communicates his own joy in learning and shares with boys and girls the best treasures of his mind. He lights many candles which, in later years, will shine back to cheer him. This is his reward. Knowledge may be gained from books; but the love of knowledge is transmitted only by personal contact. No one has deserved better of the republic than the unknown teacher.

—Henry van Dyke (1852–1933), in Percy E. Burrup, *The Teacher and the Public School System,* 2nd ed. (1960), 175.

Teacher, Remembrances of

(*See also* Teacher, Dispraise for; Teacher, Praise for)

964. George Washington High School was the first real school I attended. My entire stay there might have been time lost if it hadn't been for the unique personality of a brilliant teacher. Miss Kirwin was that rare educator who was in love with information. I will always believe that her love of teaching came not so much from her liking of students but from her desire to make sure that some of the things she knew would find repositories so that they could be shared again.

She and her maiden sister worked in the San Francisco school system for over twenty years. My Miss Kirwin, who was a tall, florid, buxom lady with battleship-gray hair, taught civics and current events....

There were no favorite students. No teacher's pets. If a student pleased her during a particular period, he could not count on special treatment in the next day's class, and that was true the other way around. Each day she faced us with a clean slate and acted as if ours were clean as well. Reserved and firm in her opinions, she spent no time in indulging in the frivolous.

She was stimulating instead of intimidating. Where some of the other teachers went out of their way to be nice to me — to be "liberal" with me — and others ignored me completely, Miss Kirwin never seemed to notice that I was Black and therefore different....

Years later when I returned to San Francisco I made visits to her classroom. She always remembered that I was Miss Johnson, who had a good mind and should be doing something with it. I was never encouraged on those visits to loiter or linger about her desk. She acted as if I must have other visits to make. I often wondered if she knew she was the only teacher I remembered.

— Maya Angelou, *I Know Why the Caged Bird Sings* (1970), 209–11.

965. I think of you so very often and of the three years I spent at your school because it is such a joy not to be there any longer and if one is at all down it bucks one up derectly to remember that *thats* all over atanyrate.... ps, I often rite to people telling them where I was edducated and highly reckomending you.

— Max Beerbohm, *And Even Now: 'How Shall I Word It?'*: "Letter From Young Lady in Answer To Invitation From Old Schoolmistress" (1910).

966. Some weeks later I was reprimanded by Miss Pulham for bad behaviour. She shut me in her study for two hours to 'think things over'. When she returned, everything on the mantlepiece and tables was on the floor. The room was a shambles.

She sat slowly down on a velvet chair and told me to put everything back.

'There's only one thing to do with you,' she said.

My throat tightened.

'Expel me, I suppose.'

'No, Mary,' she said quietly. 'That wouldn't help either of us. I shall make you a prefect.'

I stared at her with narrowed eyes, then I burst into tears, my head on her knee. . . .

From that moment I was a knight to her Queen.

—Mary Hayley Bell, *What Shall We Do Tomorrow?* (1968), 65.

967. When I try to recall my early life at my prep school, the things that come before me most obstinately are the faces of my masters and schoolfellows. They float to the surface of my mind, as fresh and as vivid as when I first saw them, and nearly every one of them resembles an animal. I seem to be living in a zoo, each inmate of which is slightly repellent, while taken all together they are terrifying because, like the figures in dreams, I have no control over them. Nor can this impression be entirely subjective, because many of the boys and masters had animal nicknames. . . .

Mr Parker Clark (or Face-ache, as we sometimes called him—not to be confused with Mr Everett Clerke, our history master, commonly known as the Pill) . . . taught us middle-form boys Latin and Greek. . . . He was famous for his original way of conducting his classes. A boy would stand up to construe a passage which he was supposed to have prepared in prep the night before. At the first serious mistake Mr Clark would put on a frown like thunder and start to shout at him. The boy would then mumble and fall into an even worse howler. 'Stand up on your chair,' bellowed Mr Clark, getting up himself and striding about the room. 'Up on your chair. We all want to look at you. Now try again.' Naturally the boy floundered more and more hopelessly. 'You're not high enough. Put a box on his chair.' A box used to keep papers in was put on his chair and he clambered up on top of it. 'Now see if *you* can construe it,' he would say turning to another boy. 'You can't either, eh? Up on your chair, then.' And before long, unless some cooler head came to the rescue, the whole form would be perched on chairs and boxes upon chairs . . . with Mr Clark pacing to and fro in front of them and bellowing. As he used to explain to us out of class, he was never angry when he shouted: we need not therefore be too afraid unless we saw him turn deadly pale and speak in a whisper: then, however, we must look out.

—Gerald Brenan, *A Life of One's Own: Childhood and Youth* (1962), 42, 49.

968. My admiration for Mr. Strassmeir [my elementary teacher] was unbounded, and he could do no wrong. I compared him, successfully, with such celebrated models of perfection as Galahad and Sir Philip Sidney, though he sometimes assumed a hostile attitude to his class or a few individuals in it, which, in the light of the legends about them, would have been foreign to the natures of the English paragons. He resembled them

physically, I thought. He was strikingly tall and slim, with blue eyes and curly hair, his cheeks slightly flushed, as if reflecting an inner fire. His manner alternated between passionate seriousness and flippancy tinged with sarcasm. He would interrupt our lessons to speak to us on the disgrace of poverty and on the callousness of government and the rich. He read to us, one memorable day, Thomas Hood's *The Song of the Shirt*, and the entire class was shaken. His skillfully modulated voice supplied a dramatic orchestration to the poem. As he intoned sadly the opening: "With fingers weary and worn," we could almost see before us Hood's tragic seamstress in her dark, airless, shabby attic, forever doomed to ply her needle for the benefit of the unfeeling rich. And when, with an inflection that conjured up the hopeless monotony of her existence, he spoke of the ever-recurring refrain: "Stitch! stitch! stitch!" some of us could bear the strain no longer and sobbed aloud.

—Samuel Chotzinoff, *A Lost Paradise* (1955).

969. In the autumn of 1923, when I entered the third year of the junior school [in Scotland], I came under the redoubtable 'Dub-Dub', Mr. W.W. Anderson, a man and teacher of old-fashioned strictness and thoroughness. He was within a few years of retirement when I came to know him as a teacher, a dour old Scot with a grey and ginger moustache and very little hair. His methods were old-fashioned, but remarkably effective. He battered the boys with a brand of irony all his own, and after bellowing at one of them for some error or piece of forgetfulness he would lean back against the mantel and say sardonically: 'You think I'm hard on you, don't you? You think I'm a Turk? You think I'm a Tartar? You're going to complain to your parents about me?' He would then pause and remove his gold-rimmed pince-nez glasses. 'Go home and tell your mother I'm a Tartar. Tell her I'm a Turk.' And he would give a curious little sibilant titter which sounded like 'sih, sih, sih'.

Dub-Dub never used the tawse, but he had his own way of keeping discipline. He was more feared, I think, than any other master in the school, and it was rumoured among the boys that he was not allowed to use the strap because once, away back in the 1880's or '90's, he had broken a boy's wrist with it. But I doubt if this was true. His moods of sternness made one tremble, and his levity had something of the quality of a jocund rattlesnake.

—David Daiches, *Two Worlds: An Edinburgh Jewish Childhood* (1959), 42.

[tawse (or taws)=*a leather strap slit into strips at the end*].

970. I started for school very late that morning and was in great dread of a scolding...

But nothing happened. M. Hamel saw me and said very kindly: "Go to your place quickly, little Franz. We were beginning without you."...

M. Hamel mounted his chair, and, in the same grave and gentle tone which he had used to me, he said:

"My children, this is the last lesson I shall give you. The order has come from Berlin to teach only German in the schools of Alsace and Lorraine. The new master comes tomorrow. This is your last French lesson."...

My last French lesson! Why, I hardly knew how to write! I should never learn any more! I must stop there, then! Oh, how sorry I was for not learning my lessons! ... And M. Hamel, too; the idea that he was going away, that I should never see him again, made me forget all about his ruler and how cranky he was....

Poor man! It was in honor of this last lesson that he had put on his fine Sunday-clothes, and now I understand why the old men of the village were sitting there in back of the room. It was because they were sorry, too, that they had not gone to school more. It was their way of thanking our master for his forty years of faithful service and of showing respect for the country that was theirs no more.

While I was thinking of all this, I heard my name called. It was my turn to recite.... But I got mixed up on the first words and stood there, holding on to my desk, my heart beating, and not daring to look up. I heard M. Hamel say to me:

"I won't scold you, little Franz; you must feel bad enough. See how it is! Every day we have said to ourselves: 'Bah! I've plenty of time. I'll learn it tomorrow.' ... But you were not the worst, poor little Franz. We've all a great deal to reproach ourselves with.

"Your parents were not anxious to have you learn. They preferred to put you to work on a farm or at the mills, so as to have a little more money. And I? I've been to blame also. Have I not often sent you to water my flowers instead of learning your lessons? And when I wanted to go fishing, did I not just give you a holiday?"...

Then he opened a grammar and read us our lesson....

After the grammar, we had a lesson in writing....

Whenever I looked up from my writing I saw M. Hamel sitting motionless in his chair and gazing first at one thing, then at another, as if he wanted to fix in his mind just how everything looked in that little schoolroom. Fancy! For forty years he had been there in the same place, with his garden outside and the window and his class in front of him, just like that. Only the desks and benches had been worn smooth; the walnut-trees in the garden were taller, and the hop-vine that he had planted himself twined about the window to the roof. How it must have broken his heart to leave it all....

All at once the church-clock struck twelve. Then the Angelus....

M. Hamel stood up, very pale, in his chair. I never saw him look so tall.

My friends," said he, "I—I—" But something choked him. He could not go on.

Then he turned to the blackboard, took a piece of chalk, and, bearing on with all his might, he wrote as large as he could:

"VIVE LA FRANCE!"

Then he stopped and leaned his head against the wall, and without a word, he made a gesture to us with his hand:

"School is dismissed—you may go."

—Alphonse Daudet (1840–97),
Selected Stories: "The Last Lesson"
(1951). As a result of the Franco-Prussian War
(1870–71) much of Alsace-Lorraine was annexed to Germany.

971. [My mathematics teacher] never brought himself really to believe that I could be that stupid about the most demonstrable facts. Often at the end of the day he would keep me in the classroom to explain to me with glaring eyes but in careful words of one syllable some simple proposition which everyone else had grasped instantly..., his despairing voice, with its curious expression of resentment, impatient but resigned.

—Michael Foster, *House Above the River* (1946), 15.

972. The teacher lived in the compound of the lord's storage office, but having some merchants' children among his pupils, he naturally began to train them in numerals. "Two times two is four, two times three is six, etc." This today seems a very ordinary thing to teach, but when my father heard this, he took his children away in a fury. "It is abominable," he exclaimed, "that innocent children should be taught to use numbers—the tool of merchants. There is no telling what the teacher may do next."

—Yukichi Fukazawa (1835–1901),
The Autobiography of Yukichi Fukuzawa, tr. Eiichi
Kiyooka (1966), 3. Fukuzawa's father was a scholarly samurai.

973. In 1891, being six years old, I was placed with Monsieur de Saint-Ange Beautier.... This good man had no great pretensions to being an educator. He taught only reading and writing.... He wore a long black beard and gold-rimmed spectacles which seemed part of his austere face....

He seemed not to be in good health; and in all my life I have never known a sadder and gentler man than Monsieur de Saint-Ange Beautier.

But we were not of an age to appreciate patience. As he questioned us ceaselessly, and as his questions were almost always the same, I took it into my head that the man could not possibly know or remember anything. He would ask us, "How much are two and two?" "Four!" we would answer in chorus. And I always said to myself, "This makes three days in a row we've told him that, and he's forgotten it again."

—Sacha Guitry, *If Memory Serves* (1936), 29.

974. I cannot pass the entire staff [of La Crosse High School] in review, but in memory Miss Lena Heidemann, who taught American history, was tops. She was an old maid, tall, thin, and angular. Her nose, that rudder of the mind, was of a commanding style, and her eyes could subdue you with a single glance. She had an innate dignity, and she expected dignity in others. She also possessed that mysterious quality developed in certain personalities of subduing you without arousing resentment.

—Howard Mumford Jones, *An Autobiography* (1979), 36.

975. In the third grade [of the Greek school] we had Periander Krasákis. What merciless godfather gave the name of Corinth's savage tyrant to this sickly runt of a man with his high starched collar to conceal the scrofula on his neck, his skinny grasshopper legs, the little handkerchief always at his mouth so that he could spit, spit, and spit as though breathing his last? This one had a mania for cleanliness. Every day he inspected our hands, ears, nose, teeth and nails. He did not thrash, did not entreat; he shook his oversized head which was covered with pimples, and shouted at us:

"Beasts! Pigs! If you don't wash every day with soap, you'll never, never become men. You know what being a man means? It means washing with soap. Brains aren't enough, you poor devils, soap is needed too. How are you going to appear before God with hands like that? Go out to the yard and get washed."

—Nikos Kazantzakis, *Report to Greco* (1965), 56.

976. Fräulein Weise (Wise) didn't live up to her name; she was malicious and that was what she should have been called, as a warning to her pupils. . . .

Fräulein Weise entered the classroom every morning without giving us so much as a glance. The desks were too small for us and we almost broke our legs so as to stand with the required stiffness while screaming HEIL HITLER, and we had to remain standing until she screamed back SIT DOWN. Only then did she take a look around her and at us, seeming surprised to find something living and breathing among the desks. Her attention was usually directed first at me; she addressed me only by my surname and in a voice which suddenly became soft and disconcertingly gentle, she sighed KNEF. It wafted through the classroom and she would ask me a question, which, since I was always startled and hypnotized afresh by this fishhead, I could hardly ever answer; she then spent about five minutes describing my inferiority, and the older I got during these stupefying years the more convinced I became that she must have passed her teaching exams at Gestapo headquarters.

—Hildegard Knef, *The Gift Horse* (1971), 10.
Americans knew her as Hildegarde (Neff), the popular singer.

977. She said the younger teachers naturally felt the strain of the life most keenly; the older ones had a more satisfying interest in their work. "What is it?" I asked her. "Perhaps I can grow into it." ."Oh, no," she answered quickly and soberly. "I wouldn't want you to. We narrow our interests until we grow fossilized, as—as I am. And then we have to make teaching fill our lives. We have to, to live. I want you to have many interests. You have much to expect of life."

—Margaret Mead, *An Anthropologist at Work* (1951), about Ruth Benedict.

978. Professor [Friedrich Knapp of F. Knapp's Institute, Baltimore, c. 1886] was a very mild and even amiable man, and much more diligent at praise than at blame. He was a Suabian who had come to Baltimore in 1850, and he still wore, nearly forty years afterward, the classical uniform of a German schoolmaster—a long-tailed coat of black alpaca, a boiled shirt with somewhat fringy cuffs, and a white lawn necktie. The front of his coat was dusty with chalk, and his hands were so caked with it that he had to blow it off every time he took snuff. He was of small stature but large diameter, and wore closely-clipped mutton-chop whiskers. His hands had a curious softness so often observed in pedagogues, barbers, and Y.M.C.A. secretaries. This impressed itself on me the first time he noticed me wiggling a loose milk-tooth with my tongue, and called me up to have it out. He watched for such manifestations sharply, and pulled, I should say, an average of six teeth a week. It was etiquette in the school for boys to bear this barbarity in silence. The girls could yell, but not the boys. Both, however, were free to howl under the bastinado, which was naturally applied to girls much more lightly and less often than to the boys.

—H.L. Mencken, *Happy Days: 1880–1892* (1940), 22. [bastinado=*a blow with a stick or cudgel*].

979. The acceptance of these ideas by the children of Park School was total, and I have often tried to account for the immense authority and prestige which the teachers enjoyed in propounding them, and indeed in asserting anything else, from the sounds of the alphabet to the multiplication table. The teacher was a person set apart and distinctly above, incapable of error, always to be believed and obeyed, the natural source of knowledge. I do not recall any child being rude to the teacher, no matter what other misbehavior might have occurred in the classroom. It would have been insufficient to say that we were docile or tractable; we were a devoted band of scholars, disciples following a stern mistress. When the fourth-grade teacher, a Miss Stapenhorst, left us to become a bride, we wept openly. I think the feeling was that here we were, just coming to grips with the rudiments of English grammar, and how could we ever expect to master them without the all-wise (and beautiful) Miss Stapenhorst?

—Charles W. Morton, *It Has Its Charms. . . .* (1966), 14.

980. There were times when I enjoyed going to school [in Garth, Scotland]; it depended on who was teaching me. I passed under a whole regiment of teachers there, male and female: teachers who shouted at me, who hit me over the head with the pointer, who strapped me (for the tawse was used vigorously), who took an interest in me, who sneered at me (and they were the worst); teachers whose personal habits I came to know as I grew older; who drank, or were infatuated with the pretty girls in their class, or had a curious walk or some curious habit. We studied them with the inquisitiveness of visitors to a zoo; for to us they were really animals behind bars. There were teachers who terrified us, could assume the hypnotic glare of an animal-tamer. I knew the appearance of all the straps in all the classrooms: there were the thick, voluptuous ones, and thin, mean, venomous ones; laid down on the desk after execution, they folded up with ruthless grace like sleepy cats. In some of them the tails had been burned over a fire to make them sting more sharply. . . . There were teachers who did not use the strap more than three or four times in a year, and others who flogged on monotonously day after day, as if they were pounding some recalcitrant substance, not the hands of living boys. I avoided the strap as well as I could; in some classes I could completely forget it, and then I liked school, for the teachers were invariably good at their work. One teacher, Miss Annan, did not use the strap at all. She had a cheerful, impudent, devoted class who only needed her presence to become inspired. She taught us English, and but for her we might never have realized what the subject meant beyond the drudgery of parsing and analysis. She opened our eyes; we felt we were a sort of aristocracy, for what we did for her we did freely. She must have been a remarkable woman; she seemed to have endless

charm, vitality, and patience. She filled us with confidence and a kind of goodness which was quite unlike the goodness asked from us by the other teachers. Yet she never put us on our honour; she simply took us as we were and by some power changed us.

—Edwin Muir, *An Autobiography* (1954), 70.

981. My next teacher [was] Judge Griffin, who lived across the street and had never taught school. To church-goers he was the town atheist, which is only more proof that the churches wouldn't recognize religion if they met it in the middle of the big road, for he was a saint. His house, where I went for lessons, was a turmoil of grandchildren, dogs, models of inventions, bundles of cotton lint, sacks of cottonseed (he was a great hybridizer), silkworms eating mulberry leaves and spinning cocoons, books on tables, on chairs, in stacks on the floor.... I anticipated golden hours and was not disappointed. We browsed and ranged and broke every law of pedagogy....

As with all great teachers, his curriculum was an insignificant part of what he communicated. From him you didn't learn a subject, but life. I suspect anyway that the important things we learn we never remember because they become part of us, we absorb them. We don't absorb the multiplication tables..., but those things that are vitamins and calories to the spirit, the spirit seizes on and transmutes into its own strength, wholly and forgetfully. Tolerance and justice, fearlessness and pride, reverence and pity, are learned in a course on long division if the teacher has those qualities, as Judge Griffin had....

Judge Griffin, Mr. Bass, Father Koestenbrock [other teachers]—their names are being forgotten in our little town, the town where they lived. They have gone the way we all take and they left no mark on the world. But before I join them, I bear testimony they left shining marks on one little boy's heart that shine still.

—William Alexander Percy,
Lanterns on the Levee (1941), 81–83, 91.

982. I remember that uproarious, unruly standard [in Carclaze Elementary School, c. 1907], forty children or so, because of the charming habit of the young woman-teacher who couldn't keep us in order and used to retire behind the blackboard to have a good cry, and then come out to face the mob again. In the meantime Bedlam broke loose; children are, in such circumstances, fiends.

—A.L. Rowse, *A Cornish Childhood* (1942), 111.

983. The teachers [of Latin School, Boston, c. 1875] . . . were surely not out of keeping with their surroundings: disappointed, shabby-genteel, picturesque old Yankees, with a little bitter humor breaking through their constitutional fatigue. I daresay that for them as for me, and for all the boys who were at all sensitive, the school was a familiar symbol of fatality. They hadn't chosen it, they hadn't wanted it, they didn't particularly like it; they knew no reason why it should be the sort of school it was: but there it stood, there they somehow found themselves entangled; and there was nothing else practicable but go on there, doing what was expected and imposed upon them. You may say that for the teachers at least, in that age of individual initiative and open careers, a thousand alternatives were, or had been, possible; and you may say that they could not have been altogether insensible of their high vocation and the high vocation of their country to create gradually and securely a better world, a world free from superstition, from needless hatreds, from unjust inequalities, and from devastating misery. . . .

Those teachers were stray individuals; they had not yet been standardized by educational departments of pedagogy. . . . In a word, they were *cultivated* men.

—George Santayana, *Persons and Places* (1944), 154.

984. Though English, Latin, and French were among the subjects [that Mr. Hunt, housemaster of Wolcott House at Milton Academy, c. 1909] taught, he himself was the subject from which his pupils learned most. . . .

Twenty-four years after he left Milton [Robert E. Sherwood] sent Mr. Hunt the kind of letter which for a real teacher is as cherished as a diploma and the justification of his labors. Said Sherwood, "I always feel close to you and deeply grateful to you for the friendship that you gave to a supremely difficult little boy. I think it was thirty-five years ago this summer that you first came to Westport and started the apparently hopeless task of trying to teach me some sense; but, although your efforts in that direction met with repeated, discouraging failures, you did give me a wonderful and unfailing demonstration of the power of kindness and sympathy.

"I am almost totally devoid of the usual 'nostalgia for the old days.' . . . I have, however, the most tremendous feeling of sentimental attachment for Wolcott House. Under you, that was really a friendly and stimulating place for a boy to grow up in. Almost all the things in which I am most interested, and about which I have written (starting with Hannibal's crossing of the Alps), can be traced back to your room and to the atmosphere of cultivation and good humor which prevailed in it.

Probably, the most important element of my enduring affection for you is the fact that I never think of you as a teacher or associate you with test-books or blackboards. My principal memory of five years in Wolcott House is of innumerable laughs."

—Robert E. Sherwood,
in John Mason Brown, *The Worlds of Robert E. Sherwood: Mirror to His Times, 1896–1939* (1962), 66.

985. The Russian writer Anton Chekhov once told a story about a man who tried to teach a kitten to catch mice. Whenever the kitten refused to give chase, the man beat it. After the animal grew into an adult cat, it always cowered in terror in the presence of a mouse. "That," said Chekhov, "is the man who taught me Latin."

—Patrick Welsh, *Tales Out of School* (1986), 150.

986. I wasn't particularly interested in the Middle Ages but I was trying to get an education and was willing to listen to almost anything. The professor [at Cornell University in 1920 was] a little old gentleman named George Lincoln Burr. He had white hair, and we students used to see him trotting briskly across the campus carrying a big stack of thick books, taller than he was himself. For the first few days, his class in history seemed pretty much like any other college class. But as Professor Burr talked, something began to happen. Somehow I seemed to be transported into another century [and] I began living in the dark ages when a few men who still called their souls free were struggling to preserve what priceless shreds of knowledge and truth the world had at that time managed to scrape together. . . . My chance encounter with George Lincoln Burr was the greatest single thing that ever happened in my life, for he introduced me to a part of myself that I hadn't discovered. I saw, with blinding clarity, how vital it is for man to live in a free society. The experience enabled me to grow up almost overnight; it gave my thoughts and ambitions a focus. It caused me indirectly to pursue the kind of work which eventually enabled me to earn my living. But far more important than that, it gave me a principle of thought and action for which I have tried to fight, and for which I shall gladly continue to fight the remainder of my life.

—E.B. White, Memorial Day speech, May 1940,
in Scott Elledge, *E.B. White: A Biography* (1984), 58.

Teaching

(*See also* Lecture; Teacher; Teacher, Dispraise for; Teacher, Praise for; Teacher, Remembrances of; Teaching Method)

987. 'You wouldn't like to go back to teaching?' asked the head suddenly.

'No, not at all.'

'Fancy! I wouldn't be without it. There's always somebody to talk to when you're teaching. Don't you ever get lonely?'

—Lillian Beckwith, *The Sea for Breakfast* (1961), 121.

988. Teachers brought their hourglass along to measure the duration of their lecture or the length of the students' prescribed study period. An Oxford don in Elizabethan times once threatened his idle pupils "that if they did not doe their exercise better he would bring an Hower-glasse two howers long."

—Daniel J. Boorstin, *The Discoverers* (1983), 34.

989. I remember when I was a child. With what joy the teacher jumped all over the paper, putting in punctuation marks! In this way she could vindicate herself . . . it was her excuse for being. It kept before our minds constantly the fact that she was superior. No matter what we would write, she could always find something wrong. It kept us in our proper place. How kind that teacher would have been if once she had praised the content rather than correcting the form.

—Natalie R. Cole, *The Arts in the Classroom* (1940), 107.

990. I have observed, on examining the natural constitutions of different minds, that there are hardly any so dull or slow of understanding as to be incapable of apprehending good opinions, or even of acquiring all the highest sciences, if they be but conducted along the right road.

—René Descartes, *The Principles of Philosophy* (1644), preface.

991. 2^{ly}: that from the begi^{n}ing of the first moneth untill the end of the 7th [the schoolmaster] shall e^{v}ry day begin to teach at seaven of the Clock in the morning and dismisse his schollers at fyve in the afternoone. And for the other five moneths that is from the beginning of the 8th moneth untill the end of the 12th m^{o}th he shall e^{v}ry day beginn at 8th of the Clock in the morning and [end] at 4 in the afternoone.

3^{ly}: e^{v}ry day in the yeere the usuall tyme of dismissing at noone shalbe at 11 and to beginn agayne at one, except that

4^{ly}: every second day in the weeke he shall call his schollers togeither betweene 12 and one of the Clock to examin them what they have learned on the sabbath day preceding at which tyme also he shall take notice of any misdemeanor or disorder that any of skollers shall have Committed on the sabbath to the end that at somme convenient tyme due Admonition and Correction may be administered....

7[ly]: e[v]ry 6 day of the weeke [Saturday] at 2 of the Clock in the afternoone hee shall Chatechise his schollers in the principles of Christian religion....

—Dorchester, Massachusetts, school rules, 1645, in Willard S. Elsbree, *The American Teacher* (1939), 58. *See* school rules for Schoolmaster Pietersen, **#994.**

992. Teaching is all right and I dont mean to speak of it with condescension. I shall have another go at it before the last employe is fired. I believe in teaching but I dont believe in going to school. Every day I feel bound to save my constituency by advising my pupils to leave school. Then if they insist on coming to school it is not my fault: I can teach them with a clear conscience.

—Robert Frost, letter to Sidney Cox, July 17, 1920, in William R. Evans, *Robert Frost and Sidney Cox: Forty Years of Friendship* (1981), 138. *See* Frost, **#993.**

993. I'm rather blue over my teaching. I don't like the boys as much as I ought to.

—Robert Frost, letter to Lincoln MacVeagh, Nov. 24, 1923, in Lawrance Thompson, *Robert Frost: The Years of Triumph, 1915–1938* (1970), 256. *See* Frost, **#992.** Despite his asserted dislike for academic life, he continued to teach for most of his remaining years.

994. 1. He shall take good care, that the children, coming to his school, do so at the usual hour, namely at eight in the morning and one in the afternoon.

2. He must keep good discipline among his pupils.

3. He shall teach the pupils the Christian Prayers, commandments, baptism, Lord's supper, and the questions with answers of the catechism, which are taught here every Sunday afternoon in the church.

4. Before school closes he shall let the pupils sing some verses and a psalm.

5. Besides his yearly salary he shall be allowed to demand and receive from every pupil quarterly as follows: For each child, whom he teaches the a b c, spelling and reading, 30 st.; for teaching to read and write, 50 st.; for teaching to read, write, and cipher, 60 st.; from those who come in the evening and between times pro rata a fair sum. The poor and needy, who ask to be taught God's sake he shall teach for nothing.

6. He shall be allowed to demand and receive from everybody, who makes arrangements to come to his school and comes before the first half of the quarter preceding the first December next, the school dues for the quarter, but nothing from those, who come after the first half of the quarter.

7. He shall not take from anybody, more than is herein stated. Thus done and decided by the Burgomasters of the City of Amsterdam in N.N., November 4, 1661.

—Instructions and rules
for Schoolmaster Evert Pietersen,
in Thomas Finegan, ed., *Free Schools: A Documentary History of the Free School Movement in New York State* (1921), 16. *See* Dorchester School rules, #991.

995. When a person teaches children—some of whom are more brilliant than others—and sees that it is disadvantageous for all of them to study together inasmuch as the brilliant children need a teacher for themselves alone, he should not keep quiet. He ought to say to the parents, "These children need a separate teacher," even if he loses by making the division.

—Judah the Pious (1150–1207),
Sefer Hasidim (Book of the Pious), sec. 823.

996. School is a conflict—mean and miserable—and I hate conflicts. I was never born to command; I do not want to command. So the lads and I have a fight, and I have a fight with my own nature, and I am always vanquished. I have been setting my foot down—nothing in the world is so hard for me as to be firm, hard, stern. I can be cruel, but not stern. So I struggle with my nature and with my class till I feel frayed into rags. Think of a quivering greyhound set to mind a herd of pigs and you see my teaching.

—D.H. Lawrence,
in Myron C. Tuman, "Prometheus Bound: The Brief Teaching Careers of Great Writers," *Phi Delta Kappan* Magazine, December 1980. Lawrence was a certified teacher. He wrote this in his first month of teaching.

997. Friday 19th [1855] Commenced school on Wednesday January 17th under rather unfavorable circumstances. Only nineteen scholars and as yet no additions. Hope to have more next week. Shall be completely discouraged if I do not. It is hard to teach and I know I sometimes feel it to be a hardship and complain more than I ought but I know by experience that it is harder still to have no school to teach. At such times I have resolved that I would never [?] because of my duties were wearisome if the Lord

would give me a field for labor and usefulness I have chosen the occupation of a teacher and I do not feel willing to resign this office for any other, but sometimes I feel almost persuaded that it is not my duty to do so thinking I am unfit for a teacher Do not feel the responsibility which rests upon me as I ought. Do not feel that anxiety to instill right principles in the hearts of my pupils which a teacher ought to feel. How often might a word dropped from the lips of an instructor prove in the youthful heart like a good seed sown in good ground bringing forth fruit to the honor and glory of God. O that all who are engaged in training the young mind might feel that we are not only preparing them for future life in this world but may we remember that there resides under our care an immortal part and while striving to to *[sic]* cultivate the intellect may we not forget the more important part but may strive to scatter crumbs upon which the soul may feed when time shall have robbed them of youth and tarnished their literary attainments.

—Amelia Akehurst Lines,
To Raise Myself a Little: The Diaries and Letters of a Georgia Teacher, 1851–18868, ed. Thomas Dyer (1982), 21.

998. Pointers for Teachers

1. Does your manner attract or repel pupils and parents?
2. Is your voice pleasing, or harsh and grating?
3. Are you pedantic and pretentious, or frank and dignified?
4. Are you fidgety and nervous, or quiet and equable?
5. Is your eye restless and foxy, or calm and penetrating?
6. Is your face deceitful, or pleasant and honest?
7. Is your walk hesitating and unsteady, or direct and firm?
8. Is your judgment wavering and fitful, or judicial and impartial?
9. Is your judgment narrow and selfish, or broad and liberal?
10. Is your scholarship weak and restricted, or comprehensive and accurate?
11. Is your health tottering, or is it vigorous and strong?
12. Is your moral nature weak and vacillating, or is it noble and elevated?
13. Have you stagnated, or are you still elastic and buoyant?
14. Is your attitude toward your school board one of helpful cooperation?
15. Do you recognize that they are the real authority in school matters?
16. Do you first find whether they sympathize with new plans before applying them to the school?
17. Do you try to follow out any suggestions they may make?

—*List of Qualified Teachers and School Officers for Wayne County, Michigan, 1900–1901.*

999. The world would be better and brighter if our teachers would dwell on the Duty of Happiness as well as the Happiness of Duty, for we ought to be as cheerful as we can if only because to be happy ourselves is a most effectual contribution to the happiness of others.

—Sir John Lubbock, *The Pleasures of Life* (1887).

1000. Children are to be sent to school at the age of six or seven years, according to the strength of the individual child and its physical development. But no child is to be sent to school under six years of age. The teacher may chastise his pupils to inspire them with awe. But he must not do so in a cruel manner or in a vindictive spirit. Accordingly, he must not strike them with whips or sticks, but only use a small strap. He is to teach them the whole day and by night. And there shall be no holiday except on the eve of the Sabbath or festival, towards the close of the day, and on festivals. On Sabbaths, pupils are not taught a new lesson, but they repeat what they have already learnt previously, even if only once. Pupils must not be interrupted at their studies, even for the rebuilding of the Temple.

—Maimonides, *Mishneh Torah (Repetition of the Law)* (1180), I.ii, in J.S. Minkin, *The World of Moses Maimonides* (1957), 286.

1001. I liked Dr. Copshews. When he found that I worked hard, he praised me. It was one of his generosities, to praise. It is a rare end, to praise. It is a rare end, when just, a noble thing to praise; few people praise enough; all ought to praise whenever they see something that can be praised. Once in a century a man may be ruined, or for the time made insufferable by praise; but surely once in a minute something generous dies for want of it. I once heard someone say: "The occupation of Heaven is praise."

—John Masefield, *Dead Ned* (1938), 11.

1002. [On her first day of teaching] Dorothy faced the class. She was not afraid of them—she was too used to dealing with children ever to be afraid of them—but she did feel a momentary qualm. The sense of being an impostor (What teacher has not felt it at times?) was heavy upon her. It suddenly occurred to her, what she had only been dimly aware of before, that she had taken this teaching job under flagrantly false pretenses, without having any qualification for it. The subject she was now supposed to be teaching was history, and like most "educated" people, she knew virtually no history. How awful, she thought, if it turned out that these girls knew more history than she did! . . .

[But she soon discovered that] they knew nothing, absolutely nothing—nothing, nothing, nothing, like the Dadaists. It was appalling that even children could be so ignorant. . . .

Dorothy tried not to hurt the children's feelings by exclaiming at their ignorance, but in her heart she was amazed and horrified. She had not known that schools of this description still existed in the civilized world. . . .

School began again at two o'clock. Already, after only one morning's teaching, Dorothy went back to her work with secret shrinking and dread. She was beginning to realize what her life would be like, day after day and week after week, in that sunless room, trying to drive the rudiments of knowledge into unwilling brats. But when she had assembled the girls and called their names over, one of them, a little peaked child with mouse-colored hair, called Laura Firth, came up to her desk and presented her with a pathetic bunch of brown-yellow chrysanthemums, "From all of us." The girls had taken a liking to Dorothy, and had subscribed four pence among them, to buy her a bunch of flowers.

Something stirred in Dorothy's heart as she took the ugly flowers. She looked with more seeing eyes than before at the anemic faces and shabby clothes of the children, and was all of a sudden horribly ashamed to think that in the morning she had looked at them with indifference, almost with distaste. Now, a profound pity took possession of her. The poor children, the poor children! How they had been stunted and maltreated! And with it all they had retained the childish gentleness that could make them squander their few pennies on flowers for their teacher.

She felt quite differently toward her job from that moment onward. A feeling of loyalty and affection had sprung up in her heart. This school was her school; she would work for it and be proud of it, and make every effort to turn it from a place of bondage into a place human and decent.

—George Orwell, *A Clergyman's Daughter* (1935), 221, 226–32. *See* Runbeck, **#114,** under "Children."

1003. She said to him one day: "You should do for your children [in school] what their parents fail to do for them. The reading, writing and arithmetic are not, after all, what they most need; it is all well and good for them to learn something, but the really important thing for them is to *be* something,—for them to become what they are meant to be, and in becoming which they so often have no guidance or help at home."

—Johann Heinrich Pestalozzi, *Leonard and Gertrude* (1781–87).

1004. I do not know that I could make entirely clear to an outsider the pleasure I have in teaching. I had rather earn my living by teaching than in any other way. In my mind, teaching is not merely a life-work, a profession, an occupation, a struggle: it is a passion. I love to teach. I love to teach as a painter loves to paint, as a musician loves to play, as a singer loves to sing, as a strong man rejoices to run a race. Teaching is an art—an art so great and so difficult to master that a man or woman can spend a long life at it, without realizing much more than his limitations and mistakes and his distances from the ideal.

—William Lyon Phelps,
Autobiography With Letters (1939), 307.

1005. The teacher must be a Leader, a Master, in many cases a Lion-Tamer, a manager of wild beasts. It is essential, then, that the man or woman who teaches should have a strong personality, a dominant, fearless disposition. He is the Captain of the ship, and is as much alone in the schoolroom as the captain is alone with his crew on the high seas. Those who have never taught have no idea of the loneliness and responsibility of a school-teacher shut up in a big schoolroom with a pack of wild boys and girls. The teacher can consult outside of hours with his superiors or colleagues; he can get advice and talk over his difficulties. But when he goes into the classroom, shuts the door, takes the lonely seat behind the desk, and looks into the shining morning faces, then he is thrown back absolutely on himself. No power on earth can help him, and nothing can save the situation if he makes a blunder. There he needs all his resources, all his courage, and infinite patience.

—William Lyon Phelps, in Claude M. Fuess
and Emory S. Basford, eds., *Unseen Harvest* (1947), 54.

1006. "Amanda, what makes you so hard?" Then she answered her own question. "Schoolteachers all get like that. They are so in the habit of laying down the law.... No, Amanda; school teaching certainly does not agree with you. So overbearing. And you come home so cross. I suppose you hold it in all day, then let me have the full benefit at night."

—Helen Hooven Santmyer,
"...And Ladies of the Club" (1982), 292, 293.

1007. Teaching is a sacred calling that is difficult enough to follow—even harder to describe. It has little to do with what is commonly called instruction. It, legitimately, demands docility of the learner only insofar as the teacher himself is caught up in a special and transcendent obedience. His client is not or not only the child before him, or the children he happens to have, or their parents, or the school system or society—still less the nation-state which may well be the enemy of all of them. It is none of these that "employs" him; indeed, he cannot be employed. His task may well be stated as the heightening of "the unity and community of minds," but only if every key word is taken in a special sense.

—John R. Seeley,
"The University as Slaughterhouse," in R.M. Hutchins
and M.J. Adler, eds., *The Great Ideas of Today 1969.*

1008. A teacher who teaches less than his fellow-instructors should be dismissed. The other teachers will become more diligent both out of fear and out of gratitude.

—*Talmud: Baba Batra,* 21a (before A.D. 500).

1009. More than the calf wishes to suck does the cow desire to suckle. [The teacher wishes to teach even more than the pupil wishes to learn.]

—*Ibid.: Pesahim,* 112a.

1010. I have thoroughly tried school-keeping, and found that my expenses were in proportion, or rather out of proportion, to my income, for I was obliged to dress and train, not to say think and believe, accordingly, and I lost time into the bargain. As I did not teach for the good of my fellow-men, but simply for a livelihood, this was a failure.

—Henry David Thoreau, *Walden:* "Economy" (1854), 71.

1011. Cunégonde . . . saw Dr. Pangloss behind some bushes giving a lesson in experimental philosophy to her mother's waiting-woman, a little brunette who seemed eminently teachable.

—Voltaire, *Candide* (1759), i.

Teaching Method

(*See also* Discipline; Punishment, Corporal; Teacher, Praise for; Teacher, Remembrances of; Teaching)

1012. To some [students] I administer the honey of the sacred writings; others I try to inebriate with the wine of the ancient classics. I begin the nourishment of some with the apples of grammatical subtlety. I strive to illuminate many by the arrangement of the stars, as from the painted roof of a lofty palace.

—Alcuin, (735?–804), *Epistolae.*

1013. If your scholer do misse sometimes, in marking rightlie these foresaid sixe thinges, chide not hastelie; for that shall both dull his witte, and discourage his diligence: but monish him gentelie: which shall make him, both willing to amende, and glad to go forward in love and hope of learning.

I have now wished, twice or thrice, this gentle nature, to be in a Scholemaster: And, that I have done so, neither by chance, nor without some reason, I will now declare at large, why, in mine opinion, love is fitter than feare, jentlenes better than beating, to bring up a child rightlie in learning. . . .

I do gladlie agree with all good Scholemasters in these pointes: to have children brought to good perfitness in learning: to all honestie in manners: to have all fautes rightlie amended: to have everie vice severelie corrected: but for the order and waie that leadeth rightlie to these pointe, as we somewhat differ. For commonlie, many scholemasters, some, as I have seen, moe, as I have heard tell, be of so crooked a nature, as, when they meete with a hard witted scholer, they rather breake him than bowe him, rather marre him, than mend him. For when the scholemaster is angry with some other matter, then will he soonest faul to beate his scholer: and though he him selfe should be punished for his folie, yet must he beate some scholer for his pleasure: though there be no cause for him to do so, nor yet fault in the scholer to deserve so. These, ye will say, be fond scholemasters, and fewe they be that be found to be soch. They be fond in deede, but surelie overmany soch be found everie where. But this will I say, that even the wisest of your great beaters, do as oft punishe nature as they do correct faultes.

—Roger Ascham, *The Scholemaster* (1570), 9.

1014. I often wanted attention and I wanted it smartly. And I trained the children in a way that is new only, maybe, in degree. Most teachers have some way of calling a room to attention; some use a bell, some rap a ruler, and most, I should think, use their voices. But where the sounds of learning and living are allowed in a room, a voice would need to be lifted and sharpened and could be unrepresentative of a gentle teacher; so, predictably, I used the keyboard. No crashing chord, no alarming octave, but eight notes from Beethoven's Fifth Symphony. What was good enough for him was good enough for me, since, whereas he demanded attention for the rest of the symphony from several thousand people, I wanted it only for a sentence.

—Sylvia Ashton-Warner, *Teacher* (1963), 16.

1015. Dynamite explodes in the same way,—according to the same laws,—whether it is used as a harmless blast in a mine or to deal death and destruction at the will of an anarchist. Similarly, the principles of educational method work in the same way whether they are to produce a theologian or a thief.

—William C. Bagley, *The Educative Process* (1926), 41.

1016. Fancy ... my ... astonishment when I was invited to conduct a class in the university. I, whose memory still stung with the birch, was to wield the birch myself; and I pray that I may not descend to vicarious revenge.

In what way does one go about a task of teaching and how may one prepare? Many years ago, for one day only, I was a substitute instructor in a Sunday school; but then a leaflet was handed out with the lesson set. I had only to brush up on the golden text and use a long pointer on the map, as harder matters were handled by the superintendent in his address at the end....

It will be terrifying, when we open in September, to see a row of eager faces shining with expectation that I have a secret to make their writing easy...; still more terrifying to behold a general nodding of curly heads or snapping after flies. This last, with a rubber band, is a harmless sport for the drowsy student and tends to rid the room of pests, but I must now forget how it was once my solace and frown upon the custom....

Suppose I run dry before the hour is out! Here on the sands of England I can compose a speech that will last the afternoon. I can swing my arms in excessive gesture and find apt references at will. But before my class, in my hot embarrassment, my flowery periods may shrivel to fifteen minutes. How do teachers fill the gap? Do they scrawl headings on their cuffs? Do they lead a song to fill the empty portion of the dawdling hour? Or will it be possible to stir the clock to a livelier pace? "My dear young ladies," I shall say, "consult for a moment the blackboard at the rear!" And then when their backs are turned, perhaps I may lunge forward secretly to push ahead the minute hand.

—Charles S. Brooks,
A Thread of English Road:
"To Be Read Only by Serious Stupid Persons"
(1924), 180. Booker T. Washington tells of pushing
the school clock ahead, but for a different reason
(*see* **#747** under "School, Remembrances of")
and Katherine Brush, using the same method, shortens her
piano practicing time (*see* **#1115** under "Women, Education of").

1017. It was perhaps because he lacked a real rapport with the boys [of Larchfield Academy, c. 1930] that [W.H.] Auden kept order in class partly by means of clowning. Margaret Gardiner, who visited him at Larchfield, noted this: 'He told me that he believed teachers ought to be clowns; if you stood on your head or played the piano with your feet, the boys would immediately attend, there'd be no difficulty about discipline. You should continually startle them into interest, he said, keep them alert by letting them catch out, trip you up.' One of his tricks was teaching boys to stick stamps on the ceiling by flicking them up on pennies. On another occasion when he had trouble with discipline he told Gabriel Carritt he had threatened 'to cut my prick off' if the boys continued to fool about. He bought a suitable piece of meat from the butcher, and next time a hullabaloo broke out in class, opened his fly, brought out this meat, and appeared to be actually carrying out the threat with a sharp knife – to horrified cries of 'No, sir! Don't do it!'

—Humphrey Carpenter, *W.H. Auden: A Biography* (1981), 112.

1018. What do I do? I go and spin flax, weave nets and catch stags. I feed orphans with the flesh, dress the skins into parchment, and write a copy of the Pentateuch. I go to a place and instruct five children in the Five Books of Moses and six children in the Six Orders of the Mishnah; then I tell them, "By the time of my return, teach each other the Pentateuch and the Mishnah."

—Rabbi Chiyya (3rd. cent), quoted in *Talmud: Baba Metzia,* 85b, in A. Cohen, *Everyman's Talmud* (1949), 174. Each boy was taught a section of the *Pentateuch* or the *Mishnah.* He in turn taught what he had learned to the others.

1019. Now, what I want is, Facts. Teach these boys and girls nothing but Facts. Facts alone are wanted in life. Plant nothing else, and root out everything else. You can only form the minds of reasoning animals upon Facts: nothing else will ever be of service to them. This is the principle on which I bring up my own children, and this is the principle on which I bring up these children. Stick to Facts, Sir!

—Charles Dickens, *Hard Times* (1854) I.i.

1020. My one pupil has begun to work with me, and I will give you a description how the lecture is conducted. It is the most important point, you know, that the tutor should be *dignified,* and at a distance from the pupil, and that the pupil should be as much as possible *degraded,* otherwise, you know, they are not humble enough. So I sit at the further end of the room; outside the door (which is shut) sits the scout: outside the outer door (also shut) sits the sub-scout: half-way downstairs sits the sub-sub-scout; and down in the yard sits the pupil.

The questions are shouted from one to another, and the answers come back in the same way – it is rather confusing till you are well used to it. The lecture goes on something like this.

Tutor. "What is twice three?"
Scout. "What's a rice-tree?"
Sub-Scout. "When is ice free?"
Sub-sub-Scout. "What's a nice fee?"
Pupil (timidly). "Half a guinea!"
Sub-sub-Scout. "Can't forge any!"
Sub-Scout. "Ho for Jinny!"
Scout. "Don't be a ninny!"
Tutor. (looks offended...)

– Charles Lutwidge Dodgson (Lewis Carroll), at age 23, humorous description of tutoring his only pupil, in a letter to his sister and brother, Jan. 31, ?1855, in Morton N. Cohen, ed., *The Letters of Lewis Carroll* (1979), I.31.

1021. Read over carefully, the lessons in Latin and Greek, in your leisure hours, that the story and Language be fresh in your memory, when you are hearing the respective lessons; for your memory is treacherous, & I am pretty certain it would confound you if you should be accosted by a pert Schoolboy, in the midst of a blunder, with "Physician heal thyself!" You ought likewise to do this with those who are working Figures; probably you may think that because the highest Cypherer is only in decimal arithmetic, is not there fore worth your critical attention to be looking previously into the several Sums. But you are to consider that a sum in the Square-Root, or even in the Single Rule of three direct, is to your Pupils of as great importance, as the most abstruse problem in the Mathematicks to an able artist; & you may lay this down for a Maxim, that they will reckon upon your abilities, according as they find you acquainted and expert in what they themselves are studying.

– Philip Fithian, advice to a friend who was considering a tutoring assignment, in Hunter D. Farish, ed., *Journal and Letters of Philip Vickers Fithian, 1773–1774: A Plantation Tutor of the Old Dominion* (1943).

1022. I had a delightful Professor of Education at Brooklyn College who taught his future teachers (me amongst them) in pseudo-Brooklynese, that to put over a perfect lesson you had to stick to one simple rule: "Tell 'em what you're gonna 'learn 'em'; then 'learn 'em'; then ask 'em: 'What did I just "learn you"?'"

—Sam Levenson, *You Don't Have to Be in Who's Who to Know What's What* (1979), 9.
See Grahame, **#435**, and Nock, **#441**, both under "Learning."

1023. The great skill of a teacher is to get and keep the attention of his scholar; whilst he has that, he is sure to advance as fast as the learner's abilities will carry him; and without that, all his bustle and pother will be to little or no purpose. To attain this, he should make the child comprehend, as much as may be, the usefulness of what he teaches him, and let him see, by what he has learned, that he can do something which he could not do before; something which gives him some power and real advantage above all others who are ignorant of it. To this he should add sweetness in all his instructions, and by a certain tenderness in his whole carriage make the child sensible that he loves him and designs nothing but his good, the only way to beget love in the child, which will make him hearken to his lessons, and relish what he teaches him.

—John Locke, *Some Thoughts concerning Education* (1693), 167.

1024. Most tutors never stop bawling into our ears, as though they were pouring water into a funnel; and our task is only to repeat what has been told us. I should like the tutor to correct this practice, and from the start, according to the capacity of the mind he has in hand, to begin putting it through its paces, making it taste things, choose them and discern them by itself; sometimes clearing the way for him, sometimes letting him clear his own way. I don't want him to think and talk alone, I want him to listen to his pupil speaking in his turn. . . .

Let him not be asked for an account merely of the words of his lesson, but of its sense and substance, and let him judge the profit he has made not by the testimony of his memory, but of his life. Let him be made to show what he has just learned in a hundred aspects, and apply it to as many different subjects, to see if he has yet thoroughly grasped it and made it his own, taking stock of his progress by the pedagogical method of Plato. It is a sign of crudeness and indigestion to disgorge food just as we swallowed it. The stomach has not done its work if it has not changed the condition and form of what has been given it to cook.

—Michel de Montaigne, *Essays:* "Of the Education of Children" (1580), I.xxvi, tr. Donald M. Frame.

1025. [On Dorothy's first day of teaching] Mrs. Creevy produced a penny notebook from a drawer and laid it open on the table.

"Just take a look at this," she said. "Here's a list of the girls' names that I've got ready for you. I shall want you to know the whole lot of them by this evening." She wetted her thumb and turned over three pages: "Now, do you see these three lists here?"

"Yes," said Dorothy.

"Well, you'll just have to learn those three lists by heart, and make sure you know what girls are on which. Because I don't want you to go on thinking that all the girls are to be treated alike. They aren't — not by a long way, they aren't. Different girls, different treatment — that's my system. Now, do you see this lot on the first page?"

"Yes," said Dorothy again.

"Well, the parents of that lot I call the good payers. You know what I mean by that? They're the ones that pay cash on the nail and no jibbing at an extra half-guinea or so now and again. You're not to smack any of that lot, not on any account. This lot over here are the medium payers. Their parents do pay up sooner or later, but you don't get the money out of them without you worry them for it night and day. You can smack that lot if they get saucy, but don't go and leave a mark that their parents can see. If you'll take my advice, the best thing with children is to twist their ears. Have you ever tried that?"

"No," said Dorothy.

"Well, I find it answers better than anything. It doesn't leave a mark, and the children can't bear it. Now these three over here are the bad payers. Their fathers are two terms behind already and I'm thinking of a solicitor's letter. I don't care what you do to that lot — well, short of a police court case, naturally."

— George Orwell, *A Clergyman's Daughter* (1935), 221, 226–32.

1026. In all justice let me observe that we teachers should not be saddled with the blame for this bombast of which you complain. After all, if the patients are lunatics, surely a little professional lunacy is almost mandatory in the doctor who deals with them. And unless we professors spout the sort of twaddle our students admire, we run the risk of being, in Cicero's phrase, "left alone at our lecterns." . . .

We are, that is, rather in the position of a fisherman: unless he baits his hook with the sort of tidbit the little fishes like, he is doomed to spend eternity sitting on his rock without a chance of a bite.

— Petronius Arbiter, *Satyricon*
(c. A.D. 60), i.5, tr. William Arrowsmith.

1027. The teacher without reverence . . . thinks it is his duty to 'mould' the child: in imagination he is the potter with the clay. And so he gives to the child some unnatural shape, which hardens with age, producing strains and spiritual dissatisfactions, out of which grow cruelty and envy, and the belief that others must be compelled to undergo the same distortions.

—Bertrand Russell, *Principles of Social Reconstruction:* "Education" (1916).

1028. First teach a person to develop to the point of his limitations and then—pfft!—break the limitation.

—Viola Spolin, in "Spolin Game Plan for Improvisational Theater," *Los Angeles Times,* May 26, 1974.

1029. I seek a situation as a teacher of a small school, or an assistant in a large one, or, what is more desirable, as private tutor in a gentleman's family.

Perhaps I should give some account of myself. I could make education a pleasant thing both to the teacher and the scholar. This discipline which we allow to be the end of life, should not be the one thing in the schoolroom, and another in the street. We should seek to be fellow-students with the pupil, and we should learn of, as well as with him, if we would be most helpful to him. But I am not blind to the difficulties in the case; it supposes a degree of freedom, which rarely exists. It hath not entered into the heart of man to conceive the full import of that word—Freedom—not a paltry republican freedom, with a *posse comitatus* at his heels to administer it in doses as to a sick child—but freedom proportionate to the dignity of his nature—a freedom that shall make him feel that he is a man among men, and responsible only to that reason of which he is a particle, for his thoughts and his actions.

I have ever been disposed to regard the cowhide as a non-conductor,—methinks that, unlike the electric wire, not a single spark of truth is ever transmitted through its agency to the slumbering intellect it would address. I mistake, it may teach a truth in physics, but never a truth in morals.

—Henry David Thoreau, letter to Orestes A. Brownson, Dec. 30, 1837, in Henry Seidel Canby, *Thoreau* (1939), 61.

1030. We schoolmasters must temper discretion with deceit.

—Evelyn Waugh, *Decline and Fall* (1938), I.ii.

1031. The mind is never passive; it is a perpetual activity, delicate, receptive, responsive to stimulus. Whatever interest attaches to your subject-matter must be evoked here and now; whatever powers you are strengthening in the pupil, must be exercised here and now; whatever possibilities of mental life your teaching should impart, must be exhibited here and now. That is the golden rule of education, and a very difficult rule to follow.

—Alfred North Whitehead, *The Aims of Education* (1929), i.

Textbook

1032. In the multiplying medieval universities there were few institutional libraries, but professors still needed books. These could be had from itinerant book peddlers, an unreliable source over whom the professors had no control. Renting out textbooks, usually at a fixed price per quire, was a valuable privilege that could enrich the university and prevent circulation of heretical texts. The earliest book list of the University of Paris, in 1286, names some one hundred thirty-eight different titles for rent. At Bologna and elsewhere every professor was required to provide the university "stationer" with a copy of his lectures so they could be transcribed and rented or sold. He was called a stationer simply because, unlike the itinerant book peddlers, he stayed in one place. Peddlers still dealt in forbidden books, and it was they who gave wide circulation to John Wycliffe's banned translation of the Bible into English. But the stationer long remained the authorized source of textbooks and writing materials, and also operated a circulating library.

—Daniel J. Boorstin, *The Discoverers* (1983), 533.

1033. The author was led to lay this small work before the publick, for the benefit of beginners; who are apt to wear out a large book, without gaining any more knowledge than they would from one of this description.

Should parents, instructors and the benevolent encourage the introduction and continuance of this little work among children, they may be instrumental in guiding millions to a true knowledge of the rudiments of our language and *receive their reward at the resurrection* of the just.

—Joshua Bradley, spelling book preface,
Vermont, 1815, in Clifton Johnson,
Old-Time Schools and School-books (1904), 209.

1034. Considering the many grammatical Improprieties to be found in our best Writers, such as Swift, Addison, Pope &c. a Systematical English Syntax is not beneath the Notice of the Learned themselves.

—James Buchanan, *A Regular English Syntax* (1767), p. vi.

1035. Dinner is ready. Come little frozen boys, come get some pudding.

Will Mama give Charles some beer? Yes, Charles shall have some beer. . . .

Do not spit on the floor. Spit in the corner.

—*The Child's Spelling-book,* "calculated to render Reading Completely Easy to Little Children; Compiled by a printer, Hartford, 1798," in Clifton Johnson, *Old-Time Schools and School-books* (1904), 191.

1036. [The] most closely conned text-book [of the first educational institutions for girls] seems to have been "Wayland's Moral Science"—a book of essays dealing with such subjects as "The Nature and Defects of Natural Religion," "Happiness" and "Reciprocity." After each chapter "Wayland's" propounded a series of questions ranging from "If I hire a house for a year, and a new street is opened which renders it twice as valuable, before the close of the year, am I obliged to pay more for rent?" to "How do you know that God did not intend you to eat the leaves of the apple tree instead of the fruit?"

—Ruth E. Finley, *The Lady of Godey's: Sarah Josepha Hale* (1931), 223.

1037. What is marketable in a textbook is what is commonly believed or what is commonly believed to be believed.

—John Kenneth Galbraith, in Frederick J. Pratson, *Perspectives on Galbraith: Conversations and Opinions* (1978), [illegible].

1038. It is indeed a great Blessing of God, That Children in England have liberty to read the holy Scriptures, when others abroad are denied it. And yet alas! how often do we see Parents prefer *Tom Thumb, Guy of Warwick,* or some such foolish Book, before the Book of Life! Let not your Children read these vain Books, profane Ballads, and filthy Songs. Throw away all fond and amorous Romances, and fabulous Histories of Giants, the bombast achievements of Knight Errantry, and the like, for these fill the Heads of Children with vain, silly and idle imaginations.

—*The History of Genesis* (1708), preface, in Clifton Johnson, *Old-Time Schools and School-books* (1904), 45.

1039. In . . . Fiske's *The New England Spelling-book,* Brookfield, Massachusetts, 1803, it seems a little odd to find "Damn" included among the "words which should be well learned by every Scholar." But words just as much out of place are not uncommon in the old spellers. To quote a textbook preface of 1828, "They contain words collected from all the departments of nature, life, and action; from the nursery, the kitchen, the drawing-room, the stable, the bar-room, the gaming table, the seaman's wharf, the apothecary's shop; from the subtle pages of the metaphysician, and the rhapsodies of the pompous pedant."

—Clifton Johnson, *ibid.*, 203.

1040. Something was wanted, in American schools to replace the lessons, which have been copied from book to book, since the reign of Queen Anne. It is the intention, in the present work to advance principles suited to the rising generation, in the United States. Beast, reptiles and insects are not represented in this volume, as the equals of rational beings; because such a supposition is repugnant to nature, science, and correct moral sentiment. Most of the fables so long employed in schools, are particularly improper for small children, who should be taught by literal examples, before they can comprehend figures of rhetoric or draw inferences from remote hints. The fancy of converting inferior animals into *"teachers of children,"* has been carried to ridiculous extravagance.

—John Franklin Jones, preface to
Analytical Spelling Book, New York (1823).

1041. One speller . . . thoroughly dominated the school field for over a century. That book is Noah Webster's "Old Blue Back." Originally conceived as the First Part of A GRAMMATICAL INSTITUTE OF THE ENGLISH LANGUAGE (1783), it became twenty years later the AMERICAN SPELLING BOOK; and in 1829 THE ELEMENTARY SPELLING BOOK. But by the common-folk it was affectionately called the "Old Blue Back," and is still so remembered. The designation comes from its blue, paper-covered board binding.

The "Old Blue Back" has sold over 100,000,000 copies—the best single-book seller of all time, except the Bible. And it still sells, even though it is older than our country.

Through its influence spelling became a "must" course in elementary schools. Spelling-bees—contests between schools to see which could "spell down" the other—were important winter social events in our pioneer days; and the "Old Blue Back" was the final arbiter as to correctness. The judges and the "pronouncer" each had a copy in hand.

—W.W. Livengood, ed., *Americana as Taught to the Tune of a Hickory Stick* (1954), 45. *See* Webster, **#1046.**

1042. A man of culture in our pioneer period could point proudly to many volumes of history in his library—Greek, Roman, French, English, and probably several on the church and the church fathers. In other words, the well-to-do recognized the cultural necessity of a knowledge of history. No such need was felt in the far-flung farm houses and log cabins of the pioneer settlers.

Still with the passing of the Revolution and the beginnings of our new Nation, the common man wanted to read about the wars, its leaders, and the doings and lives of Washington, Jefferson, et al. Hearsay was not enough, not satisfying. So histories via subscription sale began to appear. The schools woke up.

In 1822 Rev. C.A. Goodrich, using the pen-name of "Peter Parley," wrote the first United States History for schools. His Boston publisher claimed a sale of 150,000 copies in the first twelve years. By 1850 several school histories had been published.

—W.W. Livengood, *ibid.*, 67.

1043. Go little book, go
Bearing an honored name
And may everywhere that you went
Be glad that you have came.

—Pupil's inscription on the title page
of a leather-bound copy of Goold Brown's
Institutes of English Grammar (1823).

1044. In the "primary room" I learned the letters of the alphabet and how with letters you can spell words. We had a thin book with a green cover called a Primer. The one piece I remember was about a ladies' tea party. A lady pours tea into a cup for another lady and asks her in three words, "Sugar in it?" And the lady holding the cup of tea answers in the same three words, "Sugar in it." Miss Flora A. Ward, our teacher, had us read that question and the answer. One boy and then another got up and slid straight through the question and the answer in the same tone of voice. You couldn't tell by how they said it which was the question and which the answer. . . . You couldn't tell the first lady from the second; we spoke the question like it was an answer. We believed that whoever wrote the Primer was silly. If the question had been "Would you like sugar?" and the answer "Yes, I'll take sugar," we would have read it out loud like it was a question and an answer. None of us Swede boys had ever drunk tea and had never been to a tea party. If it had been a Swedish *Kaffekalas* and the question was three words, "*Socker i kaffet*?" (Sugar in coffee?) and the answer "*Ja, tack*" (Yes, thanks) we would have sailed through it. Miss Ward did her best with us and after she had asked "Sugar in it?" and given the answer "Sugar in it" about forty times we began to understand that one tea-party lady was asking and another answering. I wonder if year after year Miss Ward had the same trouble with sugar in it and sugar in it. She stayed on teaching more than thirty years. Because she unlocked secrets of the alphabet for me I am thankful to her.

—Carl Sandburg, *Always the Young Strangers* (1952), 109.

1045. These last years I've been writing a *Primer*, and now I'm having it published. It's very difficult to explain what this labour of many years, this *Primer*, means to me.... My proud dreams about this *Primer* are: that two generations of *all* Russian children, from tsars' to peasants', will study with the aid of this *Primer* alone, and will receive their first poetic impressions from it, and having written this *Primer* I'll be able to die peacefully.

—Leo Tolstoy, letter to Countess Alexandra Andreyevna Tolstaya, Jan. 12, 1872, in R.F. Christian, ed., *Tolstoy's Letters* (1978), I.240. The *Primer* was the fruit of Tolstoy's own educational theories and his experience of teaching in his school. However, it was not well received.

1046. Be cautious in listening to the addresses of men. Is thy suitor addicted to low vices? is he profane? is he a gambler? a tippler? a spendthrift? a haunter of taverns? and, above all, is he a scoffer at religion?—Banish such a man from thy presence, his heart is false, and his hand would lead thee to wretchedness and ruin.

—Noah Webster, *The Elementary Spelling-book* (1829). *See* Livengood, **#1041.**

1047. Of Man

Lord what is man! a dunghill blanched with snow, or a May game of fortune, a mark for malice, a butt for envy; He is born crying, lives laughing and dies groaning!

—*The Youth's Instructor in the English Tongue, Or the Art of Spelling Improved,* Boston (1770). See *The American Heritage History of Colonial Antiques,* **#81,** under "Childhood."

Thought

1048. His cogitative faculties immersed
In cogibundity of cognition.

—Henry Carey (1687–1743), *Chrononhotonthologos* (1734), I.i, a burlesque of contemporary theatrical bombast.

1049. There are lots of people who can't think seriously without injuring their minds. Their minds were not meant for this use, and so the more they think the feebler they grow.

The cure is simple.

Speak out opinions before you think—and before the other fellow speaks. Thus you will give your mind some chance of forming them in a natural way—unconsciously. Accustom yourself to not knowing what your opinions are till you have blurted them out, and thus find what they are. That's what talk is for—and it doesn't prevent the careful summarizing of ideas upon occasion when this is in order. Your valued father went the limit in the expression of things in writing in this improvised way, for he never knew quite what was on his mind—as he told me himself—till he wrote; and it was by this course that he made his most telling cracks: for it is only in the poetic element that truth is told. For truth to be truth must be new.

If one is dealing with such simple matters as making an engine—adding a cog to it—or finding a microbe—you may reason and ratiocinate to good ends. But if you're dealing with human nature in any form, you go broke if you reason—you're an ass to reason—you must put the thing off your mind and allow the probabilities to occur to you—and never be sure then.

—John Jay Chapman, letter to Henry James (1879–1947), 1926, in M.A. DeWolfe Howe, ed., *John Chapman and His Letters* (1937), 418. *See* Wallas, #1065.

1050. How do most people live without any thoughts? There are many people in the world (you must have noticed them in the street) How do they live? How do they get strength to put on their clothes in the morning?

—Emily Dickinson, letter to Thomas Wentworth Higginson, August 1870, in Thomas H. Johnson, ed., *The Letters of Emily Dickinson* (1958), II.474.

1051. Nobody can think our thoughts for us, and nobody can tell us what will act as dew or sun on our thinking. The book that makes us think is the book we cannot shut again after we have read one page, because we are entranced by what it says to us; or it is the book we drop on our knee after reading one page, because what it says starts us irresistibly questioning, contradicting, or supplementing. No titles, no categories can be given to you by anybody but yourself.

—Ernest Dimnet, *The Art of Thinking* (1928), III.ii.c.

1052. Look sharply after your thoughts. They come unlooked for, like a new bird seen on your trees, and, if you turn to your usual task, disappear; and you shall never find that perception again; never, I say—but perhaps years, ages, and I know not what events and worlds may lie between you and its return.

—Ralph Waldo Emerson,
Journals, October 1872. *See* Locke, **#1058.**

1053. All of your scholarship, all your study of Shakespeare and Wordsworth would be vain if at the same time you did not build your character and attain mastery over your thoughts and your actions.

—Mahatma Gandhi, in Richard
Attenborough, ed., *The Words of Gandhi* (1982), 19.

1054. I had better explain that I was a frequent visitor to the headmaster's study, because of the latest thing I had done or left undone. As we now say, I was not integrated. I was, if anything, disintegrated; and I was puzzled. Grownups never made sense. Whenever I found myself in a penal position before the headmaster's desk . . . I would sink my head, clasp my hands behind my back and writhe one shoe over the other.

The headmaster would look opaquely at me through flashing spectacles.

"What are we going to do with you?"

Well, what *were* they going to do with me? I would writhe my shoe some more and stare down at the worn rug.

"Look up, boy! Can't you look up?" . . .

I had nothing to say to the headmaster. His spectacles caught the light so that you could see nothing human behind them. There was no possibility of communication.

"Don't you ever think at all?"

No, I didn't think, wasn't thinking, couldn't think—I was simply waiting in anguish for the interview to stop.

"Then you'd better learn—hadn't you?"

On one occasion the headmaster leaped to his feet, reached up and plunked Rodin's masterpiece ["The Thinker"] on the desk before me.

"That's what a man looks like when he's really thinking."

I surveyed the gentleman without interest or comprehension.

"Get back to your class."

Clearly there was something missing in me. Nature had endowed the rest of the human race with a sixth sense and left me out. This must be so, I mused, on my way back to the class, since whether I had broken a window, or failed to remember Boyle's Law, or been late for school, my teachers produced me one, adult answer: "Why can't you think?"

—William Golding, "Thinking as a Hobby," *Holiday Magazine,* August, 1961.

1055. No result is easy which is worth having. Your education begins when what is called your education is over. . . . No man has earned the right to intellectual ambition until he has learned to lay his course by a star which he has never seen, — to dig by the divining rod for springs which he may never reach. . . . Only when you have worked alone, — when you have felt around you a black gulf of solitude more isolating than that which surrounds the dying man, and in hope and in despair have trusted to your own unshaken will, — then only will you have achieved. Thus only can you gain the secret isolated joy of the thinker, who knows that, a hundred years after he is dead and forgotten, men who never heard of him will be moving to the measure of his thought.

—Oliver Wendell Holmes, Jr., lecture to undergraduates of Harvard University, in Mark DeWolfe Howe, ed., *The Occasional Speeches of Justice Oliver Wendell Holmes:* "The Profession of the Law" (1962).

1056. It is not learning, grace nor gear,
Nor easy meat and drink,
But bitter pinch of pain and fear
That makes creation think.

—Rudyard Kipling, "The Benefactors," st.iii, *Rudyard Kipling's Verse* (1950), 339.

1057. And while the great and wise decay,
And all their trophies pass away,
Some sudden thought, some careless rhyme,
Still floats above the wrecks of Time.

—William E.H. Lecky, *Poems:* "On an Old Song" (1891).

1058. The thoughts that come often unsought, and, as it were, drop into the mind, are the most valuable of any we have, and therefore should be secured, because they seldom return again.

—John Locke, letter to Samuel Bolde, May 16, 1699. *See* Emerson, **#1052.**

1059. "Dear me," cried Mrs. Spaniel, "what will the neighbours think?"
"They won't," said Gissing, "I don't doubt they'll talk, but they won't think. Thinking is very rare."

—Christopher Morley, *Where the Blue Begins* (1922), 51.

1060. Ah! as you say, we ought to slip over many thoughts that pass through our minds, and pretend not to see them.

—Marie de Rabutin-Chantal, Marquise de Sévigné (1626–96), letter to her daughter, *Lettres de Mme. de Sévigné* (1725), lxx.

1061. Men fear thought as they fear nothing else on earth—more than ruin, even more than death. Thought is subversive and revolutionary, destructive and terrible; thought is merciless to privilege, established institutions, and comfortable habits; thought is anarchic and lawless, indifferent to authority, careless of the well-tried wisdom of the ages. Thought looks into the pit of hell and is not afraid.... Thought is ... the chief glory of man.

—Bertrand Russell, *Principles of Social Reconstruction:* "Education" (1916).

1062. Faster than spring-time showers comes thought on thought.

—William Shakespeare, *II Henry VI* (1590–91), III.i.337.

1063. The children of the mind are like the children of the body. Once born, they grow by a law of their own being and if their parents could foresee their future development, it would sometimes break their hearts.

—Richard Henry Tawney, *Religion and the Rise of Capitalism* (1926).

1064. Sell your clothes and keep your thoughts. God will see that you do not want society. If I were confined to a corner of a garret all my days, like a spider, the world would be just as large to me while I had my thoughts about me.

—Henry David Thoreau, *Walden,* "Conclusion" (1854), 313.

1065. The little girl had the making of a poet in her who, being told to be sure of her meaning before she spoke, said: "How can I know what I think till I see what I say?"

—Graham Wallas, *The Art of Thought* (1926). *See* Chapman, #1049.

Translation

1066. It seems better to me . . . for us also to translate some books which are most needful for men to know into the language which we can all understand; and . . . that all the youth now in England of free men, who are rich enough to be able to devote themselves to it, be set to learn as long as they are not fit for any other occupation, until they are able to read English writing well.

—Alfred the Great, king of Wessex,
(A.D. 849–99), preface to his translation
of Pope Gregory's *Cura Pastoralis (Pastoral Care)*
(A.D. 894). The revival of learning and his own English translation of Latin works were among Alfred's greatest achievements.

1067. Those who with nine months toil had spoil'd a play
In hopes of eating at a full third day,
Justly despairing longer to sustain
A craving stomach from an empty brain,
Have left stage-practice, chang'd their old vocations,
Attoning for bad plays, with worse translations;
And like old sternhold, with laborious spite,
Burlesque what nobler muses better write.

—Anonymous, "A Satyr on the Modern Translators," 1684.

1068. Reading poetry in translation is like kissing a woman through a veil.

—Adapted from Chaim Bialik (1873–1934).

1069. The task of translating from one language to another requires far more than a comprehensive knowledge of both languages. Inevitably the translator must play peacemaker between two peoples who are strange to each other. Bridges of understanding must be built. To create these, the translator needs psychological insight into the *spirit* of both languages.

Only after penetrating the spirit of a language is it possible to become familiar with the character of the people who speak it. When a translator achieves this familiarity, fundamental human reactions are revealed. After this the translator's task is the proper choice of words with which to convey, in another language, these human reactions, as portrayed by the author.

—Alexandra Kropotkin, translator's preface (1949) to Fyodor Dostoevsky, *The Brothers Karamazov* (1880).

1070. So of Translators they are Authors grown,
For ill Translators make the Book their own.
Others do strive with words and forced phrase
To add lustre, and so many rayes,
That but to make the Vessel shining, they
Much the precious Metal rub away.
He is Translations thief that addeth more,
As much as he that taketh from the Store.

—Andrew Marvell, "To his worthy Friend Doctor Witty upon his Translation of the Popular Errors" (1651), *The Poems and Letters of Andrew Marvell,* ed. H.M. Margoliouth (1927), I.

1071. Egad, I think the interpreter is the hardest to be understood of the two!

—Richard Brinsley Sheridan, *The Critic* (1779), I.ii.

Truth

1072. Truth even unto its innermost parts.

—Motto of Brandeis University, Waltham, Massachusetts.

1073. "Truth," said a traveller,
"Is a rock, a mighty fortress;
Often have I been to it,
Even to its highest tower,
From whence the world looks black."

"Truth," said a traveller,
"Is a breath, a wind,
A shadow, a phantom;
Long have I pursued it,
But never have I touched
The hem of its garment."

And I believed the second traveller;
For truth was to me
A breath, a wind,
A shadow, a phantom,
And never had I touched
The hem of its garment.

—Stephen Crane, from *The Black Riders* (1895).

1074. I died for Beauty—but was scarce
Adjusted in the Tomb
When One who died for Truth, was lain
In an adjoining Room—

He questioned softly "Why I failed"?
"For Beauty," I replied—
"And I—for Truth—Themself are One—
We Brethren, are", He said— . . . .

—Emily Dickinson, written c. 1862;
first published 1890, *The Complete Poems of Emily Dickinson*,
ed. Thomas H. Johnson (1951), 216. *Compare* Keats, **#1078.**

1075. When you have eliminated the impossible, whatever remains, *however improbable*, must be the truth.

—Sir Arthur Conan Doyle, *The Sign of the Four* (1890), vi.

1076. Truth is never strengthened by exaggeration.

—John Kenneth Galbraith,
in Frederick J. Pratson, *Perspectives on Galbraith: Conversations and Opinions* (1978), 256.

1077. Twixt Truth and Errour, ther's this difference known,
Errour is fruitful, Truth is onely one.

—Robert Herrick, "Truth and Errour," *Hesperides* (1648).

1078. "Beauty is truth, truth beauty,"—that is all
Ye know on earth, and all ye need to know.

—John Keats, "Ode to a Grecian Urn,"
(1820), ln.49, *The Poems of John Keats*, ed.
Jack Stillinger (1978), 372. *Compare* Dickinson, **#1074.**

1079. In the search for truth there are certain questions that are unimportant. Of what material is the universe constructed? Is the universe eternal? Are there limits or not to the universe? In what way is this human society put together? What is the ideal form of organization for human society? If a man were to postpone his searching and practicing for Enlightenment until such questions were solved, he would die before he found the path.

—Bukkyo Dendo Kyokai, *The Teaching of Buddha* (1986), 296. *See* Ruskin, #**407**, under "Knowledge."

1080. The question, What is truth? has certainly no prospect of obtaining a speedy answer; but the question, What is the spirit of truth? may be discussed with a greater prospect of agreement.

By the spirit of truth I mean that frame of mind by which men who acknowledge their own fallibility, and who desire above all things to discover what is true, should adjudicate between conflicting arguments. . . . Reason, reason alone, should determine their opinions.

—William E.H. Lecky, *History of the Rise and Influence of the Spirit of Rationalism in Europe* (1880).

1081. Truth, after all, wears a different face to everybody, and it would be too tedious to wait till all were agreed. She is said to lie at the bottom of a well, for the very reason, perhaps, that whoever looks down in search of her sees his own image at the bottom, and is persuaded not only that he has seen the Goddess, but that she is far better-looking than he had imagined.

—James Russell Lowell, *Democracy and Other Addresses:* "Democracy" (1887).

1082. Do anything, but find the truth! The middle of the road is for horses!

—Menahem-Mendel of Kotzk (1787–1859), Hasidic leader.

1083. The real advantage which truth has, consists in this, that when an opinion is true, it may be extinguished once, twice, or many times, but in the course of ages there will generally be found persons to rediscover it, until some one of its reappearances falls on a time when from favorable circumstances it escapes persecution until it has made such head as to withstand all subsequent attempts to suppress it.

—John Stuart Mill, *On Liberty* (1859), ii.

1084. He who wishes to teach us a truth should not tell it to us, but simply suggest it with a brief gesture, a gesture which starts an ideal trajectory in the air along which we glide until we find ourselves at the feet of a new truth.

—José Ortega y Gasset, *Meditations on Quixote:* "Preliminary Meditation: Worlds Beyond" (1961), 67.

1085. The truth appears so naked on my side,
That any purblind eye may find it out.

—William Shakespeare, *I Henry VI* (1590–91), II.iv.20. [purblind=*half-blind, sometimes wholly blind*].

University

See College

Wisdom

1086. Raphael paints wisdom, Handel sings it, Phidias carves it, Shakespeare writes it, Wren builds it, Columbus sails it, Washington arms it, Watt mechanizes it.

—Ralph Waldo Emerson, *Society and Solitude:* "Art" (1870).

1087. These kind of Men that are so given up to the study of Wisdome are generally most unfortunate, but chiefly in their Children; Nature, it seems, so providently ordering it, lest this mischief of Wisdome should spread farther among mankind.

—Desiderius Erasmus, *The Praise of Folly* (1509).

1088. Wisdom is not in words;
Wisdom is meaning within words.

—Kahlil Gibran, *The Treasured Writings of Kahlil Gibran* (1980), 900.

1089. The wisdom of mankind creeps slowly on,
Subject to every doubt that can retard
Or fling it back upon an earlier time.

—Richard Henry Horne, "Orion" (1843), III.

1090. My parents hoped that no matter what else, I would be a wise man. For this I already had two of the qualifications—thick glasses and the hungry look. Wisdom was the greatest glory, my parents felt. Besides, wisdom was steadier than millionairedom. Besides that, if you were wise and somehow lost your millions, you still wouldn't lose your mind.

I proceeded to bone up on the subject of wisdom and learned that according to the wisest of professional wise men, wisdom is a virtually unpossessable possession; it diminishes as it increases. The more of it you acquire the closer you come to the knowledge that you are not wise at all. Knowing that you don't know is top flight wisdom. Knowing that you are a fool is sheer genius. Admitting to it is saintliness.

—Sam Levenson, *You Don't Have to Be in Who's Who to Know What's What* (1979), 119.

1091. Accuse not Nature! she hath done her part;
Do thou but thine! and be not diffident
Of Wisdom; she deserts thee not, if thou
Dismiss not her, when most thou need'st her nigh,
By attributing overmuch to things
Less excellent, as thou thyself perceiv'st.

—John Milton, *Paradise Lost* (1667), VIII.561.

1092. What people are really looking for is wisdom. To our great store of knowledge we need the added quality of wisdom.

Wisdom is inseparable from knowledge; it is knowledge plus a quality which is within the human being. Without it knowledge is dry, almost unfit for human consumption, and dangerous in application. The absence of wisdom is clearly noticeable; the learned fool and the educated bore have been with us since the beginning of recorded history. Wisdom adds flavor, order, and measure to knowledge. Wisdom makes itself most manifest in the application of knowledge to human needs.

—Isador I. Rabi, "Scientist and Humanist," *Atlantic Monthly*, January 1956.

1093. Wisdom that exists in a man only theoretically without becoming practical is like a double rose which by its colour and perfume delights others, but drops away without going to seed.

No rose without a thorn. But many a thorn without a rose.

—Arthur Schopenhauer, *Parerga and Paralipomena:* "Similes, Parables, and Fables" (1851), tr. E.F.J. Payne (1974), II.648.

1094. *Wisdom* is a Fox, who after long hunting, will at last cost you the Pains to dig out: 'Tis a *Cheese*, which, by how much the richer, has the thicker, the homelier, and the coarser Coat; and whereof, to a judicious Palate, the *Maggots* are the best.... But then, lastly, 'tis a *Nut*, which, unless you chuse with Judgment, may cost you a Tooth, and pay you with nothing but a *Worm*.

—Jonathan Swift, *A Tale of a Tub:* "Introduction" (1704).

1095. Seven characteristics distinguish the wise: he does not speak in the presence of one wiser than himself, does not interrupt, is not hasty to answer, asks and answers to the point, talks about first things first, and about last things last, admits when he does not know, and acknowledges the truth.

—*Talmud: Aboth*, 5.7 (before A.D. 500).

Women

(*See also* Women, Education of)

1096. That sex, which heretofore was not allowed,
To understand more than a beast, or crowd;
Of which problems were made, whether or no
Women had souls, but to be damned, if so;
Whose highest contemplation could not pass,
In mens esteem, no higher than the glass;
And all the painful labours of their brain,
Was only how to dress and entertain:
Or, if they ventured to speak sense, the wise
Made that, and speaking ox, like prodigies.

—Anonymous woman, "To the Excellent Orinda," 1669.

1097. I here and there o'erheard a Coxcomb cry,
Ah, Rot it—'tis a Woman's Comedy,
One, who because she lately chanc'd to please us,
With her damn'd Stuff, will never cease to teeze us.
What has poor Woman done, that she must be
Debar'd from Sense, and sacred Poetry?...
Why in this Age has Heaven allow'd you more,
And Women less of Wit than heretofore?...
But for you half Wits, you unthinking Tribe,

We'll let you see, whate'er besides we do,
How artfully we copy some of you:
And if you're drawn to th' Life, pray tell me then,
Why Women should not write as well as Men.

—Aphra Behn, *Sir Patient Fancy:* "Epilogue" (1678). She was the first English woman author to make her living by writing.

1098. The educational institutions for women are much superior to those of Europe, and perhaps the most important work which America is doing for the future of humanity consists in her treatment and education of woman. Woman's increasing value as a teacher, and her employment as such in public schools, even in those for boys, is, in these states, a public fact which delights me. It even seems as if the daughters of New England have a peculiar faculty and love for this occupation. Whole crowds go hence to the western and southern states where schools are established and placed under their direction.

That which is most admirable in New England is the number of great schools and asylums for the education of youth, and in aid of the unfortunate. These are the offspring of a large heart, and they have a broad basis. It is a joy to see and hear children taught in these free public schools in large and airy halls. One can see that the pupils are all awake and full of life; one can hear that they understand what they read and learn. The great reformation in the conduct of the schools, and the impulse toward universal education are the result, in great measure, of the enthusiasm, perseverance, and determined resolution of a single individual, Horace Mann. This reformation is, without question, one of the most beautiful and significant phenomena of this national culture, especially since it embraces woman as well as man, and places her side by side with him as teacher of the rising generation.

—Fredrika Bremer, *Hemmen i den nya Verlden (Homes in the New World)* (1853), in Oscar Handlin, *This Was America* (1949), 221. Bremer was a Swedish writer.

1099. What, always reading, Madam, still afronting mankind by invading their province of knowledge, fye this is unnatural; a Lady should no more pretend to a book, than a sword, neither of 'em are proper to her sphere of activity.

—Thomas D'Urfey, *Richard Heiress* (1693).

1100. Women were not born to read authors and censure the learned, to compare lives and judge of virtues, to give rules of mortality and sacrifice to the Muses.... We are willing to acknowledge all time borrowed from family duties is misspent: the care of children's education, observing a husband's comments, assisting the sick, relieving the poor and being serviceable to our friends are of sufficient weight to employ the most improved capacities amongst us. If sometimes it happens by accident that one of a thousand aspires a little higher, her fate commonly exposes her to wonder but adds little esteem.... A heroine is a kind of prodigy; the influence of a blazing star is not more dangerous or more to be avoided.

—Mary Evelyn, letter to Mr. Bohun,
Jan. 1672, in John Evelyn, *Diary,* ed.
William Bray (1852), IV.31. *See* Makin, **#1105.**

1101. If I were one of you, I should cordially detest all those emancipators of the sex who are for making you into men's equals. They are urging you to take a false step. Fine promotion, to be sure, for you, to be as good as an attorney or a druggist! Take care, I say; already you have stripped off some particles of your mystery and fascination. All is not lost. Men still fight, and ruin and kill themselves for you; but the young fellows in tram-cars leave you to stand on the platform while they sit snug inside. Your cult is declining along with other things once held sacrosanct.

—Anatole France (1849–1924),
"Women," in Leo Hamalian and Edmond L. Volpe,
eds., *Great Essays by Nobel Prize Winners* (1960), 22.

1102. Their education is miserably deficient; ... they are taught to regard marriage as the one thing needful, the only avenue to distinction; hence to attract the notice and win the attentions of men, by their external charms, is the chief business of fashionable girls. They seldom think that men will be allured by intellectual acquirements, because they find, that where any mental superiority exists, a woman is generally shunned and regarded as stepping out of her 'appropriate sphere,' which, in their view, is to dress, to dance, to set out to the best possible advantage her person, to read the novels which inundate the press, and which do more to destroy her character as a rational creature, than any thing else.

—Sarah M. Grimké, *Letters on the Equality
of the Sexes and the Condition of Women* (1838), viii.

1103. Papa ... alternately scolded and teased me. "You a lawyer, Sara? That's man's work. It does no good for a woman to be educated. What will you do with your fine education in the kitchen? Besides, you'll never get a husband if you are too brainy. Men don't appreciate bright women.

Forget this foolish notion of college." His hand would stray to my hair. "Little Goldilocks," he would murmur, as he had all those years ago in Germany. . . ." Once you are a mother, you will be fulfilled."

—Sara Halbert, *Call Me Counselor* (1977), 30.

1104. There is one field of public life . . . which women may well desire to occupy. . . . There should be women on our school boards. . . .

We cannot but think that American women in general, even those who are most eager in demanding what they deem the "rights" of their sex, have failed to comprehend their duties in regard to the schools in which their sons and daughters are educated.

—Sarah Josepha Hale, "Women on School Boards," *Godey's Lady Book*, February 1871, in Ruth E. Finley, *The Lady of Godey's* (1931), 238.

1105. A learned woman is thought to be a comet that bodes mischief whenever it appears.

—Bathshua Makin, *An Essay to Revive the Antient Education of Women* (1673), 26. *See* Evelyn, **#1100.**

1106. You're not pretty, Miriam-mine, so you better be smart. But not too smart.

—Marge Piercy, *Small Changes* (1973), 88.

1107. Several gentlemen, on a visit to this country to purchase land, spent a few days at the Bluff. They were gentlemen of intelligence, learning, and politeness. While here, they had frequent opportunities of conversing with the ladies, of which they availed themselves with that taste and good sense which ever distinguish well bred people. But, alas! then it was I discovered the disadvantage a female labors under, when destitute of education; and this is still more apparent when contrasted by one of their own sex. It is well for them their ignorance effectually screens them from all knowledge of the ridiculous figure they made. If they were sensible of the pain they inflict upon those who are so unfortunate as to hear them blundering from one thing to another; miscalling some words, and misapplying others; and the no small pains they take to expose their ignorance, shame and mortification would drive them mad.

—Anne Newport Royall, ostensibly written to "Matt," a young lawyer friend, Feb. 8, 1818, *Letters from Alabama: 1817–1822*, ed. Lucille Griffith (1969), 174.

1108. [After my brother's death] I began to study Latin, Greek, and mathematics with a class of boys in the Academy, many of whom were much older than I. For three years one boy kept his place at the head of the class, and I always stood next. Two prizes were offered in Greek. I strove for one and took the second. . . . One thought alone filled my mind. "Now," said I, "my father will be satisfied with me." So, as soon as we were dismissed, I ran down the hill, rushed breathless into his office, laid the new Greek Testament, which was my prize, on his table and exclaimed: "There, I got it!" He took up the book, asked me some questions about the class, and evidently pleased, handed it back to me. Then, while I still looking and waiting for him to say something which would show that he recognized the equality of the daughter with the son, he kissed me on the forehead and exclaimed, with a sigh, "Ah, you should have been a boy!"

—Elizabeth Cady Stanton, *Eighty Years and More* (1898), 22.

1109. (An American scientist has come to the conclusion that the tendency of too much education or intellectual development in women is to make them lose their beauty.)

O PHYLLIS, once no task to me was sweeter
Than, grasping my enthusistic quill,
To hymn your charms; erratic though the metre,
It gained in fervour what it lacked in skill.
But now, alas, those charms are like to vanish.
Without preamble duty bids me speak.
The rumour runs that you are learning Spanish,
And also—simultaneously—Greek.

Those eyes, to which I loved to dash off stanzas,
No longer gaze, as erstwhile, into mine;
They're fixed on *Quixote's* deeds, or *Sancho Panza's*
Or rest on some Aeschylean line.
Or, as you spell THUCYDIDES his speeches,
Your face assumes a look of care and pain.
O PHYLLIS, heed the moral that it teaches,
And cease to run the risk of growing plain.

Shun, I implore, the vampire Education.
Be guided by my excellent advice.
You owe a solemn duty to the nation—
Simply to give your mind to looking nice.
Learning may be acquired, but beauty never:

Dry books, believe me, were never meant for you.
Be fair, sweet maid, and let who will be clever.
If brains are wanted, I've enough for two.

—P.G. Wodehouse, "'Tis Folly to Be Wise," *Punch* Magazine, 1902.

Women, Education of

(*See also* School, Advertisements for; Women)

1110. If you complain of neglect of Education in sons, What shall I say in regard to daughters, who every day experience the want of it. With regard to the Education of my own children, I find myself soon out of my depth, and destitute and deficient in every part of Education.

I most sincerely wish that some more liberal plan might be laid and executed for the Benefit of the rising Generation and that our new constitution may be distinguished for Learning and Virtue. If we mean to have Heroes, Statesmen, and Philosophers, we should have learned women. The world perhaps would laugh at me, and accuse me of vanity, But you, I know have a mind too enlarged and liberal to disregard the sentiment. If much depends as is allowed upon the early Education of youth and the first principals [*sic*] which are instilld take the deepest root, great benefit must arise from the litirary [*sic*] accomplishments in women.

—Abigail Adams, letter to John Adams, who was concerned that sons were not the scholars their fathers and grandfathers were, Aug. 14, 1776, in L.H. Butterfield, M. Friedlaender and M.J. Kline, eds., *The Book of Abigail and John* (1975), 153.

1111. When a father has a numerous issue of sons and daughters, the sons must be first put to the Grammar School, and after perchance sent to the University and trained up in the liberal arts and sciences, and there (if they prove not blockheads) they may in time be booked-learned. . . . [But we daughters] are set only to the needle to prick our fingers; or else to the wheel to spin a fair thread for our own undoings, or perchance to some dirty and debased drudgery. If we be taught to read, they then confine us within the compass of the mother tongue, and that limit we are not suffered to pass. . . . If we be weak by nature, they strive to make us more weak by our nurture. And if in degree of place low, they strive by their policy to keep us more under.

—Anonymous woman, *The Women's Sharpe Revenge* (1640), in Angeline Goreau, *Reconstructing Aphra: A Social Biography of Aphra Behn* (1980), 24.

1112. Women are from their very infancy debarred those advantages (of education) with the want of which they are afterwards reproached, and nursed up in those vices with which will hereafter be upbraided them. So partial are men as to expect bricks when they afford no straw.

—Mary Astell, *A Serious Proposal to the Ladies for the Advancement of Their True and Greatest Interest* (1694).

1113. Let all women learn in silence with all subjection.

But I suffer not a woman to teach, nor to usurp authority over man, but to be in silence.

—*Bible: Timothy,* 2:11.

1114. "We don't want her to take music too seriously." Real concern came into her voice. "We don't want her to become intense over something, and warped and queer. Such women are unhappy in later life. They don't," she rang the bell for more tea, "they don't make good wives."

—Catherine Drinker Bowen, *Friends and Fiddlers* (1934), iv.

1115. I had five years of music lessons—every Wednesday at four. How anyone could ever have thought that anything would come of this, I do not know; and perhaps no one ever really did think so. It was an era when little girls were given music lessons automatically, even as they were given rhubarb in the spring. I had to practice an hour a day, and my fixed custom of assisting the clock hands on their appointed rounds was accordingly pure humankindness. Well, almost pure.

—Katherine Brush, *This Is On Me* (1939), 11.

Booker T. Washington advances the school clock (*see* **#747** under "School, Remembrances of") and Charles S. Brooks considers doing it (*see* **#1016** under "Teaching Method").

1116. She'd a great and varied knowledge,
Absorbed at Vassar College,
Of quadratics, hydrostatics,
And pneumatics very vast.

She was stuffed with erudition
As you stuff a leather cushion,
All the ologies of the colleges,
And the knowledge of the past.

She knew all the mighty giants
And the master minds of science.
All the learning that was turning
In the burning mind of man.
But she couldn't prepare a dinner
For a gaunt and hungry sinner,
Or get up a decent supper
For her poor, voracious pa.

For she was never construed
On the old domestic plan.

—Lizzie W. Champney,
Demorest's Illustrated Monthly Magazine, late 1890s,
in Ishbel Ross, *Crusades and Crinolines* (1963), 225.

1117. The overemphasis on protecting girls from strain or injury and underemphasis on developing skills and experiencing teamwork fits neatly into the pattern of the second sex. . . . Girls are the spectators and the cheerleaders. . . . Perfect preparation for the adult role of woman—to stand decoratively on the sidelines of history and cheer the men who make the decisions.

—Kathryn Clarenbach,
Sex Role Stereotyping in the Schools (1973).

1118. Beginning in the nineteenth century a limited but formal education was regarded as a suitable genteel and womanly aspiration. Female seminaries sprang up all over the Northeast, not to train girls for work outside the home (although teaching was considered an admissible occupation for those in financial straits), but to prepare them for the responsibilities of motherhood and the rearing of future citizens. The academic curriculum was usually limited to a smattering of history, literature and languages and to a large dose of moral philosophy. Science and mathematics were considered beyond the scope of the female mind. . . . Here and there a girl managed to acquire a learning comparable to that of an educated man, but she was a rarity, and her achievement usually depended on a father who was willing to provide the necessary instruction. Even those parents who encouraged their daughters' education made it quite clear that learning was meant to contribute to a woman's domestic felicity and not encourage her to cherish thoughts of independence and personal ambition.

—Deborah Pickman Clifford, *Mine Eyes Have Seen the Glory: A Biography of Julia Ward Howe* (1978), 18.

1119. I have often thought of it as one of the most barbarous Customs in the world, considering us as a Civiliz'd and a Christian Countrey, that we deny the advantage of Learning to Women. We reproach the Sex every day with Folly and Impertinence, while I am confident, had they the advantages of Education equal to us, they wou'd be guilty of less than our selves.

One wou'd wonder indeed how it should happen that Women are conversible at all, since they are only beholding to Natural Parts for all their Knowledge. Their Youth is spent to teach them to Stitch and Sow, or make Bawbles: They are taught to Read indeed, and perhaps to Write their Names, or so; and that is the height of a Women's Education. And I wou'd but ask any who slight the Sex for their Understanding, What is a Man (a Gentleman, I mean) good for, that is taught no more....

Methinks Mankind for their own sakes, since say what you will of Women, we all think fit, one time or another, to be concerned with 'em, shou'd take some care to breed them up to be *suitable* and *serviceable*, if they expected no such thing as *Delight* from 'em. Bless us! What Care do we take to Breed up a good Horse, and to break him well! and what a Value do we put upon him when it is done—and all because he shou'd be fit for our use! and why not a Woman? Since all her Ornaments and Beauty, without suitable Behaviour, is a Cheat in Nature, like the false Tradesman who puts the best of his Goods uppermost, that the Buyer may think the rest are the same Goodness.

The Capacities of Women are suppos'd to be greater and their Senses quicker than those of the Man; and what they might be capable of being bred to, is plain from some Instances of Female-Wit which this Age is not without; which upbraids us with Injustice, and looks as if we deni'd women the advantages of Education for fear they should vye with the men in their Improvements....

To remove this Objection, and that Women might have at least a needful Opportunity of Education in all sorts of Useful Learning, I propose the Draught of an academy for that purpose.

—Daniel Defoe, *An Essay on Projects:* "An Academy for Women" (1697).

1120. Virginia, in spite of her gaiety, had been what Miss Priscilla called "a docile pupil," meaning one who deferentially submitted all her opinions to her superiors, and to go through life perpetually submitting her opinions was, in the eyes of her parents and her teacher, the divinely appointed task of woman. Her education was founded upon the simple theory that the less a girl knew about life, the better prepared she would be to contend with it. Knowledge of any sort (except the rudiments of reading and writing, the geography of countries she would never visit, and the dates of battles she would never mention) was kept from her as rigorously as if it contained the germs of a contagious disease. And this ignorance of anything that could possibly be useful to her was supposed in some mysterious way to add to her value as a woman and make her a more desirable companion to a man who, either by experience or by instinct, was expected "to know his world." . . . Virginia had until today accepted with humility the doctrine that a natural curiosity about the universe is the beginning of infidelity. The chief object of her upbringing, which differed in no essential particular from that of every other well-born and well-bred Southern woman of her day, was to paralyze her reasoning faculties so completely that all danger of mental "unsettling" or even movement was eliminated from her future. To solidify the forces of mind into the inherited mould of fixed beliefs was, in the opinion of the age, to achieve the definite end of all education.

—Ellen Glasgow, *Virginia* (1913), I.21.

1121. Messrs. Editors,

Will you allow a female to offer a few remarks upon the subject that you must allow to be all-important? I don't know that in any of your papers you have said sufficient upon the education of females. I hope you are not to be classed with those who think that our mathematical knowledge should be limited to "fathoming the dish-kettle," and that we have acquired enough of history if we know that our grandfather's father lived and died. It is true the time has been when to darn a stocking and cook a pudding well was considered the end and aim of woman's being. But these were days when ignorance blinded men's eyes. The diffusion of knowledge has destroyed those degrading opinions, and men of the present age allow that we have minds that are capable and deserving of culture.

There are difficulties, and great difficulties, in the way of advancement; but this should only stir us to greater efforts. We possess not the advantages with those of our sex whose skins are not colored like our own, but we can improve what little we have and make our one talent produce twofold. The influence we have over the male sex demands that our minds should be instructed and improved with the principles of education and religion, in order that this influence should be properly directed. Ignorant ourselves, how can we be expected to form the minds of our youth and conduct them in the paths of knowledge? How can we "teach the young idea how to shoot" if we have none ourselves? There is a great responsibility resting somewhere, and it is time for us to be up and doing.

I would address myself to all mothers, and say to them that while it is necessary to possess a knowledge of cookery and the various mysteries of pudding making, something more is requisite. It is their bounden duty to store their daughters' minds with useful learning. They should be made to devote their leisure time to reading books whence they would derive valuable information which could never be taken from them.

I will no longer trespass on your time and patience. I merely throw out these hints in order that some more able pen will take up the subject.

—Matilda, an anonymous Negro woman, letter to *Freedom's Journal,* Aug. 10, 1827, in *The Annals of America* (1968), V.225.

1122. In 1847 Lucy Stone graduated from Oberlin and was informed that one of the professors would read her graduate essay, for it would be indelicate for Lucy to read it herself "before a promiscuous audience." Deprived of the right to read it herself, she refused to have it read at all.

—Eve Merriam, *Growing Up Female in America* (1971), 14.

1123. To prove that they [girls] ought to receive an education I find four special reasons, any one of which—therefore surely all together—may persuade their greatest adversary, much more than myself who am for them tooth and nail. Then first is the custom of the country [England], which allows them to learn. The second is the duty we owe, charging us in conscience not to leave them deficient. The third is their own aptness to learn, which God would never have bestowed on them to remain idle or to be used to small purpose. The fourth is the excellent results shown in them when they have had the advantage of good upbringing. I do not advocate sending young maidens to public Grammar Schools, or to the Universities, as this has never been the custom in this country. I would allow them learning within certain limits, having regard to the difference in their vocation, and in the ends which they should seek to study. We see that young maidens are taught to read and write, and can learn to do well in both; we hear them both sing and play passing well; we know that they learn the best and finest of our learned languages to the admiration of all men. As to the living modern languages of highest reputation in our time, if any one is inclined to deny that in these they can compare with the best of our sex, they will claim no other tests than to talk with such a one in whichever of the tongues she may choose.

—Richard Mulcaster (1530?–1611), in J. Oliphant, *The Educational Writings of Richard Mulcaster* (1903), 51.

1124. Perhaps one of the indictments that may be made against the traditional Jewish scheme of life [during the Middle Ages] was that female education was overlooked. Yet the fact remains that women scribes are on record who copied with understanding highly intricate Talmudic treatises, that women were even known on occasion to answer difficult Rabbinic problems or to conduct public lessons, and that one of the granddaughters of Rashi is said to have acted as his amanuensis. Leaving such exceptional cases aside, we often find girls having lessons with their brothers from private tutors or from their parents, and a Talmud Torah [elementary Hebrew school] for girls is said to have existed in Rome in the fifteenth century; indeed, in Italy women often acted as the primary teachers.

Hence, average women . . . could read, if not write. Moreover, they knew large numbers of Hebrew words and phrases which had entered into daily speech, they learned by rote some of the standard Hebrew prayers and their meaning, they joined in singing the table hymns, they listened to discourses in synagogue, they heard their fathers and husbands discussing points of Rabbinic law, they were familiar with a vast store of legendary lore, and they were supposed to have mastered those domestic regulations prescribed by tradition which were their special care. Hence the least educated or even illiterate Jewish woman of the Middle Ages enjoyed a relatively higher degree of Hebraic culture than her more sophisticated and better-trained contemporary descendant of either sex.

—Cecil Roth, "The Success of the Medieval Jewish Ideal," in Leo W. Schwarz, ed., *Great Ages and Ideas of the Jewish People* (1956), 295.

1125. Although it had a full academic curriculum, a primary aim of Miss Pierce's academy [in the early 1800s], not unlike that of later "finishing schools," was to teach decorum, ladylike manners, and "refined conversation"—in short, the social graces. . . .

Mixing morality, religion, hygiene and diet, Miss Pierce would regularly interrogate her charges: "Have you been neat in your person . . . ? Have you combed your hair with a fine tooth comb and cleaned your teeth every morning . . . ? Have you eaten any green fruit during the week . . . ?" It was the daily scholastic counterpart of the Sabbath catechism.

—Milton Rugoff, *The Beechers* (1981), 43.

1126. Methodist parents, who would send your girls headlong to Hell, send them to a fashionable boarding-school.

—John Wesley, *Journal*, Apr. 6, 1772.

1127. The community which has not made adequate provision for the right education of its daughters, is in a sadly self-ruinous condition—and that those parents who will not sacrifice much to place their female children within reach of a first-rate education, are failing in one of their highest duties; and that even that Church membership, which fails, by properly directed effort, to secure a religious training for girls connected with their families, appropriate to the received standards of Bible truth, must be considered false to their own belief, disregardful of the future of their children, and greatly deficient in intelligent zeal for the welfare of their fellow men.

—Joseph R. Wilson, *Female Training. A Sermon Delivered . . . before the Friends of the Greensboro Female College, May 23, 1858,* in John M. Mulder, *Woodrow Wilson: The Years of Preparation* (1978), 8. He was Woodrow Wilson's father.

Word

(*See also* Language; Meaning)

1128. "A pun is the lowest form of wit,"
It does not tax the brain a bit;
One merely takes a word that's plain
And picks one out that sounds the same.
Perhaps some letter may be changed
Or others slightly disarranged,
This to the meaning gives a twist,
Which much delights the humorist;
A sample now may help to show
The way a good pun ought to go:
"It isn't the cough that carries you off,
It's the coffin they carry you off in."

—Anonymous, in Martha Lupton, ed., *The Treasury of Modern Humor* (1938), 948.

1129. An artificial stretching of vocabulary is not to be urged. . . . Nor may students exult when they have found a hard word to express their thoughts. For, in the first place, hard words make hard reading. Beneath their weight a sentence staggers like a man with a bag of coal. It is usually a pattern of easy words that gives a sentence grace, and any octosyllabic explosion blows the thought quite off its track. But secondly, and of more importance, hard words have mostly been coined for a special use and their meaning is narrow and scientific. They stiffen a paragraph to a formula. They smell unpleasantly of the laboratory and the schoolroom.

But common words have grown up with the language. They have been bartered back and forth until they are loaded with experience and association. With them life has been measured for a thousand years. To them cling both joy and sadness. Each century has left a deposit on them. Their very meaning has shifted back and forth as fashions change. Democracy or despotism, city or country preference, farce or tragedy, youth or age, power or slavery, reverence or contempt, have set them to different uses. They have lived in triumph and adversity, in gutter and palace. They have been both truth and jest and have starved and feasted. Sometimes they have started life poor and out at elbow, but have come to better fortune; or, fed in youth from a golden spoon, they have sunk to poverty.

With these common words children have been taught a lesson at their mother's knee, with them they have been sung to sleep. A million books have been made of them, and the far-off hum of cities is the fabric of their use. They have lulled multitudes to obedience, and rebellion has been stirred by them. At their sound Saxon and Roman set up their standards. By them London Tower was built. They have been shouted in mediaeval streets. Ladies have listened to their song and have confessed their love to the silly moon. With them the Magna Charta was signed and the Armada fought. They crossed the seas in the stormy Mayflower and set up their stockade against the Indians. Their common use has built America. These common words defy exact definition because they mean so much. They contain a hundred elusive overtones of racial experience and recollection. A secret of style is to make this overtone a servant of the thought.

—Charles S. Brooks, *A Thread of English Road:*
"To be Read Only by Serious Stupid Persons" (1924), 187.

1130. Many words in every language are generally thought to be synonymous; but those who study the language attentively will find that there is no such thing; they will discover some little difference, some distinction between all those words that are vulgarly called synonymous; one has always more energy, extent, or delicacy, than another.

—Lord Chesterfield, letter to his son,
Mar. 16, 1752, in Lord Mahon, ed., *The Letters*
of Philip Dormer Stanhope, Earl of Chesterfield (1845), II.234.

1131. A word is dead
When it is said,
Some say.
I say it just

Begins to live.
That day.

—Emily Dickinson, (1872?), *The Complete Poems of Emily Dickinson*, ed. Thomas H. Johnson (1960), 535.

1132. Words importing the masculine gender shall always include women, except where otherwise stated.

—English law known as Lord Brougham's Act, 1950.

1133. If a people have no word for something, either it does not matter to them or it matters too much to talk about.

—Edgar Z. Friedenberg, *The Vanishing Adolescent:* "Adolescence" (1959).

1134. The English language has several dozen words like "dichotomy" and "bifurcation" about which we can do nothing since they already mean (I believe the professional semanticists say "signify" or "connote") something. We certainly make no improvement when we infest the language with our lazy words—words like "gimmick" which does not even mean, connote, or signify much of anything at all. "Give me the picture," the boss asks the salesman. Just what in hell does the boss want?

Even worse is the word *thing*. *Thing* means or fails to mean a million situations. The financial report becomes "the whole *thing*." "The *thing* is getting out of hand," says the boss to his secretary, meaning his wife has found out about their casual evenings together at the Schwartz Motel. "Get your *things* on," says the mother to her children. She wants them to dress. "A funny *thing* happened to me..."

—Harry Golden, *So What Else Is New?:* "The lazy words" (1964), 302.

1135. Men ever had, and ever will have, leave
To coin new words well suited to the age.
Words are like leaves, some wither away ev'ry year,
And ev'ry year a younger race succeeds.

—Horace, *Ars Poetica* (20 B.C.).

1136. They sing, they hurt, they teach, they sanctify. They were man's first, immeasurable feat of magic. They liberated us from ignorance and our barbarous past. For without these marvelous scribbles which build letters into words, words into sentences, sentences into systems and sciences and creeds, man would be forever confined to the self-isolated prison of the scuttlefish or the chimpanzee. "A picture is worth ten thousand words," goes the timeworn Chinese maxim. "But," one writer tartly said, "it takes words to say that." We live by words: LOVE, TRUTH, GOD. We fight for words: FREEDOM, COUNTRY, FAME. We die for words: LIBERTY, GLORY, HONOR. They bestow the priceless gift of articulacy on our minds and hearts—from "Mama" to "infinity." And the men who truly shape our destiny, the giants who teach us, inspire us, lead us to deeds of immortality, are those who use words with clarity, grandeur and passion: Socrates, Jesus, Luther, Lincoln, and Churchill. During National Liberty Week, Americans caught between affluence and anxiety, may again give thanks for the endless riches in the kingdom of print.

—Leo Rosten, *The Many Worlds of Leo Rosten:* "The Power of Words" (1964), 24.

Writer

(*See also* Biography; Book Preface; Historian; Poet; Writing)

1137. The end of his book comes unexpectedly upon an author. And this is odd, considering that months, perhaps years, he has been anticipating the moment with almost pathological anxiety. He has been sure that he would die before his work was done, and being in palpably good health throughout, he has not liked to confess this anxiety. The feeling, however, is common to artists; psychologists I believe have a name for it. With Peter Tchaikovsky it took the form of being certain, before conducting a concert of his own music, that his head would fall off during performance—an awkward situation because conducting requires two hands, with none to spare for holding down the head.

There is an element of usefulness in this despair; it is a driving force. "I have no hope of my book, except for being done with it." So Carlyle, in the midst of writing his *French Revolution*—"that smoke and flame conflagration." With a long book, a history or biography, the anxiety is exacerbated. "Matter multiplieth toward the conclusion," said Thomas Fuller, apologizing for delay in completing the last of three volumes. Yet somehow the day arrives. Somehow, here it is, a sleeting Tuesday at twelve noon and one's book is done, over with, finished and in the mail, addressed to the publisher. In one's study the big desk is bare and the bookshelves above the desk; volumes from the public libraries have been returned.

—Catherine Drinker Bowen, *Adventures of a Biographer* (1946), 123.

1138. An essayist is not a mighty traveler. He does not run to grapple with a roaring lion. He desires neither typhoon nor tempest. He is content in his harbor to listen to the storm upon the rocks if now and then by lucky chance, he can shelter someone from the wreck. His hands are not red with revolt against the world. He has glanced upon the thoughts of many men; and as opposite philosophies point upon the truth, he is modest with his own and tolerant of the opinion of others. He looks at the stars and, knowing in what a dim immensity we travel, he writes of little things beyond dispute. There are enough to weep upon the shadows; he, like the dial, marks the light. The small clatter of the city beneath his window, the cry of the peddlers, children chalking their games upon the pavement, laundry dancing on the roofs and smoke in the winter's wind—these are the things he weaves into the fabric of his thoughts. Or sheep upon the hillside—if his window is so lucky—or a sunny meadow, is a profitable speculation. An essay, therefore, cannot be writ hurriedly upon the knee.

—Charles S. Brooks,
"Hints to Pilgrims," 1921, in Essie Chamberlain,
Essays Old and New (1934), rev., frontispiece.

1139. 'Tis pleasant, sure, to see one's name in print;
A book's a book, although there's nothing in 't.

—Lord Byron, "English Bards and Scotch Reviewers" (1809),
ln.51, *The Complete Poetical Works of Byron* (1933), 242.

1140. For myself, I cannot live without my art. But I have never placed it above everything. If, on the other hand, I need it, it is because it cannot be separated from my fellow men, and it allows me to live, such as I am, on one level with them. It is a means of stirring the greatest number of people by offering them a privileged picture of common joys and sufferings. It obliges the artist not to keep himself apart; it subjects him to the most humble and most universal truth. And often he who has chosen the fate of the artist because he felt himself to be different soon realizes that he can maintain neither his art nor his differences unless he admits that he is like the others. The artist forges himself to the others, midway between the beauty he cannot do without and the community he cannot tear himself away from. That is why true artists scorn nothing: they are obliged to understand rather than to judge. And if they have to take sides in this world, they can perhaps side only with that society which, according to Nietzsche's great words, not the judge but the creator will rule, whether he be a worker or an intellectual.

—Albert Camus, Nobel Prize
for Literature acceptance speech, Stockholm, 1957.

1141. In America only the successful writer is important, in France all writers are important, in England no writer is important, and in Australia you have to explain what a writer is.

—Geoffrey Cotterell, English writer, *New York Journal-American*, Sept. 22, 1961.

1142. I rarely play cards, but I was taken to the cleaners this evening by a couple of young women in a spirited game of "Authors." I reflected as I played upon the appearance of authors, as a class. They are a mangy lot. Shakespeare appears to have been a dapper fellow, but look at James Fenimore Cooper, who kept turning up again and again in the hands I was dealt. And look at Ralph Connor and Sir Gilbert Parker, the two Canadians included in the game. Scarecrows, all of them. Authors should be read, not seen. Their work unfits them for human society.

—Robertson Davies, *The Table Talk of Samuel Marchbanks* (1949), 97.

1143. All good books are alike in that they are truer than if they really happened and after you are finished reading one you will feel that all that happened to you and afterwards it belongs to you: the good and the bad, the ecstasy, the remorse and sorrow, the people and places and how the weather was. If you can get so you can give that to people, then you are a writer.

—Ernest Hemingway, "Old Newsman Writes," *Esquire* Magazine, December 1934.

1144. There are two literary maladies—writer's cramp and swelled head. The worst of writer's cramp is that it is never cured; the worst of swelled head is that it never kills.

—Coulson Kernahan (1858–1943), lecture in Birmingham, England.

1145. [Ring] meant it when he complained: "Where do they get that stuff about me being a satirist? I just listen." Most revealing of all was his response, with only family present, to a nephew's contention that Dickens was sentimental and sloppy. "How can you write if you can't cry?" he said.

—Ring Lardner, in Ring Lardner, Jr., *The Lardners* (1976), 175.

1146. If the writers of the world took chairs in an orchestra pit, each would hold the instrument that he plays best. There are first- and second-string fiction writers; biographers are at the oboe; historians play the cello; poets are the flutists. Somewhere in the symphony are those who love a journal.

—Laurel Lee, *Signs of Spring* (a journal) (1980), frontispiece.

1147. In other countries, art and literature are left to a lot of shabby bums living in attics and feeding on booze and spaghetti, but in America the successful writer or picture-painter is indistinguishable from any other decent business man.

—Sinclair Lewis, *Babbitt* (1922), 182.

1148. A real writer learns from earlier writers the way a boy learns from an apple orchard—by stealing what he has a taste for and can carry off. He will imitate his elders as every good writer has since the world began—even an original, even a Rimbaud—but the hunger and the pants pocket will be his own. Some of his apples will make him sick, but it will be his sickness. Others will shape his hand for life—because he picked them.

—Archibald MacLeish, *A Continuing Journey:* "On the Teaching of Writing" (1967), 229.

1149. There is a story of the famous novelist who once told his publisher that he planned to write a book about child care. The publisher, a doubting man, immediately asked what the novelist's qualifications might be. To which the great novelist replied with quiet dignity:

"I am a former child."

—William Nichols, editor's preface to Herbert Hoover, *On Growing Up* (1962), 12.

Writing

(*See also* Biography; Book Preface; Grammar; Historian; Poet; Poetry; Writer; Writing Style)

1150. "Don't begin to write yet, any of you," said the Doctor; "I have a few words to say to you first. In most cases, and as a general rule, I think it wisest to let every boy commit to paper whatever his feelings may dictate to him. I wish to claim no censorship over the style and diction of your letters. But there have been so many complaints lately from the parents of some of the less advanced of you, that I find myself obliged to make a change. Your father particularly, Richard Bultitude," he added, turning suddenly upon the unlucky Paul, "has complained bitterly of the slovenly tone of your correspondence; he said very justly that they would disgrace a stable-boy, and unless I could induce you to improve them, he begged he might not be annoyed by them in the future."

—F. Anstey, *Vice Versa; or, A Lesson to Fathers* (1882).

1151. If you're going to touch or tempt the world with what you write you'd better make the ultimate effort, and in my prose writing I'll crawl on my elbows to get it right.

—Hortense Calisher,
in Israel Shenker, *Words and Their Masters* (1974), 141.

1152. This appears to include very cliche known to the English language except "Please adjust your dress before leaving."

—Winston Churchill, note scribbled on
a pretentious and overly detailed memorandum by one
of his Ministers, in Bill Adler, *The Churchill Wit* (1965), 40.

1153. I have the conviction that excessive literary production is a social offence.

—George Eliot, letter to Alexander Main, Sept. 11, 1871,
George Eliot's Life as Related in Her Letters and Journals (1885).
See Mendelssohn, **#1163**; also Poe, **#35**, under "Book."

1154. Writing, madam, 's a mechanic part of wits. A gentleman should never go beyond a song or a *billet.*

—Sir George Etherege, *The Man of Mode* (1676), IV.i.

1155. Innumerable are the men and women now writing for bread, who have not the least chance of finding in such work a permanent livelihood. They took to writing because they know not what else to do, or because the literary calling tempted them by its independence and dazzling prizes. They will hang on to the squalid profession, their earnings eked out by begging and borrowing, until it is too late for them to do anything else—and what then. With a lifetime of dread experience behind me, I say that he who encourages any young man or woman to look for his living to "literature," commits no less than a crime.

—George Gissing, *The Private Papers of Henry Ryecroft* (1903).

1156. Among the greatest of academic frauds are courses in "Creative Writing"; one can no more be taught to write "creatively" than to love creatively; one can be taught only to write carefully, gracefully, and economically—which has nothing to do with creative power.

—Sydney J. Harris, *The Best of Sydney J. Harris* (1976), 328. *See* Macleish, #**1161.**

1157. I wrote some lines once on a time
In wondrous merry mood,
And thought, as usual, men would say
They were exceeding good.

They were so queer, so very queer,
I laughed as I would die;
Albeit, in a general way,
A sober man am I.

I called my servant, and he came;
How kind it was of him
To mind a slender man like me,
He of mighty limb!

"These to the printer," I exclaimed,
And, in my humorous way,
I added (as a trifling jest),
"There'll be the devil to pay."

He took the paper, and I watched,
And saw him peep within;
At the first line he read, his face
Was all upon the grin.

He read the next; the grin grew broad,
And shot from ear to ear;
He read the third; a chuckling noise
I now began to hear.

The fourth; he broke into a roar;
The fifth; his waistband split;
The sixth; he burst five buttons off,
And tumbled in a fit.

Ten days and nights, with sleepless eye,
I watched that wretched man,

And since, I never dare to write
As funny as I can.

—Oliver Wendell Holmes, Sr.,
"The Height of the Ridiculous,"
The Poetical Works of Oliver Wendell Holmes (1887), 12.

1158. Boston, Mch 16th 1849

Dear Mr. Sullivan.

The exersise you have given is writing a letter instead of composition, and so I thought I would write you one. But as we have got to write a short one I cannot make this any longer.

Your affectionate friend
O.W. Holmes. Jr.

—Oliver Wendell Holmes, Jr.,
age 8, to his teacher, in Mark DeWolfe Howe,
Justice Oliver Wendell Holmes (1957), I.3.

1159. Go on then doing with your pen what in other times was done with the sword: show that the reformation is more practical by operating on the mind than on the body of man, and be assured that it has not a more sincere votary nor you a more ardent well-wisher than. . .

TH: JEFFERSON

—Letter to Thomas Paine, June 19, 1792, in Saul K. Padover,
ed., *A Jefferson Profile as Revealed in His Letters* (1956), 91.

1160. No man but a blockhead ever wrote, except for money.

—Samuel Johnson, in James Boswell, *Life of Samuel Johnson*, Apr. 5, 1776 (1791). *Contrast* Montagu, **#1164**.

1161. Everybody knows by now that "creative writing" can't be taught. Nevertheless thousands of professors in hundreds of colleges go on teaching it. Which is absurd but not as absurd as it sounds.

Everybody knows, too, that you can't teach a horse to race, but Kentucky is full of racing stables with neat oval tracks and miles of expensive, whitewashed fencing which costs as much to maintain as a presentable professor. Even more.

There is one difference, of course. In Kentucky they begin with the horse's sire and dam whereas the professor of writing rarely breeds his own students and wouldn't know where to begin if he tried. Who would have picked that pair from the livery stable to beget and bear John Keats?

But otherwise the situation in Cambridge [Harvard University] is much like the situation in Kentucky. You have to have a horse that can race before you can teach it racing. You have to have a writer who can write before you can teach him how.

—Archibald MacLeish, *A Continuing Journey:* "On the Teaching of Writing" (1967), 227. *See* Harris, **#1156.**

1162. Dear Mr. White:

Since your profession is writing I don't expect you to continue this correspondence, but I just had to let you know how delighted I was to read that you enjoyed the book. . . .

It is not easy to write even a short note to a man who has just published a book on the pitfalls of the English language. You see, I write by ear. I tried writing with a typewriter but I found it too unwieldy. I then tried dictating to my secretary but after some months of futility I realized that she, too, was unwieldy.

—Groucho Marx, letter to E.B. White, Oct. 13, 1959, *The Groucho Letters* (1967), 133.

1163. The diffusion of writings and books . . . has entirely transformed man. . . . We teach one another by writings; we learn to know nature and man out of writings; we toil and repose over, edify and amuse ourselves with writings. . . . Dead letter all; spirit of living conversation none!

—Moses Mendelssohn, *Jerusalem* (1783), II.111. *See* Eliot, **#1153;** also Poe, **#35,** under "Book."

1164. A person of quality should never turn author . . . one of the most distinguished prerogatives of mankind, writing, when duly executed does honour to human nature. If done for the purpose of making money it is contemptible.

—Lady Mary Wortley Montagu, letter to Lady Bute, July 23, 1753. *Contrast* Johnson, **#1160.**

1165. I wear my Pen as others do their Sword.
To each affronting sot I meet, the word,
Is *Satisfaction:* straight to thrusts I go,
And pointed satire runs him through and through.

—John Oldham (1653–1683), "Satire upon a Printer," ln.35.

1166. Don't teach the student how to write correctly. Teach him how to think correctly. The writing will follow, and if not, so much the better. We can well do with less writing and more thinking.

—Dagobert D. Runes, *Treasury of Thought* (1966), 363.

1167. "I have written my poem. All that remains to do is to correct it."
But my father waxed wroth.
"So you write your poem first, and then correct it! But what is writing but correcting? Have you watched him modelling the clay? Correction by correction, the face emerges; nay, the very first thumb-stroke was a correction of the primal lump."

—Antoine de Saint-Exupéry,
The Wisdom of the Sands (1950), lxxxi.

1168. Whoever writes carelessly thereby confesses at the very outset that he himself does not attach any great value to his own ideas. For only if we are convinced of the truth and importance of our ideas does the necessary enthusiasm arise to be intent on the clearest, finest, and most powerful expression, everywhere with untiring persistence, just as we use silver and gold receptacles for sacred objects or priceless works of art. Therefore the ancients, whose thoughts have survived in their own words for thousands of years and who thus bear the honoured title of classics, always wrote carefully. Indeed Plato is said to have written the introduction to his *Republic* seven times, differently modified.

—Arthur Schopenhauer, *Parerga and Paralipomena:*
"On Authorship and Style" (1851), tr. E.F.J. Payne (1974), II.545.

1169. My use of the first-person singular is deliberate; few literary conventions seem more pointless to me or more misleading, than the substitution of "we" or "this writer" for the pronoun "I." Writing is nothing if not an assertion of self, an "act of saying I," as Joan Didion has put it, "of saying listen to me, see it my way."

—Charles E. Silberman, *A Certain*
People (1985), 27. *Contrast* Singer, **#1170.**

1170. Although I do write from time to time in the first person, I don't consider it a healthy habit. I'm against the stream of consciousness because it means always babbling about oneself. The writer who writes about himself all the time must become a bore, just like the man who talks all the time about himself. When the writer becomes the center of his attention, he becomes a *nudnik*. And a *nudnik* who believes he's profound is even worse than just a plain *nudnik*.

—Isaac Bashevis Singer (with Richard Burgin),
Conversations With Isaac Bashevis Singer (1985).
[nudnik=*nuisance, bore*]. *Contrast* Silberman, **#1169.**

1171. Playwriting and safe-cracking are similar occupations. Both are lonely work, tedious and tense, and, for the most part, not especially rewarding when one considers the time, the effort, and risk involved. Furthermore, unless each job comes off to perfection, as George S. Kaufman often said, the newspapers treat both the safe-cracker and the playwright as common criminals.

—Howard Teichmann, *George S. Kaufman:
An Initimate Portrait:* "Author's Note" (1972).

1172. Nothing goes by luck in composition. It allows of no tricks. The best you can write will be the best you are. Every sentence is the result of a long probation. The author's character is read from title-page to end. Of this he never corrects the proofs. We read it as the essential character of a handwriting without regard to the flourishes. And so of the rest of our actions; it runs as straight as a ruled line through them all, no matter how many curvets about it. Our whole life is taxed for the least thing well done: it is its net result. How we eat, drink, sleep, and use our desultory hours, now in these indifferent days, with no eye to observe and no occasion [to] excite us, determines our authority and capacity for the time to come.

—Henry David Thoreau, *Journal,* 1841.

Writing Style

(*See also* Writing)

1173. By *style,* I do not mean every combination of words expressing some sense; but I mean such a combination, as, in regard either of the words, or the composition of these words, or both, is some way different from ordinary discourse. It has a certain character by which we distinguish it, and denominate it the historical, the didactic, the poetic, the epistolary, and the like.

—James Burnett, Lord Monboddo,
Of the Origin and Progress of Language (1773–92).

1174. With respect to style..., I have attempted to make it vary with the subject; avoiding all pomp of words.... I have neither spare time for superfluous writing, nor spare money for superfluous printing.... It has cost me more time and pains to abridge these pages than to write them.

—Charles Caleb Colton,
Lacon, preface to first volume (1820), p. vii.

1175. You become a good writer just as you become a good joiner: by planing down your sentences.

To-day rhetoric is decried: In the Middle Ages it was called "Madam Rhetoric." I regret it: rhetoric teaches how to please, to instruct, and to touch. Ideas pass; but rhetoric is eternal.

Ah, yes! There is the simple style, the sublime style, the balanced style. That makes our young literary sparks shriek with laughter, doesn't it? In fact, it is a truism. Does anyone choose the same ink, the same pen, and the same tone, to write to the Archbishop of Paris, to his mistress, or to Potin?

—Anatole France, in Jean Jacques Brousson,
Anatole France Himself, tr. John Pollock (1925),
95. Félix Potin was the great grocer, wine merchant
and gastronomic purveyor of Paris.

1176. It is not easy to write a familiar style. Many people mistake a familiar for a vulgar style, and suppose that to write without affection is to write at random. On the contrary, there is nothing that requires more precision, and, if I may so say, purity of expression, than the style I am speaking of. It utterly rejects not only all unmeaning pomp, but all low, cant phrases, and loose, unconnected, *slipshod* allusions.

—William Hazlitt, "On Familiar Style" (1821), in Charles
Harold Gray, ed., *Essays of William Hazlitt* (1926), 223.

1177. *Elegance* of *Thought* is what we commonly call *Wit*, which adds to Propriety, Beauty, and pleases our Fancy, while Propriety entertains our Judgment. This depends so much on Genius, that 'tis impossible to teach it by Rules. To the Elegance of Words, or Style, belong all the Figures of *Rhetorick*, and to use these to Advantage requires a Judgment well form'd by Observation. In this therefore, as in learning the Graces upon an Instrument of Musick, good Examples are the best Instruction.

—John Hughes, *Poems on Several Occasions:* "Of Style" (1735).

1178. Endeavor to cultivate conciseness and elegance, do not attempt to write verse unless thou canst do it perfectly. Avoid heaviness, which spoils a composition, making it disagreeable alike to reader or audience.

—Judah Ibn Tibbon, to his son, *Ethical Will* (c. 1190).

1179. Elegance in prose composition is mainly this: a just admission of topics and of words; neither too many nor too few of either; enough of sweetness in the sound to induce us to enter and sit still; enough of illustration and reflection to change the posture of our minds when they would tire; and enough sound matter in the complex to repay us for our attendance.

—Walter Savage Landor,
Imaginary Conversations: "Chesterfield and Chatham" (1824–29).

1180. *Style* is the physiognomy of the mind and as such is more infallible than that of the body. To imitate another's style is equivalent to wearing a mask. However fine this may be, it soon becomes insipid and insufferable because it is lifeless, so that even the ugliest living face is better. . . .

We should discover faults in the style of the writings of others in order to avoid them in our own.

—Arthur Schopenhauer, *Parerga und Paralipomena:*
"On Authorship and Style" (1851), tr. E.F.J. Payne (1974) II.515.

1181. As for style of writing, if one has anything to say, it drops from him simply and directly, as a stone falls to the ground. There are no two ways about it, but down it comes, and he may stick in the points and stops wherever he can get a chance.

—Henry David Thoreau,
Letters, ed. Ralph Waldo Emerson, 158.

Youth and Age

(*See also* Adolescence; Childhood)

1182. Let's away with study,
  Folly's sweet.
Treasure all the pleasure
  Of our youth:
Time enough for age
  To think on Truth.

So short a day,
  And life so quickly hasting,
And in study wasting
  Youth that would be gay!

—Anonymous, *Carmina Burana* (13th cent.),
in Helen Waddell, tr., *Mediaeval Latin Lyrics* (1948), 203.

1183. Youth is perennially, and naturally, in revolt against age. Only by belittling the past can one assure himself and the world of his importance. Nobody, at 20, is going to admit the possibility that all the best poems may have been written, the best pictures painted, the best music composed. Even in the world of business it is not true, as is sometimes supposed, that to be a meek yes-man is the way to the top. A surer way is to challenge authority with new ideas—and prove you are right.

—Bruce Bliven, "By 1966 Half of Us
Will Be Under 25," *New York Times*, Dec. 8, 1963.

1184. Youth should heed the older-witted
  When they say, don't go too far—
Now their sins are all committed,
  Lord, how virtuous they are!

—Wilhelm Busch (1832–1908), "Die fromme Helene"
("Pious Helen"). *See* Terence, **#520**, under "Parent."

1185. Youth, what man's age is like to be, doth show;
We may our ends by our beginnings know.

—Sir John Denham (1615–69), "Of Prudence" (1650), ln.225.

1186. "I like your book, my boy,
'T is full of youth and joy,
And love that sings and dreams.
Yet it puzzles me," he said;
"A string of pearls it seems,
But I cannot find the thread."

"O friend of olden days!
Dear to me is your praise,
But, many and many a year
You must go back, I fear;

You must journey back," I said,
"To find that golden thread!"

—Richard Watson Gilder, "Youth and Age," *Poems of Richard Watson Gilder* (1908), 133.

1187. It is as well perhaps that this is not the first time I have been swept off my feet. In the days of my blessed youth there were such occasions; in what young person's life do they not occur? No, the only young people to whom this feeling is strange are those young conservatives who were born old, who do not know the meaning of being carried away. No worse fate can befall a young man or woman than becoming prematurely entrenched in prudence and negation. Heaven knows that there are plenty of opportunities in later life, too, for being carried away. What of it? We remain what we are and, no doubt, it is all very good for us!

—Knut Hamsun, Nobel Prize for Literature acceptance speech, Stockholm, 1920.

1188. Youth and Crabbed Age stand broadly for the two opposite poles of human living, poles equally essential to any real vitality, but always contrasted. Youth stands for rationalism, for the intellect and its concomitants, egotism and individualism. Crabbed Age stands for tradition, for the instincts and the emotions, with their concomitant altruism. . . . The whole art of living is a delicate balance between the two tendencies. Virtues and vices are but convenient analytic labels attached to particular forms of the two tendencies.

—Jane Harrison, "Crabbed Age and Youth," *Alpha and Omega,* 1915.

1189. They've spent their whole lives being right, those old folks. Whatever my father says, even if it's admitting he was wrong, comes out sounding like he's the one who's right and you're the one who's wrong because you're too young. It's only the old folks who have the strictly logical minds and the infallible intuition and all that, while you're too spoiled, or too confused, or too lazy, or too superficial to think straight. It doesn't matter if you're thirty years old. They still talk to you like a grown-up being patient with a child who's only being treated like a grown-up in order to make him feel good. You can't even ask them for the time of day without getting a whole complicated answer full of explanations for everything, point by point, A, B, C, D, and all that, and without being told that experience is the best teacher and that there's always another side to the coin. What you think makes no difference because you belong to a generation that never learned how to think. You can't get a word in edgewise. It's like being checkmated by someone who's playing both sides of the board because you have no pieces of your own, just your tender soul with your psychological problems.

—Amoz Oz, *A Perfect Peace*, tr. Hillel Halkin (1985), 134.

1190. The atrocious crime of being a young man, which the honourable gentleman [Horace Walpole] has with such spirit and decency charged upon me, I shall neither attempt to palliate nor deny; but content myself with wishing that I may be one of those whose follies may cease with their youth, and not of that number who are ignorant in spite of experience.

—William Pitt, Earl of Chatham,
speech in House of Commons, Mar. 6, 1741.

1191. Our [Roman] young men have grown slothful. Their talents are left idle, and there is not a single honorable occupation for which they toil day and night. Slumber and languor, and an interest in evil which is worse than slumber and languor, have entered men's hearts. They sing and dance and grow effeminate, and curl their hair, and learn womanish tricks of speech: they are as languid as women, and deck themselves with unbecoming ornaments. Which of your contemporaries [he is addressing his three sons] has any talent, any industry? Which of them is in any way a man? Without strength, without energy, they add nothing during life to the gifts which they were born, and then they complain of their lot. God forbid that the gift of eloquence should be given to their like.

—Marcus Annaeus Seneca (the elder,
54 B.C.?–A.D. 39), *Controversiae*, I.8–9.

1192. It is surely beyond doubt that people should be a good deal idle in youth. For though here and there a Lord Macaulay may escape from school honours with all his wits about him, most boys pay so dear for their medals that they never afterwards have a shot in their locker, and begin the world bankrupt. And the same holds true during all the time a lad is educating himself, or suffering others to educate him.

—Robert Louis Stevenson,
Virginibus Puerisque: "An Apology for Idlers" (1881)

1193. Youth is not a time of life—it is a state of mind. It is not a matter of ripe cheeks, red lips and supple knees. It is a temper of the will, a quality of the imagination, a vigor of the emotions. It is a freshness of the deep spring of life.

—Samuel Ullman, *From the
Summit Years, Four Score* (1920?), 13.

Author Index

References denote entry numbers rather than page numbers.

A

B

C

D

E

F

G

H

I

J

K

L

M

Q

R

S

V

W

Subject Index

References denote entry numbers rather than page numbers.

D

E

Q

R

S

T

U

V

W

Y